CU00689869

From Pit Town To Battlefields 1914 – 1916

Mexborough
&
The Great War

Bill Lawrence

Books

First published in Great Britain in 2015 by LEB Books, a division of LEB Ltd,
57 Orrell Lane, Liverpool L9 8BX

© *Copyright 2015* Bill Lawrence

All rights reserved. No part of this publication may be
reproduced or distributed in any form
or by any means, or stored in a database or retrieval system,
without the prior written permission of the publisher.

ISBN 9780993407505

British Library Cataloguing in Publication Data.
A catalogue record for this book is available from the British Library.

The right of Bill Lawrence to be identified as the author
of this work has been asserted by him in accordance with the
Copyright, Design and Patent Act 1988.
Designed by Paul Etherington.

DISCLAIMER
Whilst every effort has been made to ensure the factual accuracy of the contents, no liability
can be accepted for any use of the information in this publication.

From Pit Town To Battlefields 1914 – 1916

Mexborough
&
The Great War

Bill Lawrence

Foreword by
Dr Ian Parks

Mexborough & District Heritage Society

A tribute to the people of Mexborough for their
courage and commitment during the First World War.

Where are you sleeping to-night, My lad
Above-ground - or below?
The last we heard you were up at the front,
Holding a trench and bearing the brunt; -
But - that was a week ago.

John Oxenham

Private Albert Beal (known as John) in his KOYLI uniform. John worked for a while as a barman at the Montagu Arms, survived the war and became a bandsman with the Mexborough Concertina Band. The young mascot is George Hurst, who later became a Mexborough councillor.
Courtesy of the late Bill Beal.

For my son, Sam.

Contents

1915

1916

Appendices

Acknowledgements

My gratitude goes to many of my associates and friends. Colleagues in the Mexborough and District Heritage Society have given me valuable support and encouragement over the months it has taken to complete this book. Thanks go to the Society's member Julia Ashby, who has served our organisation for over 25 years. Julia's help has been invaluable for her in-depth of knowledge of Mexborough. The Society's committee members are worthy of a special mention. Margaret Roper, our chairperson, for her friendly encouragement and assistance in proof reading some of the text. Others who must be thanked include Molly Beardsley, Gary Barker and Graham Oliver for photos of his great uncle George Oliver. Ian Harber has been of immense help as a result of his computer skills which included the designing of the book cover.

Making up the army of proof readers were, Sue Wild (Sheffield), Susan Shaw (Barnsley), Amanda Simmonite (Mexborough). I am also grateful to my son Sam Lawrence who spared time from his post-graduate studies to proof read a large section of the text as well as making some useful comments. My good friend of many years, Nick Broadhead of Liverpool deserves a special mention too. Nick's professional writing skills have been of enormous assistance to me in the final editing of the book. The same thanks go to another 'old' colleague from Rugby, Geraldine (Gerry) White. I am forever in her debt for helping the book to become more readable as a consequence of her remarkable grasp of the English language.

I am also indebted to Mexborough's renowned poet Dr Ian Parks. Not only did he volunteer to undertake proof reading of the volume, but on my request kindly wrote a splendid 'Foreword'.

The contribution made by those who were of assistance at the research stage should rightly get a mention. I must thank the staff of the Archives and Local Studies at both Clifton Park Museum and Barnsley Museum for the efficient and friendly service I received from them. Thanks also to Steve Tagg at the KOYLI Museum in Doncaster whose knowledge of the local regiment was most useful in the preparation of the relevant parts of the book.

The Mexborough and District Heritage Society has received a number of photographs relating to the Great War over the past few years from members of the local community. For these photos we specially thank: Geoff White, Susan Shaw, Mrs Pauline Gibbons, Graham Oliver, Gary Baker, Roger Gilbert, Bill Goddard, Steve Hamilton and Barrie Dalby. Mexborough's Dave McCabe of the Great War Society has also been of great help. A special mention should go to both the late Bill Beal and Peter Robinson. My thanks also to Christine Barrett-Spence for helping to secure funding from 'Community First' to assist with the publishing of this book.

Last, but certainly not least, I must express my considerable gratitude to a man I have come to call 'Sir Ron'. If anyone deserves to be recognised for services to the local heritage movement then it is Ron James. Despite his senior years, Ron is still a selfless and tireless researcher worker for local heritage societies in the Don and Dearne area. Many thanks Ron.

Foreword

The Great War of 1914-1918 has long been recognised as a catastrophe of international dimensions. The Battle of the Somme, which raged from 1st July to 18th November 1916 was to result in 60,000 British casualties. On the first day of the offensive alone around 20,000 British soldiers fell, amongst whom were 50 from Mexborough and Swinton, serving mainly in the 8th and 9th Battalions of the York and Lancs Regiment. This bare statistic shows the magnitude of the losses suffered in these communities but does little to convey the effect it had on the families and friends of those who died. It also emphasises the fact that the Great War was not only a national tragedy but a local one too. My paternal grandfather, a Mexborough man himself, was one of the wounded during the Battle of the Somme and that personal connection – which so many of us have with someone who fought in that conflict – added to my interest when coming to this book. As the centenary of the beginning of the war passes and the war itself recedes from living memory, it is timely to look again at what it meant for those who lived through it and what it also means to us today who still, in so many ways, continue to live in the long shadow cast by it.

In this excellent and accessible account, Bill Lawrence has combined meticulous research with a narrative flare to bring to vivid life a lost and fascinating chapter in the history of Mexborough and district with particular reference to the effect it had on people on the Home Front and in their everyday lives. A glance at the contents page shows the range and depth of this book which serves not only to highlight the local dimensions of the conflict but to locate them firmly in the context of the war itself. Like all good social history, it directs the reader away from the broad generalisations and stereotypes to a consideration of the ordinary men and women who, in that and any other age, are the real makers of our collective past. The men and women of Mexborough and the surrounding areas are given the opportunity to speak for themselves across the generations and do so with disarming clarity and individuality.

One of the poets of that war, Wilfred Owen, wrote in his great poem *Strange Meeting* of 'the pity of war' and 'the pity war distilled'. Owen himself was to die in combat just days before the Armistice was signed. But the distillation he talked about was to continue in public memory and still does. *From Pit Town to Battlefields: 1914-1916 – Mexborough in the Great War* offers us an invaluable insight into why the Great War made such an impact on the consciousness of the nation and on the small part of it in which we live.

Dr Ian Parks
Mexborough
2015

Author's Preface

This book has been written for two main reasons. Firstly, it coincides with commemorations of the 100th anniversary of the Great War, or the First World War as it was to become known in 1939. Secondly, after researching the Mexborough and District Heritage Society archives, it became evident that there was a need for material which exists on the period to be written into a detailed, comprehensive volume.

As there was a gap in Mexborough's history during the eventful Great War period, it was decided to include not only events in relation to Mexborough's contribution to the struggles on the battlefields, but also the contribution made by Mexborough people on the Home Front. In describing activities on the Home Front, an attempt has been made to highlight key events and bring to life some of Mexborough's prominent and influential personalities of the war years.

But Mexborough's history concerning the war is not dominated by the town's leaders or local 'dignitaries' as they might have been called at the time. The contribution made by the 'ordinary' working class men and women is also a feature of the book. The lives of the men who stayed at home were by no means without hardship or sacrifice. Harsh discipline was evident for those at work in industries such as the railways and, more significantly, coalmining. Both of these industries were heavily relied upon to sustain the war effort.

Briefly touched upon is the way Mexborough people were entertained by such as cinema and theatre, and how they entertained themselves through social clubs, public houses and sports. Social life was greatly affected by the war and in some cases by government legislation.

No book of this nature on the First World War can be written without some mention of women's contribution to the war effort and an appreciation of how decisive these efforts were. Having said this, it is an area which is only, regrettably, dealt with in brief. Such a history of Mexborough women's contribution calls for a more detailed and comprehensive study and with it a book worthy of the subject matter. It is hoped such a book will become available in the near future.

While the book's main emphasis is on the impact war had on Mexborough and its people, it attempts to place this in the broader context of events happening nationally, especially with emphasis on government legislation and policy. Also contextualised is a brief account of events elsewhere in Europe leading up to the outbreak of hostilities. It is hoped this is useful to the reader who may have had no previous knowledge of some of the origins and reasons for the outbreak of war.

It was felt necessary to include some reference to the momentous events in the immediate years prior to the declaration of war in 1914. The events referred to took place between 1910 and 1913, years which are a backdrop to what was to follow and are taken up in the first chapter. Britain found itself in a position in which it was able to create enormous wealth, which some were keen to display, yet still lacked the mechanism to ensure a fair distribution of that wealth, despite the introduction of some welfare reforms by the Liberal Government of the day. The tensions created by poverty amid prosperity lead to serious industrial and political unrest and it is against this background that we must consider how the thoughts of those from the working classes, who readily responded to the call to arms in August 1914, might have been shaped. The book suggests that not all those who rallied to Lord Kitchener's initial call for men, were motivated by the patriotic ideals engendered in the words 'For King and Country'. Army life may have had some attractions, offering the relative security that appeared absent in the mundane, monotonous and sometimes brutal lives their employment offered.

Subsequent chapters are sectioned into the years 1914, 1915 and 1916 whilst events on the Home Front have been written thematically rather than chronologically as are events happening on the battlefields. The early 1914 chapters suggest that, by all accounts, Mexborough and district, like the rest of the country, was sleepwalking into a disastrous conflict. However, on the declaration of war there is a clear sense of collective endeavour that galvanised the local community, led by those with remarkable organisational skills. Apart from sections of the military and political establishment, the rest of society was often engaged with the 'domestic' struggles that had pre-occupied their minds for some time. As far as the Western Front is concerned, the 1914 section deals with the contribution in those early months made by Mexborough's Regulars and Reservists, notably of the 2nd Battalion of Kings Own Yorkshire Light Infantry (KOYLI) and the 2nd Battalion of York and

Lancaster Regiment (York and Lancs). The first men from Mexborough to be killed in action were to die at the First Battle of Ypres (18th October to 22nd November 1914). This battle saw a commencement of a long list of Mexborough dead and with it the beginning of an acknowledgement of the reality of war, although for many the hope that it would all be over by Christmas endured, an optimism that was evident throughout the country.

The 1915 section tells how Mexborough Regulars and Reservists faced further horrors and of the consequential stalemate on the Western Front at Neuve Chapelle, at the Second Battle of Ypres (22nd April to 25th May) and at Hooge. It was becoming evident to the military authorities and politicians at home that the war effort would need to be intensified. The 'pressures of necessity' witnessed the introduction of legislation which manifested itself in harsh working conditions and discipline in the workplace. Women's labour in vital industries was now considered a necessity, as was the belief, in some quarters, that military conscription could no longer be delayed.

As the stalemate continued and the casualties increased so did hostility towards the enemy. The sinking of the passenger liner the *Lusitania* by a German U-boat somewhat understandably exacerbated hatred for all that was German. Butchers of a German origin, who were plentiful in the Don and Dearne Valley area, were particularly targeted. The riots in Mexborough which immediately followed the sinking of the *Lusitania* liner are a sad episode in the history of a town which, it appears, previously readily accepted a German butcher into its community without question.

The book mostly deals with, in terms of the conflict abroad, events on the Western Front and does not touch upon other theatres of war, with the exception of the struggles surrounding the Gallipoli campaign. Men from Mexborough serving with both the Royal Naval Division (RND) and the 6th York and Lancs were to play a significant role in this campaign which ended in ultimate disaster. Locally many men were to join the 6th York and Lancs and their heroic story was one that could not go without finding its way into the book

The year 1915 saw desperate last ditch attempts to fill the ranks of the British army with volunteers without the need to introduce compulsory military service. The closing months of 1915 witnessed hectic activity to try and achieve the sort of numbers required to both compensate for the losses during the year and prepare for the large-scale offensives to come. Mexborough was no exception in this activity, but there were those who refused or were reluctant to accept compulsion and their story is briefly covered. This interesting part of Mexborough's wartime history is worthy of a more in-depth study.

The section on 1916 inevitably deals with the bloody catastrophe of the first Battle of the Somme. During the four and half months of the battle, Mexborough suffered more than its share of casualties. The 8th and 9th York and Lancs, two battalions well represented by local men, were to sustain casualties as high as most battalions throughout the country. A later appendix in the book has identified 50 men from the Mexborough and Swinton area who died on the first day of the Battle of Somme. The majority were men serving with the 8th or 9th York and Lancs.

Like most towns throughout the country, particularly in the industrial north, Mexborough's community was devastated with grief as the lengthy list of deaths on the battlefields of the Somme reached home by telegram, letter and through the pages of the *Mexborough and Swinton Times*. Mexborough's well known families were to suffer just as others and the names Barron and Waddington were not to be excluded from the roll call of the dead.

The preparations for the 'big push'- the offensive on the Somme - is a subject taken up in the 1916 section. The preparations themselves included the contribution of the tunnelling battalions of the Royal Engineers of which Mexborough's William Hackett was a part. It goes without saying that the story of Hackett's personal contribution is included.

The contribution made by men serving in the Royal Navy is also touched upon, with particular reference to the Battle of Jutland in the summer of 1916. Here the tragic story is told of Mexborough's youngest serviceman, who took part in this action, the last full-scale sea battle to take place with the involvement of two great opposing navies. It is the story of Mexborough's own 'Jutland Hero'.

The book contains an extensive bibliography of secondary research sources. The Mexborough and District Heritage Society appealed for any photos, letters and other materials of interest which were relevant to Mexborough and the Great War. The Society is grateful for the response we received by members of the public for material, of which a considerable amount has been used in the book. However, I am of the belief that there is probably still relevant material which is yet to be seen in the public domain. It is hoped that such valuable materials will be forthcoming to help in the writing of future works on Mexborough's contribution to the First World War.

It will be noted that there has been a significant reliance on the *Mexborough and Swinton Times* (referred to as *The Times* throughout) as a source of reference. For this I make no apology. Given that newspapers at the time were almost the only method of distributing news to the public, this type of media was usually very thorough in content, often reporting such events as meetings almost verbatim. Thus *The Times* has been an extremely valuable resource and one which evidently Mexborough servicemen at the time also highly valued as a way of keeping in touch with their community and offering them a platform to tell their own stories.

This volume can be considered as one part of a complete work on Mexborough and the Great War. Such was the need for a comprehensive coverage of the period that, given the amount of material accumulated, it was decided to take this account of the war up to the year 1916. A complete publication would have appeared too far removed from commemoration of the 100th anniversary of the beginning of the war, given the time needed for its completion. It is hoped that the second part of Mexborough's story during the Great War will not be too far from publication.

Despite this edition ending in the year 1916, the book includes an appendix of all those from Mexborough who gave their lives in the war between 1914 and 1918, together with those who died of wounds and those who served in years beyond the declaration of peace up to 1922. This appendix unfortunately excludes a small number of men whose names are on the Mexborough War Memorial, but as yet cannot be identified on the records of the Commonwealth War Graves Commission. Nevertheless, the appendix includes men who are not on the Mexborough memorial but arguably should be. The reason for their omission is complex. The list includes some men who were born in Mexborough but moved away before or during the war. It also included some who were not born in Mexborough but settled in the town and enlisted at one of Mexborough's recruiting offices. Matters are not helped by the fact that, at the time of the war, parts of what is today Mexborough were in the Swinton Urban District Council area. That is why those who can be considered as Swinton men and women occasionally appear in the book. It is hoped that this particular appendix will be of use to those readers who recognise a relative from the lists and are moved to find out more about them. Hopefully, the other parts of the appendix will be of interest, particularly the list of Mexborough servicemen who received military honours for gallantry, although this is likely to be incomplete.

The volume has aimed to fill a gap in Mexborough's history, covering a period hitherto scarcely touched upon. In no way can this contribution be considered as a definitive history as there is much scope for further research into the part Mexborough people played in the Great War. If the book is able to add to the reader's knowledge, particularly those with an association to Mexborough, then it has achieved what it set out to do. It is especially hoped that the younger generation of readers will, through the following pages, begin to have an understanding of events surrounding the First World War and an appreciation of the lives and sacrifices made by their great and great-great grandparents.

Finally, there will inevitably be errors in the text which the author takes full responsibility for, although some of the research material itself contained inconsistencies such as names, places and dates.

Bill Lawrence
Mexborough
October 2015

Abbreviations

ASC: Army Service Corps

ASC (MT): Army Service Corps (Mechanical Transport)

BEF: British Expeditionary Force

DLI: Durham Light Infantry

DORA: Defence of the Realm Act

KOYLI: King's Own Yorkshire Light Infantry

KRRR: King's Royal Rifle Regiment

MFGB: Miners' Federation of Great Britain

NCO: Non-Commissioned Officer

NUR: National Union of Railwaymen

RAMC: Royal Army Medical Corps

RE: Royal Engineers

RGA: Royal Garrison Artillery

RHA: Royal Horse Artillery

RFA: Royal Field Artillery

RFC: Royal Flying Corps

Sherwood Foresters: Sherwood Foresters (Derby and Notts) Regiment

TUC: Trades Union Congress

UDC: Urban District Council

YMA: Yorkshire Miners' Association

York and Lancs: York and Lancaster Regiment

1910 - 1913

Chapter One

Sunshine and Shadows:
Prosperity, Poverty and Social Unrest
Part One: 1910 & 1911

The First World War, or the Great War, was to change many aspects of Edwardian society. It was not, as promised, the war to end all wars, but the beginning of the end of the rigid British class system and British society's conformity to it. This chapter looks at the immediate pre-war years as a backcloth to the outbreak of the war in August 1914. It does so to examine these years in relation to the social and economic influences on the people of the Don and Dearne Valleys and the political struggles which shaped their lives. While doing this it introduces some of the significant local figures who had a part to play in the shaping of those lives. The new century was fashioned by political change and revolt, together with a rapid expansion in new technologies and industrialisation. This had brought with it a rise in nationalism, socialism and a growth in trade union membership and activity.

George Dangerfield in his classic book on this period, *The Strange Death of Liberal England*, identifies three rebellions: a women's rebellion, a workers' rebellion, and the Tory rebellion over the Irish Home Rule question. We might also include here the rebellion in the House of Lords. How did these conflicts affect the people of Mexborough and district? Certainly the workers' rebellion had a major influence upon Mexborough life. As a key railway centre within the vast coalfields of the Don and Dearne Valleys, the two national strikes of the time, in the railway and coal industries, were instrumental in forging political opinion whilst impinging upon the local economy and the welfare of the district's people.

The Liberal Party had won a landslide victory in the general election of 1906 under the leadership of Campbell-Bannerman. When he died in 1908 he was succeeded by Herbert Henry Asquith, the man who would take the country towards, then into, the First World War. The Liberal Government was always under pressure from the Irish Nationalists on the question of Irish Home Rule. They were under pressure also from the fledgling Labour Party, which was formed by the trade union movement. The Labour Party was pushing for social reform and trade union rights and had 59 MPs in Parliament who could influence the direction of Liberal policy. They had already achieved the delivery of the Trade Union Disputes Act of 1906 which gave trade unions immunity from prosecution and financial damages resulting from strike action. The Liberal Government was also to deliver on legislation benefiting Britain's miners with the introduction of the Coal Mines Act of 1908 which saw a reduction in the working day of the miner to eight hours. It also succeeded in squeezing the owners' profits which led to them seeking ways to regain the levels of profitability they had seen previously. Other concessions to Labour were to follow.

The Asquith Government's social policies were particularly directed towards welfare reform, often referred to as the New Liberalism. The origins of the Welfare State can be traced to this period. For example, unemployment and health insurance was introduced later in 1911. With Lloyd George taking over as the Chancellor of the Exchequer from Asquith, there were preparations to introduce old age pensions, again influenced as a result of pressure from the trade union and Labour movements.

The Liberal Government also wished to ensure that Britain had sufficient armed forces to meet the need to protect her interests, home and abroad. Originally, reforms to the naval programme were to be limited in cost, but the Government was alarmed by the rate at which Germany was increasing its battleship capacity year upon year. To keep pace with German naval expansion the cost would rise. Lloyd George saw the need to raise the finance to both fund military expenditure and welfare reform. He could only achieve his ambition by increasing taxes on, particularly, the property-owning rich. In order to raise the revenue required, Lloyd George put together a Finance Bill that was to become known as the 'People's Budget'. It was passed by the House of Commons on 5th November 1909. It targetted the rich, especially the aristocracy and those who sat in the House of Lords. Death duties were increased, as were duties on minerals and coal. Income tax was increased and a Super Tax was introduced for those on incomes of over £5,000. These were a few of the measures which were profoundly objected to by those most affected by them, namely their Lordships in that 'other place'.

The Conservative and Unionist's leader, Arthur Balfour, had mischievously boasted that the Conservatives and Unionists would always be able to control the affairs of the country by virtue of the built-in hereditary majority it had within the House of Lords. They could veto the will of the House of Commons on all bills put before them. But constitutionally they could not veto finance bills and the budget in particular. Their indignation got the better of the Conservative Unionist Lords and the 'People's Budget' was voted down on 30th November. The country was now in a constitutional crisis and there was talk of the King creating hundreds of Liberal peers to overturn the Lords' decision, but Asquith chose to dissolve Parliament and call a General Election in the January of 1910. It would be those who were eligible to vote who would decide the outcome of the Lord's veto. Thus Britain entered 1910 with a serious question to resolve. Although it may not have been on everyone's minds during the Christmas of 1909, Mexborough, like the rest of the country, prepared itself for a General Election in the January.

In General Elections, Mexborough was in the Doncaster Division. It had been a firm Liberal seat since the Liberal landslide victory of 1906. Previously it was held by the Conservatives. The sitting MP was Charles Norris Nicholson. He resided at 'Hazeldene', Thorne Road in Doncaster, but also had a residence in Harrington Gardens in London. Nicholson was adopted as the Liberal candidate, the Mexborough nominees being Liberal Councillors, John Hudson Watson, of Clayfield House, and a local schoolmaster William Winstanley.

The Conservative and Unionist candidate was Charles Warwick Whitworth a barrister, of 'Larchfield', Harrogate. Whitworth was proposed by Mexborough nominees Councillor Tom Athron, Henry Waddington, Thomas Barron and Mr B. Chipp.

Polling day was to be Thursday 20th January. Both candidates came to Mexborough on the evening of 11th January to rally support. Nicholson spoke at the Public Hall to a packed audience and then went on to a meeting in the Primitive Methodist Schoolrooms. His opponent, Whitworth, was said to have a meeting on the same night at the 'other end of the town'. The Unionists were concentrating their efforts down Church Street, Mexborough, trying to sell their policy of Tariff Reform and against the 'People's Budget'. Whitworth did a great deal of work with the Mexborough Conservatives, busily operating his campaign from Peter Waddington's rooms in Bank Street.

There were 21,514 voters in the Division, (an increase of nearly 3,000 voters from 1906). This included 6,000 employees of the Doncaster Locomotive Works (the Plant) and, of course, many miners within the area. It was not surprising that the sitting MP, Mr Nicholson, was returned to the House of Commons with a similar majority to 1906. The result being Nicholson, 10,564 votes to Whitworth's 7,085. The turnout in Mexborough had been about 84%, with the town showing strongly for the Liberal Party cause.

Following his victory, Mr Nicholson attended a meeting held in the Congregational Schoolroom on 11th February, in order to thank the local party workers. Councillor Watson was in the Chair at this meeting and supported by fellow Councillor John Easton Cliff and well-known Mexborough businessman Mr W.T. Tiptaft together with Mr A. Beal, the Reverend Thomas Anderson and local JP, Christopher Ward. At this meeting it was claimed that Mexborough was solidly Liberal and Mr Nicholson had secured many votes in the area which helped to ensure victory. This was despite some local industries leaning towards Tariff Reform and the Protectionist policies of the Conservative. One local glass bottle maker was to confront Mr Nicholson with the suggestion that protectionism would benefit the glass and bottle making industry. Yet so strong was the Liberal's cause in Mexborough that this meeting talked of setting up a Young Liberal Association.

The General Election saw the Liberal Party lose seats, resulting in a hung parliament. The Liberal Party had the majority of seats with 274 MPs and the Conservative and Unionist were just two seats short of this with 272. Despite this, the Liberals were able to form a government with the help of the Irish Parliamentary Party with its 71 seats and the Labour Party. Which increased the number of MPs to 40. Asquith felt in a position which enabled him to push on with his legislation which vitally depended on the passing of the People's Budget. Their Lordships thought better of resisting the Finance Bill a second time and the Budget passed into legislation.

The Lords were not so amenable to Asquith's Parliament Bill which would restrict their veto to which they were staunchly attached. The Bill was designed to ensure that the Lords could not indefinitely impede the will of the House of Commons. If passed it would see Bills passed in the Commons become enacted if the House of Commons itself passed them in three successive sessions. Again the Conservative dominated Lords were set to resist the Bill which would see their powers reduced, curtailing their ability to defeat legislation which they felt not in their Lordships' interest. Their focus at this time was the Irish Home Rule Bill.

The introduction of the Parliament Bill was in a period when King Edward Vll was in the last weeks of his life and this constitutional crisis was said to have hastened his death. The King had been in poor health for many months and overindulgence in the 'pleasures' of life were probably a greater contributor to his final demise. King Edward passed away on 6th May 1910 after suffering a heart attack following his return from Biarritz.

It was the monarch who had the ability to intervene in this present crisis over the Parliament Bill and threaten, as before, the creation of hundreds of Liberal peers. The task this time would fall upon the new King, George V. The Government felt that it would not be responsible of them to thrust this immediately on a King who had yet to establish himself in his newly acquired role. Asquith and his Government decided the best course of action, under the circumstances, was to attempt to find a compromise. The mechanism, which was to try to find some common ground and a settlement, was to establish a Constitutional Conference. This was set up in June. The Conference convened meetings between the representatives of both sides up until November, but failed to achieve its objective. The new King was not averse to the creation of peers, but only after the Constitutional Conference had run its course and on the additional condition that there was another General Election which returned a majority in favour of the Parliament Bill.

Mexborough had been concerned with its own elections. The Mexborough Urban District Council comprised fifteen councillors, of whom five were elected or re-elected each year for a period of three years. The local elections for 1910 took place on 2nd April. In order to get an appreciation of the town's characters and personalities on the political scene it is worth giving some details of the candidates for this particular election. The retiring councillors were:

> Alderman John Hudson Watson, described as a gentleman, who lived at 'Clayfield House', Mexborough. He was proposed by Thomas Chambers a well-known businessman of the town. Mr Watson had no problem in being re-elected when he picked up 585 votes, down from his previous 650. He was an Alderman, a County Councillor and a Justice of the Peace.

> Walter Turner, a newspaper proprietor, who lived at 'Brookfield', Swinton. He had served the Council for five years to this point and had been proposed by Mr William T Tiptaft, the well-known local grocer. Mr Turner was surprisingly 'thrown off' the Council as he finished just outside the winners with 449 votes.

> Abraham Lee, a builder who lived at 52, Helena Street. He had served the Council for seven years and was a County Councillor. He was re-elected with 501 votes, but was not to see the year out and died on the Christmas Eve of 1910.

> James Easton Cliff, described as a fish and game dealer of 2, Cliff Street, finished top of the poll with 620, a

considerable improvement on his last election result.

John Clayton the well-known retired businessman, described as a gentleman, who lived in Church Street. He retained his seat with 525 votes, this being a drop from his previous top of the poll 695 votes.

The new challenging candidates were:

Francis John Law, who had tried to win a seat on the council before and this was his third attempt. He was originally from Wath, where he kept the Cross Keys Hotel, and prior to that a public house in West Melton. On moving to Mexborough he became the proprietor of the Montagu Arms Hotel, described by a reporter as, 'The most important commercial hotel in the town and as one of the heaviest ratepayers he (Mr Law) has a considerable stake in the municipal enterprise of the place'. A former sprinter in his youth he was well known for his interest in a range of sports. At the time he was Mexborough boxer 'Iron' Hague's manager. Mr Law was proposed by Edgar Barron. He was to finish in fifth place with 472 votes and thus elected to the council for the first time. As 'Iron' Hague's manager he had probably been buoyed by his boxer's success in winning the English Heavyweight Championship the previous year.

Jonathan Rogers, a retired deputy overman of over 25 years, who worked at Denaby Main and lived at 52, Hallgate. He finished with a respectable 364 but was not elected.

Alfred Dryden a caterer of 37, Pitt Street who had been proposed by John Sopps, the local mineral water manufacturer. There were doubts about to whether his candidature was serious. He had wanted to withdraw from the contest, but those wishing to withdraw had to do so in person (which he failed to do) and so his nomination stood. Despite his popularity in the town, Mr Dryden's attempt to save himself from possible humiliation may have been unfortunate in that he finished bottom of the poll with a mere 41 votes.
George Fredrick Bullock a works manager at the Don Glass Works who lived at 1, Foundry Lane. This was his

first attempt at becoming a councillor but he failed to make an impression gaining only 193 votes.

There were a number of withdrawals before the polling day:

William Briggs, the proprietor of the Bull's Head in the High Street. He was also a manager of 'Iron' Hague. Mr Briggs was said to be popular and would have stood a chance of being elected if he had not withdrawn.

George Marshall, a draper who lived at Helena Street.

Alfred Raynor, a butcher of 22, Helena Street, was also proposed by John Sopps.

Charles Trafford, described as a gentleman's outfitter who lived at 52, Cromwell Road. He had been proposed by William Winstanley, a local schoolmaster and a prominent member of the Liberal Party.

Willliam Winstanley, of 158, Doncaster Road was himself to withdraw. He would try for a seat later.

On the formation of the new Council, Councillor Nathaniel Adshead, a miner and one of the first Labour Councillors, was elected as the new Chairman. Other councillors at the time were Tom Chambers, Vice Chairman, a local butcher, Charles H. Evans, described as a licensed victualler, Arthur Goulding, an innkeeper and Tom Athron another licensee who kept the Commercial Hotel. They were accompanied by Councillors J. Wood, C. Lazenby. G. H. Boyes, John Thomas Rowan and John Sopps.

In November 1910, the failure of the Constitutional Conference to bring about a solution to the crisis of the House of Lords' refusal to accept the Parliamentary Bill, again obliged the Liberal Government to threaten to create enough Liberal peers to defeat the Conservative and Unionist Lords' desire to retain its position of power. King George V was now amenable to the creation of the required peers but not without another election. Once again the Government dissolved Parliament and a general election was called to take place on 15th December, the second within the year.

Mexborough once again prepared itself for a second general election. The Doncaster Division chose the same candidates as it had done in the January election. Mr Charles N. Nicholson, the Liberal was to fight the seat again. Nicholson was to address a meeting, with a large attendance, on Thursday evening of 8th December at the Primitive Methodist schoolroom, Mexborough. The next evening he addressed another crowded meeting at the Public Hall. Here he was accompanied on the platform by Mr R. Fletcher, the secretary of the Mexborough Liberal Association, together with the Reverend Thomas Anderson, Mr A. Beal and Mr J. Hallford.

In his address, Mr Nicholson took the conventional Liberal Government line, by supporting the Irish Home Rule Bill, condemning the Lords, supporting free trade, which had brought 'bumper' exports, and approved payment for members of Parliament. Mr Fletcher, however, was to examine him on another important question of the day. "Was Mr Nicholson in favour of votes for women?" To this he replied that despite having a good deal of sympathy for working women, his sympathies were beginning to diminish as a result of the attacks being made upon the Government and its Ministers. To applause he said that this militancy was making things worse for the women's cause. This condemnation of the belligerent methods of the Suffragettes was also becoming the conventional Liberal Party reply on the 'women's question'.

The Conservative and Unionist Association again chose as their candidate Mr C. W. Whitworth to challenge Nicholson. John Dunk, the secretary of the Mexborough Conservative and Unionist Association was one of the proposers of Mr Whitworth's candidature.

The declaration of the Doncaster Division was given from the Guild Hall balcony by the Returning Officer announcing that Mr Nicholson was returned to the House of Commons, but with a decreased majority; 9,240 votes to Whitworth's 6,696.

Again Mexborough helped to contribute to the Liberal victory. *The Mexborough and Swinton Times (The Times)* had this to say about at least one section of Mexborough's residents: 'Roman Terrace again showed itself an uncompromising and undivided Liberal stronghold. It was unwaveringly yellow and searching for the modest blue was fraught with disappointment as a violet hunt in June.'

The result of the December General Election did not see any significant change in the balance of power in the Commons. The number of seats obtained by all political parties remained was almost identical to that of the January election. (Liberals, 272, Conservative and Unionist, 271, Labour Party, 42, Irish Parliamentary Party, 74). Nevertheless the Liberals were able to form a government once more with the support of the Irish Nationalists and the Labour Party. This allowed the Liberals and their allies to pass the Parliament Bill in the following year. The Lords now had to decide whether or not to continue voting against the Bill and witness the creation of enough peers that would see the safe passage of the Bill through their Lordships 'Upper House'. The House of

Lords was split, between the so called 'Hedgers' who saw no point in further resistance, and the 'Ditchers' who were still prepared to continue defiance. In reality it was a choice between death by fire or death by hanging in relation to continued resistance. It was put more eloquently by Lord Selbourne when he said, "The question is shall we perish in the dark, slain by our own hand, or in the light, killed by our own enemies." The Lords could resist no further. The Parliament Bill became the Parliament Act in August 1911 and with it a diminished power of the House of Lords, now unable to undermine the will of the nation's elected representatives. Such was the pressure on Arthur Balfour, the Leader of the Opposition, that he resigned his position as a result, it is said, from the exhaustion of it all.

The coalfield districts around the Don and Dearne, although strongly Liberal, arguably were politically on the right of the Liberal politics, certainly being somewhat conservative towards the question of votes for women. Mr J.A. Pease the Liberal MP for the Rotherham Division was, unlike his Liberal colleague at Doncaster, opposed to women obtaining the franchise.

Pease was campaigning in Rotherham on October in readiness for the December General Election when he was confronted by a group of Suffragettes. Mr Pease, who had just become the President of the Board of Education, received a deputation at the Crown Hotel, Rotherham, from the Women's Social and Political Union (WSPU). This included Mrs Slack, the Secretary of the Rotherham branch of the WSPU, Lady Constance Lytton and Mrs F. Brookshank, 'Vice Chairman' of the Rotherham Women's Liberal Association. The deputation also included Miss Adela Pankhurst, the lesser known daughter of Mrs Emmeline Pankhurst. Pease urged that there was not sufficient demand for such women's suffrage. The member for Rotherham suggested that if one was to walk down the street of his constituency one would not find a majority for the women's vote. He was not however prepared to put such a claim to the test when asked to do so by Miss Pankhurst.

Mr Pease declared he would vote against the Conciliation Bill, which was to come before Parliament shortly in November. Mrs Brooksbank urged him to support this first step to the long awaited women's vote. The Bill, if passed, would have given around one million, wealthy property-owning women the vote in a general election. The Bill was originally supported by Asquith and despite Pease's voting intentions it actually passed its first stage. Unfortunately, for the women of the movements for the vote, Asquith refused to allow it sufficient parliamentary time to proceed further. There were to be a further two Conciliation Bills in 1911 and 1912, both of which failed, despite the efforts of the militant Suffragettes, the moderate, National Union of Women's Suffrage Societies (NUWSS), the Suffragists and others, including sympathetic, progressive males.

The failure of the Bill's progress and the general refusal to meet the women's demands led to an aggressive protest outside Parliament on so called Black Friday of 18th November. Women demonstrators were rough-handled by the police authorities and many arrests were made. It is difficult to know what was most abhorrent in the minds of ordinary working class man and women: militant tactics of the Suffragettes of arson, systematic smashing of windows and the general disruption of political meetings, particularly those of the Liberal Party, or the barbaric treatment of women prisoners by the authorities. The treatment saw the callous force-feeding of women hunger strikers and the emotionally damaging use of the Prisoner (Temporary Discharge of Ill Health) Act 1913, better known as the 'Cat and Mouse' Act. This witnessed women released from prison after their health had been severely damaged by force feeding only to be returned when they were considered fit to serve the remainder of their prison sentence.

Adela Pankhurst had been sent to Sheffield in about 1908 to organise women activists in the district. In 1910 and 1911 she resided at 45, Marlborough Road, Sheffield. She had first spoken in Rotherham's St George's Hall at a meeting held on Wednesday 12th June. This was a meeting attempting to set up branch of the WSPU which would attract women activists in the Rotherham area.

By this time in 1910, Adela was beginning to have doubts over the militant's direct action tactics which favoured the use of violence. Prior to her doubts Adela had followed the WSPU line of engaging in acts of violence. She was arrested for disrupting one of Churchill's meetings in 1909, and sent to Strangeways Prison, for seven days, after refusing to pay a fine. Here she was forced-fed, as were her colleagues, including Lady Lytton, who attended the Pease meeting in Rotherham. On another occasion Lady Constance Lytton was arrested and thrown into Walton Prison, Liverpool and force-fed despite not having any medical examination. She had disguised herself as a poorly paid seamstress named Jane Warton. When her true identity became known to the authorities she was speedily released. Lady Constance Lytton was the daughter of Lord Lytton, former Viceroy of India and something of an embarrassment to the Liberal Government.

Adela Pankhurst had in fact been assigned to disrupt Home Secretary Winston Churchill's meetings at the time she was sent to Sheffield as an organiser. Conveniently for the Suffragettes, Churchill visited Sheffield during the campaign for the December General Election. The Suffragettes continuously attempted to disturb Churchill's meetings. The Home Secretary was well protected as he boarded his private railway carriage and made his way to Rotherham by rail. At the Great Central Railway station in Rotherham, Churchill's carriage was detached and stood in the station yard during the early hours of the morning of 1st December. With the carriage blinds firmly closed, the Home Secretary is said to have had discussions with the Rotherham Liberal candidate Mr Pease. This political assembly was again under the secure protection of a number of detectives including a Chief Inspector McCathey of Scotland Yard.

The Sheffield Suffragette, being given word of Mr Churchill's movements, rushed over to Rotherham to try to engage him and his political colleagues. At around midnight the Suffragettes tried to scale the walls of the station yard, with one woman disguised as a nurse. She was said to have been armed with a pot of green paint and a bag of flour. The determined militant was restrained from completing her objective by a local police officer. Mr Winston Churchill was able to continue his journey safely when his carriage was attached to an express at 2.30 in the morning to head northwards to York.

It is not known whether Adela Pankhurst was among these who sought to challenge the Home Secretary, it is simply reported that they were prominent Sheffield Suffragettes. Adela was certainly back in Rotherham for a meeting in the Town Hall Assembly Rooms on Tuesday 6th December, when she shared a platform with some distinguished speakers for women's suffrage.

Adela Pankhurst was to speak for the last time in Rotherham with her mother Emmeline Pankhurst at a packed WPSU meeting in May 1911, again at the Town Hall Assembly Rooms, presided over by the Reverend T. James of Sheffield. The second Conciliation Bill was just about to come before Parliament and a resolution asking for immediate passage through the Commons was carried unanimously. Mrs Pankhurst dominated the proceeding with her daughter taking, on this occasion, a secondary role just confining her attack on Mr Pease's attitude to the subject of women's suffrage. Pease called upon women to canvass, to do his "dirty work". Adela remarked, "A man with such a poor opinion of the intelligence of women was not fit to be a representative for such a Division".

This was probably one of the last meetings in which Adela participated alongside her mother. Her doubts over the feasibility of violent direct action as a positive method of achieving women's right to vote, forced her to leave the WSPU in October 1911. Her references at meetings to working women and their contribution to society may be a clue to the direction of future thinking. She appears to have been influenced by the approach taken by her more radical socialist sister, Sylvia. Sylvia is said to have argued that Adela, who worked extremely hard for the movement, was not given the credit owed to her in 1913. The final rift between Emmeline Pankhurst and Adela came in 1913 at which stage she made the decision to move to Australia in 1914 on a one-way ticket paid for by her mother. They were never to meet again.

Sylvia, too, had been involved in the rift. She saw the need to organise poor working class people into trade unions and associated herself with socialist and other Labour organisations. Sylvia established the East London Federation of Suffragettes (ELFS) and a branch of the WSPU. This approach was not to the liking of Sylvia's mother or her sister Christabel. Christabel and her mother's view of internal democracy in the WPSU extended little beyond their own ideas and the idea of mass working class involvement wasn't one of them. "We only want picked women", Christabel announced.

Yet it was the cause of the women belonging to Sylvia Pankhurst's group of 'Eastenders' which must impressed the Liberal Government in appreciating that their resistance to women's suffrage could not last much longer. It was the voice and deeds of the female lower orders who would finally convince the Government of the justification of votes for women. It would be the likes of Mexborough women who worked on railway carriage cleaning, locomotive cleaning, local goods yards, brickworks, glass works, and munitions factories who would most influence the decision to give women the vote. They were just a few of the working women who were to help to secure the vote with their efforts during the First World War. More generally, women of all classes demonstrated their undoubted abilities during the war, which led to the inevitable granting of the vote, for those over 30 year olds at least, in 1918.

It is difficult to gauge with any certainty the extent of the women's suffrage movement in the Mexborough area. Certainly the suffragettes, being an upper-middle-class and even aristocratic organisation would not attract, nor would want to attract, working class women into its ranks. There does not appear to be any evidence of WSPU activity in the Mexborough Area. Mexborough was largely a working class community, and Mexborough did not have a Sylvia Pankhurst to organise its women.

Certainly the campaign for women's suffrage was supported in the area. Men like Alderman Clarke, who had congratulated the Liberal Party women workers at the Liberal victory in January, was like a number of men in the Liberal Party who gave their support. Some local trade unionists too voiced their approval. At a meeting of the Mexborough and District Trades and Labour Council, a resolution favouring votes for women was carried unanimously.

The newly formed Labour Party had it supporters too. Yet the male dominated Liberal Party in the area does not appear to be over-enthusiastic with the thought of votes for women. Even some Women's Liberal Associations were subservient to the generally cautious Liberal Party line and Mexborough does not seem to have been any different in this respect. The local press, as far as the *The Times* was concerned, had no great desire to report the activities on the positive side of the women's suffrage campaigns, in fact there was a distinct lack of interest in even the most notable national aspects of the women's suffrage movement's activities. This is despite the women's campaign being one of the biggest political issues of the period. For candidates of both Liberal and Conservative parties in the Doncaster and Rotherham Divisions the question of votes for women did not show itself to be one of their priorities at either general election of 1910.

If the women's rebellion did not feature too significantly in the lives of Mexborough people then the worker's rebellion most certainly did. Mexborough saw a rapid growth in population as a result of the coalfields expansion and the allied industries. With this economic expansion came wealth which, when unequally distributed, caused poverty, ill health and often distress among the lower classes. Despite a boom in trade and relatively full employment, real wages were dropping and poor working conditions were being experienced. Industrial injuries, dangerous workplace occurrences and fatalities were inevitable with the increase in production and productivity. With the spread of socialist and trade union ideas, working men were beginning to assert themselves in pursuit of what they saw as a fair share of the fruits of their labour. Trade union membership rapidly grew, from 2.1 million 1910 to 4.1 million in 1914. As Dangerfield puts it:

> 'The instinct of the British worker was very active in 1910. It warned him that he was underpaid, that Parliament, left to itself, would keep him underpaid; it told him that good behaviour had ceased to have meaning; it asserted that he must unite at all costs. The only visible symbol of unity was the Trade Unions: to the Trade Unions therefore he turned.'

Certainly the era of the so-called Victorian working class respectability, which had been strived for without advantage, was over.

There was widespread industrial action throughout industry during 1910, but as so often, the Government's focus was turned to the coal industry. Attention focused on the coalfields of the Rhondda Valley in South Wales and the Ely pit owned by the Naval Colliery Company. This company was part of the Cambrian Combine, a holding company with little interest beyond the profits of its shareholders. Despite the Naval Colliery Company's poor profitability, the Cambrian Combine was resolutely satisfying its shareholders; this was despite the working conditions making it difficult for the miners to earn a decent wage within the existing wage structure. Ely miners worked in conditions associated with 'abnormal places' which restricted their earnings. The complicated wage structure in mining led to a future national strike and of course south Yorkshire was not excluded. The miners of Ely demanded more than the Combine were offering and were locked out with 900 finding themselves without work on 1st September.

Five days later miners at some other Naval Collieries declared a strike in sympathy. Two weeks later all the Cambrian Combine collieries were out, with 30,000 men striking in support of the dispute which the South Wales Miners' Federation made official on the question of the 'abnormal places' issue. The employers brought in 'blacklegs' in an attempt to keep the pits in some working order. As pickets were employed by the striking miners, events become hostile and the mood extremely aggressive. In November, hundreds of police were mobilised and during the riots in Tonypandy the Home Secretary Mr Churchill (reluctantly it is said) ordered troops to be employed resulting in the death of a miner and injuries to hundreds more. The strike at the Cambrian Combine Colleries went on until August 1911 when the miners returned to work on terms that they had been offered in the early part of the dispute. They had been forced to accept these out of sheer exhaustion and near starvation. The strike had been influenced by groups of Syndicalists. Syndicalism was an ideology which had its origins in France and had a strong following in the trade unions in the USA. Its followers did not believe in a socialism which involved replacing capitalism through parliamentary democracy or by political insurrection which might bring about state socialism. The Syndicalist's aim was to overthrow the capital state by taking control of the capitalist means of production, in other words factories and industrial plant and infrastructure. The main weapon to achieve this was through militant industrial action and ultimately a general strike of workers through their trade unions.

The Syndicalists did not believe in the contemporary methods of settling disputes by conciliation and negotiations. The nature of disputes, in the great 'labour unrest' of this period, was that many of them tended to be unofficial and against the wishes of the official trade union leaders.

Syndicalism was strong in the South Wales coalfields and in the big industrial areas of Glasgow and Liverpool where it filtered into that city by way of its passage from the USA. The Syndicalists were strong in the Miners' Federation of Great Britain (MFGB) and the Amalgamated Society of Railway Servants (ASRS) later the National Railwaymans' Union (NUR) in 1913. It is known that the Sheffield branch of the ASRS was influenced by Syndicalist supporters. There appears to be no evidence that they had any real influence on trade unionism in the Mexborough and district area, however. Nevertheless Mexborough did have a branch of the newly formed British Socialist Party (BSP) which was influenced by the Syndicalist movement. Certainly the BSP had no great impact on proceedings of the Mexborough and District Trades and

Labour Council, where they appear to have been marginalised.

What the militant miners of South Wales were able to achieve through their own struggles, over what they saw as unfair rates of pay in difficult coal seams, was to bring the demand for a national minimum wage to the fore. This became an aim for all miners throughout the country. The action of the South Wales miners galvanised the miners within the south Yorkshire coalfields over the question of wage rates as it did elsewhere. In February there was a dispute at Brodsworth Colliery over the difficulty with price lists for cutting coal. This saw 1,800 men idle and the spread of the dispute to Hickleton Colliery, but neither dispute lasted long. Frickley was also in dispute, with the prospects of evictions by the coal owners of the miners and their families from their homes. By May some families of Frickley miners had to be 'housed' in camps with tents in order to relieve some of their suffering.

In June, 50,000 local miners attended their annual gala or demonstration at Doncaster. The main speaker was the famous Labour MP Kier Hardie. It is clear that the mood at the gala was tense and fractious when local MP Mr Nicholson was heckled during his address to the gathered audience. This is likely to have been a reaction to his own approach to the unrest and his colleague Mr Churchill's deployment of heavy numbers of police and the military against their comrades in South Wales.

In July, the newly opened pit of Earl Fitzwilliam at Elsecar Main was already heading for a dispute involving price lists. Discontent continued, as negotiations between the Yorkshire Miners' Association (YMA) and the Earl had not reached an agreement. The reputation that Earl Fitzwilliam is supposed to have had, that of a 'considerate master', was not evident in this particular case. A reporter on *The Times* was to remark:

> 'The hope that Earl Fitzwilliam would uphold the reputation of the Fitzwilliams in their sentiment and thought for their workmen seems to be doomed to disappointment for up to the present the Earl has given no sign of recanting the position taken some weeks ago.'

The pit management had made some concessions, with slight alterations to the list for the Parkgate seam, which were not enough to satisfy the pitmen's demands. The Earl was dealing with a different and new type of employee to that which he had previously been accustomed. These men showed less compliance and deference and belonged to a strong trade union in a period where agitation over pay and conditions in the coal industry was beginning to reach its pre-war zenith.

The management at Elsecar Colliery offered a new price list which was to come into operation on 8th September. Management gave notice to the men who were not prepared to accept the new terms and informed them that they would terminate their contracts and advised them to seek work elsewhere. A mass meeting took place at the 'Croft' adjourning the Ship Inn at Elsecar to discuss this grave situation, with a majority of the men agreeing not to accept the Earl's offer. The YMA officials realised the determination of the men but wished the dispute to be settled by conciliation or arbitration. The meeting agreed that YMA officials should approach the Earl with a deputation, with a view to achieving a settlement.

The miners refused to accept the terms of a revised offer on 8th September, the men 'withdrew tools' and as a consequence were 'locked out' by their employer. The official miners' leaders were able to get their members to accept arbitration and the men returned to work on 16th September. On the last day of September a deputation of the miners was summoned to Wentworth House to meet the Earl to talk over the arrangements for the arbitration process. It is an illustration of the gravity of the situation that representatives of the Trades Union Congress (TUC) were present at this critical meeting. There was a similar dispute over the way wages were distributed in the mining industry. Often the miners' wages were distributed by men within management who had discretion over the men's remuneration. This was the case at Manvers Main where 5,000 'downed tools' over the conduct of an under-manager accused of unfairness in the way he distributed wages.

Strike action at local collieries, usually of a short duration, happened almost weekly. The big battle in the coalfields was to come in 1912, following the confrontation in the railway industry in the previous year. Trade union membership had grown rapidly in these two dominant local industries, but this growth was not confined to these particular industries. In Mexborough and district hundreds were employed in glass and bottle manufacturing. The industry had its own trade union and in 1910 the Mexborough and district glass workers were also in dispute with their employers.

Around the turn of the century, to counter the growth and bargaining power of the trade unions, employers formed their own unions known as employers' federations or associations. This gave individual employers the ability to cooperate with others in the federation or association to help break strikes by initiating lock-outs in each of the employers' workplaces. This placed pressure on the men to return to work in recognition of their colleagues' hardship. It could of course work in favour of the trade unions if collective strike action between the men's workplaces was achieved. The employers' association could be advantageous to both sides, however. The trade union could negotiate with representatives of an association over wages and conditions for all those workplaces in the association. This could deliver a satisfactory outcome for even the weaker organised trade union in a workplace and quite often the employers welcomed the control trade officials were able to exert over their membership.

At the end of April, *The Times* headline read, 'Glass Bottle Dispute' and remarked that it was a 'serious situation'. Many glass workers in the district were organised in the Glass Bottle Workers' Union. Yet there were a number of firms who were not in the Employers' Combine, (the Amalgamated Association of Glass Bottle Manufacturers). The non members of the Association included: Kilner's at Conisbrough, employing 450 'hands', Mexborough firms, Barron's, with 200 'hands', Don Glass Works also with 200 employees, P.I. Waddington and Son and the Swinton based South Yorkshire Bottle Manufacturing Company, with just 150 workers.

It was imperative that the Combine persuaded the non-Combine men to join their Association. It claimed that there was a general slump in manufacturing and the industry was being challenged by increased foreign competition. The non-Combine firms were underselling to the detriment of those in the Association. On 30th April the struggle between the two sides began with the withdrawal of labour from union members in those non-Combine workplaces who were fighting against inclusion. The workers insisted that they would not give a weapon to their employers, but that it was in the workers' interest to ensure that prices were regulated in order to remove the cut-throat policy that was resulting in underselling. This in turn was reducing wages as the employers sought to maintain profit margins. They insisted that through the British Association of Manufacturers there was an international agreement with Germany not to undersell each other and create a level playing field of 'fair competition'. It was maintained that it was in everyone's interest all local firms to be part of the Association. The union's action was undoubtedly of assistance to the Combine employers, but there is no evidence collaboration took place between the official trade union leaders and the Association.

The stoppage affected some 400 workers locally and seriously disrupted the local economy, as all the local firms were shut down. The dispute was a bitter one and by the end of May only two Don Valley glass bottle employers resisted what was described as the 'complete mastery of the British glass-making trade' by the Combine. Waddington's attempted to bring in men (blacklegs) to break the strike, but union pickets were successful in impeding them from commencing work. Despite this there was a report of a blackleg being assisted over the workplace wall by a member of the public who happened to be passing by. The response to this was to intensify and maintain the vigil of pickets.

On 24th June, after a strike lasting eight weeks, a Mr Greenwood, the secretary of the union, met with the management and trustees of the

Don Works in Mexborough and an agreement was reached that the firm should join the Association of Glass Bottle Manufacturers. The Mexborough employer's resolve had been broken and all Mexborough glass bottle workers returned to work. This left the South Yorkshire Glass Bottle Manufacturing Company as the only English firm outside the Association, leaving it in a precariously isolated position. It could not possibly defy the pressure to join its fellow employers indefinitely.

The dispute had cost the Glass Bottle Union a total of £1,500 after paying out 25/- (£1.25p) a week strike pay to its members for the duration of the eight week stoppage. Although not a vast income by the standards of the day it would have been just sufficient to maintain a reasonable subsistence. This union expenditure must have been a strain upon its funds. Whether the Employer's Association was of any assistance to the union in helping to fund such a level of strike pay will probably remain open to conjecture. Any evidence of this kind would no doubt have been embarrassing to both union and employers.

There was every indication that the railway industry was becoming unsettled with poor wages and conditions, especially for lower grades of railway workers. In the middle of the district's glass bottle dispute, the local branches of the ASRS held, on a sultry Sunday afternoon of 22nd May, a mass meeting at Mexborough Public Hall. The meeting was chaired by Mr C. W. Beardsley, of Sheffield, a representative of Midland Railway workers on the company's Conciliation Board. He was joined on the platform by Mr W.J. Ford, secretary for Mexborough No 1 Branch and three representatives from the Swinton Branch, Messrs Wood, Hill and Daniels.

The speaker and main attraction at the meeting was Jimmy Thomas (J.H. Thomas). Thomas had just being elected as the Labour MP for Derby in the January General Election. A Welshman from Newport, Monmouthshire, he had quickly risen through the ranks of the union. He had been the union's President and at the time of this meeting was an Organising Secretary. There is every suspicion that there was a degree of self-interest in the attendance of Mr Thomas at this particular meeting. There was every likelihood that he would be standing for the vacant position of the union's Assistant General Secretary; a position which he won easily in September. Mr Thomas was to become the union's General Secretary in 1916 (the National Union of Railwaymen, NUR by this time). He was offered a position in Lloyd George's wartime Coalition Government of 1917, and served as a cabinet minister in the first Labour Government in 1924. As a TUC leader involved in the 1926 General Strike he was an extremely conciliatory voice and was instrumental in assisting in the conclusion of the strike after only eight days. Some railway workers would have seen Jimmy Thomas as a clever shrewd negotiator, others would have seen him as a political careerist, opportunist and traitor to the working class movement.

The chairman Mr Beardsley described Mexborough as a "little stronghold in the railway world" in the south Yorkshire area. He voiced his discontent with the system of conciliation and arbitration operating in the railway companies and argued for more worker representation through the Labour Party. Mr Thomas initially spoke of his sadness at the death of King Edward VII, paying tribute to the late monarch. Despite the trade union and Labour movement's class approach to its struggles with Government and employers, there was a palpable sense of loyalty to the British monarchy which Edward himself had helped to create.

Mr Thomas also mentioned the sad events in the Cumberland town of Whitehaven which had occurred on 11th May 1910, a few days before this particular mass meeting of railway workers. An explosion and fire at the town's Wellington Pit ended in the death of 136 men and boys. 85 women lost their husbands in the disaster resulting in 260 fatherless children. This railwaymen's leader believed it was the duty of Government to reduce risk to miners through legislation. Such legislation was enacted the next year, but made little difference to the dangers faced by miners. On Sunday 22nd May, the same hot day as the railwaymen's meeting took place, churches and chapels throughout the district were crowded for memorial services for the victims of the Whitehaven tragedy. The sense of a great affinity with the Whitehaven families must have been palpable.

The legislation of which Mr J.H. Thomas had spoken, to improve safety in the collieries, was enacted in 1911 but in practice did little to reduce coal mining fatalities and injuries. It certainly made little difference to the dangers faced by miners, as the community in south Yorkshire coalfields were to experience in 1912. On 9th July of that year a total of 92 men lost their lives as a result of two explosions at Cadeby Main Colliery. The dreadful tragedy has been well documented over the years and need not be repeated here. It was a disaster which shook the surrounding community, having a profound impact on the consciousness of the peoples of the local area, including of course, Mexborough.

Mining communities and indeed most of Britain were devastated by yet another disaster at the Senghenydd Colliery on 14th October 1913. This was another explosion which saw the death of 439 miners in the pit community near Caerphilly, Glamorganshire. At the time it was the most serious loss of life in the coal mining industry anywhere in the world. On a weekly basis the newspapers of the period contained reports of injury and death within the local mining industry.

It is no coincidence that these injuries and fatalities in the mining industry happened at the same time as an increase in coal production. Coal production from British mines was at its highest in the period around 1910-913, these being the most profitable years before the beginning of the First World War. This expansion saw a massive growth in population in the area. In 1901 the population of Mexborough was 10,430; by 1911 it had grown to 14,308. This increase of nearly 40%, brought about by economic expansion and prosperity, came with social problems. Housing shortages, led to poor living conditions, poverty and notably a high infant mortality rate. It is not surprising that with such economic prosperity existing alongside a range of social problems, a breeding ground for militancy and unrest was created in the British coalfields. In *The Times* of 12th February 1910 a headline of 'Mexborough's Bootless Children' appeared. Many children were not attending school because they lacked clothing. Mr H. O'Neil, the Schools' Attendance Officer, appealed to the people of Mexborough for 100 pairs of boots and any spare clothing they might have. Donations were to be taken to the donor's nearest school or *The Times'* Office.

With the growth of the population, Mexborough witnessed the opening of the Secondary School at College Road in January 1910, under the headship of Mr Thomas Wilson Ireland. This splendid building of some architectural note was not fully completed until a year later with the cost of the building escalating from £13,000 to £21,000 by its completion. Mexborough councillor John E. Cliff was later to express the view that Mr Ireland's salary was too high and that with annuities Mr Ireland would be earning £500 per annum by 1919. Councillor Cliff was also concerned that preparatory classes at the school were too expensive to run and were simply a finishing school for the district's upper and middle classes.

Some had seen Mexborough Secondary School as a somewhat elitist establishment. Mexborough was in desperate need of an elementary school to accommodate the needs of children of the area which had rapidly expanded from about 1900. In response to this need, Adwick Road School was opened in December 1911, having taken fourteen months to complete. It accommodated 420 pupils and cost £7,000. The school was fully equipped with electric lighting, a new innovation to many of its pupils, no doubt. It was, nevertheless, clearly a school for working class pupils. *The Times'* report on the school's facilities indicated that much of the learning would emphasise the division of labour between the girl's future occupations and that of the boys. There was a splendid new woodworking facility for the boys and for the girls a wonderfully equipped kitchen with a Yorkshire range, 'commonly used in Yorkshire homes'.

With the growth in population and the availability, for many, of more disposable income as a result of economic growth, a need for entertaining the masses grew. This saw a spate of new cinemas and other places of entertainment. The first of these was the New Cinema House in Garden Street, opened in the summer of 1908. It later came to be called the Cosy Cinema, but later suffered from wartime decline in audiences and closed in 1915. The Olympic Skating Rink was opened on Swinton Road in January 1910 by the Mexborough and Swinton Roller Rink Company. It was reopened as a cinema in June 1911, renamed as the Empire Palace in the same year as the Royal Electric Picture Palace on Bank Street was opened. Such was the popularity of the new entertainment offered by the picture house, that yet another one, the Oxford Picture Palace, was opened in October 1912, in Oxford Road.

The growth of moving pictures did not initially undermine Mexborough's theatre life; The Prince of Wales Theatre opened in 1893 and was renamed the Hippodrome in 1913. It was able to maintain its income with some enterprising diversity, hosting public meetings and boxing contests. The Olympic, too was to become an arena for boxing, a sport that was popular in Mexborough. The sport locally was no doubt enhanced by the town's fortune in gaining its own heavyweight champion of England, one James William 'Iron' Hague, who took the title in 1909. The town can be said to have produced and developed (and arguably still does) some very fine boxing talent.

Football and cricket were two other sports which were popular in Mexborough. As far as football is concerned Mexborough Town, who played in the Midlands League, by 1910 was struggling to maintain its position of previous years. The club struggled to pay the players' wages, making it difficult to attract players of the quality needed to be competitive in a league which contained some clubs, which at the time, would have been considered 'heavyweights'. The club relied heavily on local benefactors to keep it solvent.

Cricket fared somewhat better in Mexborough. Being more of a 'gentleman's sport' devoid of what was often seen as unrefined professionalism, it was able to survive the rigour of the competitiveness increasingly evident in Association Football. Mexborough Cricket Club was able to build its own pavilion at its ground at Hampden Road, a building shared with other sporting activities. The club's lavish Annual Ball, was held after 1910 in the great hall of Mexborough Secondary School. It was a Ball which was always well supported by the town's most prominent dignitaries.

One recreational activity in which the people of Mexborough could not participate, at least in Mexborough itself, was swimming. During the period just before the war, Mexborough Council was constantly debating the issue of building public baths in the town. In April 1911, Councillor Rowan spoke of residents having to go to surrounding areas. He was aware that Wath was about to open its own new public baths a little later in June. Teachers at the National School had been granted permission to take their scholars to Wath so that they could use the new bathing facilities. Rowan suggested that it would be cheaper if the town were to have its own bathing facilities. Council Rowan suggested the Council establish a Baths Committee, an idea that was taken up.

The issue of the importance of having public baths which were conveniently located for the people of Mexborough was regularly discussed. It would benefit the town sanitarily as well as having an educational value. Councillor John Cliff had suggested swimming should be on the school curriculum. The local papers often ran a story of drowning in the River Don or the canal. One of the most tragic of these drowning incidents was to take place in May 1911, shortly before the opening of the Wath Baths. The fatality was a young thirteen year old Harold Seymour. He was in a pleasure boat with his sister and another young women, a boat which was under the charge of the boat owner, Mr Fred Woffinden, a well-known local entrepreneur and later a councillor. Woffinden had lost a leg in a pit accident some years previously and it was believed this may have caused some difficulty with the handling of the boat, which on this occasion capsized. Harold Seymour's funeral took place on 16th May 1911. There is reported to have been a crowd of over 500 mourners who lined the streets through Mexborough. The funeral was held up for an hour because of an 'unfortunate incident' at the cemetery. It can only be speculated that there may have been some possible hostility towards Mr Woffinden for his part in boat tragedy.

The 1911 local election, which took place in March, is reported as being featureless and with little public interest. The candidates were remarkably quiet, although the Liberals were to canvass every house in the Mexborough area, probably aware of the strong threat from the rising Labour Party. The result changed little but it saw the election of the popular Liberal schoolteacher William Winstanley, who was to become prominent during the war years. Two sitting councillors lost their seats, Charles Evans and also John Sopps, the mineral water manufacturer. Sopps had been fined £5 for assaulting a tenant of his the previous year, which may not have helped his cause. One of the first tasks of the 1911 Mexborough U.D.C. was to form a Coronation Committee to raise funds for the forthcoming celebration for the crowning of King George V. The committee was chaired by Councillor Tom Athron with Councillor Frank Law its secretary.

The Coronation took place on Thursday 22nd June. *The Times* reports that during the celebrations:

> *'Mexborough was not exactly a blaze of colour nor were the inhabitants given the spectacular show of a prossession in a town well qualified by experience in the*

art of demonstrating...In the first place a brass band could not be found for love or money, so the fire engine, Sunday school and club banners and the other 'regular' items of an organised march were left at home.'

Despite this, the town was not entirely without colour. Flags waved from the public buildings and the workers had decorated their houses with bunting as a very evident demonstration of loyalty and patriotism.

There is evidence that the Coronation Committee had raised sufficient funds to at least ensure the children of the town were entertained. The Committee achieved the remarkable feat of providing tea for 3,400 children between the age of three and fourteen at Doncaster Road and Garden Street schools as well as Sunday schools throughout the town. Free entertainment was provided for 1,000 children at the Royal Electric Theatre while Tom Athron and William Winstanley toured the town distributing Coronation medals to all the children of Mexborough.

The Coronation celebration continued into Friday when it was the turn of the 'old folk' to enjoy the festive events. They were entertained, too, in the Royal Electric Theatre, followed by tea in the Market Hall. The Market Hall is said to have been transformed by Mr R. Grainger into a 'place of colour and beauty'. Here all ladies over the age of 60 were presented with half a pound caddy of tea by courtesy of the Barnsley British Cooperative Society.

The Coronation celebrations can be said to have been somewhat overshadowed by events occurring in British industrial relations. The miners in South Wales were still engaged in a bitter struggle with their employers, a dispute that was now bringing untold hardship for miners and their families. There were local disputes surfacing on a regular basis throughout the coalfields over the long-standing issue of the minimum wage in the industry. This included south Yorkshire, with Fitzwilliam's pit at Elsecar in dispute in July. The pit boys at Roundwood, Silverwood, Dalton Main and other collieries in this area were also in dispute over price lists in August.

The summer of 1911 was on record as the hottest since recordings began in 1841. This long, hot summer boiled over into a major transport strike throughout the country. Seamen at Southampton were to be the first to show, with a strike which held up the newly launched White Star liner *'Olympic'* from sailing. The men won a rapid pay increase. A general transport strike Liverpool of dockers, sailors, and railwaymen broke out in June in Liverpool. It continued for some weeks with troops being called to the city and ended in violence in August, when police broke up a demonstration in which two demonstrators were killed. Of this strike wave, Lord Derby at the War Office, remarked that this was no ordinary strike but one that had the features of a revolution. The strike had an immediate impact on the local pits. Cadeby and Denaby Main were shut down in early June as a result of their coal exports being held up at Hull and Immingham. No wagons were returning from these ports to Hickleton, Elsecar and Wombwell Main, resulting in these pits being unable to work.

With the general mood of industrial unrest as it was in 1911, railway workers, too, were in no mood to remain silent about their own grievances. Not only were railway workers' wages generally falling behind those of miners in some districts, their hours of work were long: 60 hours a week was normal. The railwaymen also had justifiable grievances against the directors of their companies, many whom resisted any negotiations with their trade unions. Indeed some directors were positively hostile to trade unionism and had no wish to enter into meaningful discussion with the men's representatives. One of the major demands of the men was that their trade unions should be officially recognised by the railway companies for the purpose of collective bargaining.

Unofficial strikes broke out across the country starting on the Great Central Railway at New Holland in July, spreading to Paddington on the Great Western Railway on 10th August and then to other cities such as city as Birmingham and Sheffield. There is little doubt that syndicalist trade unionists had a hand in this spread of industrial action. It was clear that the trade union leaders of four of the major railway trade unions could not control the situation and called for a strike of united action on 18th August. Areas such as Mexborough and Wath, which employed many railway employees, were of course immediately affected.

The two main unions, the Amalgamated Society of Railway Servants (ASRS) and the locomotivemen's union ASLEF were, on this occasion, as one, in this coordinated action which became the first national railway strike in Britain. The leader of ASLEF was Albert Fox, a man who Mexborough railwaymen would have known well. Born in Aldershot, Albert moved to Mexborough to work at the Locomotive Depot, or the Plant as it was often called. He joined ASLEF in 1886, as a locomotive fireman, when he became branch secretary for Mexborough. By 1891 he was promoted to driver and by 1897 was elected on the union's Executive Committee and became its President in 1900. A year later Albert Fox was elected ASLEF's General Secretary. During his time in Mexborough, Albert Fox lived in various properties in Wath Road, and was still living at 53, Wath Road when he become ASLEF leader in 1901, although he soon moved near to ASLEF's Head Office located in Leeds at that time. During the 1911 strike Albert Fox was suffering from illness, but despite this insisted on demonstrating his leadership during a critical period in the union's history. He died in Leeds in March 1914.

Panic-stricken by the railway strike, the Government moblised the military in many parts of the country. An attachment of Gordon Highlanders arrived at Rotherham Masborough railway station as a 'precaution' to control the 30 to 40 pickets that had gathered there. The police were busy with the protection of goods, particularly food stuff, as they worked with traders to enable them to retrieve their goods from the railway yards. Miners in the area were unhappy about the railway's employment of non-union labour as 'blacklegs' and considered sympathetic action. Generally it is reported locally that the striking railwaymen were solid and would remain so until their demands were met.

The *Barnsley Chronicle* reported a 'gloomy outlook' at Barnsley's railway stations. The Lancashire and Yorkshire Railway attempted to run trains with mixed success on the first day of the strike. The same, too, can be said of the Great Central and the Midland Railway which ran trains from Court House station. The services of these two railways were described as 'dislocated'. Yet as the strike entered the second day, the men were showing solidarity with their union's strike call and the railway system generally came to a standstill.

The *Rotherham Advertiser* of 19th August illustrates the fear that the railway strike was to instil in many minds of the Liberal and Conservative press. 'Not a week goes by without a trade dispute or lockout in one part of the country or another...Class has been set against class and a state of anarchy has prevailed very similar to the state of affairs that preceded the French Revolution'. Nevertheless, the *Rotherham Advertiser* does have to conclude, despite its fears, that no violence had been witnessed in the area. A mass meeting, called by the ASRS at Barnsley, urged all men to join the strike, but union officials would condemn any violence. There were no reports of violence in Barnsley either. This certainly was not the case everywhere. This was particularly the case in Liverpool and Llanelli where serious violence occurred, the latter place witnessing the death of two men, when a crowd attempted stop a train and the army intervened. There was also violence, but on a lesser scale, in the Mexborough area.

Events in Mexborough and district give some indication of the confusion which surrounded this first national railway strike. *The Times*, before the start of the official strike action, was somewhat relieved that the Don and Dearne Valley was 'well away from the seat of the mischief', but feared that 'the mischief elsewhere was becoming a powerful influence'. The newspaper had cause to voice this concern. News of the events happening elsewhere created the 'spontaneous action' on Wednesday 16th August, when some local railwaymen attempted to persuade men working on the permanent way and at the Mexborough 'Plant', to withdraw their labour unofficially. This was not successful, as most men were waiting for official instructions from their trade union leaders.

On the evening of the Wednesday, a delegation of Mexborough railwaymen attended the Strike Committee at Sheffield. It was likely that this Committee was influenced by a small, but vocal, group of Syndicalists. The Committee instructed the Mexborough railwaymen to withdraw their labour as from six o'clock that evening. It was an instruction which the Mexborough delegation refused to carry out, though, again on the basis of their preference for waiting for instructions from their national leaders. Nevertheless it was reported that by Wednesday evening, Wath Yard was at a standstill.

Local railwaymen finally received the official strike call late on Thursday 17th August. A telegram from ASRS Head Office was received by the secretary of the Swinton Branch of that Union at eight o'clock in the evening. Head Office's communication read, 'All railwaymen strike at once. Loyalty to one another means victory.' The Swinton Branch Secretary immediately called a meeting which saw a reported 1,000 railwaymen and members of the public attending. Such was the size of the meeting that it had to be held in the yard near the Ship Inn, rather than in the Inn itself. Swinton signalman Tom Henson chaired the meeting with the Mexborough men being represented by William Hill, the secretary of Mexborough ASRS No 1 Branch. Mr F.R. Oliver was the men's principal speaker.

After the meeting a decision was made to march the assembled railwaymen into Mexborough amid a good deal of singing and chanting on what would have been a beautiful summer evening. Once in Mexborough, the march stopped at the South Yorkshire public house where 'three cheers' were given for Mexborough No 2 Branch, who were themselves meeting to discuss the situation. From here the marchers' next port of call was the Old Mason's Arms where Mexborough ASRS No 1 Branch held their meetings. The procession became larger and larger as it met in orderly fashion at the Montagu Square. The railwaymen were now being joined by members of the public and by some excitable individuals who had the potential to cause disorder. The large crowd now marched down Station Road towards the railway station, with a posse of eight policemen in attendance. When they reached the station they witnessed a few passengers anticipating some kind of train services, but also two others patrolling the platform, who were none other than Superintendent Hickes from Doncaster and Mexborough's Inspector Fairburn. At the moment the crowd arrived a train pulled in, but left without incident. As for the next arrival, some of the younger strikers called to the driver and fireman to get out of their cab and join them, but they declined.

As darkness began to descend, the mixed crowd of railwaymen and public became a little hostile and as a result two windows in the booking office were broken, probably it is suggested, by mischievous boys. The crowd's next target was the station signal box.

A number within the gathering masses shouted to the signalman to immediately leave his box. He refused, insisting he would finish his shift. This met with a mixed response, but as *The Times* reported his reply was accepted by 'the more sensible men'.

The next morning, Friday 18th August, the strike was made official and this prompted a large crowd to gather down Mexborough's Station Road. The platforms were now guarded by a considerable presence of police officers, with a number of specials by now being sworn in. Some trains did run at very irregular intervals, but a large presence of pickets in the Mexborough area ensured that the system locally was virtually at a standstill. Some men continued to work and the two signalmen at each end of Swinton Midland station had to have police protection. Pickets were not totally successful and a number of 'blacklegs' reported for work. At Mexborough, five engine drivers and a guard reported for work, but later decided to join their colleagues on strike.

One railwayman who did cross the picket line, or at least found his way through it without being detected, was Mexborough locomotive driver, John Oliver. Ironically John Oliver's brother was a local trade union leader in the ASRS, but John had decided to stay loyal to the Great Central Railway, his employers. Driver Oliver is said to have driven a locomotive of a train from Retford to Cleethorpes and in doing so was attacked at Grimsby, resulting in him requiring medical attention. He was also said to have driven a train of soldiers of the Gordon Highlanders Regiment, who were busy with protecting non-strikers, goods and services. John Oliver's loyalty to his employer made him very unpopular, particularly with the residents of Swinton.

The news came through at seven o'clock on the evening of Saturday 19th August that a settlement had been agreed between the Government, employers and trade unions, which effectively ended the dispute. The locomen hurriedly arranged a mass meeting on the cricket field at Hampton Road to organise the calling for full reinstatement on resumption of work.

The calling-off of the strike was not accepted as dispassionately everywhere in the area. At eleven o'clock on Saturday evening what was described as a 'riot' broke out when a signal box on the Midland Railway near Wath Road was attacked by a hostile crowd. The relationship between the strikers' officials and the police had been good and any violence was immediately condemned by the local trade union leaders. Nevertheless, there were those who were dissatisfied by the decision to call the strike off and elements of non-railway workers who were intent to get involved. A mass crowd, which is reported to have swelled to 3,000, gathered at the top end of Wath Road, by the cottages on Wragby Row. Their aim was to confront the signalmen at the nearby Midland

Railway signal boxes. Inspector Fairburn and about 20 to 30 men found it extremely difficult to keep order. Two officers were hit by flying bottles during the riot. It had been another very hot day and many of the rioters were worse for drink and were scarcely aware of the objective of their violence towards the police and those the police were attempting to protect. The crowd contained many women and young children, all apparently spoiling for a fight. One woman shouted, to some of the less violent railwaymen, that they, the railwaymen, were faint-hearted and looked to the colliers to fight their battles.

As the night air cooled so did the tempers of the mass crowd at the 'Wath Road Riot'. The incident on Wath Road may have been the continuation of the events of earlier in the evening. At about nine o'clock on that Saturday evening, trouble had erupted outside Swinton Midland Station. In this incident another large crowd had gathered resulting in a passing tramcar having one of its windows smashed by some stone-throwing individuals.

As daylight arrived on Sunday morning, the more moderate souls of Mexborough and district no doubt gave a sigh of relief. A meeting was held on the Leach which was attended by not just railwaymen, but by members of the Mexborough Urban and District Council. The meeting was presided over by David Humphreys, the Secretary of Mexborough ASLEF Branch. The meeting was arranged to outline the settlement that had been agreed in London the night before. Humphreys was particularly keen to ensure that his men were reinstated to their previous employment and grades. Thus the meeting was adjourned for a delegation, led by the ASLEF Secretary, to meet Mr Charles H. Hugell, the Locomotive Superintendent, for the assurances the men sought. Mr Hugell in his enthusiasm to see an end to the dispute had walked from Doncaster to Mexborough. He, like the Mexborough Station Master, gave the assurance that the men would receive full reinstatement. The locomotivemen, on the termination of the mass meeting, attended the 'Plant' to ascertain their next turn of duty. Buoyed by the satisfaction that a trouble-free return to work was possible, the assembled men of the mass meeting marched towards the town to join the Montagu Hospital Procession which was taking place that day. What *The Times* had headlined as the 'Unprecedented Labour Struggle' and a union 'Declaration of War' was now over. The newspaper the following week was happy to report the stories of the struggle under the headline, 'The Calm after the Storm'.

The strike was thus called off after just two days, as a result of the clever intervention of Lloyd George. Prime Minister Asquith, who was keen that the railway dispute should end, was not the man to handle such a delicate issue as the relationship between workers and employers. Asquith offered the unions a Royal Commission to look into their grievances, but this was rejected on the basis of the length of time such a body would take to deliver its conclusions. Lloyd George understood Asquith's solution would not 'cut any ice' with the railwaymen. He was able to get both sides 'around the table', something that had not been achieved before, given the reluctance of the Railway Directors to do so. The union was promised that Conciliation Boards, which up to then had not worked favourably for the workers, would be altered to allow union representation on them, along with a shorter period in which the Board should hear the union's demands. Lloyd George further offered them a Special Commission of Inquiry that would speedily reach conclusions on the industrial relations problems that had beset the railways for many years.

Towards the end of the year the revisions to the Conciliation Boards were seen by the men as having made little difference and the Executive Committee of the ASRS was forced to hold a ballot over the question of further strike action. Mr J. H. Thomas, by this time the Assistant General Secretary of the ASRS, was forced to come to Mexborough to attempt to calm any dissent that was potentially building amongst the rank and file. Thomas spoke on Sunday 3rd December in front of a 1,000 strong audience gathered in the Empire Theatre. The meeting was presided over by Councillor William Frow, himself a Mexborough railway signalman. To say Thomas was a moderate trade union leader is perhaps an understatement. He was a shrewd handler of mass meetings and appears to have had no difficulty in stifling any hard-line dissent and militancy which may have existed within the assembled railway workers.

The ballot for further industrial action was due to close two days after Jimmy Thomas's visit to Mexborough. Mr Thomas was likely to have some idea which way the vote was likely to go when he was addressing the railwaymen at the Empire Palace. At a meeting in Nottingham on 17th December Mr Thomas was asked to reveal the result to members of the audience, but refused to announce it, despite having the figures in his pocket. It was likely that there was a majority for strike action. The railwaymen's leaders had been alarmed by their members' enthusiasm to confront the employers again through strike action. Any future strike action might this time be more difficult to control. The result was no doubt used as a negotiating lever to encourage the railway directors to discuss an improved system of conciliation. Some men were able to achieve moderate gains under the new arrangements during 1912, but not all railway companies were as 'charitable' as others: the Great Central Railway being one of those who held back on wage increases, although some signalmen on this railway did see an increase in their earnings.. Discontent on the country's railways, like other industries, continued throughout 1912, 1913 and into the onset of the First World War itself.

Mexborough glass bottle workers c 1900. In April 1910, the Glass Bottle Workers' Union called a strike in Mexborough over union recognition.

Former Mexborough loco driver, Albert Fox, became the General Secretary of ASLEF in 1901 and led his union into the 1911 national railway strike.

This picture of William Ward outside his home in Denaby Main during the Miners' strike in 1921 shows the extent of poverty in the district. His son, Ambrose, on his right, lived into his 80's.

A tea party for the children of the poor, held by Reverend Thomas Anderson of the Congregational Church during the Christmas period of 1912.

Mexborough's UDC's Medical Officer, Dr John James Huey served Mexborough for over 40 years. Seen here in the centre wearing his distinctive top hat, pictured outside the Council Offices circa 1925. Note Sapper Hackett VC's memorial in its original position.

1910 Elsecar Main Colliery was opened in 1908. Despite the owner, Earl Fitzwilliam's reputation for consideration for his men, disputes at the pit were a feature of the labour unrest before the war.

1910-11 As the pre-war population of Mexborough grew, so did entertainment establishments. Pictured are the staff of the Empire Cinema which opened in June 1910.

In the years before the war, Mexborough men and women were enthusiastic for the newly established entertainment of cinema. The Prince of Wales Theatre became known as the Hippodrome in 1913, showing films as well as live entertainment.

Decorations in the Market Hall in preparation for the 1911 Coronation transforming it into 'a place of colour and beauty'.

Chapter One

Sunshine and Shadows:
More Unrest and One Bright Moment
Part Two: 1912 & 1913

The year 1911 witnessed many days lost through strike action, but 1912 was to see many more. The perpetual disputes in the coal-mining industry, many of which were unofficial and spontaneous, came to a head at the beginning of the year. At the MFGB National Conference held at Birmingham, the decision was made to call a national ballot over the claim for a national minimum wage of no less than 5/- (25p) a shift for men and 2/- (10p) for boys. The first day of the ballot took place in early January 1912 and there was little doubt that it would see a result solidly in favour of action. This was indeed the case when the result was announced a few days later. A mass meeting of Mexborough and district miners in mid-January took place at the Empire Palace, a meeting presided over by William Goddard, a local miner's official. Here the miners set out their demand for a district minimum of 7/6d (37.5p) a shift, a rate which was slightly inferior to that which some men at Manvers Main were already enjoying. In fact, men in the Yorkshire coalfields were amongst the best earners in the country.

There were frantic negotiations between the Miners' Federation and the coal owners, with some later intervention from the Government who were increasingly alarmed by the general mood of the workers' unrest. When it was clear that the employers were not prepared to concede to their worker's demands, the MFGB gave notice to the coal owners that strike action, the first national strike action in the industry, was to take place from 26th February. The strike would potentially see a total of nearly 150,000 withdraw their labour from the Yorkshire coalfields alone. From this total the Yorkshire Miners' Association (YMA) had 90,000 members and reserve funds of £300,000, some of it available for strike pay.

On 28th February at the finish of the day's shift, 2,500 men ceased work at Manvers Main and by four in the afternoon the last coal was drawn up. It is said the men left quietly and there was no attempt to demonstrate. Some Manvers men had little to gain personally from the strike but were prepared to show solidarity with their colleagues. Manvers Main Colliery management was, however, strongly opposed to the concept of a minimum wage. It is perhaps worth adding that the men at Manvers did not expect the strike to last more than a few days, making it unnecessary even to have to bring the ponies to the surface.

There was consideration by local railwaymen about whether or not to support their comrades in the mining industry. A joint meeting between ASLEF and the ASRS was held on Sunday prior to the start of the strike, to discuss the possibly of joining in the action in a show of solidarity. It was decided not to take action until instructions from the union's head offices were received. Such instructions were never forthcoming.

The local press reported that the two weeks of the strike were conducted with an air of a holiday spirit, although it is also remarked that the outlook was grave and certainly the strike immediately impacted upon the economy, as local factories prepared to shut down. Messrs Baker's Steel Works at Kilnhurst was forced to close because of their low coal stocks. The railways found it necessary to reduce their timetables for the same reasons. It wasn't long before the holiday atmosphere began to evaporate. Strike money, of between 12/- (60p) and 15/- (75p), was being paid but it would have been a pittance compared to the reasonable wage the men in the area would be used to. Other workers were also beginning to experience the difficulties caused by the lay-offs occurring in the local factories and by 16th March, *The Times* headlines heralded, 'Distress Spreading in the District. Soup Kitchens Opened'.

The soup kitchen soon became a regular feature of life in Mexborough and district over the next five weeks or so. The local Salvation Army was dealing with 6,000 children a day. Soup Kitchens were set up at Oxford Street and St George's schools. Miss Montagu, who had been appointed in January by the Council as Mexborough's first Health Visitor, had insisted on a charge of a penny per meal for adults and their children's meals should be repaid on the ending of the strike. Miss Montagu, a relation of the local Montagu family, remarked that her insistence on repayment of money was to prevent "pampered charity". Generally the community, regardless of class and political persuasion, was sympathetic to helping to relieve some of the distress that was now evident within the district. Mr and Mrs Briggs, of the Bull's Head public house in the High Street, help to provide meals for 400, assisted by a Mr W.R.Melly of the Cosy Picture House in Garden Street. The Montagu Arms Hotel followed the example of their fellow licensees at the Bull's Head and opened their premises to provide soup and tea. The Don Working Men's Club catered for 400 children with provisions provided by various local tradesmen.

A public meeting was held in the Council Chamber on Friday 29th March which proposed the setting up of a Mexborough Distress Relief Fund for those suffering from the hardship brought about by the strike. A committee was established with Mr Neil. B. Laidlaw as its treasurer. The well-established and respected councillor Tom Athron announced that he was prepared to donate three guineas (£3.15p), a fine gesture which prompted others to follow his example. The first list of contributors published a week later certainly contained some impressive names. Mr F.J.G. Montagu, whose address at the time was Lynford Hall, Norfolk, headed the list with a 'handsome' donation of £50. A number of Mexborough councillors contributed generously, as did working men's clubs such as the Mexborough Main Street Club, which was always generous in these situations, as were picture houses such as the Royal Electric Theatre. No doubt there was an element of vested interest in some of the donations. There were also some interesting donations including a generous contribution from the Manvers Main Colliery Company, a colliery where industrial relations were considered to be relatively good. The owners of the Denaby and Cadeby Collieries did not respond to the appeal for funds, but did give £50 to Montagu Hospital. This perhaps reflected the poor industrial relations situation at these particular collieries. Local Breweries were to donate, notably Barnsley and Bentley Breweries. Even national organisations such as Maypole Dairies and Cadbury donated some of their produce.

On 21st March, the 'Education (Provision of Meals) Act' of 1906 was invoked for the first time. This piece of legislation was enacted in order to take into account emergency situations such as many of the families were now facing. A good deal of the money raised by the Mexborough Distress Relief Fund was directed at attempts to fulfil the requirements of the Act. The Act provided that teachers in schools affected should distribute coffee, cocoa and bread and butter to those school children most in need. The Doncaster Road School logbook for 21st March records '34 children given breakfast at 8.30 a.m. in accordance with the 1906 Act.' The log book for 4th April records, 'Breakfasts this week to 55, 56, 56, 55'. The Easter holidays followed but the Headmaster, Mr Brown and two of his teachers, worked through this period to continue providing the children with at least a breakfast. By the end of the strike, Doncaster Road School had provided 996 breakfasts. The majority of schools would have been under the same obligation as Doncaster Road.

Many young people found other ways of helping their families survive. Outcropping (low level surface mining) was taking place in Mexborough Brickyards, a popular venue for such activity. Youths, mainly in their teens, were busy outcropping at the Brickyard by permission of Mr S. Oliver. Often up to 20 tons a day would be moved by a variety of transport, including carts, prams and even tin baths. A good little business would have developed over the duration of the strike. A more serious trade had developed at Wath Main, where colliery spoil was transported by barge from Wath Moor Lane and then on to Doncaster.

Just as in the railway dispute, the Government was forced to intervene to bring both sides together in an attempt to solve the crisis in the coal industry. A Parliamentary Bill was proposed to establish district Minimum Wages Boards. The Bill was rushed through all of its Parliamentary stages to become law on 29th March. On the basis of a new Minimum Wage Act, the leaders of the MFGB recommended a resumption of work. Yet most miners were initially solidly against a return to work. At Manvers only 194 out of about 1,600 were to return. At Denaby and Cadeby, 230 returned, but over 650 stayed away. The national ballot, in fact, showed more voting to reject the call to return than those in favour of going back. The MFGB rule book contained the provision that a two thirds majority was needed to reject the leadership's instruction and thus those determined to continue strike action were effectively defeated. The men were, however, right about their anxiety over the functioning of the system which was supposed to achieve fair wages in the industry. Local disputes would continue right up to the beginning of the forthcoming war.

Local pitmen, despite their misgivings about how effective the new bargaining arrangement would be, loyally accepted the position and gradually returned to work. Manvers Main, Hickleton, Denaby and Cadeby had all returned by 11th April. To the relief of many, all the local factories affected by the dispute were getting back to full production. *The Times* described the great coal strike as '40 Days in the Wilderness'.

Due to the depressed atmosphere within the town, the local Council election went almost unnoticed. The newly rising Labour Party made important and historical gains in Mexborough, with the election of miner Levi Jones and John Rowan, a compositor. Fred Woffinden, or 'Fred of the Wharf' as he was known locally, despite his involvement in the drowning incident the year before, retained his seat. The popular Tom Athron also retained his seat. John Sopps, who had lost his seat the year before, again, failed to get elected. One of the sitting councillors, Frank Law, the well known landlord and sports enthusiast, had been disqualified from office in March on the grounds of his prolonged non-attendance at Council meetings.

Amid what must have been a difficult time in terms of the nation regaining some resemblance of confidence after the coal strike, the tragic news was received concerning the sinking of the Titanic. This did at least bring some unity of sorrow to the coalfield area as it did elsewhere. Mexborough Parish Church was crowded on Sunday evening of 21st April. The Mexborough Congregational Church, where the congregation was said to be visibly affected and in tears, was similarly crowded. At the Mexborough Primitive Chapel, special reference was made by the Reverend H. MacRow to the tragic sinking. Here the organist, Mr Beal, was to play the tune, reported to have been played during the sinking by Titanic's orchestra, 'Nearer my God to Thee'.

What might be seen as one bright moment was the announcement in mid-June. The Press Association made the official announcement that the King and Queen were to visit the Earl and Countess Fitzwilliam at Wentworth House. The idea that the King and Queen should visit the communities of the south Yorkshire coalfields was that of the Archbishop of York, Cosmo Gordon Lang. The royal couple were to visit various industrial areas during the week commencing 8th July, after first visiting Conisbrough Castle. This would include a short visit to Mexborough whilst on their way to Hickleton Hall for luncheon with Lord and Lady Halifax. It was the first time in history that a reigning monarch had passed through the town and clearly generated great excitement.

There was speculation as to the route the King's motorcar would take when passing through Mexborough. This appears to have concerned members of the Education Committee of the Council when planning where to assemble the school children for the royal occasion. The route of the royal motorcar cavalcade was changed from its original plan and the royal couple finally arrived in Mexborough on 9th July. The visit was overshadowed by the Cadeby pit disaster, this event again altering the plans arranged for the Royals and thus a diversion was organised that would see the King and Queen visit the Denaby and Cadeby Main Colliery Company offices in the evening. *The Times* described the occasion in this way:

> *'The good people of Mexboro' displayed their loyalty in no uncertain fashion. Flags and streamers were flying gaily from nearly every residence, workshop, business establishment and cottage, but the awful events at Cadeby had turned the day of rejoicing into a day of sadness. Even before the royal party had passed, most of the flags had been lowered to half-mast. The children, nevertheless, waved their flags with ecstasy, and there was no mistaking the loyalty of the Mexboro' citizen.'*

The royal party had arrived in Mexborough at 12.30pm and was met by councillors and public officials at the front of the Montagu Hotel. Montagu Square was crowded by members of the public and cheering school children. The royal motor cars then took the Market Street and Church Street route where school children from Adwick Road, Garden Street, Main Street and Doncaster Road were assembled. The Parish Church choir was lined up outside the church to sing the National Anthem, reprised by scholars from the National School as the cars slowed on Church Street in order to appreciate the efforts of the enthusiastic Mexborough youth. All appears to have been an uplifting experience following the misery of the depressing events which had recently descended on the local coalfields.

By October, the question of the miners' minimum wage had again reared its head locally in the form of a walk-out at Manvers Main. The trammers had been awarded 5/9d per shift (about 28p) by the Chairman of the Minimum Wages Board, Sir Edward Clarke, but it was not being paid to them. A mass meeting at Manvers Bridge, a regular meeting place for union mass meetings at the pit, was attended by over 300 men. MFGB officials Mr Dixon and Mr Sam Roebuck urged the men to return to work, but the meeting clearly demonstrated the anger of the men. Walter Goddard, who was presiding over the meeting, had difficulty in keeping order. The meeting witnessed some rowdy behaviour and defiant language of, 'make the masters pay'. The meeting broke up in chaos without a definite decision, but resumption of work was achieved within 24 hours.

The unofficial strike at Manvers Main was, like many disputes in this period, a spontaneous 'ragout' of the type that appeared on a periodic basis. Yet there was a crucial issue concerning the minimum wage that was a predictable problem at Manvers Main. Herbert Smith, the President of the YMA, was back later, in October, assuring the miners at Manvers that the Union would never allow the men's wages to be reduced lower than that which they were earning before the national strike. Smith quoted from the Minimum Wage Act, remarking that the legislation clearly stated that any previous custom and practice or agreement should prevail. If the owners were not prepared to fulfil their part of the Act, then a stoppage would be likely. Such was the unsatisfactory nature of the settlement of the recent national coalmining dispute.

The industrial situation that had prevailed throughout 1911, and had worsened in 1912, impacted on living standards. It gave rise to fluctuations in family income and, as a consequence, affected the health and welfare of the town. There was an outbreak of typhoid in late 1911, a problem that Dr Huey argued was partly due to the hot summer, insufficient drainage and contaminated milk. This prompted the Council to appoint Miss Adeline Elizabeth Montagu, who had just completed a midwifery course at the British Lying Hospital, London, as Mexborough's first Lady Health Visitor. The Council also intended spending up to £4,000 on improvements to the sewerage system.

In her first report to the Council in February, Miss Montagu reported that there was no sign of a decline in the high infant mortality rate. In an extraordinary contribution to Council members, she stated that she believed that the figure were of little significance, "for the children who died would probably not have survived under the ministrations of the committee of angels seeing they were damned from birth". This peculiar statement, which portrays an air of determinism, must have presented the Council members with a picture of despair.

Dr Huey, the Medical Officer, gave his annual report in March 1912 to Mexborough Councillors, reiterating the Health Visitor's report. In his report he detailed that there had been 90 deaths of infants under the age of one year in Mexborough in 1911. This was the highest infant mortality recorded since 1908 and well above the national average. The Medical Officer also reported that tuberculosis was still the problem, with infected milk being a cause. In October, a locum Lady Health Visitor, Miss Thomas, reported to the Mexborough UDC that two children had died at the age of six weeks of starvation. Not surprisingly the entire Council was left in shock.

It might be argued that, despite an undoubted, genuine interest in child care, Miss Montagu was not suited to her unenviable role of overseeing child welfare. In December 1912, after a very trying year, and just twelve months after starting in the job, Miss Montagu handed in her resignation. At her penultimate meeting with the Council she was asked the question, "Was there was much poverty in the town?" Her reply suggested that there was little 'unavoidable' poverty except during times such as the recent coal strike. Yet she was scathing about Mexborough's working class in general when she remarked:

> 'It is quite evident that there is plenty of money and I suppose there is plenty of work. But there is no doubt many people wasted their money either through drinking or gambling or some other causes. There certainly is poverty, but I think there need not be any or very little indeed. There is not the slightest doubt that there are many thriftless people in this place.'

Clearly there were tensions between Miss Montagu and the Council members which may have given some impetus to her resignation. At the

Council meeting on 19th December, she was again scathing of the poor state of some housing in the town and particularly certain houses on the Leach. Yet one disgruntled councillor had to remind her that at no stage had she raised the question of these houses before, perhaps because some belonged to members of the Montagu family.

In January 1913, the Mexborough UDC, shocked by some of the social and health problems, had decided to advertise for a new Health Visitor and a Sanitary Inspector. There was an attempt to combine the positions of the Health Visitor and the School Nurse but this was not taken up. It was at this January meeting that Miss Montagu gave her last report. She told councillors that the illegitimacy rate in Mexborough was as high as she had ever experienced. Mexborough's rate was 5%, St Pancras, in London, was only 3.5%, even Swinton was half that of Mexborough. Miss Montagu argued that Mexborough, with a population on 14,500, required two health visitors rather than combining the two roles of Health Visitor and School Nurse. The retiring Lady Health Visitor, fired her parting shot by condemning the Council members for caring little for her concerns. In some parts of the town there was only one ashpit for ten houses. Miss Montagu argued that all the Council did in response to this was send around Council officials to examine the situation, but they simply smiled and did nothing. Miss Montagu furiously proclaimed, "People in this town are calling you a pack of old women. You sit by your firesides and do nothing".

Although Miss Montagu was thanked by the Council for her work with Mexborough's needy mothers, undoubtedly there were those on the Council who were not sorry to see her depart from her Council employment. She was to become a Superintendent of a School for Mothers in Holbeck, Leeds, probably a more suitable position. This is not to say that she was not capable and commitment to her role, there is plenty of evidence to suggest she was, but her upper middle class upbringing appears to have been somewhat of a hindrance in the solidly working class environs of Mexborough. Miss Adeline Elizabeth Montagu never married and died in the Lake District in 1952 at the age of 76.

Miss Montagu was replaced by a Miss Sarah Thornber in the May of 1913, but her stay was also a short one and by September of that year she too, had handed in her notice. The reason she gave for her sudden departure was that she felt unable to secure any improvement in the health of mothers and their young children until there was a dramatic improvement in sanitation in the town. A Miss M. Cussack, from Cork in Ireland, was appointed to replace Miss Thornber in October.

The year 1913 was not to be the one of relative industrial harmony some were expecting after the unprecedented unrest of the previous year. It had been hoped by those of a more moderate opinion that the 'settlement' which ended the 1912 coal strike would as *The Times* put it, 'clear the air for some years to come'. The newspaper's editorial continued, 'Storm Clouds hung persistently over the mining industry and there are sinister signs of someone spoiling for a fight' and Yorkshire was the centre of the 'mischief'.

Local disputes continued over the interpretation of the Minimum Wage Act, but disputes over the employment of non-trade union labour also became an issue. A campaign had emerged to 'encourage' men to join their appropriate union in order to strengthen their bargaining power. This move was prompted to some extent by the pending introduction of the Trade Union Dispute Act of 1913, which allowed trade unions to set up a political fund which could legally finance the Labour Party.

The non-union issue raised its head at Manvers Main, where in June, 200 miners held a meeting at Wath to withdraw their labour until the non-trade unionists were forced to join the union ranks. The call for action over the issue of non-trade union labour was to spread across Yorkshire by the efforts of the YMA. The men at the Elsecar Colliery were eager to tender notices to strike, but the union officials believed that only 'a handful were causing trouble by not joining the union' and there was no significant problem at that particular pit.

Walk-outs were not confined to the coal industry in 1913. On Monday night of 12th October, a dispute erupted at Mexborough Locomotive Depot. Young engine cleaners engaged at the depot had a habit of throwing food at each other during their supper interval. For this, the Foreman dismissed one the young cleaners leading to 60 of his fellow cleaners walking out on the grounds that their colleague was innocent and petty officialdom was to blame. They demanded his immediate reinstatement. Officials of the Great Central Railway were alarmed enough to quickly call in a Mr Lure from Gorton, to Mexborough to attempt to settle the dispute, along with Mr Charles H. Hugell, the Locomotive Superintendent at Mexborough. Both men met a deputation of three cleaners with their ASLEF Branch Secretary, David Humphreys. Not only was the young dismissed cleaner unconditionally reinstated, the cleaners were able to gain a further concession in that, after three months service, they could present themselves for an examination to become a locomotive fireman. Such was the mood of militancy in this period, a mood that even inspired the youngest of workers in Mexborough to flex their industrial muscle.

The Don and Dearne areas made their contribution to the mood of worker's unrest, with many workers locally committed to the trade unions of their occupations. The Mexborough and District Trades and Labour Council claimed to have over 20,000 affiliated members by 1913. Local workers generally had a sense of loyalty to their trade union leaders, although unofficial action was by no means out of their consideration. On the whole local trade unionism locally was of a moderate persuasion, relative to the unprecedented worker unrest at the time. There were elements of a more extreme trade unionism within the area. The Marxist British Socialist Party (BSP) had a number of members in the area, including Mexborough, but had little influence and appeared to be less than welcome in their attendance at Mexborough and District Trades and Labour Council meetings.

The moderate nature of trade unionism within the district is reflected in the politics of the area. It was strongly Liberal, but there was a developing confidence amongst rank and file trade unionists, particularly with the Labour Party now an ever-growing force. Following their success at the 1912 Local Election, two more Labour candidates, William Frow, a railway signalman, and newcomer David Humphreys, a locomotiveman, were easily elected in 1913. Significantly, William Frow topped the polling. The new developing area of Mexborough Common was now occupied by a great many miners and railwaymen, who were solidly behind the two Labour candidates. The more conservative, Councillors such as John Clayton, ('Honest John') and James Cliff, lost their seats to the rising Labour Party challenge.

As for the Tory revolt and the unrest over the Irish Home Rule Bill, the Don and Dearne area, being a Liberal stronghold, generally had no cause other than to support the proposals for a united Ireland. The local Labour Movement supported Irish independence, even showing itself in support of the Irish workers' struggles in 1913, led by the Marxist, James Larkin. Larkin had formed the Irish Transport and General Workers Union. He led a strike of 20,000 workers in Dublin for union recognition, better wages and conditions. This was mainly against the employers of the Dublin United Tramway Company and the brewing company Guinness, the largest employer in Dublin, although there were as many as 300 other employers involved. The workers were locked out at the Tramway Company and by other employers. Guinness did not operate a lock out, but did sack fifteen of its workers.

James Larkin was arrested and imprisoned for his part in the Dublin strikes. The British TUC initially supported the striking workers and donated £150,000 to their cause, but later the leadership of the TUC abandoned Larkin with some in the Labour Party disapproving of his militant tactics. Despite this, most rank and file trade unionists supported Larkin and their colleagues in Dublin and many protest meetings in support of the Dublin strikers took place throughout England. This was to be the case in Mexborough and district. The Mexborough Trade's Council held a mass meeting of workers in Mexborough Market Place in November. Although the weather was extremely bad, it was reported as a well-attended meeting. The meeting expressed the view that no workers had been more badly treated than those suffering in Dublin and called for the immediate release from prison of James Larkin. At the end of the meeting, David Humphreys, the newly elected Councillor, called for the meeting to support the following motion: 'That this meeting of workers of Mexborough and district vigorously protest against the unfair treatment which has been meted out to workers and their representatives from time to time and calls upon the Parliamentary Committee of the TUC to call together at once all affiliated unions with a view to declare a general stoppage throughout the Kingdom, unless Jim Larkin is released from prison.' The proposal was easily adopted, such was the spirit of trade union solidarity showed by the workers of Mexborough and district during this turbulent period.

The TUC leadership did not support the call for sympathetic strike action and therefore abandoned the Irish strikers. Without this support the strike, which had started on 28th August, was forced to end on 18th January 1914. The men and their families, who were already amongst the most poverty-stricken, in Great Britain, were on the edge of starvation at the termination of the dispute. They returned to work on their employers' terms, which in many cases meant a pledge that they would not join Larkin's trade union.

What influence did the women's rebellion have on Mexborough and district politics? It has been mentioned that Mexborough appears not to have produced any militancy in the campaign to secure votes for women. The year 1913 was one in which militancy, as practised by the WPSU, was probably at its highest. There was an intensification of militant, direct action after the failure of a Bill which might have seen a move towards votes for women in January. This resulted in yet more systematic arson of a variety of buildings and property and other acts of vandalism. It led to the desperate action in May of Emily Davidson killing herself, intentionally or not, as she was crushed under the King's horse at Epson Downs during the running of the Derby. (An incident in which the *The Times* appears not to have been remotely interested.) In turn, the Government reacted by introducing the infamous and barbaric Act allowing the Home Secretary to release hunger strikers after imprisonment, only to be rearrested when they had recovered from their ordeal.

These desperate militant tactics by the WPSU suffragettes was alienating even some their closest supporters in the trade unions and Labour Party. The Liberals, who not surprisingly took the Government line, were on the whole cautious on the question of the women's votes and certainly not in support of the approach employed by the leaders of the WPSU. In late January, the women of Mexborough and district Liberal Party had the objective of forming a branch of the Women's National Liberal Association. They held a meeting at the Miners'

Institution, the Main Street Club, which gave a clear indication of their views on votes for women and on Mrs. Pankhurst's Suffragettes. A speaker from London, a Miss Edith Shaw, addressed the audience, describing the members of the WPSU as "mad women." She suggested their impotent rage only encouraged the Government, who were at the point of conceding to their demands, to move back from women's suffrage rather than towards it.

The local trade union movement was widely in favour of votes for women, but not in support of the militant WPSU. At their monthly meeting, at the Mason Arms, in October, the Mexborough and District Trades and Labour Council was addressed by a guest Suffragist speaker, a Mrs Oldham, from the moderate National Union of Women's Suffrage Societies. She was there to explain the objectives of the Societies and in doing so emphasised that she and her organisation were non-militant and condemned militancy in any form.

The British Socialist Party, with its small number of supporters in Mexborough, was the only organisation which appears to have given substantial support to WPSU. At a South Yorkshire District BSP meeting in February, delegates strongly protested against the treatment and unjust prison sentences of six Suffragettes, expressing the view that this act was a 'vindictive display of class hatred'. This statement may have been some way off the mark, given the class composition of the majority of WPSU members.

There is no evidence that the Suffragette WSPU tried to organise in Mexborough, or had any desire to. It is unlikely that the non-militant NUWSS themselves ever made any serious inroads in organising women in Mexborough into its ranks. The female population of the town was predominantly working class, existing in a male dominated environment and not exposed to local politics which were monopolised by the men of the town. Even the middle class women within the local Liberal Party seemed content to follow the cautious approach to 'votes for women' pursued by the Liberal Government.

The years 1910–1913 domestically were without doubt an exceptional period of unrest and tensions. International tensions, too, were of great concern to the Liberal Government. The arms race and Germany's strengthening of its armed forces, particularly the build up of its navy, with its ambition to more than compete with the British navy, could not be underplayed by the Government. There had been a crisis in Agadir in 1911, the second crisis in Morocco within a few years, where the French and German Governments were vying against each other for additional colonial gain. It was a crisis in which Britain would have supported France, but were, as was often the case, reluctant to get involved. Two wars had broken out in the Balkans, one in 1912 and another in 1913, both as a result of the break-up of the Ottoman Empire and the rise of the Serbian nationalists. This in turn, increased tensions between Serbia and Austria–Hungary, the latter being a firm ally of Germany.

Much of Britain was preoccupied by its own internal problems. The Government, nevertheless, kept one eye on the international situation and was not completely unprepared for the possibility of conflict with the Kaiser's Germany and its known military ambitions. In 1907, the Government introduced the Territorial and Reserve Force Act, part of the Haldane Reform of the British Army. Locally one outcome of this legislation was the building of a new Territorial Drill Hall at Wath in May 1911. This would serve as the major centre in the district for the training of the new Territorial Force (TF) as a supplement to the regular army in times of conflict. Mexborough did not acquire its own premises until the 1930's and as a consequence Mexborough 'Terriers' were attached to Wath with the 5th Battalion of the York and Lancashire Regiment.

A part of the 1907 Act reform of the army's structure was the proposal to set up a National Reserve. In March, Mexborough Council received a request from the National Reserve Movement asking for the use of one of the offices in the Council Building, for just one night a week for enrolment purposes. The request was made on their behalf by Captain R.J. Jenkins of the Rotherham Detachment of the 5th York and Lancs. Council members were supportive of this approach but advised Captain Jenkins that there was no room to spare in the Council Offices and recommended to the Library Committee that a room should be found in the Free Library in Bank Street.

In some quarters the international situation was considered to be serious enough to warrant introduction of military conscription. At their monthly meeting in June, the Mexborough and District Trades and Labour Council were asked to support the Labour Movement's Anti–Conscription Committee, which it duly did. A campaign against military conscription was maintained solidly by the Labour Movement up to the inevitable introduction of conscription in 1916.

There were those who, however, held a different perspective on the possibility of war. The Member of Parliament for Rotherham, Mr J. A. Pease, was the President of the Board of Education in 1913 and also President of the Peace Society. At a meeting in May he was confident that the storm clouds of war were lifting. Pease believed that previously Anglo-German relations had been strained, but he was glad that this had now passed; "The time had arrived" he said, "When we might say we are just as friendly with Germany as any other nation." Sir Edward Grey, the British Foreign Secretary, had sent a message to the meeting that, whilst realising that there were international tensions, 'At the moment we can congratulate ourselves that an era of peace is before us'. Canon Masterman was even more buoyant and reassuring when he told the peace meeting that, "The honourable and disinterested policy of the

German Empire had done much in the past months to avert the danger of war and strengthen the bonds of peace".

The optimistic proclamations of those anxious to promote the cause of peace contrasted with the actions of local army personnel hurriedly constructing a system which would attract and enrol recruits to the military for any impending conflict. What the ordinary 'man in the street' in the Don and Dearne would have concluded from this is difficult to assess. Certainly their thoughts, time and energy over the past few years had been largely preoccupied by their struggles on the industrial front. This possible distraction from the crisis on the continent was still evident in the first few months of 1914. The workers' unrest continued into that year, particularly in the mining industry when the weaknesses in the Liberal Government's Minimum Wage Act were further exposed. The country did have the appearance of sleep-walking into a global conflict. Any debate about the prospects of future peace or war was to end in the summer of 1914 and that fateful day in August also witnessed an abrupt end to overt industrial, social and political unrest, which had been most noticeable during the years 1910-1913.

At the end of 1913, the people of Mexborough and district had a peacetime Christmas to look forward to, before that fateful summer of 1914 arrived. *The Times* at least expressed their satisfaction that 1913 had been year of economic boom. But, in its opinion, the labour unrest had disfigured and nullified the opportunity for prosperity and Christmas itself was less likely to be a merry one for some, even though a postal service strike in Mexborough had just been averted. In any case, *The Times* admits, this prosperity would not be shared by all. After a long, dry autumn, *The Times* believed its readers might appreciate an 'old fashioned Christmas', one with glittery frosted greeting cards and the prospects of snow. This might be welcome just as the Christmas pudding and cake, until the readers were reminded of the poor and needy who lacked even suitable winter clothing. The poor of the Don and Dearne were scarcely in a position to appreciate the charm of an old-fashioned Yuletide, let alone an economic boom. The years between 1910 and 1913 had been ones of sunshine and shadows.

However Christmas 1913 was celebrated, within twelve months many would have to make the best of their next Christmas in a foreign land or in a training camp somewhere in England. Hundreds of local men had responded without hesitation to Kitchener's call within a week of the commencement of war. How can this phenomenon of the rush to enlist in Britain's new volunteer army be explained? The press of the day preferred to suggest that it was a singular show of patriotism. Certainly, there was the powerful influence of a social system which resulted in a British chauvinism with its belief in the superiority of its Empire. Such a message was reinforced by the Liberal and Conservative press and in literature for youth consumption by way of papers like the *Union Jack*, the Boy's Own Paper and the penny thriller comics.

It can be questioned whether the experiences of working men, particularly during the 1910-1913 period, influenced their decision to respond to the nation's seemingly seductive call to arms. These years of unrest had witnessed industrial struggle which led to hardship, wage instability, poverty and numerous social problems. The workers were generally loyal to their trade unions and to each other, an attribute harnessed to good effect in the forming of the 'Pals' battalions. The majority were less loyal to their employers, but most loyal to the monarchy. The mining disasters of the period were particularly horrific and devastating to local communities and all this amidst an economic boom and a display of conspicuous consumption. Many had probably welcomed the opportunity of some time away from the drudgery of working life in the industrial north and the experience of seeing some foreign parts. This was certainly the observation of Willie Gallacher, revolutionary trade unionists, who led Clydeside workers during the war years. Gallacher wrote:

> *'What a terrible attraction war can be! The wild excitement, the illusion of wonderful adventure and the actual break in the deadly monotony of working class life! Thousands went flocking to the colours in the first days (of the war) not because of any "love of country", not because of any high feeling of "patriotism" but because of the new strange and thrilling life that lay before them.'*

Whether motivated by patriotism, the simple enthusiasm of youth, belief in a potentially better life or driven by a combination of inducements, the British armed forces had no trouble in attracting willing men to the ranks of the military in the first few weeks of the war. But for now, thoughts of war would, in most cases, have been far away from the minds of British people at Christmas 1913. They would have simply looked forward to a better year.

Manvers Main Colliery c 1912. The pit employed many men who lived on Wath Road. Despite industrial relations at the colliery being reasonably good, the men joined the national strike in 1912.

Blacklegs and colliery officials being escorted by police from Elsecar Colliery during the 1912 National Miners' strike.
Courtesy of Old Barnsley.

Mexborough residents digging for coal during the 1912 strike. Outcropping for coal in this way was a common activity during coal mining strikes.

The 1912 Whitsuntide celebrations in Montagu Square. The Miners' strike had just ended to the relief of many. Within three years some of the young men in the picture would be wearing an army uniform.

Crowds waiting outside the Prince of Wales theatre, Mexborough, for the arrival of King George and Queen Mary in July 1912.

The car carrying the King and Queen passes Pepper's Corner during their visit to Mexborough on 9th July 1912.

The King and Queen's car pulls into Market Square on 9th July 1912. Note the crowds who are standing on the site of the, as yet unbuilt, Montagu Building.

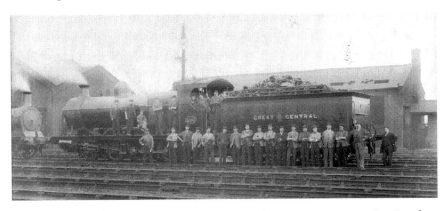

Engine cleaners at Mexborough Locomotive Depot c.1910. In October 1913, young cleaners took strike action.

1914

Chapter Two

Amid 'Gathering Storm' Clouds

The Christmas weather of 1913 in Mexborough had been described as dry, crisp and invigorating. The people of Mexborough would most likely have enjoyed their short Christmas break. *The Times* believed 1913 to be the best year the country had seen for sometime, reporting that the people should have an affectionate regard for the year and the benefits the trade boom had brought. So much so that 'in such happy circumstances we will naturally look with renewed confidence and hope into the future and await with some compliancy whatever fortune 1914 has to bestow upon us.' Yet as they entered the new year of 1914, the people of Mexborough would have had little or no perception of what would greet them in the Christmases that followed. For many of them, Christmas would be spent in a foreign country. Others would never see a Christmas again and for those at home it would be a long time before the festive season returned to such as the ones enjoyed in 1913. Life in Britain and no less the Don and Dearne Valleys, was about to change.

One of the first items of local news in the New Year which concerned Mexborough, was the announcement that the town's motor engineer, Frank Harrison, had the distinction of having introduced the first motorised ambulance in the area. Mr Harrison was chosen by the Doncaster and Mexborough Joint Hospital Board to supply the vehicle from an extensive list of motor engineers. The description of Frank Harrison's vehicle sounds splendid in both quality and appearance with its teak body, electric lighting and heating apparatus. What could not have been foreseen is that it would soon to be used to assist in a war effort.

The January weather had initially brought with it snow blizzards and very sharp frosts, causing traveling difficulties around the area. This was said to make the countryside look a brilliant and rewarding spectacle and well worth stepping out in.

Following Christmas, Mexborough returned to a normal pattern of life, complete with industrial, political, economic and social problems and challenges to debate and attempt to resolve. The economic boom of 1913 with its expansion of coal production throughout the Don and Dearne Valleys had not been unproblematic. Despite near full employment, prices were rising and money was 'dear' in terms of borrowing. The boom had seen a large influx of men and their families seeking employment in the area. In 1913, a report for the Mexborough Urban District Council estimated Mexborough's population to be 15,761. The same report said that there were 3,146 Council rate-paying houses, but the increase in the population had caused an acute housing shortage in the town. Plans for only 30 new dwellings had been laid before the Planning Committee in the whole of 1913.

At a Council meeting early in the new year, Mr T. Douglas, the Sanitary Inspector, spoke of the "evils of overcrowding." He knew of cases of ten people, four adults and six children, living huddled together in one room. Councillor David Humphreys recalled his own observation of three separate families in one house. When a neighbour of his took down her curtains for washing there was a regular rush of enquire as to the availability of renting the property.

There was an apparent air of complacency on the subject of the lack of housing in the town from a number of councillors. Councillor Humphreys' response to the Sanitary Inspector's serious statement that there was not a house to be got in Mexborough, drew laughter. There was further laughter when Councillor Tom Athron suggested that perhaps some soldiers' tents should be purchased. The Chairman of the Council, Mr John Thomas Rowan, was a little more responsive to the appalling situation the town found itself in. It was clear to him that private enterprise was unable to provide the houses that Mexborough desperately needed. It appears that the Council had let the Housing and Town Planning Committee lapse and had taken its 'eye off the ball' on this issue. Mexborough had fallen behind other councils in the district who better provided for their residents. A motion calling for the Housing and Town Planning Committee to begin meeting again at the earliest possible date was passed.

The problem of limited housing in the town was clear. Many houses were sub-standard, not fit for purpose and needed demolishing. Although without immediate prospects of new builds, this course of action would have forced tenants into common lodging houses. It was clear to some in the Council that they themselves had to take a hand in solving the problem, as the free market had not brought forth a solution. It was suggested that the Council might borrow money to stimulate private building in the area. Chairman Rowan, previously a strong opponent to municipal building, now spoke out for municipalisation of housing by encouraging owners of existing housing to sell to the Council, although it is not quite sure how this might increase the housing stock

A major opponent of the implementation of municipal housing was Councillor John Hudson Watson J.P., who had a self-confessed interest in property. While admitting that private enterprise was not sufficiently furnishing adequate provision, Watson blamed the high cost of building material and labour difficulties for the housing problem. He made no suggestion as to a solution to the building stagnation and simply argued that the situation in Bolton-upon-Dearne was worse. Even an editorial of *The Times* was staggered by Councillor Watson's approach. They described the fierce interior struggles which were taking place within the Council between the 'progressives' and what they referred to as the opposing party. Newspaper reports suggest that there was no clear political direction to local politics in Mexborough at this time. A resolution was put forward at a meeting in February, that the Council seek funds and purchase housing to try to alleviate the housing crisis. The resolution was defeated by three votes to six with only Councillors Rowan, Humphreys and William Winstanley voting in favour. Councillor Watson was the main protagonist against the proposal. Mexborough's desperate housing problem was no nearer a solution. The editorial of *The Times* of 21st February commented on this decision in relation to the town's housing problems:

> *'Is this highly insanitary congestion of the population of the district to remain un-remedied? Stories of plural families herded together in small and mean tenements leaves the Council unmoved. These gentlemen say that this horrid state of things which exists in this town today does not represent an evil acute enough to justify a meaningful housing scheme.'*

There were properties in Mexborough that were placed on the open market at an auction held at the Montagu Arms on Monday, 11th May. There was a large attendance at the auction, including a number of Mexborough councillors. Councillor Ward was present as was Councillor Athron, who both appear to have had an interest in the property.

Some of the auction lots didn't reach their reserved price and other property secured no interest. Nevertheless, six dwelling homes in Regent

Place, which were situated off Schofield Street and property of the late Thomas Schofield, were secured for £600 by Councillor Athron. These properties were said to gross £77.7s (£77.35p) annually in rent. Whether the councillors attending the auction were conscious of the deficiencies of the housing stock and the consequences of overcrowding in Mexborough, or their thoughts were of self-interest is beyond our ability to assess.

The inadequate housing situation brought with it associated health problems. At a Council meeting in February, the Medical Officer Dr John James Huey gave his monthly report advising councillors of nine cases of scarlet fever and four of diphtheria. These outbreaks had caused overcrowding at the Conisbrough Isolation Hospital, owing to scarlet fever being endemic in the district. Such was the crisis that a Dr McClure suggested that the all of the town's schools should be closed. Again, Councillor Watson was unsympathetic to this view.

A case of scarlet fever was discovered at Adwick Road Mixed School. A child from Victoria Road had said something to his teacher which alerted the school to the issue. Dr Gardener was called along with Dr Huey, and the two doctors found the boy in an advanced state of desquamation (or peeling). The boy was sent home and the school was closed and disinfected throughout.

Dr Huey, an Irishman from County Tyrone, was to become established in the area for over 40 years and was continually in conflict with some Mexborough councillors. During the scarlet fever crisis in March, the Local Education Authority believed that fumigation of books and material was a satisfactory way of dealing with it. Dr Huey thought this inadequate and insisted in books and materials being destroyed. This is most vividly illustrated in Dr Huey's attempts to address councillors with his annual medical report in April, a report which offered the statistic that infant morality had doubled in town in the previous twelve months. Whilst giving his report, two of the established councillors chose to take the opportunity for a gossip and a smoke in an adjoining room of the Council Chamber. Clearly there were some unwholesome tensions existing within the Chamber. There was however some appreciation of Dr Huey's persistent efforts to draw the Council's attention to the poor state of health within some areas of the town, from the more 'progressive' members of the Council.

Dr Huey's report to the Council in July observed no improvement in the health of some of the Mexborough population. Scarlet fever continued in seven cases, diphtheria was still present and there was a prevalence of tuberculosis (TB), whooping cough and chicken pox. Such was the extent of these problems that Dr Huey advised that Garden Street, Central and Doncaster Road schools should close. The Medical Officer's report in October reports similar illness as July. Of the 30 deaths in the month of September, eleven were infants under a year old. Eleven of these deaths were from diarrhoea. The weather in the summer of 1914 had caused sanitary problems with enormous numbers of flies created from privy middens.

The Health Visitor had made 400 visits to mothers and their babies. The unsanitary conditions had caused this high death rate among youngsters, but some blame was attached to the mothers themselves by the Health Visitor, who argued the women gave their babies infected milk, improper food and failed to dispose of refuse effectively.

Unsanitary conditions were not helped by the situation which prevailed with the water supply. From the beginning of the year there was a fight for control over Mexborough's water supply between the Urban District Council and the Mexborough Water Company as a result of the latter's irregular and unsatisfactory delivery of supplies. Councillor Humphreys at a Council meeting in March raised the question of intermittent water supply and its impact on public health. Again, Dr Huey commented that no warnings had been given by the Mexborough Water Company when the water was to be turned off and this was prejudicial to health.

Despite the Water Company's pledge to improve supplies, the Council in its fight for ownership of the town's water called a public meeting in January. The meeting was not well attended but a resolution that the Council, 'Acquire the undertaking of the Mexborough and District Water Company Limited', was passed by twenty votes to nineteen. Such was the closeness of the vote that a Mr White demanded the vote be taken again, but he was overruled. White then called for a poll of the people of Mexborough, which again was dismissed, but it was enough for *The Times* to suggest the electors had demanded the takeover.

The result of the public meeting prompted the promotion of a 'Water Bill' before Parliament and both parties to the proposed takeover entered into negotiations over detail and price. The Mexborough Urban District Council's 'Water Bill' was passed in the House of Lords in April with the Water Company withdrawing their own 'Bill'. In May, it further passed through the House of Commons unopposed and went forward for Royal Assent. *The Times* editorial of 16th May comments; 'So that for all practical purposes the sanitary authority of Mexborough is from today the Water Authority'.

The Council was aware of another public health issue when it decided to seek a loan to build a public baths in Mexborough. At its meeting in February, it received permission from the Local Government Board for a loan of £5,960. The Council considered the tenders for the project and recommended that the lowest tender be accepted. When the lowest tender was received, it exceeded their estimate by nearly £2,000, a sum which would have put a penny in the pound on the rates. It may have come as no shock to the people of Mexborough that the Council was divided on the issue. Originally, the scheme to build the baths was agreed, but then referred back to see if costs could be reduced to somewhere near the original estimate. The public baths were never built. If the people of Mexborough wanted to enjoy the delights of public bathing they would have to visit their nearest public baths, situated in Denaby Main and Wath. The situation today remains very much the same.

In *The Times* of 21st March, the nomination for five seats on the Council were announced for an election which was to take place on Saturday, 4th April. This was at a time when the eligibility to vote was limited. Just 3,000 Mexborough people had the right to vote, mostly adult male householders, although a few females did have the right in local government elections. The actual number of votes cast for this 1914 local election was 1,296, about 43%.of electors.

There were nine candidates, all males as was the norm of the time. The contest saw two 'Labour' men, Mr W.C. Bramham, an engine driver of 39, Wood Street and Walter Ward, a railway foreman of 150, Doncaster Road, nominated by the Mexborough Trades and Labour Council. Neither was elected. Three retiring councillors were successfully returned to the Council. Arthur Goulding, an innkeeper, topped the poll. High Street butcher Tom Chambers was second with school teacher William Winstanley third, and Christopher Ward, an insurance agent from Crossgate, fourth. There was one newcomer to the Council, pork butcher George Schonhut of 47 High Street, who took the fifth seat. He was proposed by two other local businessmen, William Tiptaft and Ernest Clayton. Schonhut, according to the press was expected to do well and this prediction turned out to be correct. He was described by *The Times* as a 'successful businessman who is very popular in his adopted town.' In the coming months, a good deal of this popularity would disappear.

The poverty of some areas of Mexborough was in great contrast to the aristocracy, housed in country houses in the surrounding area. It was reported in July that the Earl and Countess of Fitzwilliam had entertained 550 guests at their London residence in Grosvenor Square in London. Their guests included the Duke and Duchess of Devonshire, the Earl and Countess of Scarborough and the Duke and Duchess of Norfolk. For this lavish social gathering, flowers had been sent from the Earl's South Yorkshire residence at Wentworth Woodhouse. Such opulence was openly displayed and well reported in the press in some detail. Long detailed accounts of the local hunt were described to the readers. In the summer of 1914 *The Times* had this account of others within the Fitzwilliam family:

'Lady Fitzwilliam is doing a good deal of entertaining this

summer for her pretty debutante niece Miss Dorothy Fitzroy, the daughter of Lord and Lady Southampton. She is a fine rider to hounds. Though this is the age of the motor car Lady Fitzwilliam still uses carriages of quite unusual smartness. These are yellow, like Lord Lonsdale's, but drawn by grey not chestnut horses and the servants wear grey liveries with yellow and silver facings.'

What the thoughts of the poor of Mexborough were as to these observations we can only speculate upon, but even the lives of the aristocracy would eventually have to change as a result of the conflict the nation was about to become embroiled in.

The housing problem in Mexborough may have been due to the Urban District Council's lethargy in tackling the crisis, but the shortage of properties was in part the result of the rapid expansion in the local coalfields in the few years prior to the beginning of the 'Great War'. The rich 'Barnsley Seam' saw the opening of new seams within the coalfields of the Don and Dearne. At the end of May it was reported that the newly sunk Barnburgh Colliery had reached coal and was a 'sensational sinking success' being good news for the area. By 1919, Manvers Main, Barnburgh, Wath Main, Hickleton, Denaby Main and Cadeby, Warren Vale and Hickleton Collieries were employing 14,000 men and boys. This saw a massive influx of workers from areas with less employment prospects. This influx massively exacerbated the housing problem and with it the lack of sufficient public of transport was highlighted.

Barnburgh pit employed 3,000 men at the beginning of production in 1914, yet the majority of these men would be required to walk some considerable distance to the pit, for the nearest centre of population was at least three to four miles away. To cater for the miners and general public, it was proposed that a new tramway, to be called the 'Dearne District Light Railway' should be built. Such a system would, from the initial starting point at the Alhambra, Barnsley, reach Wombwell, West Melton, Wath, Swinton, Bolton- upon-Dearne, Thurnscoe and hopefully Mexborough.

Local Urban Councils supported this proposed tramway scheme and Mexborough Urban District Council was certainly in favour. Councillor Watson, a West Riding County councillor and Mexborough councillor for 37 years, spoke out strongly in favour at the Inquiry into the scheme at Barnsley Town Hall on 26th February. Watson believed that the tramway would be of great benefit to Mexborough. The Mexborough and Swinton Tramway, opened in 1904, demonstrated the advantages of this type of transport, but as yet there was no direct conveyance between Mexborough, Goldthorpe, Thurnscoe, West Melton and Brampton. Mr A.J. Ram said that the people of Mexborough were now using trams to travel as little as a few hundred yards and had "acquired the riding habit".

Despite this, Mexborough Urban District Council had petitioned against the scheme. However, this was purely on financial grounds and the petition was only to give the Council what Councillor Watson called some "standing"at the Inquiry and Mexborough did not intend to indicate any hostility to the scheme. It was envisaged that there would be a great deal of expenditure in the process of obtaining land and acquiring property, an expenditure which would fall upon the ratepayer. Mexborough Urban District Council was at this time always anxious to keep any 'burden' on the rates down as much as possible.

There was wide-spread enthusiasm for the new tramway, particularly from the representatives of Labour. The Rotherham Trades and Labour Council supported it as did the Yorkshire Miners' Association (YMA). They raised the existing concerns over the length of the journeys, usually by foot, pitman were required to travel. Yet strong opposition was expressed by those with a vested interest. A meeting took place in Wath in January, organised by local property owners who believed they might be affected.

Ironically, one of the leading antagonists against the Dearne District Light Railway was Lieutenant Colonel Mitchell, owner of the Mitchell Main Colliery, who was concerned about the surrounding land which would need to be developed. Mitchell's objections contrasted with the views of John Edwin Chambers, the Colliery Manger of Cortonwood Colliery which employed 1,650 men, most of whom resided around the Wombwell Church and Brampton Church areas. The only access to Chambers' colliery was by road. He claimed that when the weather was bad, the officials had difficulty in getting the men to work at all. The effect of this walk was, he said, to "devalue the men's work". The nearest station to Cortonwood colliery was the Great Central Railway's station at Wath. Because of this, his colliery management favoured the building of the tramway.

It was, in fact, the railway companies, mainly the Midland Railway and the Great Central Railway, who were collectively opposed to the new tramway system. The Great Central Railway had the most significant interest in opposition to the scheme. Even the renowned General Manager of the Great Central, Sir Sam Fay, was to make an observation of the area in the latter part of January. The railway had argued that the motor bus service between Barnsley and West Melton had an adverse effect on the company's traffic receipts. They further claimed that half a million passengers travelled between Barnsley and Mexborough per year, and that the shorter five-mile journeys would see travellers diverted to the tramways.

What the Great Central Railway and other railways in the area had to prove to the Light Railway Commissioners, was that they could provide a sufficient service within the area. This was something that the railways were unable to do. A House of Commons committee declared that it was not enough for the railway companies to give the undertaking to accelerate the existing services. Instead, the test was for them to prove that what they provided was 'reasonably adequate to the requirements of the district'.

Even in the initial stages of the new proposed tramway system, Councillor Watson and Mexborough were to be disappointed. It was decided the system was not to reach Mexborough itself. There would be no direct connection between Wath and Mexborough and the tramway would terminate at Wath Staithes. The tramway system was finally approved, culminating in the Dearne District Light Railway Order of 1915. Owing to the necessities of war, the scheme was to lay in abeyance. There were a number of amendment orders after the war and finally it opened in July 1924 with a total of 30 single deck, 36 seat cars. It was the last tramway to be built in the UK until the 1990's. The system never did reach Mexborough, but connected with a trolley bus service at Manvers Main. Under strong competition from motor buses of Yorkshire Traction it was closed in September 1933.

Although the vast expansion of the coalfields brought prosperity to the area, amid pockets of real poverty, the industrial relations between men and their employers were always precarious, creating an instability which had an enormous impact upon the town. The cost of living had risen sharply from the beginning of the century and another major concern of the miners was the problem of the complex and chaotic wage structure. The strike of 1912 forced the government to introduce the 1912 National Minimum Wage Act. The Act solved little and the continuing chaotic nature of the wage payment system reflected itself in some strikes in local collieries. By mid February miners were again in dispute, including 2,100 men on strike at Rotherham Main, together with 4,000 men withdrawing their labour at Silverwood. The Denaby Main branch of the YMA resolved to support the Rotherham men over the failure of local employers to interpret the provisions of the 1912 Act with acceptable awards.

Towards the end of the February, problems were brewing at Manvers Main, a pit which is said to have had good industrial relations, over a minimum paid to Trammers who were paid by their fellow colliers. This appears to have elements of the 19th century 'butty' system where wages were controlled and distributed by some miners themselves. This dispute didn't last more than two days before there was a return to work, yet it does illustrate the fragile nature of industrial relations that persisted in the Dearne and Don coalfields at this time.

Negotiations over the details of the 1912 Act took place at District level. The years 1913 and 1914 were spent with these details being worked out between the Owners' Federation and the YMA. Negotiations were tense and often concluded in breakdown, as did the meeting between the YMA and owners at the Royal Victoria Hotel in Sheffield on Monday, 2nd March. As a result of the breakdown, the members of the YMA voted by a large majority, at a meeting in Barnsley the next day, to take strike action.

On 2nd April, local pits ceased to 'turn coal' and 200,000 men from the whole of the West Riding of Yorkshire went out on strike. This was not followed by strikes in other areas of the country. During the strike, the YMA were able to allocate strike pay from their accumulating funds of nine shillings per man (45p) plus one shilling (5p) for every child under the age of fouteen. Sir Joseph Walton MP maintained in a speech in Barnsley that the YMA spent £180,000 on strike pay. Indeed the President of the YMA, Herbert Smith (later to became the President of his national union, the MFGB), boasted at a meeting at Moorthorpe that there was £210,000 in the Union's war chest which would be used to fight the coal owners.

Although the strike did not last particularly long, it would have, yet again, caused distress among many Mexborough families and certainly curtailed spending power within the community. A settlement was reached by mid-April when the majority of local miners voted 27,239 to 11,333, to return to work. A fixed-rate minimum was agreed via conciliation at the Minimum Wage Board for the district. Nevertheless, the agreement was still contentious in that it gave a lower minimum to what the employer considered to be less deserving grades of employee. It was argued by *The Times* that the strike cost £5,000,000 in lost production, profits, strike pay and wages. This was a huge, but probably distorted figure, when the paper itself reported that Derbyshire pits carried on working during the strike, even exporting coal into Yorkshire to help fill the shortage caused by the strike, thus increasing production and profit elsewhere. Nevertheless, it did cause a trade slack within the Yorkshire area, once more impacting on the Mexborough community.

At the same time as the action over the subject of the minimum wage, a strike was called by the local branches of the National Amalgamated Society of Painters. They were seeking to improve their terms and condition through an improved conduct of works rules. Mexborough, Swinton and Wath workers associated with this trade were paid less than their colleagues in Sheffield, Rotherham and Barnsley and thus they demanded an increase of 1d per hour, bringing their hourly rate up to 9d (about 4p). It was many years since an increase had been advanced to the painters and a meeting to resolve the dispute took place in the South Yorkshire Hotel, Mexborough, between the union officials and the employers.

It is clear that the mood of the trade unions was one of militancy, with an atmosphere of solidarity amongst many workers which had not passed Mexborough by. Mexborough was economically dependent upon the railway and coal industries, and there was a close relationship between workers and trade union representatives of these industries. Solidarity had its roots within this closeness. This inclination towards sympathetic action amongst workers extended to transport workers, including tramway and motor bus staff. At the national level, there was recognition of the interdependence between these workers when it came to pressuring employers and government to concede to what the trade unions saw as legitimate demands. The workers, through the unions, were flexing their muscle and confident in the process; their ranks had swollen from a membership of just under 2.4million in 1910 to nearly 4 million in 1914.

George Dangerfield remarks in his noted book, *The Strange Death of Liberal England:* 'Between January and July (1914) there were no fewer than 937 strikes', albeit that these were small scale strikes compared to the mass national strikes of 1911 and 1912. Such conditions led unions to acknowledge the benefits of union action and in doing so, the formation of the so called 'Triple Alliance' in April 1914. This was an informal organisation consisting of about one and half million railwaymen, miners, and transport workers, brought together through their unions; the National Union of Railwaymen, MFGB, and the National Transport Workers Federation. The Triple Alliance was influenced by the Syndicalist movement, whose ideology was based on the principal of revolutionary trade unionism and whose aim was to take over the running of the state by utilising the weapon of the general strike. There was a likelihood that such a general strike would materialise in the autumn, but the approaching war curtailed this ambition, or as Dangerfield famously puts it: 'The great General Strike of 1914 was forestalled by some bullets at Sarajevo and had slipped away into the limbo of unfinished arguments.'

Life in Mexborough in 1914 was not wholly consumed by political and industrial struggle and conflict. Sport played an important role in providing recreation, particularly being relief from the harsh realities experienced by the pitman. Mexborough Cricket Club held its Annual Ball at Mexborough Secondary School in early-January. The Council's Medical Officer, Dr Huey, was its chairman, making arrangements for what appears to have been a glittering and fashionable event. Reporting on the event, *The Times* described some of the guest list of 140, along with a detailed description of the fine ladies' dresses. Apparently the only downbeat feature of the otherwise successful event was the shortage of gentleman in attendance. The town's cricket club, who played in the Mexborough and District League, were strong and successful in the pre—

war years. They opened the season in May with an away win by beating Rawmarsh very soundly and a little later achieved a victory over Hickleton, with Mexborough's Tom Thorpe scoring 100 not out. They were not defeated until June, but again Thorpe demonstrated his batting ability with a fine 57, becoming the league's second-best batman with an average of 62.6.

Watching and playing cricket was a favourite pastime in the summer months. It was an activity in which Mexborough's women, too, were able to participate. A novelty match on Thursday 9th July took place between a 'gentlemens' team and a 'ladies' team to raise funds for the proposed new Children's Ward at Montague Hospital. The women won easily assisted by rules hampering the men, one of these rules forced the males to bat with broomsticks. There is little doubt that, during the era, this would have been considered as a chivalrous gesture on the part of the men, rather than any patronisation.

The fortunes of Mexborough's football team were not as successful as their cricketing counterparts. In January, Mexborough Town was at the bottom of the Midland League, although they did achieve a much needed 3-2 win over Hull City Reserves in the same month. In desperation, the club's manager announced that they would drop Jackson and Murray from the team indefinitely, bringing Billy Hargreaves to left back instead of his usual position of outside left, a position he played at Goole. A hardy reserve player called Scothern was to come in at centre half.

A month later, the 'Town' were still struggling at the bottom of the league with only four wins from twenty games, although they had played three games fewer than Leeds City who had just one point more. By the end of February the club was on the verge of folding and in danger of not being able to complete the fixtures for the remainder of the season. Player's wages and expenses for the away games had been funded by two unnamed benefactors who, by all accounts, were refusing to dip into their pockets any further. It had been argued that the Midland League was too expensive for Mexborough Town to complete in.

However, the club did believe it would be able to raise money from various activities which could attract players of the right quality. A 'whist drive' was arranged at the Public Hall on Thursday, 5th March. Frank Harrison, owner of the local motor garage in Bank Street, offered a prize of a bicycle worth £8 8s (£8.40p).

These fund raising activities appeared to have been reasonably successful, for in mid-April the club called a public meeting in the town's cricket pavilion. The meeting was presided over by Mexborough Town FC president Mr Pepper, with the club secretary, Tom Brown in attendance. The meeting was not well attended by members of the public, but there was a good turnout by local tradesmen on whom the club heavily relied. Mr Pepper admitted money was owed by the club to various businessmen.

Mr Brown announced that there was an expectation that the Football Association would give the club monies from their benevolent fund. It was agreed at the meeting that the club should continue to the end of the season and apply for re-admission to the Midland League for the next season. Re-admission would nevertheless cost the club £100.

It was announced in late May that the club would run another season in the Midland League. Mexborough's businessmen had changed their minds about refusing to finance the club further. Money was to be guaranteed by, Messrs. F.J. Law, T. Athron, C. H. Athron, W. Briggs, F. Hillerby and G. Jones.

Mexborough Town FC finished towards the bottom of the Midland League in the 1913/14 season, winning just ten games from 34 and finishing with the worst 'goals against' column of 84. They did, however, win their last game of the season 2-0, beating the highly positioned Chesterfield. Dick Ebden, a goalkeeper on trial from Mexborough Great Central Railway Locomotive Department team, apparently had an excellent game for the 'Town' giving some promise for the forthcoming season. Yet the future of many of the players would be determined by the impending war. Some would no doubt be a welcome addition to their regimental football team.

Boxing contests, another sport associated with Mexborough, took place in the town on a regular basis. On Saturday 1st March, Mexborough's Tommy Stokes fought a renowned American called Dixie Kid, described as a slippery and cunning fighter. Although Stokes 'floored' Kid half way through the bout to be ahead on points, Dixie Kid evened to seize a draw.

Cycling was also popular in Mexborough, as it was throughout the country. The Mexborough Free Christian Church had its own cycling club and announced to the press in May that it had been necessary to cancel its proposed trip out to the Maltby Model Village because of bad weather. It would however be taking a run out the following week to Wentworth on a Saturday afternoon. Experienced cyclists were to become an asset to the armed forces by way of the cycling battalions.

The Mexborough and District Angling Association held its annual presentation in The Plant Hotel in early July. This included a presentation of medals and cups by Mr Brookes from 'The Plant' and Mr T. Venables from the Mason Arms.

Mexborough was also an area blessed with talented musicians. The much acclaimed Mexborough Concertina Band, winners of the English Championship in 1906, were successfully performing at the Hemsworth Hippodrome in late-July, at the so called Hemsworth Concertina Party. Some members of the Mexborough band would be joining the armed forces in a war that was now only days away.

With the world crisis of July 1914 approaching, the people of

Mexborough appeared to be almost unaware of the pending dark clouds that would break and lead the country into the bloodiest war in history. Although the Easter was spent amid a pit strike, it nevertheless was celebrated with something approaching normality. Whitsuntide fell on Sunday 31st May in 1914 and the usual festive mood prevailed. *The Times* of 30th May described the mood in this way:

> 'We approach Whitsuntide with a good more light heartiness. Last Easter Yorkshire coal strike obscured normal joyousness. We experienced the somewhat eccentric May weather with piping hot sun and frosting nights with intervals of rain, but the prospects were bright. To the children in their pretty white frocks and sashes and proudly displaying new suits it is the happiest time of the whole year.'

For many of Mexborough's working class, a trip to the coast would have been an exciting treat. Cleethorpes was a common destination, often by railway excursion down the Great Central Railway by way of Doncaster and Grimsby. *The Times* noted that the east coast had become very popular in the ten years prior to 1914: 'many people were attached to Bridlington with its beautiful bay and beach, its bracing air and its almost unrivalled bathing. The rush from south Yorkshire to Bridlington is expected to be more emphatic and pronounced this Whitsuntide than ever.'

Such confident predictions of a blissful Whitsuntide holiday do not convey a mood of impending gloom and thoughts of a forthcoming war, a war which was probably the last thing on the minds of the Oxford Road Church choir. They and their many friends took their annual trip to the delights of the Dukeries on Whit Tuesday. It was reported that the group were up early to catch the 7.52am train from Mexborough station, had tea at Worksop, and arrived home in Mexborough at 9.00pm. An enjoyable day was had by all.

The Mexborough Fair and Feast took place on Sunday 21st June. In slightly showery weather, what was called the Mexborough Hospital Demonstration was played out in front of a big crowd on the Cricket Field which included a choir conducted by Councillor Winstanley. The Fair and Feast was seen as a major event in Mexborough's calendar, being a focal point for enjoyment and pleasure and according to *The Times*, unlikely to 'lose its pride of place' on the evidence of 1914's turnout.

In order to raise funds for Mexborough Montagu Hospital, principally for a new Children's Ward, Mexborough and district held its first Alexandra Rose Day on 18th July. A Mrs W. Cook, of Bolton upon

Dearne had suggested this event to the hospital's Ladies Committee. It was to become an annual event to which the Ladies Committee devoted their efforts. Among the flower sellers were school girls from the local girls' schools. A Mrs M. Thompson of 180, Doncaster Road was busily committed to the event, asking shops and households to decorate their fronts in a show of support.

Again, this optimism in the lives of Mexborough people would remain very much unaltered despite it being a matter of weeks before war was declared. It was a theme routinely conveyed by *The Times*. The paper reported in its 1st August edition, four days before the declaration of war, that on the previous Tuesday, some of the staff of Mexborough branch of Barnsley Cooperative Society took advantage of the annual trip to Blackpool.

The Times would not have wanted to appear to scaremonger in its editorials on international affairs. However, there was a tendency for those newspapers which supported the Liberal Party to show less awareness of the implication of what was happening internationally than those supportive of the Conservative Party. The paper featured an article in late May on the possible expansion of the south Yorkshire coalfield, quoting continental financial interest in new prospective collieries. It notes that; 'the introduction of a German syndicate at Harworth may prove to be only a first stage of foreign capital in the conversion of the district from an agrarian to an industrial character'.

As for the people of Mexborough themselves, their awareness of international political events would probably have varied. Awareness of the possibility of war may have been compelling for some and their holidays may have been taken in the knowledge that the good times would soon come to an end. Others may have been oblivious to the international crisis and concerned only with their own social and economic circumstances of whether next week's wage would stretch until the following week. For the children, of course, we can assume that there would have been a blissful naivety and the sentiment that the holidays were to be enjoyed and very little else mattered.

Nevertheless, there had been discussion about the possibility of a war with Germany at least from the beginning of the century. Much of this talk would have been more emphatic within the household and circles of the well-heeled. The thought of Britain as a supreme power being challenged by the German nation, both industrially and in terms of military force, was of profound concern to businessmen and the armed forces. A show of strength at some point was seen as being unavoidable. This feeling, engendered by the right-wing press, created anti-German sentiments, unfettered by class divide. The theatres and music halls, frequented in part by the working classes, rang with chauvinistic songs proclaiming Britain's superiority in every sphere of life and in every corner of the world. Certainly the music halls were used to good effect to aid recruiting campaigns in the early part of the war. The male impersonator Miss Vesta Tilley, who become to be known as 'Britain's Best Recruiting Officer', inspired young men to join the ranks with songs such as, 'The Army of Today's Alright' and 'Jolly Good Luck to the Girl who Loves a Soldier'.

What has been called music hall imperialism was popular from as early as the 1850's with Victorian and later Edwardian audiences. The Germans were the target of intense, bitter attacks in music hall and literary expression from the 1890's, with the arrival of German immigrants that were believed to have deluged the labour market around this time. How such expression of hostility affected the people of Mexborough's attitude towards German immigrants has not, as far as is known, been researched. However judging by the popularity of the German butcher, George Schonhut with his election to the Council prior to the war itself, it may have had little impact upon the majority. It is probable that most of Mexborough were not jingoistic idealists of an extreme disposition, but certainly many were ready to heed the call and serve King and country if and when it arrived.

However, it would not be true to say that all in Mexborough were of a patriotic tendency. There would have been the conscientious objector, whether it be the religious pacifist of the Quaker, or the internationalism of the Socialist or Marxist whose ideology would favour the 'class war' as opposed to an imperialist one. But there was, within religious and educational institutions in particular, a strong systematic indoctrination towards a sense of national pride and belief in Britain's supremacy within the world. This could be seen up and down the country in the nation's celebration of Empire Day, which in 1914 took place on Monday 25th May. The day would have been celebrated in all the schools in Mexborough. *The Times* described the events at Main Street School. The children at the school, after the Chair of Governors made a speech to them were 'in high glee dispersed to their homes'. Songs of the stirring nature were sung by the excited children, including 'God Who Made Our Empire Great', 'What Can I do for England'? 'Son of the Empire'and 'Land of Hope and Glory', rounded off with the National Anthem. This atmosphere would have resonated throughout the town amongst all ages and levels of society, as it was intended to do, given the international crisis being shaped by events in the Balkans.

The British Establishment had more than an eye to the pending crisis and the likelihood of conflict and was aware of the patriotism engendered by festivities such as Empire Day. Such enthusiasm for the British Empire and all that it was said to stand for would soon be in need of harnessing. Major F.E. Ashton, the commanding officer of the York and Lancashire Regiment (York and Lancs), announced that a recruitment march would take place, passing through Mexborough and district on Wednesday, 25th March. The march would start at Bolton-upon-Dearne railway station, then commence to the Drill Hall at Wath, forward to West Melton and then on to Swinton, finishing in Mexborough. The battalion in attendance, with their drum and fife band, was the 2nd Battalion of the York and Lancs, at that time stationed in Limerick, Ireland.

Major Ashton described the York and Lancs as the territorial regiment of Mexborough and district. Many Mexborough, Swinton and Denaby men were at that time serving with the 1st Battalion in Jabblepore, India and with the 2nd Battalion in Limerick. It was many years since such a march had taken place and consequently this march was to, as *The Times* put it, get the locals reacquainted with their 'own regiment'.

The battalions arrived accordingly when the band detrained at Bolton-upon-Dearne in the company of Colonel T.W.H. Mitchell of the 5th Battalion of the York and Lancs, whose barracks were at Rotherham. Mitchell, who lived at Sandygate House in Wath, was due to retire from command of this regiment after 32 years service and this was his last official engagement. He and the assembled battalions moved off towards Mexborough where they were reportedly met by thousands of Mexborough citizens who were readily waiting to hear speeches made from a platform which had been erected at the east entrance of the Market Hall. Here, the battalions were received by Urban District Council representatives including Councillor J.T. Rowan, the Chairman and Mr J.H. Watson, JPCC.

Major Aston, whilst not appearing to reflect on the possibilities of a forthcoming war, expected Mexborough to help fill the ranks of the Regiment. The Major drew some laughter when observed the many young men that he would have preferred to see on the barrack square at Pontefract with him putting them through a few drills. To great acclaim, and with a hint of reference to conflict, he said that the great Empire of these young men had been, "won by the sword and would have to be held by the sword".

Major Aston's patriotic call may have had less influence on prospective recruits than the words of one of the recruiting officers, Captain Birch. Many of those at the recruiting rally were shortly to be thrown into another industrial dispute and the uncertainties that could bring. Strike pay was scant consolation when trying to feed a family. Pit life must have been experienced as a constant struggle with the employer for better pay and conditions and a dangerous, insalubrious and often miserable existence. There is little doubt that army recruiters within the coalfield areas were conscious of these facts. Tempting young men with the prospect of a 'better life' was part of the recruiting strategy. Captain

Birch assured those young men who joined that they would be given a heart-warming introduction to army life, plenty of comradeship and "a jolly good time into the bargain". The young men would be "well clothed, well fed and carefully attended to when they were sick". An attractive proposition, but for many, their experiences in the trenches would be somewhat different. The Captain further promised that when their period of service had expired, the army would make every effort to find them employment. This pledge would never be realised for many.

With the recruiting party having fulfilled its mission, the battalions with their bands marched along Doncaster Road. From here they went into Church Street, before returning to Market Square to play some more regimental selections, no doubt hoping to catch the attention of potential recruits. From Mexborough, the regiment's representatives proceeded to catch the train from one of the Swinton stations and on to their barracks at Pontefract.

The Times did not record the extent to which the exercise was successful or otherwise. The York and Lancs Regiment's journal, *The Tiger and Rose*, does, however, have this to say:

> 'Our visit to Mexborough was most gratifying. The principal streets and the Market Square where one dense crowd of people, who gave us a real Yorkshire welcome. As one gentleman expressed it, 'we have over 30,000 people in the town, and you have seen them all; as a matter of fact the only thing left in the houses were the cats and canaries.' Mexborough, however is showing sympathy in a very practical way, viz, by the number of men it is sending to join the Army. Last September, for the first time for many years, a recruiter was stationed there, and the response has far exceeded expectations.'

Whether the recruitment exercise was successful or not, the events elsewhere in Europe would ensure that in the not too distant future Mexborough would see the urgent return of the recruiting officers.

Chapter Three

The Breaking of the Storm Clouds

The assassination in Sarajevo of the Archduke Franz Ferdinand, the heir presumptive to the Austro-Hungarian throne and his wife, on 28th June 1914, was the spark that ignited the explosion of violence that came to be known as the Great War. Yet, as Liddell Hart remarks in his distinguished book on the war, 'fifty years were spent in the process of making Europe explosive, five days were enough to detonate it.' Events moved rapidly from that fateful day, but the cocktail of combustible material was produced over many years.

Britain had developed, or was perceived to have developed, a foreign policy of 'splendid isolation' under the premiership of Disraeli and Salisbury in the 1870's and 1880's. It is argued by historians however that the two men never used these words. Nevertheless any idea of 'splendid isolation' was about to disappear, given events in Europe.

Britain had been the first industrial nation, but lost ground as the leading industrial nation as a result of challenges from developing international competitors. By 1914, the USA had become the leaders of industrial world, but Germany would pose the biggest challenge to Britain in Europe, particularly in the iron and steel industries and to a lesser degree the coal industry. Germany was becoming a prominent nation state, developing rapidly under the leadership of Chancellor Bismarck, following German unification in the 1870's. Britain was becoming more and more dependent on imported products from a economically expanding German nation.

The major industrial powers of Europe - Britain, Germany, France,

Austria–Hungary and Italy - all needed markets with which to trade. They also wanted colonies to increase their imperialist aspirations - a process that had caused tension prior to the 1870's, although Germany was a late-comer to colonialism. A congress in Berlin, at the request of Austria-Hungary and overseen by Bismarck, was convened in 1878. Here the major European states were to take critical decisions on how territory in the East and the Middle East, central Asia and the Balkans, might be annexed or gained. The Congress of Berlin only served to increase tension. This was particularly so between Russia, who wanted to expand into the Balkans, and Germany. Russia claimed it was undermined by Germany and Austria-Hungary over the gains it had made into Turkish territory. As a result, new alliances began to be forged.

Bismarck sought to create alliances with other European powers in order to establish some security against possible French aggression in reprisal for its defeat, and the annexing of Alsace Lorraine in the Franco-Prussian war of 1870-71. This Bismarck was able to do by forging a Triple Alliance between German, Austria-Hungary and Italy. At the same time Russia's ambitions could only, in its view, be realised if it allied with France. This alliance was established initially by an agreement of 1891, only to be reinforced in 1892 and 1894 and further strengthened, although under some secrecy, in 1912.

With the European powers developing their foreign policy, Britain could no long stand isolated from the formation of alliances. The 'splendid isolation' may be said to have ceased with the Anglo-Japanese Alliance of 1902, but it was certainly dead with the signing of the famous 'Entente Cordiale', the Anglo-Franco agreement of 1904. This alliance had in a small way been assisted by the great Francophile, King Edward VII. The Anglo-Russian Entente, a little later in 1907, also had some royal influence in that there was a closeness between Edward and his cousin, the Tsar Nicholas II.

Towards the end of the reign of Edward VII, the power relationships were set around two potentially opposing alliances; the so-called Central Powers, primarily of German and Austria-Hungary on the one hand, and the Allies, mainly of Britain, France and Russia - the Triple Entente - on the other. There were other developments in the first decade of the 20th century which were bound to lead to tension. The German Kaiser's ambitions were to establish his nation as a supreme colonial power, particularly in the continent of Africa. A measure of this vision was his nation's production of a massive naval fleet between 1898 and 1914. Such activity was recognised as threatening by Britain. During the whole of the previous century, 'Pax Britannic', with the might of the British Royal Navy was seen as a major deterrent. In response to Germany's inclination to enlarge their navy, Britain began to embark on their own programme, building large battleships named the 'Dreadnoughts', the first of which was completed in December 1906. This building programme was largely welcomed by the British public. The Liberal Government of the period did not allow itself to be drawn into a 'guns or butter' argument, but chose to adopt what might be termed a 'guns and butter' policy, introducing progressive welfare reform alongside its spending on defence. Songs and sketches in the music halls portrayed the popular opinion that Britain had to expand its navy and army. Walter Tilbury's song, with reference to the building of the Dreadnought battleships was popular in the music halls at the time.

The Balkans, a region in south eastern Europe connecting western Europe with Asia, had become the focus of attention by the time of the death of King Edward VII in 1910. For four centuries, this area had largely been under Ottoman rule. By this time the Ottoman Empire had come to be known as the 'sick man of Europe' and breaking up under an intense rise in nationalist sentiment. Bulgaria, Montenegro, Greece and Serbia gained independence from the Ottoman Empire, although the Ottomans still ruled. These countries formed what was to be known as the 'Balkan League' and attacked Ottoman rule in October 1912, this being the first Balkan War.

The first Balkan War ended with the signing of the Treaty of London some seven months later, but a second conflict broke out within weeks, in June 1913. Greece and Serbia had made a secret agreement to divide up gains made in Macedonia to the exclusion of Bulgaria. As a consequence, Bulgaria was aggrieved and attacked its former Balkan League partners. Greece and Serbia defended themselves and counter attacked. Bulgaria lost land it had gained in the first war as a result of the Treaty of Bucharest which concluded the end of the second Balkan War.

Germany had been substantially involved in Ottoman politics since the Congress of Berlin in 1878. This was a meeting of the main European powers and the Ottoman Empire attempting to reorganise the Balkan countries and bring some stability. Austria gained territory, but Russia was unhappy about the outcome which increased tension between the Russia and Austria–Hungary. Russia nationalists were also to target hostility towards Germany. At the time of the two Balkan Wars, the Austro-Hungarian Empire was under threat. Serbia had increased its territory, causing what Austria-Hungary saw as 'The South Slav problem'. Between 12th and 14th of June 1914, Archduke Franz Ferdinand met Kaiser Wilhelm II in Vienna to discuss their countries' future and the problems Austria-Hungary were facing from Balkan nationalism.

On June 28th, the Archduke, along with his wife, visited Sarajevo, the capital of Bosnia-Herzegovina, to witness the Austria-Hungarian army on its summer manoeuvres. The Archduke, who was vehemently opposed to Serbian nationalism, along with his wife, were shot dead on a second attempt by Gavrilo Princip, a young disaffected nationalist student and a member of a secret society, with the melodramatic name of the 'Black Hand' who were bent on liberating Slav lands from Habsburg rule.

Austria-Hungary's unproven belief that the Serbian government was complicit in the assassinations was probably well-founded. Seizing on the opportunity to stamp its authority on the situation and solve the 'South Slav problem', Austria-Hungary demanded that those responsible should be brought to justice. It did however seek to go beyond simply justification for the murders and placed an ultimatum before Serbia on 23rd July that would virtually destroy Serbia as a state. First World War author Liddell Hart describes Austria-Hungary's demands in this way, 'its terms not only demanded the repression of all propaganda against Austria, but Austria's right to order the dismissal of any Serbian officials that she cares to name and to post her own officials in Serbia. This directly violates Serbia as an independent country'. Such a demand was unlikely to be accepted, Austria-Hungary knew it but it gave them, in their view, justification to declare war.

Serbia was given 48 hours to respond, which it duly did. She accepted all demands, except those undermining her independence. Yet mobilisation was, in effect, already taking place and Austria-Hungary declared war on Serbia on 28th July. Serbia, while protesting her innocence of the assassinations, appealed to Russia to assist in the event of a conflict. On 29th of July Russia began to partially mobilise against Austria-Hungary and a day later commenced full mobilisation of its armies.

Germany agreed to mobilise in defence of Austria-Hungary, despite originally urging her to take a road of mediation and arbitration. Germany had, in effect, given a blank cheque some days earlier, which Austria had gratefully cashed in. With the Russians now joining the conflict, Germany were conscious of the alliance between France and Russia and demanded, on 31st July, their neutrality in the affair and asked France to give up its fortress towns of Toul and Verdun as a sign of their commitment to remain neutral. Such an unreasonable demand was unsurprisingly rejected and France ordered its own mobilisation of troops on 1st August, the same day as Germany occupied Luxembourg and declared war on Russia. This was quickly followed by a German declaration on of war on France on 3rd August.

Germany was now at war with Russia and France. This triggered the implementation of the 'Schlieffen Plan' designed, a number of years previously and completed in 1905. It was designed to deal with the eventuality of having to face a war with Russia and France at the same time. This audacious plan, watered down from its original conception, was to pass into Belgium by way of Luxembourg and the Netherlands. From here the plan was to advance into northern France, encircle and defeat the French armies and then proceed by the railway network to engage in battle with the Russians who would, theoretically, be held in check by other German army divisions. With both Russia and France at war with Germany, Britain had a crucial decision to make about its position in the European conflict. As late as 29th July, the British government had no desire to commit itself to an engagement against Germany and support its allies France and Russia. Sir Edward Grey, the Foreign Secretary in Herbert Asquith's Liberal Government, told the French Ambassador in London that Britain was still to make up its mind on whether or not to support France if it and Germany became embroiled in conflict. However, the French ambassador insisted that Britain should uphold its obligation under the Anglo-French entente.

The Liberal Cabinet was largely made up of those who wished to see Britain remain neutral, whether by indecision or anti-war sentiment. Even as late as 1st August, the Cabinet refused to give any assurance to France. However on Sunday 2nd August, Grey was able to persuade the Cabinet to sanction an assurance that the British navy would protect the French coast from German attack. Winston Churchill, then the First Lord of the Admiralty, ensured the British Fleet was in a position to undertake the task.

The Times of 1st August featured an editorial headlined 'War Clouds.' It remarked: 'The task which is before Sir Edward Grey today namely that of keeping Great Britain clear of the war will test the splendid ability of the Minister to the full'.

It was the question of Belgian neutrality which became the pivotal factor. Britain and other countries, including Prussia (Germany), had signed a treaty as long ago as 1837 pledging Belgium neutrality. In order to implement the 'Schliffen Plan', it was necessary for the German army to enter Belgium and be allowed a free passage through Belgium itself. The Belgian government made it clear that it would not have its neutrality violated. Such was the force of public opinion set against an invasion of this small relatively militarily weak country that the Cabinet's opinion hardened and came in line with this public sentiment. Such an invasion would now make it difficult for the wavering Liberal Cabinet to procrastinate further.

Chapter Four

Declaration of War

That the Bank Holiday Monday of 3rd August was a tense day for the British people in that war was almost inevitable. Any holiday celebrations were tempered by prospects of war and the mixed emotions that the British public would be feeling. On the morning of 4th August, Germany did indeed invade Belgium. The British Government had demanded that such action should not take place and sent an ultimatum to the German Chancellor, Bethmann Hollweg, imploring that Belgian neutrality should be respected. Failing this, Britain would support Belgium in resisting the German army and thus enter the war. The ultimatum expired at 11.00pm British time (midnight in Berlin). The British Government had heard nothing to the contrary by the deadline and so declared war on Germany.

That evening Sir Edward Grey was in the Foreign Office anticipating the worse. Looking through his office window at the street lights peering through the darkening summertime evening, he spoke these prophetic words; "The lamps are going out all over Europe: we shall not see their light again in our lifetime." Others were even more prophetic in the belief that the world would never be the same again.

On Wednesday morning, 5th August, Mexborough, as the rest of Britain, woke up to the news that their country was fully involved in a war of a vast tangle of the world's nations, a war which was soon coined the 'Great War'. Within days, the Central Powers of Germany and Austria-Hungary (later to be joined by Turkey) and the Allies of France, Russia and Britain with its Empire countries (later to be joined by Italy, Japan and USA) were now engaged in what transpired to be the bloodiest and most bitter conflict the world has ever witnessed. Kaiser Wilhelm had promised his troops a swift conclusion to the war, telling them they would be home before the leaves had fallen from the trees. Similarly, the British public was promised that the war would be over by Christmas. Both proclamations were tragically misconceived.

Britain's response to establishing itself on a wartime footing was remarkable, given that the Government had been so indecisive just days from the declaration of war. On 4th August, a committee for the 'Prevention and Relief of Distress' was set up with a committee of Cabinet ministers serving on it. On 6th August, the Prince of Wales appealed for support for a National Relief Fund which again contained Cabinet members. Railways and mines quickly came under State control. The Trade Unions in these in these industries had long called for their Nationalisation. Their plea was rejected by governments on the ground that this would be difficult to do. However, on the onset of war, the railway and mines were brought under government control within 24 hours, demonstrating that this had been a plausible eventuality, had the government of the day willed it. Indeed, the government took a grip on most aspects of life with the introduction on 8th August of the 'Defence of the Realm Act' (DORA). A second DORA appeared on 28th August, and amendments and revisions to the Act were made in 1915 and 1916.

The editorial in the first edition of *The Times,* after the declaration of war was on 8th August, was sombre, but also upbeat regarding the righteousness of the British cause:

> *'The long dreaded European war has come upon us at last with terrible suddenness. Within a week Great Britain has been converted from a busy commercial nation into a military engine powered ready to strike for liberty and freedom.'*

Efforts of both Government and the people were concentrated against the common enemy of a German nation set on imperialist expansion and domination. The women's movement, mainly through the Suffragists and Suffragettes, began to show the zeal of the convert by putting their full weight behind the war effort. Members of the less militant National Union of Women's Suffrage Societies (NUWSS) (who were known as Suffragists) were asked to do so by Mrs Millicent Fawcett, its President. Their announcement to suspend all political activity, until the war was over, was made only two days after the declaration of war. They did, however, continue to demand the vote throughout the war and effectively promoted women's activities in the war effort, particularly of industrial production, to substantiate their case for the vote.

The smaller Women's Social and Political Union (WSPU), who believed in 'direct action', ceased their militant activity. The WSPU, led by the Pankhursts, negotiated a deal with the Government, who on 10th August released all suffragettes from prison on the proviso that the organisation end its activities and put its full weight behind the war effort. This they did and Mrs Emmeline Pankhurst announced that all militants of the WSPU were to "fight for their country as they fought for the vote". Mrs. Pankhurst moved her attention to recruiting campaigns to attract men to the forces and began to appear on recruiting campaign platforms with those who at one time she would have regarded as her political enemies. Her move to this conservative position was complete when, in April 1915, the WSPU launched its new paper, *The Britannia*, and ceased to publish *The Suffragette*. The slogan adopted by the paper was, 'For King, For Country, For Freedom'. Needless to say, this conversion did not meet the approval of all female opinion. Mrs Pankhurst's daughter Christabel was in agreement with her mother but her sisters Adela and Sylvia, both pacificists and anti-capitalists, were not in favour of their mother's change of direction, earning them a rebuke from Emmeline and Christabel. Declaration of war had clearly caused this internal division within the women's movement.

The Labour Party also converted their sentiments so much so that the chairman of its Parliamentary Party, Ramsey MacDonald, was forced to resign as a result of still holding anti-war convictions. Councillor James Walton, secretary of the Mexborough Trades and Labour Council, demonstrating what was described as a 'united front', remarked in the Council's 24th annual report:

> *'All our difficulties and differences, whether political, social or trade union, for the time being sink into insignificance beside the great crisis which is upon us, not as a section or party, but upon us as a united nation and people. Our difference and dissensions have disappeared as by magic.'*

Despite this, Walton was quick to recognise that there could be no glorification of war remarking that, "we must ever live with this realisation present with us that it is the workers of one nation and people who are being used to spread death, destruction and destitution amongst workers of another nation".

Councillor Walton was to go so far as to attend a Parliamentary Recruiting Committee in Doncaster a committee formed to promote the recruiting effort and made up of the major political parties of Liberal, Labour, Conservatives and Unionists. He told a meeting of the Mexborough and District Trades and Labour Council in December, that it was unique, sitting on a committee which saw the three parties in "perfect harmony", for they only had one desire to do what they could to safeguard the nation's interest.

The Labour Movement's modification of its anti-militarism was applauded by both the right-wing and liberal press, such as *The Times*, who described James Walton's change of views as those of 'the more intelligent body of Labour Opinion'. Yet the Mexborough and District Trades and Labour Council's annual report mentions a split in the Movement over the direction it was embarking upon. The local British Socialist Party (BSP) intended to stand a candidate in the Doncaster constituency, who was described as being one in the 'socialist interest'. Although a militant trade unionist and socialist vigour against a capitalist war had most certainly waned, elements in the Labour and Trade Union Movement had 'unfinished business'.

Another formidable source of political tension, the struggle over Irish Home Rule, was influenced by the beginning of the war, initial attitudes towards the Government of Ireland Act or the Third Home Rule Bill being affected. The struggle over Irish Home Rule evolved over many years but the Act to provide Ireland with self-government was finally enacted in September 1912 amidst great controversy, splitting the Irish nation into two factions. Liberal, Labour and the Irish Nationalists favoured home Rule, but the Conservative and Irish Unionists did not. Such was the hostility between the two sides that, in Ireland itself, two armed units in the form of the pro Home Rule nationalist Irish Volunteer Force, and their opponents the Ulster Volunteer Army, were forged. As a result, Ireland was on the brink of civil war. Yet again, onset of the Great War caused both sides in the Irish conflict, at least momentarily, to support the British Government and the war effort.

John Redmond, the leading Irish Nationalist, gave his support to the Government, showing indebtedness to the Liberal Government's willingness to ensure the passage of the Home Rule Bill. Redmond encouraged men from the Irish Volunteer Force to join the existing Irish regiments of British Army in order to demonstrate a commitment to the Government, in return for its acceptance of Irish self rule. Some dissenting Irish Nationalists defied Redmond and engaged in a rebellion against the British state, with some assistance from Germany, which culminated in the 'Easter Rising' in 1916. Likewise, the Ulster Unionist, Edward Carson, encouraged members of the Ulster Volunteer Force to enter service for the cause on the understanding that Irish self government would be suspended, at least for the duration of the war.

Like other political struggles of the day, Irish Home Rule was now on the back burner. Nevertheless, tension between the Irish factions was evident. Redmond wanted the Government to distinguish between Catholic and Protestant soldiers by some method of identification, including the suggestion of a separate Irish Brigade. The British Government were apprehensive about Redmond's demands in that it might prove to be a source of a ready-made force of disciplined armed men after the cessation of the war against Germany. The Government did however grant the Ulster Unionists its own 36th Ulster Division, and later the Government conceded to a 10th and 16th Irish Division in recognition of Redmond's request. In all, 44,000 Irishmen from both sides of the sectarian divide enlisted in 1914. Catholic and Protestant soldiers fought alongside each other, transcending the sectarianism their political leaders were, it appears, keen to perpetuate.

The 10th Irish Division served in Gallipoli, Palestine and Salonkia. Both the 36th Ulster and the 16th Irish Division were to suffer great losses at the Battle of the Somme in 1916. It is estimated that over 200,000 Irishmen fought with the British Army, of whom 30,000 lost their lives. There were also many Englishmen who fought in Irish regiments, including a number of Mexborough men.

For the moment at least, sport in Mexborough continued as normally as could be expected. At the beginning of the war, Mexborough's cricket team were in second position within the Mexborough and District League, finishing a respectable third for the year overall, with Wath Athletic taking the Championship. The report of *The Times* of 15th August, remarked that, 'against the overshadowing of the war, cricket continued on Saturday at a distinct disadvantage', with crowds being thin on the ground. An almost public school disposition seems to engage the reporter, who remarked that, 'this summer pastime seems tame tack in comparison to the thrilling European game now proceeding'.

Mexborough Town Football Club had secured a place in the Midlands League, but did no better in the 1914/15 season than it had done in the previous one. By November, they had only won three games from thirteen. By the end of the year, there was little improvement as they were third bottom with just four wins.

In contrast to cricket, crowds at local football games, and indeed those nationally, were not affected by the war as might be expected - at least initially. Cup matches as well as the normal fixture continued, including the traditional 'Montagu Cup'. Amongst a great deal of young men, there was a greater passion for Britain's national sport than for the British Army. This was brought to the attention of the Prime Minister Asquith himself. Sir John Lonsdale, a wealthy businessman and Ulster Unionist MP for Armagh, asked in the House of Commons whether Asquith was aware that recruiting meetings which had been arranged in connection with football matches were not successfully fulfilling their purpose. Lonsdale pointed to the 'fact' that at one football match in London, attended by thousands of football supporters, only one recruit offered himself for army service. Lonsdale was of the belief that legislation should be introduced to ban professional football for the duration of the war and that football grounds should be used for military purposes although the Prime Minister did not believe such steps to ban the game would be necessary.

Before the declaration of war, preparation had been taking place to mobilise the existing professional British Army, an army which was well trained, experienced and disciplined. Orders issued by the Home Office had been sent out on the evening of the Bank Holiday Monday, 3rd of August, to begin an initial mobilisation. The next day, orders were issued for the Army reservists and the Territorials to be mobilised. The Sheffield Bank in Mexborough was opened up for recruitment purposes on the Tuesday and the Wednesday 4th and 5th August. Newspapers were claiming that young from the district were responding splendidly to the nation's call to arms and that 40 men on the Wednesday had handed in their moblisation orders at Mexborough railway station and were being dispatched to their garrisons throughout the nation. Britain was mobilising its forces at an extraordinary speed.

Britain, unlike other nations, did not have a conscript army in 1914. The British army was made up of Regulars, Reserves and Territorials ('Terriers'), the latter being similar today's part-time serving soldier. The Territorials were established as a result of the Haldane Reforms of 1908 in response to the potential threat of growing German military power.

A regular soldier would sign up for twelve years service for a set period, usually of seven years, before becoming a reservist for the rest of the statutory period. On 4th August, the British army consisted of just short of 250,000 Regulars, just over 300,000 Territorials, and could call on 228,120 Reservists.

A list of the Mexborough Division of the National Reserve, under commanding officer Mr Nichol. B. Laidlaw of Bank House, Mexborough, was printed in *The Times* of 8th August. This division, known as 'C' company and attached to the Rotherham Battalion National Reserve, numbered 58 men, most of who had served previously with the army and had seen action in the Boer War. One such reservist who served in the Boer War was Trooper W.S. Pettit of 49, Park Road, formerly of the Yorkshire Dragoons. Another familiar Mexborough name on the list was William Waddington, son of Harry Waddington, the Mexborough auctioneer. He was swiftly off to Chelsea Barracks to link up with his old regiment, the Coldstream Guards. He had served in the South African War along with his brother Sergeant Harry Waddington, who was killed in that campaign.

By Thursday 6th August, 100 hundred reservists had been paid out at Mexborough Post Office with their mobilisation money (known as blood money by some) and given railway warrants in order to join their regiments. By 22nd August, many had left the town and would soon be sailing with the British Expeditionary Force (BEF) to France and Flanders. Another reservist was Lance Corporal J. Johnson, who was called up into the 1st Battalion Lincolnshire Regiment. He was a foreman porter on Mexborough railway station at the time.

Isaiah Blunt was also a reservist. He had joined the 2nd York and Lancs at Pontefract on 22nd July 1903, with the service number 7365. He was at this time employed in colliery work, probably at Denaby Main where he was born in 1884, and where the family lived at 6, Thyburgh Terrace. In March 1904, he departed with his regiment for service in India, returning to England after spending two years and 36 days overseas. He became a reservist from July 1906. Isaiah's father, also known as Isaiah, was a miner from Staffordshire. Isaiah senior, who had deceased by the start of the war, was the well-known and first landlord of the Albion public house in Mexborough, a pub that was nicknamed the 'Staff'. It is believed this nickname was derived from the landlord's place of origin, Staffordshire. Isaiah senior's eldest brother, Edward, took over as the head of the household, at 6, Thryburgh Terrace, Denaby Main by 1901, when Isaiah and his wife Ann took over the Albion. Isaiah senior had two other sons Frank and Adam. Frank and Isaiah junior, both miners, were boarders living with Edward by 1901. Edward himself had a son by the name of Harry.

Isaiah junior married a Manchester woman named Bertha in Collyhurst, Manchester on 19th September 1908, after which they moved to 24, Flowett Street, Mexbrough. He was still employed as a miner by 1911. Isaiah reported the loss of his reserve papers and his training notice in a letter to the Army in April 1913, his concern being he wished to apply for permission to go to Canada. He was granted permission and appears to have moved to Manchester in readiness to depart for Canada. He eventually sailed on the SS Arabic, of the White Star line, from Liverpool to his destination on 29th May and arrived in Portland, Maine. Isaiah's wife did not sail to Canada with him, for her name doesn't appear on the passenger list for the SS Arabic voyage in May 1913. Isaiah's address prior to leaving England was 76, Stuart Street, Bradford, Manchester. He had moved back to Manchester before making the decision to emigrate to Canada, and as a consequence separated from his wife Bertha.

As a reservist he was obliged to return to Great Britain which he did on 3rd September 1914. He returned to his old regiment and was notably recorded as being attached to the Canadian Division. After a short period, he was moved to Pontefract on 17th September, from where he embarked for France with the British Expeditionary Forces (BEF). Private Isaiah Blunt was sent out to the battlefields of Flanders to take part in the conflicts associated with the 'Race to the Sea', the fight to hold German forces pushing through to northern France from its positions in Belgium.

It appears that, that while fighting out in Flanders, Isaiah disputed the entitlement of his wife to separation allowance as a deduction of his pay. Bertha Blunt wrote to the Paymaster of the 3rd York and Lancs (a depot regiment) on 13th October claiming she had sent her marriage certificate but had not received her papers to claim the allowance. On 5th

November the Army decided that Mrs Blunt should not receive the allowance as the Paymaster had seen evidence of her misconduct. However the army would consider the allowance if there was some reconciliation between Private Blunt and his wife. Correspondence on this matter was being dealt with up to 24th November. By that time, Private Isaiah Blunt was dead. He died on 8th November, fighting around the Ypres Salient, at Messines or Armentieres. Private Isaiah Blunt is remembered at Ploegsteert Memorial (colloquially known as 'Plug Street') in Belgium. He was 33 years of age.

It is clear that the Blunts were keen to emigrate and Adam and a Richard Blunt were both on the S.S. Canada, bound from Liverpool to Quebec on 29th April 1911. Edward Blunt's son, Harry and his nephew Frank Marshall, were also to emigrate and joined them in Hamilton, Canada. Whilst in Canada, perhaps influence by Isaiah's return to England, all three volunteered and returned to their homeland to serve King and country. Adam, aged 23 and Harry, aged 21 by 1914, both single men, joined the York and Lancs, Canadian Division, as did Frank Marshall. Richard Blunt, a married man of 25 by the outbreak of the war, joined the Scottish Highlanders, again being recruited in Canada. George Hurst, Edward Blunt's son in law, was also recruited to the colours. This offers an illustration of one closely-knit family's enthusiasm to serve their country, but with it came shared grief. The eldest son of Isaiah Blunt senior, Frank, was within two years himself a casualty, killed on the first day of the Battle of the Somme in 1916.

The government had appointed Field Marshal Lord Herbert Kitchener as Secretary of State for War at the War Office and quickly authorised an appeal for the recruitment of 500,000 men, with the first recruitment appeal being order on 7th August. Famous recruiting posters featuring Kitchener's image began to appear, appealing to men between 19 and 30 (raised later to 38 as a special appeal to married men to join the ranks of Kitchener's Army. (The Royal Navy had an age range of 15 to 40).

Although the appeal was overwhelmingly well received, only 100,000 men had been recruited by 25th August. Yet by 12th September, the figure of 478,893 volunteers had been reached. September 11th saw the highest ever day for recruitment, with 12,527 men attracted to the call. In the fortnight after 30th August as many as 301,971 rallied to the colours.

Mexborough must have been a hive of activity in the first few weeks of August. Not only were the Reservists and the Territorials actively readying themselves for service, but there was a good response to Kitchener's call. The local recruiting officer was Sergeant Sudbury of the York and Lancs. Sergeant Sudbury was originally responsible for the Mexborough and District area which included Denaby, Conisbrough, Swinton, Bolton-upon-Dearne, Goldthorpe, Thurnscoe and Kilnhust. His recruiting office at his home on Wath Road was besieged with willing recruits to the extent that he complained of severe domestic inconvenience. Sergeant Sudbury returned to Pontefract Barracks to drill new recruits towards the end of September. His place was taken by Sergeant J. Oddy, formerly of the 2nd Dragoon Guards. Later, much more suitable recruiting facilities were found by using the Market Hall and the Labour Exchange in Bank Street.

By the end of August, Mexborough was becoming better organised to deal with the surge of its brave young men, who for whatever reason, were committing themselves to the nation's cause. Sergeant Sudbury appealed to local owners of motor vehicles to put them at his disposal. His request seems to have been successful and one can only imagine the hectic scene of young eager and exited men being ferried around the streets of Mexborough, experiencing their first taste of military life.

Volunteers were leaving their places of work in large numbers. The mining industry was to dominate the exodus of workers to the ranks. By October, the miners' union, the YMA, boasted that up to 13,000 of its members had joined up. There was a big response from every local pit, this including Manvers Main, Wath Main, Denaby and Cadeby and other surrounding pits. In November, when recruitment had begun to taper off, 50 men at Barnburgh volunteered so as their skills for digging trenches could be utilised. At a recruiting meeting held at Hickleton, 28 men signed up on their way through the colliery gates. By the end of the year, the Wath Main Colliery's 'Roll of Honour' contained 220 men who had joined the colours and Denaby Main Colliery had also released 300 men.

The railway industry, too, released its employees from their railway service. 'The Plant', the Mexborough locomotive department on the Great Central Railway, was reported in *The Times* of September 1914 as contributing many 'youths, principally cleaners and spare fireman'.

Army life did not suit every young man's fancy and there were desertions even in the early stages of the war. On Thursday, 15th October, Mexborough police were alerted to the fact that a young deserter from the York and Lancs was on the loose. Mexborough's PC Battersby was vigilant enough to spot the young recruit in the Adwick Road area. The police constable gave chase across fields and allotments towards the Waterworks and through Clay Lane in the direction of Denaby. The soldier was eventually caught, spent a period of time in the Town's police cell and was then handed over to the Military Authorities on the following Monday. The pursuit of deserters would become a regular duty of the nation's police for the next few years.

Recruiting campaigns saw many 'dignitaries' attending mass rallies nationwide. Locally, Lord Charles Beresford, MP for Portsmouth, appeared at a mass rally in Swinton early in September which was attended by many of Mexborough's own 'dignitaries'. To a large gathering he spoke of "the Empire's loyalty" and the "finest specimens of manhood" who were "surely thrilled with pride when they see what the Empire is going to do". He continued, to a chorus of cheers, "King George rules over a quarter of the world's inhabitants and they are tumbling over themselves to help us". This was a clear and probably successful attempt to stir a patriotic fervour within the young men gathered to hear the noble Lord. His words may indeed have been successful in that *The Times* reported at the end of September, since the outbreak of the war, 477 men in Mexborough had volunteered, principally with the York and Lancs, with a further 650 joining at Wath.

Arrangements were made for drilling instruction of the volunteer army to take place on the cricket field on Hampden Road, as well as consideration being given to the use of the Market Hall. Drill was also to take place under the direction of the Mexborough Rifle Club under commanding officer Mr Laidlaw of the Mexborough Company National Reserve. Mr Oliver, the proprietor of the Mexborough Grand Roller Rink, was also prepared to free up two nights for drill practice at Mexborough 'Rink'. The Mexborough Free Library in Bank Street placed its 'Ladies Reading Room' at the disposal of the military. Another recruiting officer of Mexborough was a Sergeant Booth who appeared before Councillors to call upon them to help facilitate another recruiting meeting at the Public Hall on Thursday, 29th October. His request, not surprisingly, was successful.

At this time a recruit could join the regiment of his choice. Most men chose to join with their colleagues in one of the Yorkshire based regiments, either the York and Lancs or the King's Own Yorkshire Light Infantry (KOYLI). It was work colleagues from the local collieries and the railways who initially responded to their nation's call. There were no 'Pals' Battalions formed in the Mexborough area as there were to be in localities such as Barnsley, Sheffield and Leeds. Yet from the beginning of recruitment in 1914, there were a number of the York and Lancs Battlions that can effectively be called a 'Pals' Battalion as far as Mexborough and district was concerned. Many Mexborough men, joining early in August, were recruited into the 6th York and Lancs and found themselves, within twelve months of joining, fighting in the horrors of Gallipoli. The 8th and 9th York and Lancs were also well sustained by men from Mexborough and the district. These two battalions were to suffer enormous casualties, particularly at the Battle of the Somme in 1916. These Service Battalions of Kitchener's New Army came into being from the September. The 10th Service Battalion of the York and Lancs, which also contained a good many Mexborough men, also began its existence in this early period.

New recruits from the area were quickly sent to the barracks at Pontefract. As this depot could not provide for the deluge of enthusiastic recruits, they were also accommodated in the local skating rink and tents, as well as being drilled on the local race course. The 8th and 9th Battalion of the York and Lancs were a little later in the year moved to Frensham Camp by train. The history of the 9th York and Lancs tells us that during the journey their train stopped at Grantham, where 'there was a regrettable rush to the Station Refreshment Room'. It does not elaborate further, but one can only be imaged the scene of chaos, given that such train journeys under war time condition tended to be long and arduous. On arrival at Frensham Camp, the 8th and 9th York and Lancs were situated on the opposite side of the road to that of the 11th Battalion Sherwood Foresters and the 8th KOYLI. These Battalions formed the 70th Brigade, of the 8th Division of the Fourth Army, in the forth coming campaigns on the Western Front.

The difficulties experienced at the beginning of the war at Frensham Camp are typical of those faced by the army in trying to raise Kitchener's New Army. Initially at Frensham there were no trained clerks and they had to be drafted in from the civilian population. A loyal group of boy scouts were initially to act as orderlies. There was one typewriter, little stationery and two motor cars, although two grey polo ponies turned up in early October, minus saddlery, for the use of the Commanding Officer and the Adjutant. Battalion transport consisted of a horse-drawn Lyon's delivery van which was used to deliver sandwiches to the troops when on route marches. Lyon's and Company originally dealt with the messing arrangements.

There were occasional letters from local Mexborough men in *The Times* concerning the lack of uniforms and equipment. Troops of the 8th and 9th York and Lancs arrived at Frensham Camp in a mixture of clothing, ranging from their civilian clothes, scarlet tunics, blue trousers and the very occasionally khaki. The men's emergency blue uniform did not arrive until the middle of October. Volunteers would often be without the proper khaki for months, sometimes even longer. The emergency blue was the blue serge known as 'Kitchener's Blue'. This was originally a substitute for the official khaki uniform, which initially relied on dyes imported from Germany, until alternative supplies could be organised. The 'Kitchener's Blue' uniform was not popular as it appeared to set men apart from their 'regular' colleagues. The 8th and 9th York and Lancs did not receive their khaki uniforms until February 1915. Things were so bad at Frensham Camp that two officers who had some connection with the clothing trade, obtained the funds to order boots and 20,000 suits of underclothing. Equipment was also a problem. There was a short supply of rifles. It was not until 8th November, three months after the first call for volunteers, that serviceable Lee Metford rifles arrived. Early in October, the Battalions were restricted to a few obsolete rifles for drill purposes.

Recruiting officer Captain Birch of the York and Lancs had promised new recruits would find comradeship and "a jolly time into the bargaining" during a May recruiting campaign in Mexborough. This promise could not to any great degree be extended to the soldier's life in the trenches, but conditions, at least initially, were not too 'jolly' in British training camps either. Although Frensham Camp was described as being 'situated in country of rolling pine hills and heather land', the battalions and regiments training here did not have, by all accounts, an easy time in this idyllic setting. To a large extent, originally at least, washing and bathing took place in Frensham pond and by mid-October with the onset of the winter, tents, which had no floor boards, became flooded and consequently large numbers of men were vacated to hospital with influenza and rheumatism.

The other regiment to which Mexborough and district men rallied was KOYLI. The 2nd Battalion KOYLI, of regular soldiers, were quickly mobilised and found themselves in the early fighting in Mons and Marne. The 1st KOYLI arrived in France and Flanders in early 1915. The territorials were the 1/4th, 2/4th and the 1/5th and 2/5th. The volunteer, 'New Army' (Service Battalions) of the KOYLI's were the 6th, 7th, 8th, 9th, 10th and 12th, the reserves being the 3rd, 11th and 13th. The 12th or the 'Miners' Battalion' was raised on 5th September and sometimes regarded as a 'Pals' Battalion. Many miners also joined the 6th KOYLI along with many from the Great Northern Railway Locomotives Works at Doncaster. Men who joined these battalions were raised mainly from the Pontefract, Wakefield and Doncaster areas, but some Mexborough men were to find themselves attached to these battalions.

It was clear that Kitchener's call for volunteers, with its legendary publicity campaign, had captured the minds and enthusiasm of the nation. The rush to engage with the recruiting sergeant would have been inspired for a variety of reasons. A release from poor working conditions endured by many workers at this time would have been a rationale for many unskilled industrial workers. Many would have been driven by a sense of adventure, and the prospect of a 'visit' to the continent. Many would have only travelled as far as the east coast, to resorts such as Cleethorpes, on works' outings on Bank Holidays, if indeed that far. But there would also have been a sense of comradeship and empathy with their colleagues who were already at the 'Front' as news was heard of the BEF's initial misfortunes with its retreat following the Battle of Mons.

The rate of recruitment was beginning to wane by October, despite the efforts of the War Office's tenacious recruiting campaign. The reasons for the decline in recruitment of volunteers would have been varied. There were always going to be 'diminishing returns' with the initial rush of the impetuous enthusiasm of Britain's young men. The military had also tried to be strict with regards fitness and even height. It raised the standard height requirement to 5 feet 6 inches in September, only to be altered to 5 feet 4 inches and again further down to 5 feet 3 inches when it became clear the military authorities had exceeded their expectations. The less optimistic news reaching the British public may have galvanised some but also had a reverse effect on others. The pre-war recruiting sergeant promise of comradeship and 'a jolly good time into the bargain' may have been wearing thin, with reports that not all the home comforts were being provided in the 'New Army' training camps.

Many articulate soldiers and sailors wrote letters to the local newspapers often with a plea to men to come and join them in the service of their country. Responding to the need to increase the momentum to raise the number of recruits to the 'New Army', a Private William Rutherford Tiptaft, wrote to *The Times* of the need for young Mexborough men to heed the call to join the colours. Writing of the British army's struggles which saw heavy casualities incurred to the regular and reservists, Private Tiptaft wrotes, 'For the last month we have only held our own with the Germans.... So it's obviously one's duty to enlist and equally obvious is that unless men are forthcoming we shall be beaten.' Private Tiptaft continued by extolling the virtues of army life whilst playing up the chances of survival. While sounding like a recruiting sergeant he wrote, 'we shall have an excellent opportunity of seeing other countries which up to the present we have merely heard about'. He appealed to the 'chap' who was yet to enlist to get it out of his head that he would have a rough time. Taking a rather public school ethos, Private Tiptaft continues, 'Mexborough has always had good place where sport was concerned and I know that everyone is anxious to keep up its old traditions by furnishing a good proportion of its population for service of the country'.

Private William Rutherford Tiptaft was the eldest of son of the well-known grocer, William Tiptaft, who after moving from Berkshire owned shops on the High Street, Mexborough and also one in Rawmarsh. Born in Mexborough, Private Tiptaft originally lived above his father's shop at 67, High Street, known as Tiptaft and Sons. Before joining the army, he worked in his father's business and was educated at Mexborough Secondary School. By the outbreak of the war, the family was living at a large house in Kilnhurst named 'Beechwood'.

William Rutherford moved to London and was one of the first to volunteer in September 1914. He is recorded in the local press as joining The London Battalion of Clerks and Businessmen, although his letter to the *The Times* indicates he was with the Royal Fusiliers stationed at Epsom in Surrey. He was not a private for long. He was given commission and raised in rank to second lieutenant. He finally became a Lieutenant with the 3rd Reserve Battalion of the Duke of Wellington (West Riding Regiment) attached to the Machine Gun Corps in September 1916, by which time he was serving in France in the Somme offensive. This son of a grocer, who had expressed clear patriotic sentiments in his letter to the press and quickly rose through the ranks, was killed near Ypres in September 1917. He is remembered on the war memorial at Kilnhurst.

Grocer William Tiptaft had a younger son, Cyril Paxman Tiptaft, also born in Mexborough. He, too, enlisted in the army in December 1915 and rose to the rank of Second Lieutenant in the Royal Army Medical Corps (RAMC). He survived the war and lived at Braunston House near Rotherham, eventually establishing himself as an accountant, with premises at 1, Cliff Street, Mexborough.

The equivalent to the Second World War's Home Guard was, in Mexborough, known as the Mexborough and Swinton Home Corps. In late September, they were anxious to bring their regular membership up to 200 men and instigate practice drills. These organisations were mainly for men in key occupations or those over military age, with others who were of suitable age and fitness being expected to join Kitchener's army. The Corps were often organised by former regular army volunteer officers.

By December the Mexborough and Swinton Home Corps were considering affiliating to the Central Association of Volunteer Training Corps, a voluntary home defence militia. This is probably because local defence groups, or town guards, had no legal status at this time. The Government were uneasy about the existence of these spontaneous units which were essentially private armies. In response to this, they set up the Central Association of Volunteer Training Corps under its president Lord Desborough on 19th November. This legitimised the local volunteer groups who affiliated, with an issuing of rules by which they were to conduct themselves. They had to be self-financing, allowed no weapons other than dummies which were approved by the local Territorial Army for drill. They were not allowed to wear khaki, but adopted a uniform of Lovatt green accompanied by a red arm band with the initials 'GR' (Georgius Rex) emblazoned upon them. This led to plenty of derision from uncharitable individuals, who labelled the members of these Corps with such derogatory names as 'Government Rejects', 'Grandpa's Regiment' and 'Genuine Relics'.

Local defence groups set themselves up in most towns and joined into county-wide units. An attempt was made in 1915 to legalise these impromptu citizen armies with a Private Member's Bill in Parliament. Despite this Bill failing, Parliament uncovered a forgotten piece of legislation, the Volunteer Act of 1863, which had escaped repeal. This allowed these organisations to grow, so much so that towards the end of the war, nearly 300,000 men had volunteered for them.

Chapter Five

Dawning of the Realities and Consequences of War

One of the consequences of mobilising for war was the general distress it caused to the working classes. This was a major concern at the time for the recently formed Labour Party and the Trade Unions. Income tax was to rise, albeit for the better off, although tax on tea and beer rose, as did prices generally. Most importantly for working class families, despite a separation allowance, they were to lose the 'breadwinner' who was now serving in the forces. The Prince of Wales National Relief Fund was set up in an attempt to combat these problems, as well as anticipating the plight of the unemployed. As Arthur Marwick puts it, 'Where there was distress in the first months it was acute: in patriotically turning their minds from dress to higher things, women of the middle and upper classes helped to throw out more than 40% of their labouring sisters out of work or on short time.' However these preparations for tackling the problems of unemployment were short lived and women in particular would later begin to fill the vacuum left by the shortage of labour.

The Government was keen to ensure that local communities organised relief networks in their area. The Local Government Board issued a circular which alerted local authorities to the possibilities of unemployment and distress as a result of the dislocation of trade. Mexborough Council responded to this when, in mid-August, it called a meeting to set up a 'Public Relief Fund'. A committee was set up with Councillor Christopher Ward JP as its chairman, with joint secretaries Mr Dennis Wood and Mr C. Brumpton. Donations to this fund were quickly received, including donations from some well-known local names; Dr J.A.E. Lee, Mr A. Barron, Mr H. Cliffe and Canon Bateman, the vicar of Mexborough at the time. Other familiar names were generous with donations. Joseph Hartley donated £5.5s (£5.25), whilst Councillor Tom Athron and Councillor George Schonhut each gave £3.3s (£3.15). Monies for the fund were to be paid either to the joint secretaries, at the newly built Oriental Chambers in Bank Street, or just down the road at the Mexborough branch of the Sheffield Banking Company. The relief itself was distributed from the Public Hall on Friday evenings.

An appeal went out to employers in the area to support the relief fund initiative. They were to ask their workers to give a voluntary levy. This appeal was successful and regular donations began to fill the coffers of the funds. In the first week of September, the fund had raised £150. Weekly donations of this order were being received:

Wath Main Workmen: £7 .0. 0.
Waddington's Workmen: £1.14s. 6d
Barron's Workmen; £3. 0. 0
Prudential Assurance Company (via Mr D.V. E. Dodsworth) £12. 0 .0
Staff of Doncaster Road School (via Mr Brown): £1.10s.6d
British Westalite Limited: £26. 5s 0d.
J Whitakers and Company: £5. 5s .0d.
Mr G. Bennett, Ferryboat Inn: £1.0.0

There was certainly a benevolent spirit about the town and probably a good deal of moral pressure placed upon those who may have been otherwise less sympathetic. The agent of a Mexborough houseowner was reported in the *The Times* as having taken possession of a soldier's wife's furniture as payment for her weekly rent. The landlord seems to have found his moral compass for he promptly brought the furniture back with his blessing and the welcomed news that she could remain in the house for the duration of the war. However, this particular landlord may not have given any thought as to how long the war might last.

The general public, in pubs, clubs, picture houses, theatres, schools and places of worship, were all encouraged to get involved in raising monies for the various relief funds. Volunteers were divided into various areas of the town and given a responsibility for collecting subscriptions and contributions. An additional role of these volunteers was to gather information on who was in need of help from the fund and report back to the Executive Committee of the Public Relief Fund. A concert was held at the Royal Electric Theatre, promoted by its popular manager Mr W.H. Melton. A so called 'Patriotic Concert' was held at the Empire, followed by a highly a successful concert in late October at the Hippodrome, for which credit was mainly attributed to Mr H. Leyton, the manager, and

Mrs Arthur Brown. Prior to this Mr Leyton had handed over £5 to the relief fund, the proceeds from Mr Will Casey's performance of 'Her Ruined Life'. Mexborough Main Street Working Men's Club members enthusiastically believed that a distress fund was essential and decided to hand over the sum of £2.2s. (£2.10p) per week to the local relief committee.

Despite the successful nature of fund raising and the most charitable response from Mexborough people and local business, controversy, was as ever, never far away. There were other distress funds which were set up nationally. The Prince of Wales Fund and monies from the Soldiers and Sailors Families Association could be drawn on from the appropriate applicants. The latter organisation decided that it would assist the families of Territorials as well as regulars. The Mexborough and District Trades and Labour Council met in the Old Masons' pub, their usual meeting place at this time, in late September, under the chairmanship of Mr B.L. Smith, to discuss those who were at that time affected by the problems created by a shortage of work at Denaby and Cadeby pits. The Labour Trades Council wanted funds from the Prince of Wales organisation to help those suffering from this shortage of work, only to be disappointed when told the fund was only for the dependents of soldiers and sailors. The meeting dealt with other issues which were considered to be adding to the distress of local workers and their families. The question was raised about the distribution of relief. Mr A. Roberts made reference to the point that he had information that some women had to stand waiting from six o'clock to eleven o'clock at night outside the relief office, for what he described as "a paltry five or six shillings". He suggested that relief should be taken to the women's homes by members of the relief committee.

Furthermore, one delegate, Mr Levi Jones, had observed that some relief was distributed by way of 'Tommy Tickets'. This was the practice of employers issuing their workers tokens which had no specific value to spent at 'Tommy Shops', shops which were owned by the employers themselves. This had been a long held grievance of the trade unions. The practice had in fact been made illegal by Act of Parliament from the early Victorian period. It was argued by some of the delegates at the meeting, that some tradesmen did give change when presented with 'Tommy Tickets'. Nevertheless delegates insisted that contributions from any Manvers Main Colliery worker was given on the strict understanding that it was to be distributed in cash. The meeting resolved that Manvers Main Colliery workers should be urged to cease paying their levies until the 'Tommy Ticket' system was discontinued.

There was better news in the first week of October when the committee of the Mexborough Relief Fund announced an increase in allowances to dependents. All families receiving relief (numbering roughly 100) were now to receive 20 shillings (a pound) per week for the wives, plus 2/6d (12.5p) per child, whether or not they were receiving relief from the Soldiers and Sailors Fund. It was clear that wartime charity was somewhat unsystematic in that it was often duplicated by the enthusiasm of supporters eager to promote good causes. The funds and charities were not always administered with complete efficiency and on occasions suffered from fraud and dishonestly. By 1916, the War Charities Act attempted to bring some government direction and control over the way the numerous charities were handled.

The question of the plight of the Belgian people was, at least initially, one that commanded the sympathy of many British people of all classes during the first months of the war. The violation of Belgium's neutrality by the German army was courageously and stubbornly resisted by a tiny Belgian force of 117,000 men, one tenth that of the enemy. It took only two days for Liege to surrender to the German army, the fortified city falling on 11th August. Despite this, those Belgian troops occupying the forts themselves, fought on until 16th August, finally being overcome by the might of a heavy German siege, greatly assisted by the Howitzers of their artillery. The surrender of Brussels followed four days later, with the remaining Belgian army of around 70,000 troops withdrawing further to the coast in an attempt to defend Antwerp. With the Belgian Government by this time having withdrawn to Le Harve, Belgian forces finally lost Antwerp to the Germans on 10th October, although its evacuation was ordered some days earlier. This was despite the efforts of the British, notably the Royal Naval Division, which landed in Zeebrugge and took part in the operations of the defence of Antwerp. Yet they themselves were to retreat and join Belgian troops who were dispirited and thrown into disarray. These forces, along with thousands of refugees, tried to make their way to Ostend on the coast. Ostend itself fell to the Germans on 15th October.

Refugees and the British sailors of the Royal Naval Division made their escape to neutral Holland, where many British servicemen were interned for the rest of the war. This included two Mexborough seamen of the Collingwood Battalion 'D' Company, Arthur Lunness and George Hyde of Cromwell Road, along with Sam Lyall, Bert Shaw, Chris Speak of Swinton and R. Bradshaw from Bolton-upon-Dearne. By mid-October, the much depleted Belgian army held a diminutive piece of land which it and its commander, King Albert of Belgium, defended until it recovered its land at the cessation of the war.

The Belgian's courageous resistance had at least allowed the French and the BEF to stall the 'Schlieffen Plan' and thus the German advance into France with their prime objective of taking Paris. This was nearly achieved when the Germans came within artillery range, just miles from the city, causing the evacuation of the French Government and half a million Parisians. The BEF, along with French troops, moved to engage German units near Mons on 23rd August, fighting a rearguard action from which they finally retreated from on 5th September. Pushed back over the River Marne and suffering from sheer exhaustion and a lack of supplies, the BEF were pursued by a German army facing similar problems. The Germans also retreated back over the River Marne and took up defensive positions on the north bank of the River Aisne. The tide of German advance was stemmed after a bloody, but nevertheless short pocket of combat, the Battle of Marne, which concluded on 15th September. This was a victory for the Allied forces and with it died the last vestiges of the 'Schlieffen Plan'. It was known as 'The Miracle of the Marne' by the French, for it had saved Paris from German capture and occupation. From this point a war of attrition began as the opposing sides constructed their trench systems – these stretching from the Belgium North Sea coast to the border of neutral Switzerland. From now until the German offensive of spring 1918, fighting was practically at stalemate, each side attacking each other across lines which altered little for the next four years.

Former Mexborough foreman railway porter, Lance Corporal J. Johnson, wrote home of his experiences at Mons and Marne. In a letter to Mr and Mrs Chadwick of Rowms Lane he was to wrote:

'At Mons we lay under shell fire for nine hours. My pals were dropping both sides of us. We lost 68 in my company alone. I gave myself up hundreds of time in that nine hours. The place was alive with shells. One shell dropped right behind me and did not explode so I can say I was lucky... The worst part about it was that we had no rest. I had not three hours sleep in a fortnight. You are lucky if you get a wash... Rough living, hard times and shell fire completely shake you to pieces. I have had some ups and downs I can tell you... But among it all I never got down hearted. I always kept my pecker up. The Commander of my regiment got a special praise from the General at Mons for the way we fought against enormous odds... After Mons we marched 140 miles in four days and nights fighting every day and three days without food except what we could get for ourselves – carrots, turnips and apples. I slept in barns, haylofts, ploughed fields, wet roads, every place you can image, even a hen-run. We had some queer times.'

Letters such as this were already arriving back home to relatives and friends in the Mexborough area, bringing with them the horrors and reality of war – a far cry from the perception of glory that some easily expressed and some easily accepted. The language of the soldiers' letters contrasts greatly with that of the official media and its commentators. The journal of the York and Lancaster Regiment, the *Tiger and Rose*, ceased to be published from September 1914 only resuming publication at the end of hostilities. Its editorial penned this final message:

> 'We bid our readers what we trust in only a temporary farewell. We do not know how many of them will have the good fortune to see active service abroad, but to one and all we wish the best good luck and we hope that the Regiment's paper will some day be restarted when the Army of the King in conjuncture with our unconquerable Navy shall have beaten England's enemies and brought to our Empire a lasting Peace and Honour.'

Such sentiments were already beginning to wear thin as a result of soldiers' battlefield experiences.

In a further letter, Lance Corporal Johnson remarked upon the plight of the Belgian people. Writing when wounded and in great pain he remarked; 'It is murder out here. You people live in Paradise compared to these poor people in Belgium. I have seen plenty like the poor old dad without homes.' News of the Belgian people's often dreadful treatment at the hands of the German occupiers was told by soldiers and press alike. Despite resistance, German units placed Belgium under a state of martial law, a move which often had brutal consequences for the occupied peoples. The German occupying forces conscripted hundreds of Belgians to work for them in the war effort and took revenge on anything they considered to be forceful resistance, such as sabotage. It is estimated that the German army executed up to 6,500 of those who were in defiance between September and November. Such acts of atrocity, especially against women and children, were seized upon by the British and French press and utilised for propaganda objectives.

It was not difficult to stir the emotions of the British people with tales of what was called the 'rape of poor Belgium'. Despite a previous mood of anti-alien sentiment, the British Government offered to the Belgian people what it called the 'hospitality of the British nation'. As a consequence, a central body called the War Refugees Committee was set up which gave guidance to local committees on how to accommodate Belgian refugees in their area. Many local Belgian Refugee Relief Committees were established throughout the cities and towns of Britain. The towns of the Don and Dearne Valley were no exception.

On 17th October, *The Times* reported that refugees were being distributed after what it called 'careful planning' throughout England. Rotherham was to house refugees in the town and also in the Rotherham

Golf Club. Some were to be housed at Hickleton Hall as well as the Village Hall. The Denaby Relief Committee had, with assistance from Cadeby Main Colliery, furnished ten houses in Blyth Street for refugees, which probably included some Belgian miners. Bolton, Goldthorpe and Swinton Relief Committees were set up and eager to give their hospitality. Belgians were also housed at Thyburgh Hall.

There was at this time little mention of Mexborough's contribution. Activity was taking place, for the *The Times* mentions that Mr John Clayton of Ingle Nook, Church Street, had been acting on behalf of the Belgian Relief Fund and had in a week collected £29. By the first week in November, the Mexborough War Relief Committee launched an appeal for Belgian refugees, announcing that a party of refugees was to arrive in Mexborough and that the Committee were making arrangements to accommodate them. One of the Committee members remarked, perhaps conscious of Mexborough's lethargy in the matter; "The whole community is awoke to the great debt we owe to the Belgian nation. Shall Mexborough lag behind in this great work securing these homeless wanderers? We hope not."

Collections for the Belgian refugees were taking place in Mexborough as early as mid-September. By mid-November, the Committee had set up a separate Belgian Fund and immediately raised £19 as a result of a charity concert at which the Orpheus Glee Singers were the main entertainers. Funds were not coming in as quickly as was hoped (Christmas was approaching), although there were regular subscriptions from the usual benefactors – local businesses and sympathisers from other areas of the Mexborough. Barron's and Waddington workers were donating a weekly sum of £3 and £3.12s.11d. (£3.65p) respectively. The school staff at Adwick Road, Garden Street Infants, Central Girls' and Infants Schools were giving the Belgian Refugee Fund £1 a week at this time, while one last appeal went for household goods such as beds and bedroom furniture.

By the beginning of December, Mexborough at last was prepared to take its first influx of refugees and arrangements were made by the Mexborough War Relief Fund to receive the arrival of three Belgian families, two from Antwerp and one from Malines, on Saturday, 19th December. An appeal for the use of a motor car was made to assist in the transportation of the refugees' worldly goods. The families were to be met at Mexborough station with a procession headed by the local Salvation Army Brass Band. The newly arrived were to proceed to the Primitive Methodist schoolroom where they would be entertained with what one imagines would have been a much appreciated tea. The Primitive Methodist Chapel was particularly sympathetic to the Belgians with the Chapel holding regular concerts in their aid.

Eventually the families were accommodated in the cricket pavilion, provided by the Mexborough Cricket and Athletic Club. Accommodation was temporarily provided for them in rooms in the Montagu Hotel prior to their settling into the cricket pavilion. Their Christmas was made as comfortable and agreeable as was possible in the circumstances. Mr Dennis Wood, the Secretary of the Mexborough Distress Committee, received from an anonymous Swinton resident, a Christmas tree decorated with presents. This was set up in the cricket pavilion to the delight of the Belgian guests who were to receive visitors over the Christmas period. Despite the obvious language difficulties, *The Times* reported that communication by way of, 'glad looks and bright smiles were eloquent enough to convey their meaning'. Various caroling parties visited the cricket pavilion on Christmas day, including the Parish Church Choir, who preferred to donate their few pence reward for their services to the small Belgian children. In the evening, a family concert was arranged and attended by Salvation Army string band. There were both English and Belgian contributions to the concert.

Fundraising for the Belgians continued into 1915. The people of Mexborough tried to offer some home comforts for the refugees with the arrangement of what was called a 'Belgian Concert' in the Public Hall in early February 1915. The main performers were the Mexborough Glee Society, but the promoters had secured the services of one, Henrie Dubois, who was described as a famous baritone from the Royal Opera House in Liege. Some considerable effort must have been made on the part of the organisers to entertain the Belgian families with such a renowned countryman of theirs.

The Central Register for Belgian Refugees attempted to keep records of those who had arrived in Britain. The National Registration Act of 1915 had deemed that men and women between the ages of fifteen and 56 should register, a move that was to aid the administrative process for the forthcoming compulsory conscription. This registration process had recorded that there were approximately 225,000 refugees who came to Britain to escape German occupied Belgium. However the registration process was said to be unreliable and it is estimated that there was probably about a quarter of million Belgians who arrived during the war, the highest intake of war refugees ever to enter Britain before or since. Statistics of 1921 show that nearly 10,000 remained although the vast majority returned to Belgium.

Generally there was little problem with Belgian refugee integration, though there was always an element of xenophobic sentiment under the surface. Locally, it was reported that there were those who believed that the male Belgian refugees should be fighting for their country and not immune from the armed forces. It was pointed out in *The Times* of 26th December that a local Belgian youth of eighteen had offered his service to join his country's armed forces, but it was not within the Belgian

King's proclamation to accept men of this young age.

In early February of 1915 the question of what should happen to the able bodied male refugees was brought up in the House of Commons, when Mr Thorne MP raised the issue of military service for abled-bodied Belgian males. The President of the Local Government Board, at the time Herbert Samuel, dismissed this unease which had surfaced, when he remarked that, "the question is not one for the Government but for the Belgian military authorities and the Belgian refugees themselves" (*Hansard*, 8th February 1915).

The forthcoming crisis of the inadequacy of shell production would see the mobilisation of labour from new areas of recruitment, including Belgian males deemed suitable for working in armaments factories and allied industries. Yet this in itself was to cause a problem in the eyes of the trade unions. They were originally fearful that the influx of Belgian refugees would saturate the labour market with cheap labour who employers would exploit at the expense of existing British workers.

At the end of April 1915, the Council's Medical Officer Dr Huey, who was also on the General Committee of Montagu Hospital, received a letter from the Belgian Relief Committee asking if Mexborough could offer a Belgian woman a bed. She was suffering from appendicitis and there were no beds available in Sheffield or Barnsley. This was granted with no committee member voting against, although only after some discussion as to whether or not it transgressed hospital rules.

Support for the Belgians continued well into the mid part of the war. Headteacher Arthur Brown of Doncaster Road School wrote in his log book concerning 'Children's Belgian Day', which was to take place on 20th July 1916. He made reference to, 'the District Sub Committee had this question before them on Wednesday last and decided that on July 20th schools should re-open at 1 o'clock and close at 3pm in order that the children may assist in the movement.'

As the war continued, ever increasing grief and financial hardship of families focused attention more towards the immediate plight of local people and less to the needs of the Belgians. It can be said that after the initial hospitality and rally to the cause of the plight of Belgian refugees, they become concealed from much attention and disappeared into the mist of history for many years. Remarking on this, Arthur Marwick writes:

> 'On the whole it can be said that, in the early stages at least, the British people rallied magnificently to those felt to have suffered unjustly in a common cause, giving a sign both of timeless human generosity and of moral idealism of the first part of the war. But as the months wore on many an unfortunate Belgian found himself in the passion of the much-adored kitten which has grown up into the unwanted cat.'

Despite the waning enthusiasm for the cause of Belgium's refugees, at least the people of Mexborough had played a part in giving some comfort to a few Belgium families who, as civilians, had seen and suffered the ravages of war first hand.

Clearly heavy demands were being made upon Mexborough townsfolk's pockets to support the ever-increasing charities that had grown as a result of the war. It now became a question of prioirity. Donations towards the completion of an additional building to the Montagu Hospital began to decline. The building of a new Children's Ward was proposed back in 1912, with firm proposals being finally being decided in April 1914. A piece of ground was selected on the north-west side of the existing building and tenders sought from contractors within the area. The contract was duly awarded to the lowest bidder, Mr E.E. Dickinson of Bolton-upon-Dearne, who was engaged to build the new ward at the price of £1,243.10s. (£1,243.50p). The Buildings Committee hired the services of Mr C. F. Moxon as their architect. To help finance the new ward, a decision was made to print small books of tickets, each ticket representing a brick, with each ticket costing one penny.

In April the Buildings Committee could not have envisaged that raising funds was about to become increasingly difficult due to the onset of the war. With the increase in the price of building materials, and thus building costs, the Hospital Building Committee found itself postponing building and with it the proposed new Children's Ward. The Children's Ward was finally opened on 25th July 1915 by the Chairman of the Committee, John Clayton.

As the months progressed, it became apparent that the war would not be one of short duration and casualties would be many. In the early days of the war, the Mexborough Montagu Hospital Committee had written to the Red Cross Society offering accommodation at the hospital for wounded soldiers. By early September, the Red Cross Society wrote to the Committee confirming acceptance of this offer and the first batch of wounded were to arrive that month. Considering its size, Montagu Hospital and its staff played a significant role in the treatment and nursing of Britain's wounded servicemen. An honorary member of the hospital staff, Dr Frank Harvey, was appointed the officer of the military wards at Mexborough hospital. Dr Harvey was attached to 3rd Northern General Hospital, Sheffield and later joined the army and saw active service in France himself. The military wards, as well civilian wards at the time of the war, were under the control of Matron Miss Wesley who became known as the 'Commandante'. As a result of her military work in the hospital she was mentioned in dispatches in 1915.

Public subscriptions provided the Montagu a large reception hut which the hospital used to receive sick and injured servicemen. The Swinton Tennis Club provided a billiard table, which by all accounts was much appreciated by patients. Concerts provided by local musicians and entertainers become a regular feature throughout the stay of the invalided soldiers and sailors, who would, despite their injuries, perhaps have felt themselves to be somewhat fortunate to be back in 'Blighty', Mexborough Montagu Hospital was a much more welcoming place than the front line. Benches were donated by charitable individuals and organisations which were placed in the town centre for the comfort of wounded soldiers while on recreational visits to shops and no doubt public houses. One can imagine the sight of the blue suited wounded socialising with the Mexborough public, who no doubt were eager to hear something of the serviceman's war experiences whilst treating them like the heroes they believed them to be. A number of more affluent residents offered their motor cars to take trips into the countryside to the delight of the soldiers and sailors who were fortunate to be chosen for the privilege.

Throughout the war period, Mexborough Montagu Hospital treated over 2,000 troops and a small number of sailors, receiving a payment of £4,318.15s. (£4,318.75p) for the medical care it provided. The growing number of casualties arriving from the Front was beginning to place pressure on hospitals like Mexborough Montagu as the war developed into the horrific drawn-out affair we are aware of today.

Chapter Six

News from Flanders and Managing at Home

The early Battles of Mons and Marne, important and costly as they were, were of relatively short duration. The longer, bloody battles of attrition were about to begin. The Allies had been able to secure a small part of Belgium from Germany occupation. The Germany Army had been unable to penetrate into a section of western Belgium which was of strategic important because of its access to seaports on the Belgian and French coasts. This included the port of Nieuport in Belgium and Boulogne, Calais and Dunkirk in France, which were not only important ports as supply points for the Allied forces but staging points for a possible invasion of Britain by German forces. Thus began the final stage of the 'Race to the Sea'. Nieuport, situated at the mouth of the Yser, saw a battle to hold the area for the allies. King of Belgium took the drastic action of flooding the land around this area to halt the advance of the German forces.

From October the Allies focused their potential offensive around the city of Ypres. Both the Allies and the German's saw the importance of holding the terrain around the city. The city was strategic for its network of railways and major road convergence including the Menin Road. The British Commander in Chief at the time, Sir John French, centered the BEF in this area for the deployment of incoming troops and supplies. The German forces had already pushed their way through Ypres in August, but had been pushed back after their advance on Mons. By October, they had withdrawn to the area around Ypres, occupying the high terrain around the city by forming a curvature on the north, east and south east sides of the city, hoping that this would give them a defensive advantage. This area surrounding the allies (British, Belgium, French and Canadian troops) was to be known as the Ypres Salient, an area very vulnerable to enemy offensives. Three significant battles were to be fought around the Ypres Salient over the next three years. The area become one of the most savage and brutal sectors of the whole war.

The Germans began an attack on the Allies on 19th October, under the command of General Erich Von Falkehayn. He had taken over from Helmuth Von Moltke who paid the price for his failure to achieve the objectives of the Schlieffen Plan with the retreat from Marne. On the 24th, the Germans launched a massive attack with heavy artillery and on the 29th succeeded in breaking through the allied lines at Gheluvelt - just five miles east from the centre of Ypres. In two bloody battles they were bravely pushed back in large part by the regular soldiers of the British army. The German Army in the area was largely composed of young German volunteer recruits who, despite their gallantry, were inexperienced and no match in quality terms for the well-trained and disciplined men of the British regular army. These young soldiers suffered great losses at the Battle of Langemarck, a battle that was to become known by the Germans as 'Kindermord' - the 'Massacre of the Innocents'.

The First Battle of Ypres was officially to end on 22nd November. As with other battles to come, little was gained by either side and ended in mass slaughter with both armies exhausted. The French saw 250,000 of its men killed with a further 250,000 injured. The Belgian army was reduced by half to 19,000 men. German forces of 80,000 were to suffer with the loss of nearly 35,000 - killed, wounded or missing,

The Allies did however, hold the strategic area around Ypres for the duration of the war, which at least gave some spirit of belief in the resilience of the Allied forces, in particular for those men of the BEF. General Edmonds summed up the position when he remarked that "the line that stood between the British Empire and the ruin (*city of Ypres*) was composed of tired, haggard and unshaven men, unwashed, plastered with mud, in little more than rags."

There was a heavy price to pay at the First Battle of Ypres of over 54,000 BEF casualties. This effectively witnessed the end of the old 'Regular Army'. As Liddell Hart elegantly wrote, 'Ypres saw the supreme vindication and final sacrifice of the old Regular Army. After the battle was over, little survived, save the memory of its spirit.' The BEF was relatively small in numbers from the beginning of the fighting in August, but by the end of the year it had seen over 80,000 casualties with many battalions being greatly depleted. Kaiser Wilhelm is mythically supposed to have called the British regulars, "that contemptible little army." True or not, it was enough for the survivors of the regular army to proclaim themselves the 'Old Contemptibles'. The gaps in this much-depleted force were to become filled by reservists, Territorials and soldiers from all parts of the British Empire.

Mexborough was now receiving news of its dead, its injured and the horrible reality of war. Mexborough's first fatality was the son of a miner from 14, Hampden Road, Private George Ernest Jones, who died on 11th September, albeit in circumstances far removed from the heat of battle. Private Jones was at the outbreak of the war a regular soldier serving with 1st York and Lancs Regiment in India. He had served out there for seven years, enlisting at Pontefract. Kitchener requested the India Military to release a number of battalions to England in preparation for duty on the Western Front, these initially being replaced with Territorial units and other regiments. This left just 15,000 men in the British garrison in India. The 1st York and Lancaster Regiment was ordered back to England via Bombay on 19th November, but despite this Private Jones, who was now 25 years of age, appears to have found himself in Abadan in Persia, where he met his death by way of a tragic mishap. His family in Mexborough received the news that he had been killed in an accidental discharge of a pistol fired by a colleague, a Private Grant. The Home Office letter claimed that Grant was cleaning his Browning pistol in a routine manner, but was unaware that the gun was loaded. Private Grant held the gun up to Private Jones' person to demonstrate how effectively it worked. There was an assertion by the Army that neither Grant nor Jones were experienced in the use of the Browning pistol, which seems remarkable given that Jones, at least, had served seven years as a regular soldier at the time.

While serving in India with the 1st York and Lancs, Private Jones was at the same time accompanied by other Mexborough and district men. These were the Mexborough born, James Gayman, Harry Glancy and Walter Stead. Walter was himself to be killed on 3rd July, 1915. The others were Swinton's Ernest Oxer and John Bramhall, Wilfred Hallford from Wath and Hiram Prince. Hiram Prince was also to lose his life in 1915 when he died of disease in a Le Havre Military Hospital on 4th October during the Battle of Loos. Private Prince had originated from Mexborough and moved to Rawmarsh to live with his uncle, whose surname he adopted. He is remembered as Hiram Foote on the Mexborough War Memorial.

George Ernest Jones had an elder brother in the army, a Private Richard Alfred Jones who was serving in 'A' Company of the 2nd Battalion of the King's Own Yorkshire Light Infantry (KOYLI). Private R.A. Jones, no doubt feeling the loss of his brother, witnessed two of his close comrades losing their lives in the Flanders operations. The 2nd KOYLI were in the thick of the fighting from the beginning after arriving at Le Havre on 16th August. Jones and his colleagues were at both the Battle of Mons and the Battle of Marne and fought at La Bassie and

Messines and at the First Battle of Ypres. Private Jones was fighting with his battalion around the Ypres area when he sent a letter to a Mr W.L. Worsley of 76, Annerley Street, Denaby Main, concerning the death of two comrades in his battalion, Private Joe Morley and Private William Hutchinson. The letter is very poignant in the way it portrayed the horrors the regular and reservist soldiers of the BEF were experiencing. It also depicted the discipline and bravery of these men. For this reason it is worth quoting it in some length:

'Dear Mr Worsley:-

You will be surprised to have a letter from me. Poor Joe was killed on Wednesday, the 28th October. At a place between Bethune and Lille in trenches with only one line of us against two German Army Corps, and our orders were to hang on at all costs. Joe got hit on the side of the head at first, a bad graze. I bandaged him and told him to keep under cover until dark when we would get him away. But Joe wouldn't; we were getting attacked so hotly that he kept on firing and of course the white bandage made him a better mark to get hit and he got one though the brain. Poor Joe died a hero. We were relieved a few days after by the Ghurkas and came up into Belgium where we had another 'do' on Saturday and Sunday, the 31st and 1st November. We were driven out of the position and Bill Hutchinson was missing. I think he is captured.'

Private William Hutchinson had not been captured: he too was killed on 28th October whilst fighting with the 2nd KOYLI. Privates Morley and Hutchinson were buried together, along with Private Fred Archer, another Mexborough man who died on 30th October. Joe and Bill had gone to school together, worked together at Wath Main Colliery and even lodged together at the home of another miner Joe Sinister and his wife Charlotte at Murphy Row, 84, Wath Road, Mexborough. Both decided to join the KOYLI at the same time in response to Kitchener's initial call. Mexborough did not have its own 'Pals' regiment but Joe Morley and Bill Hutchinson's closeness was to be repeated by other pals throughout in particular the York and Lancs and KOYLI regiments

A comrade of Joe Morley, a Private Frank Mathers whose home was at 6, Freedom Street, Walkley, Sheffield, described a moving story about Joe Morley's bravery. He relates how Morley refused to fall out of the line, despite his serious head wound, because he acknowledged his colleagues were 'short-handed'. His life would have been spared, remarked Private Mathers, if his comrade had chosen to fall out of line like he was sure most men would have done. Frank Mathers recalled that his pal Joe Morley 'died in my arms'.

Judging by the 2nd KOYLI Battalion's diary, the Battalion as a whole had suffered a terrible ordeal. The Battalion had to relieve the Durham Light Infantry (DLI) on 20th October at Lorgies and march to the trenches under heavy night attack at 2:30 in the morning of 21st. On the 22nd, the diary described how the King's Own Scottish Borderers (KOSB) made a bayonet attack on the German trenches with the Battalion being under consent shell fire throughout the day. By 26th October, the Battalion's trenches were under extremely heavy bombardment from the German artillery which consisted of the so called 'Jack Jackson's' (named after the heavyweight boxer of the time) – the 789 lbs Lyddite shell. Aircraft, too, attacked, breaking up 40 yards of trenches. Owing to the light soil, two men were buried alive and others were lucky to escape. Overall, seven were killed and 25 wounded. On the 27th, the Battalion was again under bombardment throughout the day when a group of German troops broke through on the left flank. The diary reads, 'our trenches through some error were evacuated. However on retiring on to the main road all were killed and the trenches retaken and most Germans netted. Some 30 killed while 6 to 10 prisoners were taken.' This intense fighting and the chaos it must have caused had been continuing for over a week when Joe Morley and William Hutchinson fell on Wednesday, 28th October. The diary entry for that day and the following day reads:

> *'Still in trenches. Heavy shelling and heavy casualties. Captain Richmond killed. 'A' company trenches get worst of shelling, though other companies had their share. Captain Carter's trench lost, 9 killed and about 12 wounded. French artillery firing short accounted for a great many of these.'*

The 2nd KOYLI Battalion diary recorded a similar day on 30th October, the day that another Mexborough born man, Fred Archer, died in Flanders. What these men had to endure, the horrors of the killing, the sounds of death and destruction, is difficult for us today to comprehend. Their suffering was hidden, for a while at least, from a community in Mexborough who, too, would have had little understanding of the true nature of this appalling war. A memorial service at the Mexborough Free Christian Church, taken by preacher Reverend Thomas Anderson, was held on Sunday evening, 20th December in memory of Private Hutchison. It was attended by Bill Hutchinson's sister, Mrs Parker of Dolcliffe Road and other relatives.

Joe Morley and Bill Hutchinson's comrade Private Richard Albert Jones was killed three years later in July 1917 (he was a sergeant by that time), in very much in the same area as Privates Morley, Hutchinson and Archer had been in 1914. This fact provides an indication of the state of stalemate existing on the Western Front over a long period of bloody conflict.

Mexborough suffered its first death of a Royal Navy seaman with the demise of Leading Telegraphist, Alfred Henry Perry. Seaman Perry, aged 23, was aboard the heavy cruiser *HMS Good Hope*, the flagship under the command of Rear Admiral Sir Christopher Cradock. Perry had served seven years in the Navy before war broke out and previously served on the *HMS King George*. He had lost his father who died of fever whilst serving in the South African War. The *HMS Good Hope* was engaged in the Battle of Coronel off the coast of Chile on 1st November. German warships led by Vice Admiral Graf Maxmillian von Spee defeated a British squadron which led to the sinking of the *Good Hope* when it was hit by Graf von Spee's flagship, *Scharnhorst* and the Gneisenau that night. Mexborough's Alfred Perry did not survive, nor did Craddock or any of his crew. Seaman Perry had a sister, who lived on Race Common Road, Swinton. She received a postcard on Sunday 27th December from her brother, which was written to her on 20th October, simply wishing her a Happy Christmas. Sadly, she had already received a letter from Winston Churchill at the Admiralty informing her of her brother's death. One can only attempt to empathise with Miss Perry on her receipt of her brother's last words to her. Seaman Alfred Henry Perry and the rest of the crew of *HMS Good Hope*, including Stoker J.W. Parker from South Elmsall, are remembered on the Naval Memorial at Portsmouth. A short few weeks after the sinking of the *Good Hope*, Graf von Spee was to lose his life at the Battle of Falkland Islands. *The Scharnhorst* was hit and sunk by British ships on 8th December. Like his British counterpart a month earlier, von Spee was lost with all hands.

Although he never reached the battlefields, the last recorded death of a Mexborough serviceman in 1914 is that of Private Harold Rodgers. Born in Mexborough, Harold, who played for Kilnhurst Football Club, was one of the first Mexborough volunteers to respond to Kitchener's call. He was a steelworker, single and just approaching 20 years of age when he enlisted in the 10th York and Lancs on 5th October. Harold was in training with his regiment in the Bedfordshire area when he was taken ill. He died in his billet, at 2a, Saulbury Road, Linslade near Leighton Buzzard, of what was described as a lymphatic heart on the 28th November. According to official army correspondence, Harold's father, as next of kin, had travelled to Linslade to identify Harold's body. Harold's father was Arthur Rodgers a landlord of the Commercial Hotel at Kilnhurst who had played football for Mexborough Town. In the turmoil of the early months of the war, the Army appeared to have confused matters over Private Rodger's death. The Army believed Harold to be a Private Horace Rodgers, a miner from Rawmarsh, who had attested at Rotherham and sent Harold's personal affects to Horace Rodger's next of kin, whom, we can only assume, would have been shocked and perplexed on receiving a dead man's personal belongings.

Private Harold Rogers served just 55 days and was denied frontline action, something which he was probably looking forward to as a new army recruit. His funeral took place on Wednesday, 2nd December, his body conveyed from Leighton Buzzard on the previous Monday. The coffin, covered by a large union jack, was reportedly accompanied by 500 of his comrades from his Battalion as far as Leighton Buzzard station, before being brought to Kilnhurst. From here, the coffin was taken to St Thomas Church, Kilnhurst, watched by hundreds who had assembled. The service was conducted by the Reverend P.W. Shepherd, along with the Reverend W. Douglas Steadman, the army chaplain. Harold's sergeant, G.H. Cooper attended, along with some of his other comrades, Privates J. Baugh, H. Whitehouse and M. Duggan. There was a sizeable turnout from the family, relatives and friends, for what was a memorial occasion the scale of which the majority of war dead was simply never afforded. Private Rodgers is buried in the churchyard extension of St Thomas Church. His gravestone overlooks what would then have been the small community village of Kilnhurst.

It often took some time for news of the death of Mexborough men to filter back to their families and into the pages of the local newspapers and into the public domain generally. News of the ever-increasing lists of wounded and captured was also received by the Mexborough and district populace. Hearing that their loved ones had been captured may have come for some as welcomed with relief. Private William Lockett, of Dodsworth Street, had been a regular soldier with the 2nd KOYLI since 1911. He was captured as early as September by the Germans whilst fighting at Mons or Marne and was taken to a prisoner-of-war camp in Crefield, Germany. While in captivity, Lockett was able to write to his sister back in Mexborough. He wrote:

> 'Dear sister,
> Just a few words to let you know that I have been shot and have now been in hospital 5 weeks. They have been very good to me and look after me. The shot is in the back and the left arm... I have been in pain for weeks, but I am getting better now. We are not to tell how the war is, but I shall be glad when it is finished so that I can come back to England for good. Will you send some Woodbines and a handkerchief for I do not know when I will get better.'

This letter gives us an alternative to media propaganda which claimed to highlight the brutal nature of the German enemy. It also illustrates the ability of prisoners to communicate with their families with relative ease.

News of another Mexborough soldier, Private Joseph Newey, reached his parents by postcard. Newey, who was in the KOYLI's, was initially reported as missing, but later listed as a prisoner of war in Dorbritz, Germany. He, too, wrote of his reasonable treatment; 'I have been taken prisoner and was captured in France. I am quite well and am being treated properly. Hope you are well as I am. You can send me some money or tobacco, but inquire which is best. I am hard up for smokes'.

News, too, of Private Joseph Sherwood, another regular soldier serving with the 2nd York and Lancs, reached the local newspapers in October. Sherwood, who lived at 12, Simpson Place, Mexborough, was to suffer wounds to the arm while fighting in the early battles in France. He was evacuated to England and spent time in Colchester Hospital.

Private James Lenton, of the 6th York and Lancs, was able to write home to his father at Cambridge Street, Mexborough. He wrote, possibly from around Ypres Salient:

> 'We are about 300 yards from the Germans, but the cowards won't come out and fight in daylight. They attack at night, but we are ready for them with our maxims and rifles and on a clear moonlight you can see them go down like skittles... I am rather lucky to have been in the line for 5 weeks and have kept my skin. I saw a shrapnel shell burst the other day and didn't half kill some of the men.'

Private Lenton had written his letter back home on 29th October, but the Home Office was to confirm that he, too, was wounded on the very same day. Another Mexborough man, Driver J. E. Buxton of the 2nd Battery RFA, was invalided home to 25, Manvers Road with a diseased jaw in late October.

The life expectancy of Britain's young men in the forces was reducing by the month, with reports of mass casualities now reaching the British public. Given this it perhaps isn't surprising that the question of drinking and drunkenness had become a national issue. There were concerns over servicemen on leave and of others in the workplace whose prospects might also have appeared depressing. David Lloyd George, at that time the Chancellor of the Exchequer, increased tax on incomes in the November in order to raise revenue for the war effort. Those on wages between £150 to £500 per year were to be taxed double, raising their income tax to 1s 6d (7.5p) in the pound. Income tax for those above £500 was also raised. This did not affect the majority of the working class who were exempt from income tax upon their earnings. Lloyd

George at the same time increased the tax on beer by a penny a pint, raising the price of a pint to 4d and thus the working man was taxed in this way. The tax on tea was increased more severely, from 3d per pound to 8d. This latter tax was met with in indignation by teetotallers and Temperance Societies, particularly after Lloyd George had said the tax was to catch the "teetotaller classes" who were as "difficult to track as the Emden" (a reference to the elusive German battlecruiser which caused havoc with allied shipping up until December). Lloyd George was to take an even tougher position on alcohol when he became the Minister of Munitions in May 1915.

Representatives of the working man were critical that workers, many who had volunteered to the King's service, were already contributing to the war effort and were now being made pay an additional price for the small pleasure of a 'drink'. At a meeting in December of the Mexborough Trades and Labour Council (at their usual venue at the Old Mason's Arms), the subject of the beer tax was raised. The Chairman of the meeting remarked he had seen a number of "good" beer drinkers give up the ale as a consequence of the new tax. However, a member of the Trades Council made the curious suggestion that tax should be placed on dormant bank balances and bicycles as an alternative to the beer tax. Some delegates were not impressed with this proposal which might have seemed to them somewhat bizarre.

A meeting was held at the Primitive Methodists Chapel in December, under the auspices of the United Kingdom Alliance, to discuss the affect of alcohol on the nation's efficiency in fighting an effective war. The secretary of the United Kingdom Alliance, Mr G.B. Wilson, remarked that the temperance reformers had been vindicated by the Government's concern over alcohol. He described alcohol as the "greatest enemy of efficiency and the greatest cause of waste." Mr Wilson went on to describe his observations on a Sheffield railway station. It was shameful, he said, to see on one afternoon at the station, "at least a dozen young fellows being helped into the carriage by a sergeant." The secretary continued that he had been talking to the sister of Lord Kitchener on the subject and gathered from their conversation that Kitchener was in favour of closing all public houses at eight o'clock in the evening.

The Government's primary concern over alcohol consumption and drunkenness was that it would become an impediment to the war in terms of industrial production and not just a problem relating to army discipline. Several 'solutions' were put in place. Apart from taxation and the increase in prices of liquor, it was also decided to nationalise local breweries and public houses which were close to prominent munitions factories, in a hope of curbing heavy drinking in these areas. Many felt that the key remedy to the problem was the restriction on the hours made available to drinkers in licensed premises. For many years, there had been a need for premises to seek their license from a local magistrate who would determine their opening and closing times on an annual basis. This meant that there was no standard opening and closure of a public house. London had the most 'generous' hours, with closing times as late as 12.30am, some opening as early as five in the morning. In other parts of the country, drinking could generally take place between 6am and 11pm. Taking this into consideration, in can be inferred that the Government's and Kitchener's concern may have been justified.

The records of the 9th York and Lancs tell us that crime in the training camps was practically unknown – apart from drunkenness. However, the best source in overseeing the problem of drunkenness was that of the local police forces. The Intoxicating Liquor (Temporary Restrictions) Act introduced on 31st August gave the local Chief of Police the power to impose restrictions, as he saw fit, on the hours in which alcohol might be sold.

The local government West Riding Authority, of which Mexborough was a part, met in December in Wakefield to address this question of alcohol consumption and the uniformity of licensing hours for public houses. The item was raised before the County Councillors under the unembellished title of 'Soldiers' Drunkenness'. It was Alderman Gummer, representative from Rotherham, who spoke against the suggestion that the greatest problem could be found amongst the army population. He insisted that the problem was equally widespread in every walk of life, including aristocratic circles and the gentleman's clubs. The Alderman, who had three sons serving in the forces, had more than a valid point in defence of the soldiers and the ordinary working man. The King, who pledged to give up alcohol in 1915, was said to have been disappointed that the same stance was not taken by other prominent leading figures. Nevertheless, as the result of a motion moved by the Mayor of Batley, Alderman Turner, the West Riding Authority resolved to recommend that pubs and clubs should have their hours of opening restricted between the hours of 8.30am to 10.00pm. The drinking time restriction would be in force as Christmas approached.

Private James Lenton's letter to his father's home in Cambridge Street was optimistic about the progress of the war. His letter stated that it was his belief that, 'there would not be many Germans this time next year.' He was also in hope that good luck would see him home for Christmas dinner. Yet as Christmas approached the anticipation that Britain's soldiers and sailors would be home was fast becoming fantasy. Private Lenton we know was injured and may have spent Christmas in a field hospital, or if lucky a military hospital in England. This was the fate of Private Joseph Sherwood of the York and Lancs, whose home was at 12, Simpson Place where he lived with his brother Lance Corporal A.

Sherwood also of the York and Lancs and also a casualty. Private Joseph Sherwood had been engaged in fierce fighting in Christmas week in the final phase of the battle around La Bassie when he was hit by shrapnel in the lower back. He spent Christmas in a hospital in Birmingham. Joseph had suffered wounds to his arm fighting in some of the early battles of the 2nd York and Lancs. Some wounded soldiers would have found themselves at home in Mexborough for the festive season, no doubt feeling more than fortunate to be in the position they were.

Many who volunteered for the 'New Army' were training in the camps and depots throughout the country and were most likely receiving a few days off and returning home on Christmas leave. Certainly this was the case of the 8th and 9th York and Lancs, who had earlier in December been ordered to take up winter quarters in Aldershot's Barasa Barracks. These Battalions contained a good number of Mexborough and district men. The history of the 9th Battalion tells us that every man, without exception, overstayed his Christmas leave in what appears to be an act of solidarity. They all received the punishment of 'confined to barracks' as a result of being 'absent without leave', a price some would have probably believed to be worth paying.

But there were of course those who would not return to England and were unfortunate to have to spend their Christmas in their trenches and billets in France and Flanders. An appeal to the public by the Mexborough Urban District Council was made to support the Princess Mary Fund and prepare Christmas parcels to be sent, along with a presentation box of cigarettes, to the troops who would not be getting Christmas leave. Princess Mary, the only daughter of the King, became the figurehead in the organisation of these boxes – brass cases bearing the words 'Christmas 1914'. The box itself contained a picture of the Princess, a Christmas card, cigarettes and tobacco and a pencil. It was supplied to all members of the armed forces, with non-smokers being provided with alternatives such as sweets and other appropriate gifts. Councillor William Winstanley, the local secretary of the Princess Mary Fund, organised a concert and musical service on Sunday, 6th December at the Primitive Methodist Chapel to raise funds for the cause.

Cigarettes were arriving at *The Times* office on a regular basis just prior to Christmas in response to the newspaper's appeal. On one occasion they received 1,470 cigarettes inscribed with the message, 'from the boys at the Low Drop, Montagu Arms Hotel'. These were destined for the soldiers and sailors interned in Holland.

Letters received from some Mexborough men indicate there were cigarettes in plentiful supply. Private Dustan of the 18th Fusiliers wrote to his mother, who lived off Dolcliffe Road, asking her not to send more than six packets of 'cigs' as he received 'cigs' 'every week. A similar message was expressed by Private T. Fisher serving with the 2nd York and Lancs in a letter to his brother, who lived at 4, Bank Street, Mexborough. The private wrote, 'I received your welcome letter and Christmas card...We are well looked after here. We have plenty of food and tobacco, so we must not grumble. Tell mother not to send that box of cigs as I have 200 packets of cigs and 6lb of tobacco'.

We know that the Belgian refugees were enjoying their Christmas despite being away from their homeland. Patients at Mexborough's Montagu Hospital (including the early intake of servicemen invalided out to the care of hospital staff) were not forgotten in this festive season, despite the increasing pressure on charitable sources. The hospital was grateful to the continued generosity of local businesses. The local Wath brewery, Whitworth's, supplied a goose and a turkey. Another turkey was donated by Mr H. Cliffe, with the local branch of the Barnsley British Cooperative supplying a box of fruit. George Schonhut, the local pork butcher, donated his customary offering of pork pies. In what would today be seen as an extraordinary gift from those of the medical profession, Dr Harvey gave presents of cigarettes, tobacco and Dr Ram bottles of beer. The patients were also entertained by the choirboys from St John's Parish Church. It seemed that during the Christmas of 1914 George Schonhut was regarded and regarded himself, as an integral part of Mexborough society.

The question of those who might now be considered to be foreign 'aliens' was raised in *The Times* in October. An article on the subject remarked:

> *The Government have at last decided to put an end to the possibility of all male aliens of military age in this country giving assistance to the enemy. Orders have been issued by the Home Office calling upon the police throughout the country to arrest Germans, Austrians and Hungarians of military age'.*

The 'Aliens Restrictions Act' had been introduced by Home Secretary Reginald McKenna as early as 5th August. Britain had already introduced the '1905 Aliens Act' as the country became less liberal towards asylum seekers. By 1914 the prevalence of spy scares created the atmosphere for the introduction of further legislation as hostilities against Germany and its allies began.

Initially the 1914 Act was limited to selected enemy aliens, but by late 1914, 10,000 were arrested and interned. Women, children and men above and below military age were encouraged to return to the country from which they originated. Other enemy aliens were restricted in their capacity to move about the country. It was with the sinking of the *Lusitania* in May 1915 that all enemy aliens were subject to internment, unless deemed exempt by a tribunal. Despite his evident popularity with many in Mexborough, George Schonhut would not be excluded from the wave of hostility which was about to thrust upon some of the overseas-born in Britain.

The Christmas Eve service at St John's Parish Church may have been somewhat different to previous festive seasons in that its vicar of 20 years, the Reverend (Canon) William Henry Fraser Bateman, had left Mexborough shortly before Christmas and moved to Wistow near Selby. He was replaced by the Reverend Edmund Hope, previously the vicar of Marske-by-the-Sea, before being in charge of the Holy Cross Mission in Middlesbrough. Here he worked in the Parish of St Paul's, a working class area of 30,000 containing the poorest 10,000 of Middlesbrough and described as containing 'low class music halls with a drinking saloon surrounded by public houses'. Evidently *The Times* believed he was eminently qualified to take over his clerical duties in a town like Mexborough, perhaps due to his experiences working with Middlesborough's working classes. 'He is a man', the paper said, 'of fine physique and gives one the impression of that physical and moral strength which is desirable in a man appointed to the arduous and exacting duties of a large and difficult parish like Mexborough.' His duties would indeed be arduous. His first Christmas in his new parish in this period of uncertainty, could not have been easy.

Whilst the Christmas Eve service was being held at the Parish Church, a short distance away on College Road, the non-conformist Free Christian Church was holding a service of a different kind. The congregation witnessed the unveiling, by Reverend Thomas Anderson, of a tablet inscribed with a roll of honour of all young men from the church who, at the time, had volunteered to serve in the armed forces. The tablet was engraved with the following words; 'A roll of honour of the members of the Free Christian Church who are serving their King and country. God save the King.' There were sixteen names upon the tablet and it is worth recording them all as it was a unique undertaking to honour these men so early in the war.

The sixteen were: Sam Threthaway, (York and Lancs), George Cheswick (RHA), Peter Clark (KOYLI), Clarence Dainty (RFA), Jack Dainty (KOYLI) , Fred Durose (York and Lancs), Herbert Hakin (York and Lancs), George Hakin, Alf Hargreaves (York and Lancs), Tom Hargreaves (York and Lancs), William Hughes (York and Lancs), Taylor Collingwood, (RAMC), Seamen Fred Elliott, Joe Elliott and Gordon Strawberry.

This list illustrates the large number of men who joined the two main local regiments, the York and Lancs and KOYLI and the likely fact that men from the same family were inspired, often by each other's example to join up.

The Reverend Thomas Anderson had spoken of the courage and self-sacrifice of these young men which reflected the character of those associated with the church. He hoped that before long they would return home safe and sound. Sadly that was not to be the case for a good number of these courageous men.

The local cinemas and theatres in Mexborough attempted to maintain an uninhibited portrayal of the festive season. The Hippodrome theatre was showing the traditional pantomime, *Dick Whittington*, with what was claimed to be an 'all-star cast'. The Royal Picture House was showing a lighthearted *Keystone Cops* comedy, perhaps in order to divert minds away from the more serious happenings in France and Belgium. Yet some of the titles of films would not allow the audience to stray far from thoughts of the serious conflict the country was engaged in. The Royal was also showing a film called *Our Enemy Spy*, whilst the Oxford picture house was showing *For King and Country* and the *King's Will*.

No doubt many, including those on leave, chose to take in a football match over the holiday period. If supporters were expecting Mexborough Town FC's performance to be better in the 1914/15 season then they would have been disappointed. The 'Town' were fourth from bottom at Christmas, with just five wins and three draws from sixteen games. The matches over the Christmas period characterised the club's inconsistency. Town had beaten Doncaster Rovers by three goals to nil, but then lost by the same scoreline to Halifax Town in the following game.

The Times offered a bold interpretation of how Mexborough and its community might engage in the Christmas spirit of 1914. It claimed that prospects were good as a result of the steady prosperity of the coal industry. The effectiveness of the army authorities and Distress Committee to maintain an income to families would ensure that Santa Claus would not be short of gifts for the Mexborough and district's animated children. The newspaper's editoral appealed to the adult population to shield the children from the oppressive influence of war, in order that they, at least, should enjoy a joyful Christmas. The local paper's editorial of Boxing Day continued to gloss over the realities of the true nature of the conflict, when it remarked in an exhaustive paragraph:

> *'During the last few days most of our south Yorkshire towns have been lavishly sprinkled with khaki clad and blue habited figures of recruits home for a few days furlough in honour of this festive season which comes upon us at a time when steadily victorious as we are proving in the great struggle, we are less justified for the festivity than at any previous period in our history.'*

The last few words have the greatest validity in that Britain was now facing a different war from those which it had faced before and by the Christmas of 1914 the British public began to appreciate this fact. The local newspapers had reported the shelling of Scarborough, Whitby and Hartlepool by a squadron of German cruisers on the morning of 16th December. Within a short 30 minutes more than 100 people had been killed in these coastal towns. Despite the British naval fleet being close by, the German cruisers slipped quietly away unharmed and the supremacy of the British Navy, something previously held as a truism, was undermined. The first Zeppelin raids were about to be begin on Britain's towns and cities – a phenomenon not experienced before which saw the civil population become involved with some of the realities of warfare.

Veterans of the Boer War were to comment on the difference between that conflict in South Africa and the one they now faced in France and Belgium. Private Richard Alfred Jones of the 2nd KOYLI, a regular correspondent on his experiences, comments, 'the South African war was bad enough, but not a flea bite on this one'. Private Jones and his comrades were indeed in a different conflict. They were engaged in a war across Europe and over vast sections of the globe, a war which was to cause hideous annihilation as a consequence of a rapid industrialisation of nation states and development of new weapons of mass destruction. The way the war was unfolding was baffling even to the Generals. Sir John French, the Commander-in-Chief of the BEF, was perplexed by the enemy's disregard for 'the rules'. French, an old cavalry man, believed that the German's initial use of gas was a "barbarous disregard of civilised war". As far Sir John French was (initially) concerned the cavalry charge still had a place in modern, so called, civilised, warfare. Yet the way both sides would conduct themselves during the war was anything but 'cricket'.

As far as the men on the Western Front were concerned, there would be a brief respite from the daily slaughter. According to the south Yorkshire newspapers, the fabled Christmas truce between Allied and German troops, the fraternising, carol singing and exchange of gifts, appears to have been authentic enough. Perhaps, for a brief moment, the troops on both sides might have thought that sanity had taken hold. Today's observer might remark that the politicians and commanders of the warring parties, who unsurprisingly disapproved of the events surrounding the Christmas truce, were not given to sanity. Thus the war entered into another three Christmases and with it more misery, slaughter and destruction.

The original premises of Frank Harrison in Bank Street. In early 1914, Harrison supplied the first motorised ambulance in the area. This would soon be used to transport wounded soldiers to Montagu hospital.

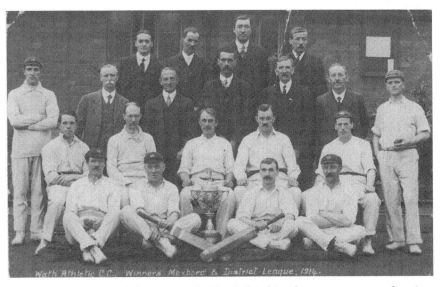

Mexborough Cricket Club team finished third in the 1914 season, despite their top batsman, Tom Thorpe, being in good form. Wath Athletic Cricket Club, shown above, finished top of the league.

Mexborough Water Works. Because of lack of water supplies, leading to poor sanitation, Mexborough UDC was forced to take over control from the private water company.

Amongst the wide variety of sporting activities in Mexborough was the Rifle Club - soon called upon to offer its skills to the military.

The first 'Alexandra Rose Day' to raise money for Montagu Hospital took place in July 1914. Pupils of Mexborough schools wore roses during the event. Headteacher of Mexborough School, Mr Thomas Wilson Ireland is middle row, left.

Recruiting offices were set up in Council Offices (Market Hall) and the newly formed Labour Exchange in Bank Street. The Free Library, also in Bank Street, offered its premises for recruiting purposes.

Some early recruits in the Mexborough area. The first of Kitchener's recruitment appeals started on 7th August 1914. Within three weeks, 100,000 men joined up. By mid-September the figure was nearly 500,000.

Many new recruits from Mexborough joined either the York and Lancs Regiment or the KOYLI. After joining they were transported to Pontefract Barracks, pictured right, c1914.

145

In the early part of the war, traders took advantage of events and, initially at least, some did not take the threat too seriously. This mood was soon to change as the dangers of war became apparent.

Mexborough reacted more slowly than other areas to the appeal to accommodate Belgian refugees. Surrounding districts took refugees as early as October 1914. These refugees were pictured at Eastwood House, Doncaster Road, Rotherham c 1914. Courtesy of Rotherham MBC Archives and Local Studies (Photo No 10319).

The Orpheus Glee Singers were the principal entertainers at a charity concert in November 1914 to raise money for the Belgian Relief Fund.

An artist's impression of the Mexborough Cricket and Athletic Club's pavilion, built in 1910. Mexborough received its first Belgian refugees in December 1914 and housed three families in the pavilion.

Private George Ernest Jones was the first Mexborough man to die in the war, although not on the battlefield. He was said to have been accidentally shot in September 1914 in Persia when cleaning his pistol. Jones was a regular soldier who lived at 14, Hampden Road.

George Hyde of Cromwell Road, who took part in the defence of Antwerp, then later interned in Holland.

Sailors from the Royal Naval Division were in the forefront of trying to hold back the advance of the German army in Belgium. After retreating, many were forced back into neutral Holland, where they were interned.

1915

Chapter Seven

Further Stalemate and the Call for Recruits

The enormous number of casualties sustained within the first few months of the war in 1914 and depleting recruitment figures were of national concern. This is despite recruiting exceeding expectations in the early two months of the outbreak of war. There was, at this stage, no desire to introduce conscription, in the belief that this would not be necessary. There was a belief that no true British man would fail to rally to the cause and therefore compulsion would not be necessary. However it was now necessary to rally potential recruits with a series of further meeting and assemblies. Such a meeting in Mexborough was called under the auspices of the Doncaster Parliamentary Committee and held at the Public Hall on Tuesday, 19th January. It was important enough to engage the support of Mr H. Neild K.C. MP and Lieutenant Milner-Barry. Well-known local dignitaries such as Dr Ram and his wife, Councillor L. Jones and the Headmaster of Mexborough Secondary School, Mr Thomas Wilson Ireland.

Mr Neild extolled the righteousness of a volunteer army when he said, "Doubtless amateur recruiters had been derided in Germany and that cartoons of Lord Kitchener and even the King imploring bricklayers to join the Army, had been printed with grotesque caricature." Mr Neild thought, however, that the Germans were beginning the see the effects of this effective voluntary system. Yet doubts where beginning to ferment in the minds of some that perhaps did not accept the noble gesture of joining on a voluntary basis. Neild had noticed that a local speaker had mentioned that there were still a great deal of men in Mexborough and district who could have enlisted but had chosen not to do so. But Mr Neild remarked, "Those young men had no right to expect that a portion of young manhood of the country should bear the burden of the fight for them". Yet he continued that he believed the nation did not really want to be forced to do its duty and a spontaneity to join the Army came 'naturally' to true Englishmen.

The meeting, which was said to have been well attended, exhibited the patriotic fervour that all those attending these recruitment rallies came to expect and thoroughly approved of. The speeches themselves were interspersed with songs, such as *Land of Hope and Glory*, sung by Miss L Beal and accompanied by Mr Arthur Beal, all designed to stir patriotism.

The patriotism at the time was held together with not just the symbolism of the songs and music of the war, but initially also impassioned belief in the ability and suitability of the British Army commanders. Mr Neild told the audience at the meeting that there was a great strain upon the first British Expeditionary Force especially during what he called, "The masterly retreat from Mons, a retreat which established Sir John French's reputation for all time, if it had not been previously established." Neild received applause for these words relating to the BEF Commander in Chief. But Field Marshal Sir John French's ability was already under question and he would not survive the year at the head of the British Army. Britain had at this time just entered a year which began to change the perception and attitude to the conduct of the war and which engendered a disillusionment among sections of the population. During the evening the well-known Mexborough Recruiting Officer, Sergeant J. Oddy, stated that since he took up his duties in Mexborough on 10th October 1914, he had recruited 561 men.

Sergeant Oddy had recruited some notable Mexborough personalities in the period of the opening months of the War. Mexborough's boxing hero James William, 'Iron' Hague signed up in the December of 1914, joining the Grenadier Guards. Iron Hague's brother, Johnny, may well have been inspired by his brother's eagerness to join the colours and he, too, joined the KOYLI in early 1915. The Hagues' were joined by another Mexborough boxer, Tommy Stokes, in this period.

Sergeant Oddy had been busy from the beginning of the year. He had given an interview of his experiences to *The Times* which gave some interesting insight into difficulties that were occurring in recruiting. Some men over and under the recruiting age were more eager to join then those officially eligible. Sergeant Oddy relates a story about a 59 year old who attempted to join the colours. The old man, eager to pick up his 'King's shilling' insisted the he was "very spry" for his age but Oddy simply remarked, "You are too old dad". At the other end of the age scale the sergeant was confronted by a young boy of fifteen who also insisted on volunteering. Oddy directed him to the nearest boy scouts group. Similarly another young man entered the recruiting office but was suspiciously too young. This young man was unsure of his age which ranged in his faltering memory from seventeen to nineteen. "Sorry", said the recruiting sergeant, "you are hardly big enough, I don't think you will pass." To this the lad replied, "Well sergeant I've done more than those who are old enough and won't come." Hearing this Sergeant Oddy agreed to take him.

There are many stories of brave, underage men being desperate to join His Majesty's forces often without their parent's knowledge or consent. There are also many stories of recruiting sergeants, like Sergeant Oddy, turning a blind eye to the age of the applicant. This was something which was assisted by the fact that the 'attestation form', which a new recruit was required to fill in, provided a loophole. It did not ask for the recruit's actual age but rather only their 'apparent age.' Likewise the Army's Medical History form asked for the soldier's 'declared age'. It is apparent that this loophole was often exercised, despite the Army's official policy of discouraging the recruitment of underage young men. The eagerness to recruit such young men in the early part of 1915 does give an indication of the Army's and the authorities concern with the decrease in the recruitment figures and with the desperate need to fill the gaps in the depleted regular British Army.

In January the numbers on average recruited at Mexborough were about 50 per week. By February it had dropped to around 30. Yet local companies continued to release men for active service. At this time 220 men from Wath Main were recruited, despite the increasing pressure for labour that was beginning to result as a consequence of the Government's frantic efforts to secure men without resorting to conscription. The drift from the workplace would however bring an inevitable shortage of labour which would soon be filled by youth and female labour.

The 9th York and Lancs, which contained many Mexborough recruits, where during their training period, billeted at Minley Manor. On 22nd January they were due to be inspected by Kitchener himself. The inspection was scheduled to take place at 2.30pm Snow fell all that morning and by 12 noon the snow was four inches thick upon the ground. By the afternoon heavy rain fell to create appalling conditions under foot. The men at this point had not been issued with their khaki uniforms. Wearing their initial blue serge uniform and civilian overcoats the men of the 9th Battalion were soaked to the skin awaiting the arrival of the Secretary of State for War. Lord Kitchener didn't arrive until 3.30p.m. to inspect these members of his New Army, but when he did arrive he dismissively drove past the assembled Mexborough men and their comrades. No one from the Battalion effectively saw this war leader and certainly Kitchener had no time to exchange words with the troops, which may have given them some compensation for what they had endured. The Mexborough men of the 9th York and Lancs, along with their colleagues, could not have been too impressed with their initial experience of their 'superior' war commander's attitude towards them. As a result of Kitchener's fleeting visit, an endeavour was made to quickly dry the men's clothing in an effort to prevent, or limit, the illness that would ensue from the Battalion's experience.

In the early part of the war, the French attempted to pressure the Germans, particularly around the Champagne area in the south of France and the more northern area of the Artois. In Artois, the weather was appalling at the time and the French made little progress at the expense of thousands of casualties. In the Champagne region the situation was much the same and the fight was abandoned because of this and through sheer exhaustion of the troops. Fighting resumed in February and a ceasefire came on 17th March. In many respects the French offensive in Artois and Champagne was a failure, with the Allies making marginal gains. Figures vary, but one source refers to the Battles of Artois and Champagne leading to the deaths of over one third of a million Frenchmen with the Germany Army suffering similar numbers of casualties. During the early part of the year, Mexborough, lost its first serviceman to die this year. Although he lived at Denaby at the time, Mexborough born Private James Hill, of the Royal Scots (Lothian Regiment) was killed on 23rd February.

The British Army had not been able, in the initial part of the year, to give the assistance that the French would have desired. Sir John French had believed that the Eastern Front might prove to be where the war could be fought decisively. He did, however, realise he needed to assist the French on the Western Front and activate his troops after their endurance in the trenches of a depressive winter. The British War Council also discussed the possibility of a concentration of operations in the Balkans and Dardanelles which might be a more positive option with resources possibly having to be switched to accommodate this theory. Senior British commanders in France being conscious of these views, quickly ordered an offensive to take place, the first of which was to take the village of Neuve Chapelle which lay about twenty miles on the south side of Ypres. The village had become a German stronghold, well fortified, causing a bulge in the British defensive lines. More significantly behind Neuve Chapelle lay a section of high ground called Aubers Ridge which was of strategic importance to the German forces.

The Battle of Neuve Chapelle began on 10th March with Sir Douglas Haig's First Army involved. The attack started with a heavy bombardment. At 7.30am the bombardment commenced with 350 guns for a period of 35 minutes which saw 17,000 shells of all sizes dropped upon the German trenches. The infantry ascended over the parapet at five minutes past eight. Ferocious fighting took place and it was only a short time before the British infantry took their objective of the village Neuve Chapelle. After a further two days of fighting the Germans were able to quickly bring forth supplies and reinforcements, build new trench lines, and consolidate those positions. The German major defensive strongholds were still intact. As a consequence, Haig called a halt to the advance, consolidating the British positions and strengthening them against German counter-attack.

The British had advanced no more than about one mile, at a vastly disproportionate expense in casualties to the amount of advance they made, if it is so possible to make such a calculation in this way in relation to human life. The cost of these three days were, 7,000 British casualties and 4,200 allied men from the India Corps. Of these there were 190 Officers and 2,337 from other ranks killed. This ratio of officers to men gives an indication of the high sacrifice made by young officers from the British middle and upper classes, elegantly expressed in Vera Brittain's moving and powerful book *Testament of Youth.*

One Mexborough man who witnessed the horrors of the Battle of Neuve Chapelle was Lance-Corporal Amos Jones serving with the Grenadier Guards as a reservist. He lived at 39, Highwoods Road, Mexborough before serving at the Front. He wrote a letter to *The Times* from his trench only 40 yards from the German trenches. He wrote, '*The Mexboro and Swinton Times* reached me once more and I notice a reference in the Marconigrams to Neuve Chapelle. I am sorry to say more men fell there than ever will be accounted for. The people at home must be at all times prepared to hear the worst'.

Amos Jones wrote of being one of the lucky ones. He had been out at the Front from the beginning in August 1914 and somehow survived the onslaught of the Germans who he described as "very barbarous". Referring to his experience of fighting to capture Neuve Chapelle he said, 'All along our line are the bodies of our comrades who fell in the last attack. We cannot reach them to bury them as they are only a few yards from the German trenches.' What is a continuous theme in letters home to the front is the plea for those at home to understand the horrors of war. 'People at home do not realise the dangers and horrors of this war. The bombardment of Neuve Chapell was hell upon earth for those who were in the trenches at the time. The men who fell went bravely to their deaths.'

Perhaps another lucky soldier was Private Henry Cavell, a former miner at Cadeby Main, who was serving with the 2nd Leicestershire Regiment, attached to the Indian Expeditionary Force. He arrived on the Western Front in December 1914. Private Cavell lived at 25, Dolcliffe Road, Mexborough. He may have been lucky but he was also without question brave, for he was awarded the Distinguished Conduct Medal (DCM) in June 1915 for his bravery between 24th and 26th January. In a letter to his aunt he told of his luck, but in some way the letter may be said to tell a one-sided story of his experiences at the Battle of Neuve Chapelle, 'At Neuve Chapelle we paid off for old scores with Kaiser Bill. I saw Germans piled up three or four high. It was not a pleasant sight but a welcome one as we had been itching to go at em for weeks'. Private Cavell was the first Mexborough man to be awarded the DCM although he was soon followed by Bombardier Eric Downing and a little later by Private A. Gwynnette of the 1/5th York and Lancs in winning one of the most prestigious honours awarded to the lower ranks.

One of those who went bravely to his death was Sergeant-Major Arthur Jackson Goulding of the Wiltshire Regiment. The son of Edward Goulding of Pinfolds Lane, Mexborough, Arthur was reported missing on 12th March, but later recorded as died on that day. Arthur was an 'old' regular soldier who worked himself through the ranks. He had originally joined the Coldstream Guards seventeen years previously when he served in the South African War. Sergeant-Major Goulding was a regular writer of letters home, which found their way into the pages of the The Times. The last letter he sent home was in contrast to previous correspondence which was of an optimistic character. By the time the letter was received at home he would have been dead. He told his wife that he was going into action at dawn the following day and made her aware of the possibility that he would not return. His letter continued that he was prepared to face death calmly, acknowledging that his loved ones would be looked after. For a veteran soldier to be so conscious of his imminent demise may give an indication that even with his experience Sergeant-Major Goulding knew the Battle of Neuve Chapelle was going to be different.

The Battle of Neave Chapelle ended on the day that Sergeant Major Goulding had been killed. It had lasted for only a brief period, but, despite this, had taken many lives on both sides. Phillip Stevens remarks of these losses, 'Remembering that the battlefront was no longer than two miles, it can be calculated that the BEF suffered more than one death or wounding for every single yard of Front, for each day of the battle'. All this misery was for an advance of just one mile.

Sir John French's own interpretation of the high casualty numbers was probably seen a little differently by the family of Sergeant Major Goudling. Whist he recognised the severity of losses, he believed on the other side of the balance the results were, 'wide and far reaching'. French was of course talking in military terms and not about the fact that notification to families of their relative's death at the Battle of Neuve Chappelle were now spreading wide and far across Great Britain.

The Germans had originally captured Neuve Chapelle in October

1914. During the operation of its capture the German forces released shells in the form of a chemical weapon containing a mild chemical which caused its recipients to violently sneeze. They further experimented with a liquid form of tear gas, on the Eastern Front, against the Russians, in January of 1915, which was not successful from the German's point of view, but went on to use a tear gas against the French at Nieuport in the March.

There was plenty of evidence that the Germans were attempting to perfect effective chemical weapons. This is despite the use of chemical weapons being banned under the Hague Convention of 1899 which all the major powers, except the USA, ratified at the time. The Convention was ignored but the major powers during the war continued to 'refine' chemical weapons, particularly the British and Germans. Tear gases had been designed to make the enemy ineffective as a fighting force rather than to cause death. As the war progressed and desperation gripped the conflicting powers more deadly and horrific chemical weapons were developed.

Three types of gases were used, each one getting progressively more dangerous to those who were to come in contact with them. Firstly chlorine gas was used. Although it could be lethal, it was at least detectable by smell and visible to those being attacked. Later phosgene was used, which although had no instant effect, would slowly attack the lungs filling them with fluid leading to a dreadful death. The final development was mustard gas, a blistering agent, introduced in 1917. Although this was a gas which could kill by destroying the lungs, it was designed to severely incapacitate the victim by producing painful blistering of the skin and temporary blindness. Originally gas was released from cylinders which relied on the direction of the wind being suitable to direct the poison gas clouds towards the enemy. Because of this reliance upon the prevailing wind more sophisticated gas shells were developed.

There was originally no protection against the effects of poison gas and the British authorities frantically sought ways to introduce something which would offer adequate protection. Initially the men used makeshift masks from cotton materials, sometimes soaked in urine. As the war progressed and the use of poison gas became more extensive, a very effective gas mask, the box respirator, was issued as a standard piece of equipment in August 1916.

The first gas attack by the Germans on the Western Front took place on 22nd April. Just prior to this, the British captured what was known as Hill 60 around Ypres. This was a man-made construction from spoil dug during the making of a nearby railway line. It nevertheless gave elevation providing tactical advantage as it overlooked the important strategic target of Ypres. The battle for Hill 60 took place between 17th and 22nd

April and its capture was, again, at great cost with 3,000 casualties. More lives were to be lost in the pursuit of this piece of earth. It was recaptured by the Germans in May only to be recaptured by the Allies again the following month. Such was the pattern of warfare on the Western Front at the time.

On the second day of the battle for Hill 60, Private George Henry Dickenson, who lived in Frederick Street, was amongst those killed in the futile attempt to establish a hold on this supposedly strategic piece of land. Fighting with 2nd KOYLI Dickenson he had been employed as a lampman on the Great Central Railway. He became the first of Mexborough's railway workers to die in the war and is remembered on the Mexborough Station memorial, despite his name being spelt Dickinson. He was just 22 years of age when he met his end.

The German Army had the objective of advancing their lines closer around the City of Ypres which would give them the ability to bring up supplies to the front line. The Second Battle of Ypres, commenced at 5.00pm on the evening of 22nd April. The German Fourth Army was to attack the French part of the Allied forces around the Ypres Salient. First they bombarded the allies with heavy artillery. They then released nearly 6,000 cylinders of chlorine gas towards the allies' positions. German forces followed up behind the clouds of gas which drifted into trenches. Despite there being some knowledge of the German ambitions to use chemical weapons and some intelligence reports as to their intended use, the reports were largely overlooked. Because of this the Allies were unprepared for the gas attack and the French, being unprotected from the effects of the gas, had their lines broken by the panic of this fearful 'new' weapon. A hole was pushed into the Allied lines leaving the Canadian Division particularly exposed. The Germans weren't able to exploit this rupture in the Allied defences, because, as on other occasions they had insufficient reserves. The German forces were also not helped by the quickly failing light and the fear that they would be exposed to their own gas. Despite this they had pushed their front lines to within two miles of Ypres.

Liddell Hart described the City of Ypres on the first day of the battle by remarking, 'It had merely the dreariness of an incomplete abandonment momentarily relieved by the fragrance of the spring day's sunshine.' But by the end of the war was to be described by him as a 'vast heap of tumble ruin'. The Cathedral and the famous Cloth Hall would become only recognisable for the symbol of the horror and destructive nature of war. There were to be many descriptions of the destruction of this once beautiful City after four years of war, but the 'Abomination of Desolation' is perhaps the most apt of all.

The Canadians and the British allies were able to re-establish their defensive line and attempted two counter-attacks between 23rd and 26th April. They failed to recover any lost ground and suffered yet more heavy casualties, 1,500 dead on 26th April alone. The Second Battle of Ypres continued on to 25th May, in which the Allies confronted four more gas attacks. The BEF suffered 58,000 casualties, in various battles which constituted the Battles of Ypres, yet the Germans still controlled three sides of the Ypres Salient. Liddell Hart, in his book on the war, described this waste of life as 'criminal.'

Liddell Hart believed there was no reasonable chance the Allies gaining advantage, 'For such 'manslaughter', whether it springs from ignorance, a false conception of war or want of moral courage, commanders should be held accountable to the nation'. At this time the commanders were not held accountable and those at home were still generally unaware of the severity of the battle. Under the headline, 'Enemy's Violent Attack on Hill 60', together with 'An Unscrupulous Foe' a report in *The Times* of 8th May 1915, played down the horrors. The report, in a positive vein, remarked on the feeble attack by the German forces east of Ypres, which was proceeded by poison gas, that was 'easily repulsed', with the British artillery inflicting severe losses on the enemy.

What could not be avoided was news of the Mexborough and district men who fell during these furious battles around the Ypres Salient. Mrs Addeliza Harriot Gilbert, of 40, Oliver Street, Mexborough was the first to hear of her brother's death. He was Bandsman Charles George Higgins of the 2nd Battalion York and Lancs Regiment who died on 2nd April. Charles Higgins, a small man of five feet three inches tall and weighing just 113 pounds, had been enthusiastic about joining the army. He was born in 1895, originating from Nottingham. He was a young pit lad of fourteen years of age, and enlisted in the army on 29th November 1911, falsely giving his age as eighteen. Little remains of his army records, but it was quickly discovered that he had lied about his age and was discharged under Kings regulations on 2nd of January for making a 'mis-statement as to his age'.

It is likely that a letter from Charles' colliery manager brought to light the real age of this over zealous new recruit. He had worked at Mitchell Main Colliery, Wombwell, where his manager was asked to write a reference as to the lad's character. In this reference the manager wrote, 'This is to certify that the bearer Chas. E. Higgins was employed at the colliery from being 14 years of age until he was 16 or just over and during that time carried out his duties as a pony driver to entire satisfaction. He was a good hard-working boy very attentive to his duties and punctual in his attendance, he left on account of his parents going to another colliery'. The other colliery referred to is probably Cadeby Main, where the family moved to. Here he resumed his job as pony driver and became a member of Denaby Ambulance Band.

There is no record of when Charles Edward Higgins rejoined the army, but it can be assumed that he would have been first in the queue in

August 1914, ready to fulfil his ambition. Like many brave young men, his army career was short, as was his life, for he did not live to see his twentieth birthday. The news of his death in a Versailles hospital was received by his sister, a Mrs Gilbert, who was married to Private Henry Gilbert a member of the KOYLI. The news she received made it clear that her brother Charles had died from shrapnel wounds. In a letter that Bandsman Higgins had written shortly before his death, he described the events leading up to his wounding. He was writing a letter home, in a dressing station, with the message that he was alright, when the dressing station was heavily shelled. It had been snowing heavily and he caught a chill as he was being carried to the field ambulance. It must have been particularly devastating for Addeliza Gilbert, for she is said to have brought Charles up from a very young age. The news was conveyed to Mrs Gilbert in a letter by a nurse at the Versaille hospital. In the letter the nurse mentioned that Bandsman Higgins had won the Distinguished Conduct Medal (DCM) and that he wanted his sister to receive it. There is no record of him receiving the DCM and one can only speculate Bandsman Charles George Higgins believed he was about to receive this honour.

It was another Mexborough woman, Mrs Mary Whitehead of 52, Church Street, who was the first to be notified about the death of her son, Private Isaac Whitehead. He joined on 8th February 1915 and, on his arrival at the Western Front, on 4th April, was attached to the 1st Battalion of the York and Lancs. Issac, was a single man, born in Mexborough and lived at 12, Doncaster Road, but moved to Carcroft, Doncaster where he was employed as a coal miner. Private Whitehead's military records cynically states that he 'became non-effective' as having been assumed dead, although previously recorded as missing on 8th April 1915.

There was more bad news which arrived by letter to 49, Victoria Road. Mrs Worthington had received official confirmation from the War Office that her brother, Driver Wilfred Drury, of the Royal Field Artillery (RFA), had died of wounds on 11th April. The letter was from a nurse at the hospital in Boulogne where Mrs Worthington's brother had died, at the age of 21 and then laid to rest in Eastern Cemetery near the hospital. Wilfred Drury, formerly a miner who worked at Cadeby Main, joined the RFA at the beginning of the war on 11th November 1914. While he was living in Mexborough he stayed with his step father, a Mr Hobson of Schofield Street.

Mexborough then learnt that it had lost one of its well-known cricketers, Herbert Heald, who played for the Mexborough Cricket Club second eleven. Private Herbert Heald had been an old soldier during the South African War, but re-enlisted in September 1914. He arrived at the Front with the KOYLI on 7th April but died there just three weeks later on 27th April. His wife had been anxious for a number of weeks about his whereabouts and was left with four children.

There were yet more press reports of those lost in and around the 'hell-hole' that was the Ypres Salient. Private Wilfred Higgins of the 2nd KOYLI, a soldier who was previously wounded in the battle for Hill 60, but returned to front line in May, was reported missing in that month and never heard of since. He is recorded as having died on 7th May. He had lived at 10, Clayfield Lane, Mexborough.

Just one day later, the Calladine family, who suffered greatly as a family with grim news from the Western Front, lost Private John Calladine on 8th May. John, a miner, was one the first of Mexborough men to enlist in 1914, joining the 1st York and Lancs on 29th December of that year. The May of 1915 must have been a desperate time for John's family. John had been posted to the Front on 1st May a little more than a week before his death. His mother Mary and his father, also named John, heard the news that their son was 'missing'. There is little left of Private John Calladine's service records but a letter does remain which is typical of those who wrote letters pleading for news of their relations. Writing to the Army Records Office, father John made the all too frequent request for news. 'Please sir would you be kind enough as to let me know if you have heard any more news about my son John, he was wounded on the 8th of May but his whereabouts is not known, Your Obedient Servant John Calladine.' Private Calladine's records have the words, 'Presumed dead for official purposes' written across them. John's father received a reply to his letter on 18th June 1915, that his son was recorded as wounded and then missing around the Ypres Salient. Private John Calladine had died on the day he had been reported missing. He was just 24 years of age.

Private Richard Robert Douglas, who was on the teaching staff at a Goldthorpe School, enlisted in the Royal Army Medical Corps (RAMC) in November 1914. While he was in France and Flanders he repeatedly volunteered for duties which brought with it additional perils. During one of the battles around Ypres, Private Douglas joined a party of volunteers from the RAMC Sanitary Corps whose task it was to spray a substance which was meant to counter-act the fumes of the Germans' gas attacks. The operation was carried out in the face of a ferocious bombardment which lasted for nearly twelve hours. Private Douglas never returned from the operation and he was pronounced missing on 15th May, and recorded as died on that day. Richard had lived at 'Esk House', Dolcliffe Road, Mexborough.

Mexborough's Private Walter Stead, a regular soldier, joined the York and Lancs as a young man of eighteen in 1908. He was previously a glassblower by trade. Walter had served with the York and Lancs out in India at Karachi and Jubulpore. He and his regular army comrades sailed home to England for a brief period, aboard the steamer *Alnwick Castle* before embarking to France in March with the 1st Battalion York and Lancs. He was killed on 3rd July.

Towards the end of the engagements of the Second Battle of Ypres, Mexborough lost other 'old' regular soldier. He was Private John Boynton, who lived at 42, West Road and served with the 2nd York and Lancs. Little is known about his death but he is buried in Etaples Military Cemetery which suggests he died of wounds in the hospital, perhaps prior to attempting to return him to England.

Reports in the local press featured many who had been a part of Mexborough in the past. The Barnsley Chronicle of 29th May, reminded Mexborough of their former respected Vicar of the parish church, Canon W.H.F. Bateman. He had just been notified that his son, Lieutenant Wilfred Bateman, was missing whilst fighting around Ypres with the 1st Battalion KOYLI Regiment. Wilfred had been missing since 11th May. Wilfred Bateman had a privileged education as a public schoolboy at Marlborough and was a potential Cambridge University undergraduate, but his education was cut short by the outbreak of the war. Reports that he had been killed arose from the fact that as he was talking to his company sergeant, the latter was hit and killed by shrapnel. It must have come of great relief to the former Mexborough churchman and his family to receive the news that, although wounded, Wilfred was safe, despite being a prisoner of war in Guteraloe, Westphalia, Germany. Press reports said he was generally treated well by the German Red Cross.

The local newspapers were by now being overwhelmed by reports of deaths, those believed to be dead, wounded and those that were suspected of being taken prisoner. Week after week the papers were filled with reports of ever increasing casualties.

News was received by the Sherwood family who lived at 12, Simpson Place, that Private Joseph Sherwood, previously wounded in October 1914, had now been wounded at Hill 60. On this occasion he was forced have a limb amputated. His brother, Corporal Arthur Sherwood, was also wounded at Ypres. Both men were in the York and Lancs.

Despite news of ever increasing casualties published in the local press, the bad news was interspersed on occasions with more fortunate and happy news which brought at least some relief from the dismal aspects of reports from the front. It must a have been a relief for families to hear the news that their loved ones were prisoners of war, rather than suffering the anxiety of receiving the message that they were 'missing'. There was at least the satisfaction that they had survived and with reasonably humane treatment they would return home one day. Private Joe Newey wrote to his parents at 37, Wood Street, from a prisoner of war camp in Germany, with what sounds a heartening letter in the circumstances. The rather demanding Joe wrote:

'I have received two parcels with thanks. I am enjoying the cocoa and tobacco and the cake came nicely whole. Send a

*loaf of bread and a couple on tins of condensed milk, some
salmon, anything useful, more soup and cocoa, and a book.
Keep sending the parcels, the more the merrier. Send
smokes cake, pork pies, bacon, butter, tinned food, tin of
golden syrup, Sorry to keep troubling you.'*

Perhaps conscious of the fact that his letter is more concerned
about his own welfare rather than that of his parents, he briefly asked
them if they were well, but ends the letter by reverting back to his major
preoccupation of his own dietary requirements, by remarking, 'Not
enough snap'.

There was good news for Mr and Mrs Collingwood, of 58, Carlyle
Street, Mexborough, whose son Private R. Taylor Collingwood who also
was a prisoner of war in a camp in Gottingen in Germany. Private
Collingwood had been serving with the 22nd Field Ambulance when he
was captured in October 1914. He was released in the spring, being one
of the contingent of disabled non-combatants who arrived back in England.
He arrived in England and was initially moved to the King George Hospital
in Waterloo before returning back home to Mexborough.

It would be probably correct to say that the war increased the
occurrence of newly weds. Some couples who may have otherwise waited
to take the marriage vows were no doubt hastened into marriage with
the thought of unwelcome separation. There may have been a pecuniary
reason for marriage, in that a separation allowance would be
forthcoming and the more sobering thought of a widow's pension. On
the question of marriage and romance, Arthur Marwick, remarks, 'The
safest generalisaton about the First War World would be that it was a
time of powerfully heightened emotional activity and responses.' Often
this meant earlier and hastier marriage, reflected in the fanstatic 1915
figure of 19.5 marriages per thousand inhabitants......Marriage in haste
often meant divorce at leisure'.

Indeed divorce increased 300% in the decade between 1910 and
1920. This does not come as a surprise given the pressures placed upon
any marriage during the war years.

Whatever the outcome of a marriage, the news of such a marriage
occurring was at least a pleasant sight for the readers of the local press,
whose pages were all too often full of gloom. So it must have been
satisfying to read in *The Times* of 3rd April that Private H. Wheatley of
the RAMC, a man who had served at Mons and Marne, had married a
Miss S. Gill of 4, Woodfield Avenue, the daughter of Mr and Mrs John
Gill. The newly married Mrs Wheatley had four brothers, all who were to
join the army. Harold, Bert, Andrew and John who was to became a
Company Sergeant Major in the KOYLI and a recipient of the DCM.
Some dejection may have struck the readers, however, when the news

article informed its readers that the marriage took place just two days before Private Wheatley's departure back to the Western Front.

The Mexborough Free Church was, in its history, to perform many weddings, but its first ever wedding was reported in *The Times* of 8th May under the headline 'Mexborough Naval Wedding'. This was the marriage between Leading Seaman John William Oakley, who was serving on the *HMS Temeraire* and a Miss Francis Parker. Miss Parker was the youngest daughter of Mr Edward Parker who lived at 10, Orchard Street, Mexborough. The newly installed Reverend Thomas Anderson (he had defected from the Congregational Church) conducted the service. The couple were said to have honeymooned in London and Weymouth

Despite the more joyous news, the pressure of the war lay heavy on the minds of those at the battle front and on the Home Front, where more than a hint of desperation was evident. This could be tempered with some optimism as in the words of Buglar A.W. Trout, 5th KOYLI, of 30, Victoria Road, Mexborough. 'Those who are at home have no idea what it is like out here. We are making trenches with sandbags in the night it is a bit warm too sometimes... A party of Germans gave themselves up, they waved their hands because they were with the British. You can gamble it will be over before the Doncaster Races.' The Doncaster St Leger week of 1915 came and went in the September, as it did for the next three years, with no signaling of the end of war. The false optimism was increasingly becoming a cruel illusion, but hope was something that was continually held on to.

There was, by mid-year, a distinct restlessness about what might be happening with able young men who had yet to offer themselves up to serve their nation. Private C. Carr, a Mexborough Territorial with the 1/5th York and Lancs, wrote to his brother and sister about sport that was still to take place back home in Britain. Private Carr suggested that pursuits such as horse racing and cycling should not go on 'when men are getting slaughtered and undergoing the hardship they have to go through'. This uneasiness in the minds of men, who were witnessing death and slaughter on daily basis, about those at home who they believed were too keen to avoid the armed services, persisted until military conscription was finally introduced in 1916.

Chapter Eight

In the Shadow of Ypres

The horrors of war were now impacting on a nation whose hopes were initially for a quick end to hostilities. With stalemate on the Western Front, the increasing casuality rate and the introduction into the war of barbaric new weapons such as poison gas, society on the Home Front began to absorb the realities that faced it. The effect on the Home Front in Mexborough and district was much the same as elsewhere. Life began to be immersed to the needs of war and the ability to defeat the enemy. The necessities of war such as manpower, resources and finance also inevitably had consequences for the lives of people at home.

The cost of living was still to rise relentlessly. In a Parliamentary debate in February, Labour members claimed that those men who were undertaking menial and labouring work were now only getting one substantial meal a day. Herbert Asquith, the Prime Minister, had to confess that the cost of living had risen, dramatically in some cases, in the previous year. Sugar and flour were up by over 70%, coal 15% and meat was up between 6% and 12%. Despite these statistics being accepted by the Government, it was not inclined to intervene to help ease the situation.

There were even complaints by the people of Mexborough that postage for parcels and letters to the front had risen considerably since the beginning of the War. The miners' trade union, the YMA, condemned these increases, blaming the shipping companies, and denounced their, 'inexplicable greed and lack of patriotism' and blamed these companies for exploiting the nation's situation. They urged the Government to take control of all shipping supplies to relieve the situation, something in light of Asquith's approach to the issue, it was unlikely to do.

A large meeting at Denaby Main in February was addressed by Mr B. L. Smith, President of the Mexborough and District Trades and Labour Council. Smith made similar arguments on the costs of living and those who were allegedly exploiting the wartime situation. He reiterated that prices had risen 72% in a year and 66% on average over the previous three years. If the Government could take control of the railways then, Mr Smith argued, there was no reason why the same measures could not be exercised in the control of shipping and foodstuffs.

In an article in the *The Times* in May, the headline ran, 'Your Meat will Cost You More.' However, the local butchers were initially insufficiently united in their desire to raise prices of their meat in a show of collective unity, thus, for a while at least, keeping some stability in the meat trade locally. The local newspaper was not convinced that this state of affairs would last long and that in prevailing fashion the butchers would 'tax the consumer'. The Local Association of Butchers was to call a meeting of its organisation to combine to revise prices in the local trade. They felt the time had come to pass on the increase in wholesale meat to the consumer.

With price rises as they were, the most militant of the workforce, the miners, were still seeking what they believed to be a fair and just living wage. In the early part of the year the Council of the YMA met at Barnsley to call for a ballot for strike action over the owner's refusal to give a written undertaking to pay a minimum wage under an agreement of a legal judgment made in July 1914. In late April the miners in the area did win an increase in the existing wage scale of 4/- (20p) 5/- (25p) a day, and 6/- (30p) shillings to up 7/6d (37.5p) a day. It was hoped that this would safeguard against further disputes over the minimum wage agreement.

In response to increased wages to the colliers, the coal owners increased their prices, with the consequence that coal prices for industry and domestic use rose. These increases were passed on to the consumer thus putting further pressure on those on the Home Front who were already hard pressed with often a decrease in their family income. The price of gas rose as a result of the increase in coal prices. In late May the Swinton and Mexborough Joint Gas Board announced an expected rise in their prices.

All sections of society were looking to maintain their standards of living in the face of rapid rising costs and prices. The Mexborough and District Property Owners' Association met for one of their general meetings, in May, in the Oriental Buildings. The meeting included the Vice President, Councillor Christopher Ward, Secretary Mr I. W. Chipp and Treasurer, Dennis Wood. Mr Ward emphasised that it was important that the owners of property in Mexborough and district should come together in the light of the pressure they perceived themselves to be to be under. It appears some tenants were given some leeway in their argument about their inability to pay the rent. Despite the tenants having some 'protection' over payment of rent, some believed, argued Mr Ward, that they didn't need to pay anything as the law protected them in any event. Mr Ward assured the meeting that for anyone coming before the Doncaster courts, the magistrates would make sure they paid if they were in receipt of a reasonable income. The meeting was concerned that those tenants in arrears with rent payments were not being dealt with strongly enough to resolve the issue.

There was a tendency for housing rents to increase as landlords took advantage of the wartime shortage of housing, due to the cessation of house building. This caused protests over the increase of rents which included rent strikes in parts of the country, notably Glasgow. The house owners of the Mexborough and District Property Owners' Association seemed to anticipate the enacting of the Increase in Rent and Mortgage (War Restrictions) Act 1915. This was a measure which was to be in force for the duration of the war, preventing landlords raising rents, apart from in exceptional circumstances. It also restricted the right of landlords to eject tenants from their property. Mr E. Fowler the Chairman of the Association, believed they should appoint their own bailiff for dealing with matters that might arise between themselves and their tenants. This was particularly in light of the fact that the Council had so far made no provision for such a bailiff. The meeting took up this suggestion and well-known auctioneer and dealer, Mr J. E. Cliff, was appointed to undertake this task. It might have been that the members of the Mexborough and District Property Owners' Association were hoping for a few additions to the local Urban District Councils who might favour the landlord's cause. They would have at least some chance of influencing which personnel would serve on the local Councils, for polling day was on Saturday 27th May for Mexborough, Swinton, Wath, Bolton and other towns within the district.

In Mexborough there was a total of seven candidates to fill the five seats 'up for grabs'. The well-known Thomas Weston had initially sought election but decided to withdraw from the contest. Those re-contesting their seats were: licensee Tom Athron, John Wood, described as 'gentleman', John Thomas Rowen, a compositor and also the former vice chairman of the Council. Those also seeking re-election were miner, Levi Israel Jones, and the well-known character Frederick Woffinden, described as a 'billiard hall proprietor'.

There were two new candidates who were seeking election for the first time. David Sharratt, who was said to be prominent in public life with the trade union movement, being the Denaby Main Branch Secretary of the YMA. The other was William Shephard Pettit. The name Pettit was a well-established within the Mexborough district then as it is today. The local press described Mr Pettit, who was in the boot and shoe trade, as representing an old and esteemed name in Mexborough. It continues, 'His father was for many years prominently identified with public affairs in the town and he himself is well known. He is credited with a considerable business shrewdness and is considered a very eligible candidate.' As this was the first council election since the beginning of the war, it was not surprising it saw the lowest turnout on record. Just over a total of 900 votes were polled, only 31% of the electorate. There were, of course, many absentees whose war service prevented them from casting their vote. The result saw the return of Wood, Athron, Rowan and Jones, but Fred Woffinden failed to be re-elected.

Fred Woffinden, who lived at 'Strawberry Villa', Church Street, had won his seat in 1912 with a reasonable 408 votes, even beating Tom Chambers, the popular fruiterer who just scraped the last seat of that election. Woffinden at the time of the 1912 election was a wharfinger. He was known by the locals as 'Fred the Wharf', and was said to a have donkey, which he used as a 'sandwich man', which trotted around the town advertising Fred's business. As Fred lived in Church Street he had been a popular candidate, particular in the Doncaster Road area. Fred Woffinden had lost a leg as a young man and had an artificial limb or 'wooden leg'.

Woffinden had won a seat on the Council in 1912, despite him being involved in a controversial boating accident the previous year. Mr Woffinden hired out pleasure boats for the public to use on the local canal. In May 1911 he was in charge of a boat which capsized, resulting in the drowning of a young thirteen year old boy named Harold Seymour. There was some argument as to whether Fred Woffinden's artificial leg was an impediment to his ability to navigate the boat satisfactorily, although he had done so for many years. Further, Woffinden's evidence that he dispensed with his wooden leg to enter the water in an attempt to rescue the boy was disputed by a witness. Nevertheless the incident did not hinder success in the local elections the following year. His popularity had waned in the subsequent three years and he polled the lowest of all the candidates with just 271 votes. Mr Pettit also failed to gain a seat on the Council.

The election was a success as far as the Labour Movement was concerned. Both Rowan and Jones were returned for 'Labour' and fellow miner Daniel Sharratt, was to take Fred Woffinden's place on the Council, bring the strength of 'Labour' to five councillors, just one third of the council's fifteen seats.

Fred Woffinden may have had mixed feelings over the loss of his Council seat He could now concentrate on his a new venture as an owner of the billiard hall on Swinton Road. The role of a councillor was becoming more arduous, greater demands were placed upon the Council as they took over the stewardship of many activities to ensure that the needs of a community at war were met. Lloyd George earlier in the year had warned local authorities against the extravagance of introducing costly measures and that they should concentrate on schemes which created work for the unemployed.

Certainly the Council heavily involved itself in activities which were designed to help the community without burdening the ratepayer too significantly. At the Council's April monthly meeting, the Council resolved to set up a committee to inaugurate the first 'Union Jack Day'. This was an event which it hoped would raise money to assist the ever increasing numbers of wounded of His Majesty's forces. It was necessary for the event to be organised on an annual basis and it was envisaged that monies would be raised by the sale of flags of a 'special design'.

A special meeting was arranged in the Council Chamber on 5th May to select a committee and a sub-committee which was to be made up of ladies, who no doubt were to advise on the question of distribution of funds. The ladies committee consisted of wives of two councillors, Mrs Christopher Ward and Mrs Dennis Wood. Other notable names being Mrs J. Senior, Mrs Harrop, and Mrs Lister. The ladies were said to have wasted no time in discussing their role concerning the event, by holding their first meeting on the same night as their committee's formation.

The main positions on the committee were taken by Councillor Winstanley, chairman Dennis, secretary and Mr Nicol. B. Laidlaw, treasurer. The local press reported:

> 'The proceedings of this, the first 'Union Jack Day in Mexboro' will go to the local War Relief Fund. An effort is being made to build up this fund, so the Committee will be able, at the close of war, to ameliorate the lot of those brave men who are fighting for us against a ruthless and barbarous foe. A great many will doubtless need all the care we can bestow upon them, and we strongly appeal for the united assistance of every citizen.'

The event took place on Saturday 22nd May and succeeded in raising just over £71. After expenses the Mexborough Relief Fund were able to receive £58.10s.

There was a great need for relief for the dependants of families who were suffering the consequences of the war. The 'Mexborough Distress Fund' Committee now had over 341 families on its books, representing over 1,000 dependents. This fund's expenditure for one month had reached £963.2s out of a total fund of £1,032.4s. Funds were depleting so fast that the Committee were considering reducing the scales of allowance. This may have been prompted by the Government's announcement in early May of an increase in the 'Separation Allowance' for the wives and children of those engaged in the forces. A wife was to receive 12s 6d (62p) with the addition of 5/- (25p) for the first child and less generous allowances for additional children.

Yet funds were still flowing into the 'War Relief Fund', mostly from workplace contributions, from such as Waddington's, Barron's, and The British Westfalite Company at Denaby and staff from various local schools. April's collection also included the proceedings from a concert at the Hippodrome which amounted to £6.2s 3d.

Funds were desperately needed for the work that Montagu Hospital and its staff were doing as part of the war effort. The hospital was very congested as, on most occasions, there were no spare beds. On 20th May the second contingent of wounded soldiers arrived at the hospital, where two wards were set aside for the military. Seven of the wounded were Canadians, all the men being wounded in Ypres. All were young men suffering from shrapnel wounds and were in Montagu for the purpose of convalescence. All the men had been conveyed to the hospital by motor car by those individuals who were in a position to own such form of transport at the time. The individuals being, Mr T. Winter, Mr J Willis, Mr G. Groom, Tom Athron and the local garage owner, Frank Harrison. Dr Huey was now also in a position to offer his motor car having acquired the vehicle as replacement for his familiar horse and trap. As the convoy of motor cars passed Adwick Road School they were said to have been greeted by the cheers of students and staff.

Mexborough UDC continued to operate in what must have been stressful and difficult circumstances at times, dictated by wartime conditions. Pre-war conditions of the lack of housing and poor health in parts of the town were still a problem for a town struggling with the additional burdens placed upon it. At its monthly meeting in April, the evil of overcrowding was again raised, as was the issue of fly infestation which persisted in homes with poor sanitary conditions. Cases of diphtheria and scarlet fever were still being reported by Dr Huey.

The Health Visitor continued to raise the question of the lack of discipline shown by some children. Visits to school had been made when it was observed that some children could barely keep awake and were considered not to be physically or mentally fit to attend school. It had been noted that children were allowed to roam the street at night. In the view of the Health Visitor, parents were lacking in carrying out their responsibilities for the welfare of their children. With many male parents away from the home it might be argued the absence of a 'father figure' may have contributed to this state of affairs.

The problem of child poverty was a central theme of Dr Huey's Annual Report to the Council in June. There had been no improvement in the health and lives of the poorer section of the town from the previous year. The birth rate had increased from 1913-14, with 493 registered births, well above the national average, of these there were 23 illegitimate births. Overcrowding problems was still a major issue, together with some poor parenting. Referring to the report of the Health Visitor, Miss Margaret Cussack, Dr Huey remarked that there were some women in town who lacked the basic skills and knowledge of parenting and took no interest in their children whatsoever. Child poverty was a pressing issue in Mexborough and Dr Huey wondered if it would not be better for some of the most neglected children to be taken charge of by the State. Dr Huey's report also contained the depressing news that the infant mortality rate within the town was up on the previous year. There were 79 deaths of children under the age of one year, again well above the national average. Dr Huey described these as avoidable deaths.

By the beginning of the year, Mexborough UDC was focusing attention on the threat of German air raids in the form of Zeppelin attacks. The German Kaiser had given his approval to deploy these airships in the January of 1915. The first attacks on the British mainland come on the night of 19th and 20th of January, when two Zeppelins attempted to drop bombs around the Humber. Bad storms forced the Zeppelin crew to be content with an attack in the East Anglia areas of Great Yarmouth, Sheringham and Kings Lynn. The raids killed four civilians. Zeppelins were used throughout the war, right up to 1918 when the last attack took place over Kent in June of that year. These bombing raids were significant in that between 1915 and 1918 they caused the deaths of 1,913 people, along with many thousands of pounds worth of damage to property.

With the Zeppelin raids, the British civilian population faced a new threat which brought the horrors of war to their doorsteps. Initially in parts of the country reports of raids were played down. The effectiveness of Zeppelin raids were not as the Germans would have hoped for. Nevertheless the playing down of Zeppelin menace in the press was a tactic to calm the nerves of the civilian population who were now experiencing a whole new dimension to the war on the Home Front. Bombing raids on the outskirts of London during the summer of 1915, received very few column inches in the press. *The Times* of 17th April, reporting the Zeppelin targets in Northumberland, makes a cursory comment describing the raids as 'feeble' and 'futile' which leaves the nation 'unperturbed'. Yet the paper was open enough to realise the potential threat that these new aircraft posed. The paper continued to say, 'The very fact of a successful crossing of the North Sea by the bulky leviathan whose airworthiness has often been contemptuously questioned, gives occasion for thought and preparation, if not alarm'. Certainly it was alarming enough for the people of London to have to take to sheltering in London Underground 'Tube' stations after the worst raid on London in 1917 had killed 162.

Clearly some preparation was needed and the raids did concentrate the minds of both the authorities and the public as the war continued as it was clear that some air raid preparation was needed. Under Regulation 12, established under the DORA, the local authorities, including the police and the local military were bound to consider the necessity of introducing some form of blackout.

The nervousness which existed for some, in relation to the threat of air raids by Zeppelins, was expressed by Councillor Chris Ward at a Mexborough UDC meeting in June. He raised his concern that there was an exceptionally glaring light at the bottom of Adwick Road. To laughter he remarked, "The Germans may not know where Mexborough is on the map but we don't want to tempt their Zeppelins."

In the September of 1915 Mexborough UDC resolved to order that Mexborough be in darkness by 10.00pm every night expect Saturdays when an extra hour was permitted. As for motor vehicles, the Home Office advised motoring organisations that from January 1916 there were restrictions, in England and Wales, concerning electric acetylene and oil lamps on motor vehicles. Motor car electric lights were to be obscured, in what it called a 'certain manner', 30 minutes after sunset and until 30 minutes before sunrise.

It is claimed in article by Ted Brook that Pontefract was bombed in December 1916 and Pocklington was alleged to have suffered a raid also, although the Pocklington press could not report this incident, presumably on the premise of 'public safety'. Overall, Yorkshire did not appear to suffer the ordeals of other parts of the country. York was, however, bombed as a consequences of a raid in May 1916 in which nine were killed. The obvious target of the steel city of Sheffield was also a German ambition in 1917. On the night of 24th and 25th September 1917, Zeppelin L45 attempted to reach this strategic target, the usual hazards of poor flying conditions prevented success and the airship was destined to drop its bombs on London and Northampton. This is in contrast to the raid on Sheffield a year earlier in 1916.

Mexborough and district was not seriously threatened during the period of Zeppelin raids, although the prospect of raids was probably never far from the minds of the Don and Dearne Valley population. The 'Log Book' of the Doncaster Road School has this interesting entry for 26th September 1916. Headteacher Arthur Brown remarked, 'Attendance poor – children up late through Zep (Zeppelin) raid – raider passed over here'. Clearly the event must have caused some excitement and fear especially among the young, whose lateness to bed was a good enough excuse for their absence from school the following morning.

The Zeppelin was in fact the German Navy's L22 making its way to its intended target of a steel works of Sheffield. The Zeppelin had planned to drop high explosives on the Norfolk Steel, and the Atlas Steel and Iron Works around Attercliffe. The works escaped any serious damage, but tragically the L22 succeeded in damaging 62 houses, mostly in Corby Street, killing 28 and injuring 19 of its residents. At this time anti-aircraft defences were poor. The Royal Flying Corp (RFC) did not respond and Zeppelin L22 was able to bomb parts of Sheffield without being engaged by any resistance. The appearance of the Zeppelin L22 over Mexborough and its subsequent raid on Sheffield was not reported in *The Times* owing to press censorship. A report simply states that there was a raid by a Zeppelin in the North Midlands.

The biggest threat to the Home Front was not from the air but what was happening at sea with the threat to merchant shipping. The rise in prices to the consumer was met with protests throughout the country. The Mexborough and District Trades and Labour Council held a meeting in the Public Hall, in February, to protest against the rising cost of food. Mr B. L. Smith, presiding over the meeting was to argue there was no legitimate reason for the necessities of life rising by "leaps and bounds". Councillor Humphreys similarly believed that increased prices were artificially high, through what he called "speculative gambling" and excessive profits. This argument had some validity at the time, for there was without doubt a tendency by some to profiteer from war conditions. Later, however, it was difficult to ignore Germany's attempt to seriously curtail British import of foods and raw materials from other allied or neutral counties such as the USA.

Both Britain and Germany were dependent on imports of raw materials and foodstuff to sustain its economies and its 'war machine' on both the battle and Home Fronts. Cutting the supply of imports to the enemy was the intention of both nations. Germany was to declare the seas surrounding the British Isles as a war zone and declared that allied shipping was at risk. The German government took the decision to launch a submarine campaign in order to achieve its objective of restricting Britain's lifeline of its import trade. Prime Minister Asquith announced to the House of Commons on the 1st May that Britain would retaliate by blockading German ports and other access to its import trade.

Asquith declared that the submarine campaign was "piracy and pillaging" and without precedent in history. The Government response was to declare that British and French navies would detain and escort into port any vessel carrying goods destined for enemy ports.

Asquith's statement on Germany's submarine campaign can be viewed as mainly propaganda. In actual fact the British had already established its own blockade against German shipping at the outset of the war in August 1914 and in November 1914 declared the North Sea a 'War Zone'. The announcement by the German government was itself a retaliatory response to what it saw as British aggression. The British blockade was seen as against international law and a blatant tactic to starve the people of Germany into submission. However, it has been argued the prolonged blockade was justified in that it hastened the collapse of the Kaiser's Government in 1918

The British Navy was without question a superior force upon the high seas to that of the German Imperial Fleet. The Germans did, however, have a superior submarine force, the U-boats, which they decided to deploy against Allied merchant shipping as well as the Royal Navy. The German U-boats at the beginning of the war were prepared to act within international law when engaging their enemy. This meant, under The Hague Convention of 1907, that merchant ships would only be sunk in the event of the crew and any passengers being able to leave the ship prior to the sinking. As it become came clear that the war would only be won if 'no holds were barred', unrestricted submarine warfare by the German Government was to become the norm. From February the Allies were warned that they risked serious consequences within the 'War Zone' from the German U-boat fleet.

One act of unrestricted submarine warfare particularly caused an outrage in Britain and internationally. The sinking of Cunard's liner the *RMS Lusitania* was the subject of one of the most appalling events in wartime history. The great luxury liner left New York on 1st May on its regular transatlantic voyage, bound for Liverpool, with nearly 2,000 passengers and crew. The crew included violinist Ernest Dixon Drakeford, who once lived in Swinton but had moved to Liverpool by this time. The German Embassy in New York had placed an advertisement in 50 newspapers warning passengers not to sail as they were likely to be in danger. The threat was taken seriously by the British Admiralty but not so seriously by the Cunard Line itself. There were recommendations to captain of liners under wartime condition to steer a zig-zag course in order to create difficulties for the U-boat commanders. Captain Turner of the *Lusitania* did not follow this advice and at two o'clock in the afternoon of 7th May the liner was hit by a torpedo (or two it is argued) from the German submarine U-20. The massive liner sunk within a short space of eighteen minutes off the south coast of Ireland. The scale of death from the sinking of the *Lusitania* was shocking. A total of 1,195, mostly British and Canadians, were lost, including nearly 100 children. Ernest Dixon Drakeford was one of the survivors.

The German authorities had argued that the liner was carrying arms and therefore was a legitimate military target, but nothing would persuade the civilised world that the sinking was anything else than a horrifying act of brutality. Of the 139 Americans on board 128 died. This single act of aggression began to turn the tide of public and political opinion in the USA, which saw that country finally supportive of the Entente powers. British politicians were 'naturally' outraged and measured language for some was difficult to find. One of the most extreme utterances on events was from Lord Derby. He was to remark, "This country calls no longer for men to fight a honourable foe. It calls for men to hunt down and crush once and for all a race of cold-blooded murderers". Such language was only likely to fuel the flames of what was to happen immediately following the news of the sinking, as it reached the British public.

There had been riots from the early months of the war, in London, Keighley and Crewe, against those of German descent living in Britain, although anything German was a target for many of the rioters. With the news of the fate the *Lusitania*, the rioting spread further afield. Riots in Liverpool, the home port of the liner and home to many of its crew members, broke out on 8th May and continued for some days. Similar riots broke out in London and elsewhere. Again the targets for the 'mob' were people of German descent, mainly businessmen and predominately it seems German pork butchers of whom there were many who emigrated from Germany in their hundreds from the 19th century.

It probably came as no surprise that Mexborough's own German pork butcher, George Schonhut, would now become the centre of attention for those who decided to vent their anger, at this German atrocity, in the same way some outraged Liverpudlians had chosen. Yet George Schonhut did not expect to become a victim in the same way as others of German descent. There is some justification for Mr Schonhut's belief that Mexborough people would not react as others throughout the country had done. He was a town councillor, winning his seat quite comfortably, was seen as generous and charitable person and no doubt popular with his customers. Yet Councillor George Schonhut must have had some reservation about making any public appearance within the town. A service at the Primitive Methodist Chapel took place on Sunday 9th May, at which, as expected, the *Lusitania* tragedy was a prominent part of the proceedings. It was customary for all town councillors to attend this service. Every councillor did attend apart from Councillor Schohnut. George Schonhut did however contribute £10 to the Mexborough War Relief Fund in June, probably in a last attempt try to demonstrate his commitment to the British cause.

On the evening of Monday 10th May, what was described as a public disturbances broke out in Mexborough High Street. Just before 9.00pm two men entered George Schonhut's butcher's shop and were met by his son Albert. The men were intent on confronting Mr Schonhut senior himself but he was out of his premises. Some heated conversation was exchanged between Albert Schonhut and the two intruders. Events may not have led to anything too serious if it was not for someone's decision to throw a large missile at the shop's large plate glass window. The assailant was believed to have been the wife of a local soldier. The smashing of the window prompted large crowds to gather.

The local police, led by Sergeants Dobson and Blyth, were called, in an attempt to ensure there was no escalation of problem, while at the same time advising Mrs Schonhut and her family to remove quietly from their premises. Any hope of containing potential outbreak of rioting was to disappear. A tramcar passed up High Street giving cover from police observation for another stone thrower, whose missile caused further damage to the Schonhut shop. This allowed further missiles to be thrown causing the crowds to become more hostile, with some shouting out references to the *Lusitania*. By 10.00pm, Schonhut's large plate glass window was smashed with the mob now steadily bombarding the property, which resulted in every piece of glass within it to be completely destroyed. As the evening progressed some of the crowd began to fight amongst themselves. The police had anticipated serious trouble and took the precaution of calling for enforcements from neighbouring districts. By 11.00pm the High Street was thronging with excited crowds, including many women, stretching almost its full length. The High Street rang with the sound of clapping and shouting of approval for the appalling events.

It had taken sometime for the police from other areas to arrive, but by 11.30pm, after many taxis had arrived, the local police were relieved to acknowledge the presence of over 100 police officers. With this substantial police strength they were able to force the crowds back 50 yards either side of the Mr Schonhut's shop. Despite this, some of the crowd who remained attempted to continue their 'demonstration', with a small number of people remaining to the early hours of the morning. There was a police presence throughout the night and next day, in an attempt to stop any re-occurrence of ugly events.

The Times' headlines the following week described the attack on George Schonhut's property as an 'Anti-German Riot'. It was said to have been the most serious disturbance since the 1896 'Miners' Lockout' which resulted in the reading of the Riot Act. During this riot, however, the reading of the Act was deemed unnecessary.

Just when things appeared to have calmed, in the week following the attack on his butcher's shop, George Schonhut's sister became subject to threats. She had married an Englishman, Mr Wedgewood, a mineral water manufacturer, and was living with him at the Brickyard in Mexborough. Mrs Wedgewood was threatened by women and youths at midnight, causing damage and attempting to force the door to her house. Mrs Wedgewood, who was subjected to 'exceptional animosity', was to leave the house for a safer place. Mr Wedgewood felt safe enough to remain in the town. The disturbance had led to a number of Mexborough residents of German origin to leave the town, including the Schonhut family and a Miss Boesch, a member of staff at the Mexborough Secondary School.

Another anti-German demonstration took place in east of the town at the property of a Mr Steckchuis, on the corner of Pitt Street and Doncaster Road. A fitter at Denaby Main Colliery, Steckchuis had lived in Mexborough for many years but had never taken it upon himself to become naturalised. His two sons had been interned in York Castle at the beginng of the war but released, later after taking out naturalisation papers. The Steckchuis residence had its front windows smashed and furniture taken. A Mr Beecroft's house, where it was suspected that some of Mr Steckchuis's furniture was stored, also suffered a similar fate. A German family called Deganhart residing in Dodsworth Street, suffered a similar fate as others with any German connection during this particular period of anti-German sentiment.

After the sinking of the *Lusitania* it was evident that to be a target of anti-German sentiment, it was not even necessary just to have a German or foreign sounding name; the mere suspicion of non-Englishness was sometimes enough. John Wordsworth of the Park Hotel wrote a letter to *The Times* on 15th May pleading that, despite rumours to the contrary, he was a true Englishman. So desperate was his concern about being mistaken for a 'foreigner' he offered £50 (a very considerable amount in 1915) to anyone who could prove he was anything else than Yorkshire born and bred. Such was the fear factor from the riots which were sweeping Britain.

There were other disturbances in the area, including, Denaby, where one of George Schonhut's shops was attacked and Conisbrough where Mr and Mrs Walters, both of German origin, had their shops ransacked and like others found it necessary to flee the district. The most serious riots in the district were, however, to take place at Goldthorpe. Here a Mr S. Elsbury, a native of Russia, was verbally abused, as was Mr J R. Bakewell, residing at a shop owned by the London Tea Company. Bakewell was attacked for allegedly being a German Jew. Perhaps not unexpectedly the riots targeted the premise of Mr Fred Schonhut, a distant relation to George, and his pork butcher business. These attacks were of a most serious nature, with fire arms being used by some of the rioters, ending with a number of serious injuries being sustained. One man, John Eades, a local footballer of some repute, was shot in the abdomen several times, causing injuries from which he eventually died. The Goldthorpe riot was estimated to have caused over £1,300 worth of damaged property.

The reporting by *The Times* of the local disturbances was a little more measured than the hysterical utterances of Lord Derby, although the newspaper did anticipate there would be reaction within the locality. The newspaper was of the opinion that the sinking of the *Lusitania* could only be avenged by smashing Germany and all that Germany stood for, not by smashing German's and German property in England. Yet curiously this advice came under the headline, 'English Hate'. Clearly the riots were a spontaneous explosion of hate, assisted by some official propaganda that was constantly delivered and easily accepted by some susceptible groups of the public. The British War Propaganda Bureau, based in Wellington House, London, was constantly busy with ideas for propaganda materials and posters, which often did little to engender some proportionality into the analysis of events.

The sinking of the *Lusitania* led to Prime Minister Asquith announcing in the Commons, on 13th May, a strengthening of the Government policy to enemy aliens. All Germans of military age (18-47) were to be interned and females to be repatriated. Those born in Germany who had become naturalised were allowed to be at liberty, unless deemed to be a threat. Those at liberty would need to regularly report to the authorities as to their whereabouts. By November of 1915 those interned reached over 32,000. By July it was the responsibility of all lodging house keepers, hotels and boarding house proprietors to keep a register of all their guests. Registration records were to be in a book of authorised forms, available for purchase locally at the 'Times' Office' and made available for police inspection.

As a result of these announcements on German aliens, George Schonhut's future hung in the balance. George Schonhut was born on May 18th 1861 in a small town called Oberhof in the German Kingdom of Wurtenberg. He maintained he had a dislike for the German military system in the then unified Germany, a dislike which prompted him to come to England in 1878 as a youth of nearly seventeen. On his arrival in England he spent time in Bradford and Sheffield and after ten years moved to Rotherham.

After the riots, Schonhut attempted to claim some compensation for damage his property had sustained. This meant producing papers to the local constabulary including, as a native of Germany, papers confirming naturalisation. George Schonhut failed to produce proof that he had registered as a British citizen when asked to do so by Inspector Barraclough. As a consequence of this he was charged with not having registered as an alien and brought before the Magistrates Courts in Doncaster on 25th July.

At the hearing, Superintendent Minty claimed that, until 16th July, the police had no idea that Mr Schonhut was not a British citizen. The police had known Mr Schonhut for many years and as a member of Mexborough Urban District Council assumed he had naturalisation papers. Schonhut employed a barrister, a Mr T.E. Ellison, to defend him. Ellison offered the defence that it was Schonhut's service in the Queen's Own Yorkshire Dragoons, from 1896, that led him to believe, after legal advice, that it was not necessary for him to obtain naturalisation papers. Mr Hattersley, Schohut's Mexborough solicitor, said that his client was advised that taking the oath to join the armed forces deemed it unnecessary to obtain papers under the 1870 Naturalisation Act.

George Schonhut's defence failed and he was ordered to pay a £5 fine, although not before making a last desperate plea to the court. He said his heart and soul was with England. He had no property in Germany and his elder brother, who was once in the German Army, had also decided to leave Germany on account of German cruelty.

Schonhut suffered one last setback when told by the magistrate that although he had eventually registered himself as an alien on 17th July, he had no right to be serving on the Mexborough UDC. This was to make no difference for Schonhut was never to return to the Council. After six months of non-attendance of Council meetings he automatically lost his seat. Although some reports say Schonhut was interned, this may not have been the case, due to his age and length of residency, but he certainly remained in seclusion until after the war and was never again to run his butcher's shop in Mexborough in person. Like many with German roots at the time, he was to change the family name. Following the example of King George V, who was from the German family Saxe-Coburg-Gotha and the first of cousin of the Kaiser, George Schohnut's family found a suitable English alternative surname. The Royal family changed their name to Windsor; by 1916 the Mexborough family of butchers had changed theirs to Sinclair.

George Sinclair (Schonhut) died in the 1924 no doubt believing that he had served Mexborough well both through his business and in his public life as a councillor. One can only speculate as to his state of mind following the disturbances in May 1915. The hate generated by this war was to manifest itself in many cruel ways.

The war was having a profound effect on the social life and activities of the community. This was clearly observed in press reports and other commentaries of the day. Easter Monday fell on 4th April, but as *The Times* put it, the Easter spirit was modifed with 'no junketing and very little feasting of any kind'.

The Whitsuntide holidays fell on the weekend of 22nd May in what was favourable sunny weather. There was some effort to focus the occasion around activities to give at least some joy for the children, with the Annual Children's Festival. Sunday saw the children from the Non-Conformist Sunday Schools come together in an assembly of hymns in the Market Place.

On the Monday, the theme of a children's occasion continued, with the children of the Primitive Methodists, the Wesleyan Chapels and the Congregational and Oxford Road Churches marching through the street of Mexborough, headed by the Swinton Wesleyan Band. The march was followed by tea in various schoolrooms and later 'games and romps' on the playing fields of Mexborough. The Free Christian Church held its own march with a possession around Mexborough Common.

The Mexborough Salvation Army's annual possession started at Dodsworth Street at 2.00pm headed by the Attercliffe Brass Band which led the parade around Mexborough's principal streets. The parade had not forgotten the men of Mexborough who had so far given their lives in this depressing war. A dray in their honour proceeded through the town flanked by the Red Cross. They were joined by nurses who walked in respect alongside the decorated dray, which was followed up by another dray displaying the words, 'Ready for the Front'. The participants in the possession were to partake of tea and then in recreation on a field owned by the Hope Working Men's Club Cricket Club. Profits from the event were to go to the 'Young People's Work Fund'.

The Midland and Great Central Railways decided that they would not run excursion trips on this particular Whitsuntide. It was said that the seaside resorts were not a popular destination now that the war was entering its second year, but trippers were still travelling by rail more locally to such as Sheffield, Leeds and Bradford. Many preferred other forms of transport in the form of waggonette trips to the countryside. The Mexbrough Wesleyan Bible Class chose a ramble to Edlington Woods, while the Free Church Cycling Club visited the old favourite venue of Roche Abbey and Blythe. Roche Abbey was also the destination of the Mexborough Parish Church Bible Class. They were to visit their former vicar, the Reverend Bateman, who was now living in Wistow but were conscious of the clergyman's anxiety over the welfare of his son, Lieutenant Wilfred Bateman, who was once believed missing but was in fact taken prisoner.

It was on the occasion of the holiday breaks that perhaps some of the melancholy which had generally descended upon the town was briefly put to one side. Sport had been affected by the gradual loss of players and members of clubs and societies. Mexborough Town Football Club was certainly one sports club which was feeling the pressures of the wartime environment. At the beginning of May the club, again, announced its doubts as to the viability of it remaining in the Midland League, a league which, at that time contained some formidable clubs. Mexborough Town had originally entered the Midland League in the 1886-87 Season. The following season it was to win the Championship with Barnsley St Peter's, later Barnsley FC, being runners up. The club had beaten such teams as Sheffield United reserves, Doncaster Rovers, Lincoln City and Rotherham Town to the title.

The 'Town' had, before the war, produced some outstanding footballers. The most notable was Walter Bennett, described as one of the greatest wingers who ever played the game. Bennett went on to be a Bramall Lane favourite. Others were Fergus Hunt, who went on to play for Preston North End, 'Titch' Tyas, and Hardy. Two sets of brothers, the Whitehouse brothers and the Mawson brothers were said to be pretty handy too.

The Mexborough club had just completed an indifferent season, although it had only lost two games at home, beating some of the strongest team in the league such as both Sheffield clubs, Rotherham County and Chesterfield. The away form of 'the Town' was quite the opposite, as they failed to win a single game. The last game of the season saw them lose six goals to nil to Scunthorpe. The club was only able to send six men to complete this final fixture of the 1914-15 Season, with a team having to be made up of some Scunthorpe men who hurriedly signed for Mexborough before stepping on to the field.

Inevitably there was a reduction in the number of spectators attending games as well as the inability of Mexborough FC to find eleven fit players on a weekly basis. Money was 'tight' within the town and consequently this impacted on the club's ability to maintain its status within the Midland League. *The Times* explains Mexborough FC's lack of finance in a way that does not sound unfamiliar 100 years later:

'The whole secret of the failure of Mexborough (and Denaby) is the rapid increase in the cost of running the Midland League football. And that cost is entirely due to the fact that the big First and Second Division clubs have fielded highly paid reserves in this competition and have forced up the footballer's prices beyond the means of small clubs like Mexborough and Denaby.'

This, *The Times* remarked, has led to clubs like Rotherham and Doncaster having wage-bills that were previously undreamt of and as a result the Midland League was no longer suitable for clubs like Mexborough or Denaby.

Some Mexborough sportsmen would have found themselves drafted into the sports teams or sporting activities pursued by their individual army regiments. Both 'Iron' Hague and another well-known Mexborough boxer, Tommy Stokes, volunteered to fight on behalf of their regiment. While in the first few weeks of his army training, Hague was offered the chance to ply his old boxing skills, something he had not done seriously for some time. It was believed that army training and discipline was something which would restore 'Iron's' fitness and an appetite for the sport, which some critics claimed he had lost.

Guardsman Hague's first contest, against a Frank Wright, proved he was still capable of being a competitive fighter, by beating Wright on points. The fight against Wright however was not seen as a particularly sufficient test for the ex-English Heavyweight Champion. His next serious fight was to take place at the West London Stadium, Edgware, on 25th February against a very experienced Dick Rice, who was also serving in the army.

Hague was, by all accounts, well supported at the north London stadium and his supporters were hoping to see the ex-champion from Mexborough put on a performance reminiscent of the best days of his career. Despite some moments in which Hague showed why he had at one time being regarded as one of the best 'white hopes', he lost on points. He was generally out-boxed by Rice, described as 'ugly and ungainly' who was always in overall control of the fight. Reports suggest that 'Iron' showed remarkable restraint although he was subjected to provoking tactics by Dick Rice. This restraint, it was said, contributed to Guardsman's Hague defeat. This characteristic in the past would have been somewhat alien to the Mexborough man. The report in *The Times* suggested that Hague,'was not at home, he did not exhibit that fire and dash which made him so terrible opponent when he was in the very freshness of his career'.

The *Sporting Life*, which covered the fight, was not so complimentary about 'Iron' Hague's past or his gallant display against Rice. Hague's suffered from 'too solid flesh' and 'never in the least fond of training'. He was too slow and laboured against Rice, although the *Sporting Life* did comment that they were not watching the Hague of old, but did at least recognised the glory days of 'Iron's fighting career.

Guardsman James William Hague went on to fight a number of further contests as a part of his army career. By the time of the last two fights, 'Iron' was out with his regiment in France. The very last of these, which took part in Harfleur, was against Gunner Joe Mills, a fight which he won with a knockout. The fight took place on 9th September, but within weeks Guardsman Hague, like many other men who come from his home town, was engaged in a different kind of fight, at the Battle of Loos.

The Headteacher's entries in the 'Log Book' of daily events at Doncaster Road School are revealing in that they give us an indication of the disruption that wartime condition brought to the education system. Mr Arthur Brown, the Headteacher, wrote on January 6th 1915 that Mr Edward Alfred Phillips was granted permission to take time off to attend a medical examination to enlist in the forces. Mr Phillips duly attended his medical the next day at 9.00a.m with Mr Brown recording, 'Mr Phillips passed into the Sheffield City Battalion (reserves)'. He was followed later in the year by Mr Frederick J. Horne, enlisting in the RAMC, again as a reservist.

Staff disruption was to become a problem. The sickness rate amongst the teachers seems high and staff were constantly moving to other schools to fill the places left by teachers who were either ill, left for personal reasons or who decided to respond to the call for more recruits to the forces.

The pupil attendance rate appeared to be a regular problem but clearly it was not helped by the chaos and confusion created by the war.

As early as 28th August 1914, the Doncaster Road School 'Log Book' records that, 'Two (pupils) made poverty the reason for absence. Father called up; no pay yet'. The disturbance to 'normal' family life was no doubt to take its toll. With the rush to join up in 'Kitchener's Army' and the sudden disruption to a child's life it was little wonder that children played truant, with both the child and parent finding reasons, genuine or not, to declare them absent from their formal education.

School absenteeism and the disruption of children's education were not helped by the gradual increase of the shortage of labour. In early May the Mexborough Education Committee discussed a letter from the County Council (CC) concerning the engagement of child labour for agriculture. The chairman of the CC had received many requests from farmers requesting certain amendments to employment conditions of children be made to allow them to work on the land to compensate for labour lost to the forces. The CC was of the opinion that perhaps children could be released from schools for the purpose of working solely in agriculture, subject to certain conditions. There were those on the Mexborough Education Committee who bitterly opposed this measure. Mr Watson had no sympathy for the farmers. They were, he stated, trying to exploit the shortage of labour by acquiring even cheaper labour than they already employed. Mr Humphries was of the same view. Humphries urged the Education Committee to consider the children's attendance at school and the education lost from which they would never recover. Probably recognising the plausibility of Watson's and Humphries' position, the Committee resolved to 'keep close watch' on the situation, but without making any clear decision on the farmers' request.

On May 25th the Liberal Government was in turmoil. Prime Minister Asquith's Government was heavily criticised for the British failure in the initial campaign in the Dardanelles. This saw Admiral John Fisher, Lord of the Admiralty, resign his position. Further criticism was aimed at Asquith over what was to be called the 'Shell Scandal'. Sir John French had blamed failure in the battles around Ypres on ammunition shortage and in particular on the shortage of shells. The ruling Liberal Government was disbanded and a wartime coalition formed containing members of the former Conservative opposition. Shaken by the criticism, Asquith moved quickly by appointing Lloyd George to the position of Minister of Munitions to try to improve shell production.

It is clear that some measures were in place even before the formation of the Coalition to try to rectify what was believed by the military commanders at the time as a major deficiency in the execution of the war. A Mexborough UDC meeting in April, received a letter from the British Westfalite Company in Denaby Main, who had the intention of applying to the magistrates for permission to extend their works, in order to facilitate the output of ammunition. An article appeared in 29th

May edition of *The Times* concerning John Baker and Company, at Kilnhurst. The article read, 'Shell forgery is a special product of these works and output is increasing as the whole of the available accommodation is adapted to the rapid manufacture of a weekly Government order'. It went on to mention that as a result of this expansion new employees would be wanted. At that time the company employed 300 men who were working a considerable amount of overtime. Those working overtime were said to have been provided with tea, which was free and a 20 minute break. The fact that there was no evidence of 'slacking' on the part of the workers may be attributed to this gesture made the employer.

John Baker and Company were probably among the first in the area to consider some welfare concessions to their workforce. The more progressive thinking employers were slowly becoming aware of the link between productivity and the physical conditions in which their employees worked. Lloyd George himself had recognised this important observation and a Special Welfare Department was set up in his Ministry of Munitions in attempt to boost shell production.

The shortage of labour, particularly skilled, was a serious concern to both Government and employers. Given this shortage, John Baker and Company devised a local scheme which tried to attract as much male labour, at least initially, as was possible. The company's idea was to encourage enthusiastic men, from lower middle class occupations, such as clerical workers and teachers, to work on a casual basis in their 'sparetime', until full-time labour could be found. In order to fill the vacancies with full-time skilled labour it was necessary to set up the Mexborough Munitions Works Bureau, which worked on behalf of munitions companies within the district. The Bureau's manager was Mr B. Jepson, who operated from an office in the Oriental Chambers, Bank Street. The Bureau's opening hours were for just three hours in the evening during the week and Saturday and Sunday afternoon. It was reported that skilled men would rewarded with high wages and be presented with 'a handsome certificate suitable for framing' inscribed on the rear recognising the fact that they were engaged upon 'special Government work in connection with the war'. *The Times* was active in assisting John Baker and Company in recruiting workers. Unskilled workers were told in July they could now register themselves at the 'Times Office'. Workers, particularly volunteers, were now informed they now had an option to work on Sundays, a day which became to be known as 'Shell Sunday'.

Any news items relating to John Bakers' in the early part of the war only refers to male workers, there was no mention of women. In July 1914, before the start of the war, just over 200,000 women were employed in the munitions industries. A year later this number had only increased by a further 50,000 despite, by then, the Government realising that there was a need to step up shell production. With the big expansion in the munitions industry in the later part of 1915, combined with military conscription in early 1916, female employment had doubled to well over 500,000. Up to the summer of 1915, female employment in the engineering industries was still low. There were probably two main reasons for this. One was society's attitude towards women, reflected in the discrimination and sexism of the time, the other was the trade union's fear that female labour, being unskilled in engineering, would undercut wages and conditions of its male membership.

In the early part of the year, the Liberal Government took action, anticipating that the trade unions would try to maintain their role and defend their members wages and conditions, with a possible resort to industrial action. Lloyd George, after discussions with the Labour Party's Arthur Henderson and some more compliant trade union leaders, agreed a deal which would curtail the trade union's ability to organise against the so called 'dilution' of labour. The agreement was that the unions were to forego their 'right to strike' with disputes being settled by compulsory arbitration and certain union practices were also to be suspended until the end of the war. This was supposed to cover all those engaged in what was said to be 'war work'. In return the trade unions were given an assurance that existing wages and conditions would be honoured. Later, under the Munitions Act, the Coalition Government promised that there would be a limit to the employers' profits in any munitions establishments under Government control. The Amalgamated Society of Engineers' Union (ASE) was initially reluctant to sign the agreement but finally agreed to the terms on 25th March. The miners' union MFGB stood aside from the deal. The ASE's decision, to agree to suspend their right to take industrial action effectively, gave the go ahead for women to become accepted into the labour force of munitions factories.

The Vicar of Mexborough Parish Church, the Reverend Edmund Hope, chose Sunday 13th June to deliver what was called by the press a powerful recruiting sermon. Taking part of his sermon from Judges Verse 23, 'Curse ye Meros', The Reverend Hope was of the belief that this text from the bible gave him every justification to condemn the trade unions for insisting on war bonuses, threatening industrial action and generally disrupting war production. As the role of the trade union was to protect its members from what it saw as an attack on living standards, this sermon was not well received by the Mexborough and District Trade and Labour Council. The Reverend Hope's provocative address to his congregation was raised at the June 'Trades Council' meeting to outraged delegates. A delegate from Wath, Mr G. Lees, believed the vicar, who had "found a good steady wage and a job for life", had failed to understand industrial conditions and the position workers often found themselves in. "He was no friend of the worker", Mr Lees remarked. Another delegate tried to move a proposal that the Reverend Hope be "shifted". This latter suggestion prompted the secretary of the 'Trades Council' to call for a more rational proposal and it was suggested that the Reverend Hope should apologise for his remarks. Eventually the matter was settled by a unanimous decision with the passing of the rather pious resolution, 'That this Council cannot find anything to justify the statement of the Vicar of Mexborough that we are suffering from the tyranny of the trade unions today.'

Certainly the Reverend Hope did not have grounds to take issue with many trade unionists themselves. The local painter and decorator, Walter Nicholson, lost eight of his painters to the armed forces by the early part of the year. One of these was Sergeant J. M. Atkinson who was a former recruiting officer at Conisbrough. Nicholson's men would most probably been in the Painters Union which lost 7,000 of its members to the army.

Society's attitude to women workers, with its male dominance over almost everything, is perhaps well illustrated in *The Times* editorial of 3rd July. The newspaper recognised that women were anxious to play their part, over and above what was called 'ordinary services', such as collectors of funds, preparing parcels for the Front, the nursing of wounds and the making of tea. *The Times* noted a radical proposal for the time and referred to the 'obvious direction in which women could play their part was in schools'. With male teachers now joining the armed forces in considerable numbers, efforts were now being made to induce back into the profession women who had been forced to leave it upon their decision to marry. Of course the engagement of these women would not be permanent; their services would be dispensed with when 'normal conditions were restored'.

The Editor of *The Times*, however, noted with satisfaction that large numbers of women were, by the summer of 1915, being employed on the railways and tramways. In April the Great Central Railway, in Mexborough and surrounding districts, announced that they were requiring temporary female labour as carriage cleaners and porters. The press reported that there was a flood of applications from what it described as 'women of all types'. Yet here *The Times* was able to maintain a familiar masculine discourse by commenting, 'Most women want carriage cleaner as this employment appeals to them.' It was suggested the appeal was because the work was congenial to women as they were already had an expertise in cleaning.

The railways saw many of their employees flock towards the armed forces in response to Kitchener's call for volunteers. This was particularly the case locally when dozens of employers from the Great Central Railway, at Mexborough, Wath and Conisbrough, were recruited in the early days of the war. This created enormous problems for the railway companies, which caused them to approach the Government to end this flood by insisting that their employees first need permission from management. The railway trade unions had already agreed an 'industrial truce' as early as October 1914, although by the summer of 1915 over 80,000 men had left the industry. The shortage of labour opened up opportunities for women in a number of grades. The railway industry, unlike engineering, had already employed over 4,500 women by July 1914. By the end of the war over 56,000 women had become railway workers.

In the same way as the railway industry, coal mining industry locally saw hundreds of its workers join the armed forces early in the war and in subsequent calls for volunteers. For example Cadeby Main Colliery was to release nearly 900 men in the first twelve months of the war. Up to February 1915 there were 191,170 employees working in coalmining who were released from the industry to join His Majesty's forces. This amounted to more than a 13% reduction in the labour force of July 1914, with a corresponding reduction in coal production, as *The Times* reported in June. The Departmental Committee set up by the Government and chaired by Sir Richard Redmayne, Chief Inspector of Mines, came to the conclusion that if the numbers leaving the industry continued at a similar rate then the production of coal would be at a serious low. The Departmental Committee did recognise, however, that the numbers lost to recruitment to the forces was tailing off.

The employers and the trade unions were anxious to retain a full complement of employees and members respectively. The Government too, were anxious that both industry and the military had the numbers required, in order to sustain the needs of war. The Government then had the dilemma of keeping men in the factories, railways and mines to maintain wartime production and at the same time satisfying the demands of the British Army for more troops and more shells. The prospect of introducing large numbers of women into employment, particularly in munitions related industries, was now something beyond debate.

On 15th July, the Coalition Government introduced 'National Registration' for all those, both male and female, who were between 15-65 years of age. The first day for registration was 15th August, when the majority of the British population was required to complete a form with their personal details including age and occupation. Even a register of lodgers in lodging house had to be kept, as was a register by boarding house proprietors of their guests. Registration books were open to police scrutiny. The government was determined to have a clear indication of where potential recruits might be found.

The production of this national register was a bold step for the Government to take. Many who were opposed military conscription believed, quite rightly as it turned out, that it was the first step towards enforced recruitment, although Prime Minister Asquith denied it at the time. There were indications that the voluntary system of recruitment was beginning to fail to meet Kitchener's demand for 300,000 more men, following his initial call for 100,000 in August 1914. The voluntary system could not have been helped by the news of carnage on the Western Front reaching the notice of young men still at home. Yet neither could it have been helped by a Government pleas for men to show their patriotism in the factories while at the same time urging them to fight at the Front.

There were those who still showed their faith in voluntarism, seeing no need for conscription that hitherto had been alien to Britain's military arrangements. In June, *The Times* ran an article called the 'Triumph of Voluntary System.' The newspaper remarked with some conviction, 'The splendid wave of patriotism confirms our faith in the voluntary system, which we believe will come triumphantly through its tremendous trial and make the name of Britons illustrious in world history.'

The local trade union's position on the prospect of compulsory military conscription into the armed forces was by now becoming ambiguous. At its normal monthly meeting for June, the Mexborough and District Trade and Labour Council placed the issue on their agenda. While the Chairman, Councillor Tom Rowan, welcomed the voluntary system, the Secretary James Walton believed it was now against the country's interest to continue to resist the introduction of compulsory conscription. A resolution proposing that the 'Trade Council's' policy should continue to oppose conscription was not put to the vote. A number of members voiced the opinion that the country was now in a serious state and this was not the time to make a decision on this controversial subject. Despite this concern the 'Trades Council' continued their opposition.

The Government and its propaganda machinery continued to produce materials and posters to rally more men to the Kitchener's call. Yet the calls came not only from 'home' but also from the Front itself. The press were only to eager to print letters from the Front which demonstrated the frustration of the those fighting in the frontline towards those men they saw as evading an experience that would bring them flocking to assist them. Corporal James Chapman of the 1st York and Lancs, a regiment that had been out at the Front from the beginning of the conflict, wrote to his landlord in Catherine Street, Mexborough, a letter which was published in June. Corporal Chapman reflects; 'I was surprised to see Bill Sinclair had enlisted. I don't think he was justified as there are plenty of younger men who are lounging about and I wish they would realise what sort of job we have got here. What about the *Lusitania*? Can our young men swallow this and stay at home. I hope not'.

Similar frustration was voiced by Drummer G.H Walker of the 1/5th York and Lancs when writing home to his parents at 73, Schofield Street. 'We get The Times every week and heard about 'raiding' in Mexborough. I think if the fellows who started it would put some khaki on it would look better for them.' Private William Waddington in one of his frequent letters home to Mr Nicol B. Laidlaw, wrote of his own observation on the local Lustania riots when he remarked, 'I see trouble around Mexborough. They ought to be out here to make a row and help us move the Germans.' Drummer Walker's battalion colleague Lance Corporal H. Roberts, wrote similarly to his wife at Park Road Mexborough: 'If these single men who are walking the street today were to wake up to the facts they would not need asking a second time to fight.' Yet another man from the 1/5th Battalion of the York and Lancs, Private C. Carr, went as far as to condemn the continuation of sports at home for diverting young men's thoughts away from the slaughter taking place on foreign battlefields.

Gunner Tom Walton of the RFA, wrote to his father, James Walton, Secretary of Mexborough and District Trade and Labour Council, expressing his frustration at what he perceived was happening at home. Published in the Barnsley Chronicle of 17th July he wrote of the horrors he had just witnessed:

> 'We came out of action on Saturday which was another sight that every young man in England who had not joined up should see and I guess he would break the record to nearest recruiting office.... Think of London in ruins. Not a house standing and us coming across Trafalgar Square. Every rein blazing and every gunner and driver and fancy horses, wagons and men blown to bits, lying about the Square with shells bursting over head.'

There were continuous pleas from those who were already serving in the forces along with the production of an increasing number of official propaganda posters. These appealed to single and married men alike and to women who might influence the male with a more feminine approach to that adopted by the local recruiting sergeant. As the first anniversary of the war drew near there appears to be sense of panic that the voluntary system of recruitment was failing the nation's requirements. There were contradictory statements about the flow of recruits attesting at the Mexborough's recruiting offices. However reports tend to suggest that Sergeant J. Oddy, Mexborough's well-known recruiting sergeant, was performing his function adequately with a steady flow of new men joining up.

There had been a recruiting march on Wednesday 12th May led by an attachment of the York and Lancs and accompanied by the

Regimental Band. The weather was described as being 'favourable for the occasion'. The troops were welcomed by Councillor Winstanley and given refreshments at the Montagu Hotel, by the proprietor, Mr Frank Law, with the event being followed enthusiastically by the public. There is no report as to whether the event was successful or not. One could speculate that perhaps the level of recruitment was not what had been hoped for.

Another recruiting event quickly followed on Monday 13th June, with meetings held at both Swinton and Mexborough. Both meetings were addressed by a Colonel L.B. Hirst and preceded by a parade of the York and Lancashire Regiment's Pontefract Depot Band. The Colonel made an impassioned speech in which he took the sentiments of a well-known recruiting poster. "Men should don the khaki and show the stuff they are made of", the Colonel said. "When the soldier's little children ask him what he did in the 'Great War' he would then proudly show them his medal and say that he went as a true Britisher and fought for his country. But what would the slacker say. No I did not fight".

The single man was, by now, not the only target for the recruiting establishment; the married man was by this time clearly in their sights. Colonel Hirst's words appear to have largely fell on deaf ears. A press report on the event commented, 'We venture to think that the eloquence was wasted at Swinton where at best a few seemly eligible young men followed the audience'. However things were said to be somewhat better at the Mexborough meeting.

It appears that circumstances were difficult in terms of attracting a sufficient flow of recruits. Even the Mexborough and Swinton Home Defence Corps were struggling to attract volunteers. Early in the year, one of their meetings was so sparsely attended that Mr Nicol B. Laidlaw, the Corps Commandant, declared that the Corp's work and activities would have to be suspended.

The second annual Alexandra Rose Day in Mexborough was to be a relative success. Mexborough Feast Sunday, always on the third Sunday in June, was similarly a relative success along with the Mexborough Hospital Demonstration on the same day. The weather was favourable for such occasions which took place as usual on the Cricket Ground. Again it was the children who were more likely to be blissfully unaware of the events elsewhere in the world. Even under difficult circumstances the procession of children is reported to have been nearly a mile in length.

With the 'Feast' behind it, Mexborough prepared for the August Bank Holiday and the first anniversary of the beginning of the war. Here was an opportunity to once again attempt to rally reluctant young men to the cause of King and country. Colonel Hirst, the Barnsley and Mexborough District Recruiting Officer, set up an extensive 'Local

Recruiting Scheme'. This was to take place between 30th July and 6th August, with meetings in Mexborough, Wath, Swinton, Wombwell, Bolton and Denaby. This was clearly a massive effort to revive the dwindling recruitment figures. The meeting would be attended by military bands, many public bodies, the clergy, the Boy Scouts, the Ladies recruiting committees, recruiting officers and men who had returned from the Front and even parents of local servicemen. There were calls for assistance of owners of motors cars and for the local women to attend the meeting to distribute badges and ribbons to the new recruits. Colonel Hirst was anticipating that this effort would raise 500 recruits from every meeting held in the Northern Command area.

On 5th August Mexborough hosted a recruitment meeting and parade. The meeting took place in the Market Square, with the usual town dignitaries in attendance, in particular on this occasion, Mr William Winstanley, Dr Huey and Mr Nicol. B. Laidlaw. The primary concern of the rally was to attract men to the Royal Engineers (RE) and for this purpose the parade was led by a detachment of RE men and headed by a bugle band of the KOYLI. The meeting was as the press headlines described it, 'An Appeal to Mexborough's Manhood.' At the end of the meeting Mr Winstanley led a rousing cheer to, 'King and country and the lads who had gone to the Front.' After the rally the detachment of Royal Engineers left to travel to Doncaster by rail. The meeting of 5th was quickly followed up by another in the Hippodrome theatre the next day.

Just prior to the August Bank holiday, the Mexborough UDC received a letter from the military authorities seeking the council's assistance in raising a company of men solely from the Mexborough area. The letter read, 'Are you willing to raise a local company of soldiers of the Yorkshire and Lancashire Regiment in the Mexborough district as shown on the map in the recruiting office? Please 'wire urgently'. The Chairman of the council replied that Mexborough town's people would do their best.

On the conclusion of the anniversary recruiting campaign a large advert was placed in *The Times* of 24th August appealing to the men of Mexborough to join this proposed Mexborough Company, of the 11th York and Lancs. Recruiting sergeants were stationed at Mexborough, Conisbrough and Wath in readiness to facilitate this appeal. The advert noted that it believed local patriotism was 'a degree more intense than general patriotism.' The advert concludes by saying, 'The credit of your district is at stake. See that your district in not let down. It has poured men generously into the ranks of all branches of the Forces. It is now a company of its own. Make it a good one'.

The appeal for Mexborough's own local company was to attempt, on a smaller scale, to replicate the 'Pals' battalions that had been established mainly in other parts of the industrialised north of England. These regiments were drawn from men who lived and worked together in tightly knit communities. Barnsley had their 'Pals' battalions as did Sheffield, Leeds, Bradford and Hull. The theory behind their formation was that such men, who would have built up a bond of loyalty and comradeship, would carry this ethos on to the battlefield, invigorating them for a taste of conflict. The idea was later to prove a catastrophic failure when the 'Pals' regiments suffered enormous casualties at the Battle of the Somme in 1916. Whole communities from where these men came from suffered a collective grief which would have caused a debilitating lowering of moral of those at home.

The Recruiting Committee of the Town Council were faced with a number of difficulties in achieving the objective of raising a Mexborough company of 'Pals'. The anniversary recruiting campaign was considered a success, seeing Mexborough sending more men to the colours than any other part of the Pontefract area, but many had not chosen to join the Mexborough Company. By late August only 70 men had been recruited to the Company. Councillor Winstanley, the Chairman of the Recruiting Committee, was of the opinion that the 'cream' of the district had offered their services many weeks before. All new recruits would now be less likely to be personal friends. There also rose the difficulty of sparing men from local industry which in itself was creating difficulties in the country's attempt to mount an efficient and effective war effort on the Home Front.

It was clearly the case that many men, who were close personal friends, had already joined the colours in the initial and subsequent call from Kitchener to form a 'New Citizen's Army'. Other towns and cities had assembled their 'Pals' battalions in the early weeks of the beginning of the war. The initiative to form a Mexborough Company one year later was too late in the day to become a reality. It was a last effort to recruit local men before the introduction of compulsion. If Mexborough did not have its own 'Pals' battalion it can be argued that the nearest Mexborough came to this was within some of the York and Lancs Battalions. The 8th and 9th York and Lancs Battalions (and to a lesser extent the 6th and 10th Battalions) were to attract a good complement of Mexborough and district men. Three days after the appearance of the advert in *The Times* of 24th August calling for men to join the Mexborough Company, the 8th and 9th York and Lancs were arriving in Boulogne ready to move up to the Western Front.

Of the 50 men from Mexborough and Swinton who had been identified as being killed on 1st July 1916, the first day of the Battle of Somme, 24 were from the 8th Battalion and 14 from the 9th Battalion of the York and Lancs. The 8th Battalion, in particular, suffered one of the highest casualty rates of any unit on this fateful day, even higher than the famous Accrington Pals.

Chapter Nine

The Gallant Sixth in the Hell that was Gallipoli

Such was the lack of progress and the stalemate on the Western Front, that the British War Cabinet looked towards the possibility of other 'theatres of war' in order to make a positive breakthrough. Was there a possibility of taking Constantinople by capturing the Turkish defences along the Dardenelles Straits and in theory, eliminating Germany's ally Turkey from the war? If this was possible it would open up a sea route, by way of the Black Sea, enabling supplies to reach the Russian forces fighting the Central Powers' forces on the Eastern Front. The plan was always controversial in that resources of arms and manpower would, in the view of some, be unreasonably diverted away from efforts on the Western Front. Winston Churchill, the First Lord of the Admirality, was a keen advocate of this strategy and a key figure in influencing the go-ahead for the Gallipoli campaign which was finally authorised on 15th January 1915.

The Dardanelles expedition was to some extent in the making just before the end of 1914, when British warships bombarded the entrance to the Dardanelles Straits which included the sinking of a Turkish vessel by a British submarine. However this only served to alert the Turks to the possible future intentions of the British and by March 1915 the Turks had strengthened their artillery and laid numerous mines in the Dardanelles Straits. There were attempts to take the Straits between February and March, with attacks from both British and French warships which ended with three British Warships being sunk and others damaged. The placing of mines in the Straits, which was in places less than one mile across, had made it extremely difficult to penetrate and take out the Turkish artillery. The attempt to take the Straits by naval power was to be deemed a failure, which ended with the resignation of Churchill as the First Lord of the Admiralty.

With the failure of the naval initiative, another form of offensive was contemplated. The Turkish guns would, according to the perceived plan, be eliminated by an amphibious attack from the other side of the Gallipoli Peninsula, an attack that 'intelligence' suggested the enemy were not in a position to resist. Thus the Mediterranean Expedition Force (MEF) was assembled under the command of General Ian Hamilton. Hamilton's forces were made up of 77,000 men drawn from across the Allied forces. There were 18,000 men from the Australia and New Zealand Army Corps (ANZACs) who famously suffered some of the most ferocious fighting on the Peninsula. There was also a French Division, the British 29th Division and men from the Royal Naval Division (RND). The RND was a formation of Royal Marines and sailors trained up as infantry who were not required to serve on British warships.

Mexborough and district had contributed a good number of its men who saw service with the RND, men who were now pressed into service to fight in the Dardanelles. The local press soon recognised the part which they had played in the war. *The Times* noted in late June that the RND already had a place in history particularly for the men's gallantry in operations during the Gallipoli campaign. They were described as 'This splendid body of men' who are 'Daily winning glory at terrible cost in the effort to dominate the Dardanelles'.

Seaman Albert Robinson, from Frederick Street, Mexborough, was one of those who served with the RND, Bristol Division at Gallipoi and was wounded in the early stages.

Seaman George Hakin was another man in the RND, this time with the Drake Battalion. He was wounded in the early offensives in the Dardanelles. He suffered a bullet in the leg. Hakin wrote home to another Mexborough man, 'You can take it from me it was hot work up there (Gallipoli) and it is only British Pluck and doggedness that has enabled us to succeed so far. Everyone down here deserves a Victoria Cross (VC) and most of all the sailors.' He describes the sound of the shell burst as giving off a 'musical ring' which made him think of the picture hall, but it was evident that the young George Hakin had clearly distinguished the reality of the battlefield from the fiction of the picture house film. He continues, 'Although we have only been left the old country three months it seems like years and I am longing for the time when the world will be peace and we shall be able to rest.'

Mexborough miner, John Hepworth, was living at 39, Simpson Place (also known as the Brickyard) when he decided to enlist on 8th September 1914 at the age of nineteen. Like George Hakin, he, too, joined the Drake Battalion of the RND and served alongside his

Mexborough colleague at Gallipoli. Able Seaman Hepworth survived the horrors of Gallipoli, but he and his surviving colleagues found themselves fighting on the Western Front from November 1916 until the end of hostilities in 1918. John Hepworth's luck held and he was able to return to Mexborough and marry in 1919. He died in 1978.

Edward Lancaster Baker (Ted), whose family lived at 6, Alexandra Road, became an Able Seaman with the RND and served with the Hood Battalion's machine gun section. Ted succumbed, like many, to dysentery and was evacuated out to Alexandria to recover. He, too, was fortunate enough to survive the war and return to Mexborough.

The first landing at Gallipoli took place on 25th April, giving the Turks ample time to prepare even more solid defences as well as assembling additional troops. The Allied troops were to land on Ari Burnus (what was to become know as ANZAC Cove) and at Cape Helles. In the face of fierce resistance by the Turkish forces, attacks on these positions fell well short of their objectives. There were to be many casualties on both sides. Despite the early signs that the Gallipoli Campaign would be likely to fail, given the strong strategic position Turks were in, it was decided to launch a further offensive in August with landings at Suvla Bay.

It was decided to use fresh divisions for this renewed offensive and among these were the 6th Battalion of the York and Lancs. This battalion was one of the first 'Service' battalions to be formed at the very outset of the war in 1914. Among its number were a good few Mexborough and district lads who had responded to Kitchener's initial call in the August of 1914. One of these men was Private William Ernest Bird, or Bill as he was known to his family. Bill had arrived in Mexborough, like many young men just prior to the war, seeking work in the ever expanding coalfields of the Don and Dearne Valley area. He and his friend, Jim Hope, cycled to Mexborough from West Bromwich in 1910, with Bill first taking lodgings in Wellington Street. He quickly settled down and met Florence (Florrie) White who he was to marry on 20th July 1912. The couple soon moved into their newly rented home at 79, Victoria Road, where they lived for the rest of their lives. Bill Bird would, like his comrades, have attended one of the local Mexborough Recruiting Offices, probably the Council Office in the Market Hall or the Labour Exchange on Bank Street. Here he joined the 6th Battalion of the York and Lancs. He would have gone through the attestation certification process, swearing the oath of allegiance to the King and country, received the 'Kings shilling' and quickly sent on a journey to Pontefract Barracks. This was probably the shortest journey during his Army service. He could not have imagined at the time the longer journeys that lay ahead.

The 6th York and Lancs came into existence, under the command of Colonel F. E. Ashton, on 19th August 1914, the day Bill Bird signed his attestation papers. Private Bird was to join many other eager young recruits on that day from the Mexborough and district area. Their Battalion moved from Pontefract to the Grantham area in April before going to a camp at Witley near Godalming, Surrey. King George V and Queen Mary visited Witley Camp on 1st May and inspected the 6th Battalion remarking on how healthy the horses looked as well as giving some praise to the men themselves.

The 6th York and Lancs was one of the battalions that sailed to Gallipoli in July to reinforce the existing forces out there, after it was believed they could be spared from the British offensive on the Western Front. They landed at Sulva Bay and were soon engaged in furious bloody battles, starting on 6th August, against Turkish Ottoman Empire regiments. These battles included the Battle of Scimitar Hill and the attack on what was called Hill 60.

We are fortunate enough to know a little about Bill Bird's journey and his experiences in Gallipoli with the 6th York and Lancs. Private Bill Bird's granddaughter, Susan Shaw, who has taken a keen interest in her family's history, came across some intriguing documents that had, for many years been hidden away in the family bible. One of the documents was a letter, rewritten by Bill's wife Florrie, relating to her husband's experience during the Gallipoli Campaign. The letter was written without the use of paragraphs and is quoted as such below, yet it makes no difference to Private Birds' fascinating story:

> 'It was on 19th August (1914) that I enlisted in the 6th Battalion of the York and Lancaster Regiment and went to Pontefract on the same day. I was stationed there until September 17th then I was drafted to Grantham in Lincolnshire. We had very hot weather while there, we stopped there until Easter Monday and then marched to Rugby. It took us 3 days and we had a grand reception when we marched through Leicester. The people gave us cigs and cake, in fact they gave us all sorts of stuff. At last we got to Rugby. They billeted us in a School. We stopped there the night and the next morning we marched off to the station, we had no idea where we were going. It took us 12 hours in the train. Of course they took us a long way round. At last we landed at our camp and found that it was a place called Witley in bonny Surrey. We had some very hard work while we were there. I don't know the dates that I was granted leave. But I know I took one on my own while I was at Grantham. The reason I took it was that while I was there my daughter died. I paraded for a pass so that I could go to the funeral. But the Colour

Sergeant passed it off and said it was too late. Well I passed it off as well as I could, but it went down hard. Well shortly after that my grandmother died and they would not let me go to her funeral so I thought I would wait my time and one day I had a letter from my wife to say that the other daughter was ill. I paraded in front of the Captain for a pass but I could not get one so I got my wife to send me the fare. On the Monday there was a big route march. I did not go on it. I went to the butts with a firing party and got back about 1 o'clock and as I sat down, I thought now is the time to go, so I got changed into my clean shift and got to the station about 10 minutes to six. I had a lot of trouble to get a ticket but luck favoured me that day. I only had to wait 5 minutes for a train. Well I got home about 10 minutes to eight. They did not expect me. I had a week at home and when I got back I was tried by the C.O. I explained everything, but I got 7 days defaulters that was my first crime. I will now get back to where we were at Witley. While we were at Whitley we had a surprise visit of Lord Kitchener and later on we were received by the King and Queen. It was on the 28th June 1915 that we had orders that no one was to leave camp and we could not send any letters. We were given our thin suits and helmets. Of course when they gave us those we had a good idea where we were going. On 1st July we left Witley for Liverpool. It was in the afternoon and we were travelling all night. We passed through Birmingham, West Bromwich and we passed within 200 yards of my mother's house and as I passed I looked out of the window and wondered if ever I should see them again. Well we arrived at Liverpool at 5.30 next morning and we had a lot of stuff to carry. We marched onto the Aquitania at 7.30.pm. she was one of the biggest ships afloat it was just like a floating palace. Well they got everything aboard and she steamed out of the dock in the night and set sail for the hell upon earth place called the peninsula. We had not been sailing long before a submarine sent 2 torpedoes at us. It was 4 o'clock when it happened the first one was about 3 yards away the second about 12 yards. They would have got a good catch as there was between 8 and 9 thousand troops aboard and there was no guns on her except machine guns. Of course they were put at every corner of the ship and ready for firing in case we came upon a submarine. Well as I say, we set sail from Liverpool on the

Saturday afternoon and it was a splendid voyage. We never stopped until we got to Lemnes we landed there on 11th July we left on 23rd July for Mudros a place 15 miles from the peninsula. It was terribly hot while we were there then came the order on 6th August to get ready for moving. There was a number left back as reinforcements. All the boys went with a good heart. Although they did not know the fate that was waiting them. It was on the 6th August they landed on the right of a place called Salt Lake they had orders that not a shot was to be fired everything had to be taken by bayonet. While we were landing they were bombarding Anjas and Ashe Baba to draw the Turkish troops from Suvla Bay. It was a terrible spot was Salt Lake we named it Death Trap. We lost very heavily although we drove the Turks back about 3miles, and if there had been another Division to follow us up we should have been well on our way to Constantinople but that was where the big blunder was made. Well those that was left behind came on the next night and when we landed it was awful to see the chaps that was wounded, it was my first experience on a battlefield and it made my blood run cold. I was all day before I got over it. We sat down and had a bit of bully beef and biscuit. General Hammersley came along and he was quite pleased when he knew who we were. At last we marched to where the remainder of the Battalion were and we was not long before we set off to capture a village called Anaparta but it was too late the Turks had got their reinforcements up. It was while we were marching that a bullet missed me and killed the next chap on the spot, so I thought that was a bit of luck. At last we found out that we could not advance any further, so we all laid down in a field as we had no trenches. As night time grew on the order came for us to form a square and dig ourselves in. Well we got nicely dug in when another came for us to retire back onto another position. Well we were marching all night and in the middle of the night the order came back for us to about turn and go back to the position we had left. It was while we were going back that a mysterious thing happened. There was 2 men guiding us and our Colonel asked them where we were they could not answer so he pulled a revolver out to shoot them but before he could do so, one of our lads put a bullet in the pair of them and they turned out to be 2 Turks, it was a good job for us that we did stop else we should have been surrounded and God knows what would have happened to us. The order came to dig ourselves in again. We had only been digging half hour when the order came to advance. So we set out and the sun was telling on us all. I am sorry we lost some men too. We were surrounded by snipers and the smell from the dead and dying was awful. A chap had only to be dead about half an hour before he would be maggot eaten. Well we held that position for 2 days when the Welsh Territorial came to relieve us. We left them and we had not been gone many minutes before they started to retire and we had to fall back and take that position back again. At last we got away and we were forced to get back over to a place called Salt Lake. It was fairly a death trap the shells were flying in all directions. I shall never forget it but some of us managed to get to the beach safe. We were only out 24 hours when we had to go back, and as we were going back over Salt Lake they started to shell us again and don't forget they gave us sock.'

It is evident that Private Bird was an articulate working class man. His granddaughter also found a poem along with his description of his experiences in Gallipoli. The poem, called, *The Landing at Suvla Bay*, just may have been written by Private Bird as the poem is officially attributed to an anonymous author. A member of the 8th Battalion of the Duke of Wellington's Regiment is claimed to have written the poem, but it also attributed to a member the 8th Border Regiment. Both these other battalions fought around Suvla Bay and a number of individual battalions have placed their own character on various versions of the poem. Private Bird and his comrades had ensured that the 6th York and Lancs were clearly emphasised in one of the verses of their particular version which is called *'Our Gallant Fighters'*.

Our Gallant Fighters

You may talk of Balaclava,
And of Trafalgar Bay.
But what of the 11th Division.
That landed at Suvla Bay.

We are a part of Kitchener's army,
Some of us left parents, children and wives.
But we fought for England's glory,
Yes we fought for our very lives.

It was on the 6th of August,
We made that terrible dash.
And the Turks along the hillside,
Our boats they were trying to smash.

The order came to fix bayonets,
As out of the boats we got.
Every man there was a hero,
Who was facing the Turkish shot.

The funnels of our boats got smashed,
While the sea in parts looked red.
But we fought our way through the ocean,
To the beach that was covered with dead.

Creeping at last up the hillside,
While shot and shell around.
We made a last desperate effort,
And charged over the Turkish ground.

The Turks at last gave it up,
When they saw our bayonets play.
For they turned their backs on the British,
And retired from Suvla Bay.

There were Lincolns, Dorsets, Stafford,
And Notts and Derbies too.
The Borders were there,
The rough and ready crew.
Then we got the Manchesters,
With the Lancashire Fusiliers by their side.
The boys who came from Lancashire,
Will fill your hearts with pride.

The Yorks, East Yorks and West Yorks,
And the Duke of Wellington's as well.
We fought for England home of beauty,
Were among the lads that fell.

The fighting sixth were at it hard,
All Yorkshire lads you know,
The sixth York & Lancs were on their guard,,
And pushing back the foe.

And far away on the hillside,
Laying beneath the clay,
And some of the lads that died,
While trying to win the day.

So remember the gallant 11th Division,
Who volunteered to go.
And fight for England's glory,
Against the determined foe.

What might be argued, with some confidence, is that the above poem was written from the hand of a working class soldier, despite the doubt as to its original author.

Private Bill Bird had also written letters home, one of which survived. It was written on 23rd August, shortly after he had seen some horrendously bloody fighting. The letter begins 'My Darling Wife and Child. Just a few lines in answer to your welcome letter of this morning and to thank you for the box of cigs......I have been longing for your letters every time the mail comes'. He also asks for writing paper and envelopes in order that he can write home and for copies of the *Mexborough and Swinton Times*.

Interestingly Private Bird makes reference in his letter to a number of his comrades who are possible to identify. He mentions, 'They may be sending Percy's lot out here that is if they have not come already?' Percy is almost certainly his brother-in-law Percy Oswald Sale, a miner who also lived in Victoria Road. Percy Sale was in the 9th York and Lancs and died on the Somme in October 1916. He also refers to Charlie, again almost certainly another brother-in-law, Charles Christopher White, also a miner who worked at Manvers and lived near to Bill Bird in Victoria Road. Charlie White also died at the Battle of the Somme being one of those who fell on the first day, 1st July 1916.

Significantly Private Bird mentions in his letter his comrades, his pals, of the 6th Battalion. He wrote, 'We came out of the trenches last night after a long battle, I am sorry to say Haywood, Earp and Briggs got wounded, but not bad'. Private J.T. Earp had lived at 7, Cresswell Road, Private Haywood at 51, Dolcliffe Road.

In his letter Bill Bird also refers to another of his comrades when he remarks, 'I hope you got my letter in which I said Green was wounded, he should be going on nicely now'. This is likely to be Private F. Green who lived at 15 West Street, Mexborough, prior to joining up.

Private William Henry Briggs did not survive the battle his comrade Bill Bird described earlier and is remembered at Helles Memorial. Born in 1889, Private Briggs had joined the 6th Battalion on the same day as his friend Bill Bird and they were probably close throughout their time together in the army. He stood only just over five feet four inches tall but weighed some ten and a half stone. Bill Briggs married Catherine Higgins, a Mexborough woman two years younger than her husband, at Mexborough Parish Church in the February of 1908 and had a son John William.

Briggs' comrade Bill Bird could not have known his friend's fate when writing his letter home on 23rd August. Private Brigg's records simply record, 'Wounded and missing' and 'To be regarded for official purposes as having died on 21st August 1915'. Like many others his body was not found. His widow, who was living at 10, Foundry Lane, received a letter in February 1917, from York and Lancs H.Q. in York informing her that her husband had left 'No Effects'. There was simply nothing left for Catherine Briggs to cherish, perhaps apart from one thing. On 14th March 1916 she gave birth to William Henry Brigg's son, a boy that he was never to see. The boy was baptised on 4th April 1916 and named William Henry after his father. This sad story was a legacy of the war which was repeated in many families elsewhere.

Mrs Catherine Briggs had received 'Separation Allowance' of 17/6d and 3/6d 'Allotment Pay' deducted from her husband's pay up until 6th August 1916, after which she received a widow's pension of 18/6d. Like many who became widows as a result of the war, she no doubt found it difficult to fend for her children and struggled on the meagre pittance of an army pension. Catherine married again before the end of the war, become Mrs Bunging and moved to her new home a few 'doors' down the street to 6, Foundry Lane.

There is another reference made in Private Bird's letter, this time to a Mr and Mrs Wright, 'Tell them I hope to see them someday and I don't think it will be long'. This is probably a reference to a Mr and Mrs Henry Wright who are likely to have been Bill Bird's landlords. Henry Wright, a Mexborough engine driver, died, in his seventies, shortly after Bill's reference to him. However the reference to the Wrights could have in connection with another pal, Jesse Senior, who lived with his parents, Mr and Mrs H Wright living at 258, Wath Road. Mr Wright was a member of the Roman Terrace Working Men's Club. Private Jesse Senior is recorded as being killed on 8th August fighting on the Gallipoli Peninsula with the 6th York and Lancs in the early days of the fighting. Mrs Wright, who had remarried, hence the different surname, had five sons serving in the army.

Three days after the death of young Jesse Senior, on the 11th August, yet another 6th York and Lancs man lost his life at the carnage in Gallipoli. He was Private James Timmins who is remembered on Helles Memorial, the same as his comrades Jesse Senior and Bill Briggs. James' parents, who lived on Garden Street, received a letter from Private J.W. Johnson, a pal of his who lived at Bolton-upon-Dearne. The letter is a further reminder of what the men of the 6th York and Lancs had to endure, particularly when first landing on the Gallipoli Peninsula. Private Johnson wrote:

'I was by his side almost until I got wounded and he was alright not taking much heed of the shells and bullets whistling passed him, beyond observing necessary caution. Before we landed on the Peninsula, with the bullets pinging over the ship, Jim would pass a joke with everyone around him. The day he was killed he was carrying messages all day under very heavy fire and it was whilst he was carrying the last massage that he was sighted by a sniper.'

In sending his 'heartfelt sympathy' to James Timmin's mother and father and to his 'sweetheart', Private Johnson remarks that his comrade 'died without pain' which may have been of some comfort to loved ones.

Throughout September and October *The Times* is full of news and photographs of men who had died or who had been wounded in the Dardanelles carnage of August. The Don and Dearne Valley area suffered more than its share of casualties. Jesse Senior was the first of Mexborough's 6th York and Lancs lads to fall. Two days later, on 10th August, Private Thomas Humphries also fell. His parents lived at 5, Chapel Walk, Mexborough. Mr and Mrs Humphries had another son, Ernest, also of the 6th Battalion, who was wounded on the same day and another son Harry who had joined the 11th York and Lancs. Thomas Humphries is remembered on the Dioran Memorial.

More wounded Mexborough men were to be reported in the local press. Mexborough's Private Clarence Whitham of the 6th Battalion lived at 7, Orchard Street. Clarence was said to be only sixteen years of age when he enlisted in September 1914. Private Whitham was in the forefront of the 6th August offensive when he was wounded. In a letter home to his mother he described how the Battalion landed at Sulva Bay at 11.30 at night so as not to alert the Turkish enemy. The Battalion were ordered not use rifle shot, but fight with bayonets. Whitham wrote, 'Our company commander got killed while leading us and several of my mates got killed as well.' He goes on to describe how he got shot in the shoulder and was lucky not to be blown to an atom and remarks, 'I saw six poor fellows blown right into the air, legs, arms and heads flying in all directions.' To this youthful soldier these dreadful scenes must have been unimaginable when he first left his home in Mexborough for Pontefract Barracks less than a year before.

Private Lewis Aubrey of the Kings Own Scottish Border Regiment, who lived at 34, Lorna Road, was wounded in the arm during the August fighting. He wrote home to his parents, on 22nd August, while in a Hospital in Malta. He recalls his experiences on the night of 10th August, 'We had been out on the night to bury the Turks because of the smell. I got caught on the barbed wire and was forced to crawl back when I was caught by a Turkish bomb'.

Private Walter Bennett another member of the 6th Battalion York and Lancs, lived on Glasshouse Lane, Mexborough. A lad, who had not yet reached the age of nineteen, was reported to be the son of 'Tip' Bennett 'The most brilliant footballer from Mexborough', who for a number of years captained Barnsley Football Club. Walter's left leg was so shattered during the fighting that surgeons were forced to amputate in order to save his life.

Yet another 6th Battalion man, Private W. Shenton of Clayfield Road, a married man, was wounded by shrapnel on 31st August. *The Times* is full of similar reports of casualties from south Yorkshire who were attached to the 6th Battalion York and Lancs.

On 28th July, reinforcements were sent out to the Dardanelles on the Royal Edward, a commandeered Canadian passenger ship. At Avonmouth 1,367 officers and men embarked for service with the 29th Infantry Division. These numbers included a good many men of the RAMC. The transport ship arrived in Alexandria on 10th August and then set sail for Moudras, a staging point for vessels on their way to operations in the Dardanelles. On 13th August, the Royal Edward was hit by two torpedoes from the German U-boat UB14. The ship took only six minutes to sink, taking with it nearly 1,000 men to their deaths, although reports of the death toll varies. It is said that about 500 men, which included crew members, were picked up by a passing hospital ship and other vessels in the area. Local newspapers reported that eight men from Wath and West Melton went down with the Royal Edward. They were men all serving with the RAMC and included Corporal T.H. Wild and Privates Williams, A. Clarke, John Allan Mansbridge, Enoch Garbett and Lance Corporal Thomas James Pyott.

Deaths from the Royal Edward sinking also included another RAMC man, the twenty year old Private John Galbraith Hunter, who lived on Highwoods Road. He is remembered on the Helles Memorial in the Dardanelles but does not appear on either the Swinton or Mexborough memorials. Private Hunter's RAMC colleague Corporal Wilson Baldwin, who also lived on Highwoods Road, was reported as being one of those who were fortunate to survive. Corporal Baldwin was a member of the Wesleyan Chapel on Roman Terrace.

On Sunday 19th September a memorial service took place at the Primitive Methodist Chapel in Mexborough for yet another RAMC victim of the sinking of the Royal Edward. On this occasion the congregation gathered to remember the life of Private John W. Smith. The congregation included representatives from the local St John Ambulance Brigade, an organisation of which John had been a member.

Mexborough and district paid a heavy price for Britain's involvement in the Gallipoli Campaign. *The Times* of 16th September 1915, in an editorial, headlined 'The Gallant Sixth', pays testament to the contribution of the 6th Battalion York and Lancs with these words:

> *'The 6th York and Lancs suffered severely in the general fighting at the Dardanelles and their losses come home especially to this district from which so many fine lads went to share its fortune. Probably this district has been more hit by the splendid sacrifice of the 'Sixth' than by any other section of casualties since the Mons fighting and the bombardment of the 1/5 York and Lancs and the RND in the early stages of Gallipoli.'*

The high casualty rate began to impress upon the minds of the military authorities, in both the Dardanelles and Britain, that the campaign in Gallipoli might well be a disastrous misadventure. On 16th October, Kitchener ordered Sir Ian Hamilton to return to home to England. On his return he briefed the British War Cabinet on his assessment of whether or not the continuation of the Gallipoli Campaign was feasible. Hamilton never returned to the Dardanelles, he was replaced by Sir Charles Munro who took over the command of the MEF. When Munro arrived on the Peninsula he reported back to the War Cabinet, putting forward a convincing argument that the campaign should be terminated and the Allied forces withdrawn. Kitchener, who visited the area himself, was of the same opinion. He had at the same time wanted to withdraw some British and French troops for service in Salonika which would have weakened the Gallipoli forces still further. By the beginning of early November, Munro recommended the evacuation of the Peninsula. This was confirmed by the British Cabinet on 7th December and thus this disastrous misadventure was about to come to an abrupt end.

By the end of August, Hamilton had decided on a defensive strategy when the Bulgarians entered the conflict in support of the Central Powers thus assisting the German's in their efforts to re-arm the Turks. The 6th York and Lancs had occupied Jefferson's Post on the Karakol Dagh during the months of September and October. Here Turkish snipers were busy causing further British casualties, despite the official war diary of the Battalion reporting there was no action during these months. It wasn't just snipers who created danger; severe heat and poor sanitation and an outbreak of dysentery killed and incapacitated many on both sides.

The 6th York and Lancs had another two of its comrades, associated with Mexborough, to mourn before they were able to finally depart from the hell of Gallipoli. One of them was Private Robert Carroll, a former engine cleaner employed by the Great Central Railway at Mexborough Locomotive Depot. Private Carroll was just 20 years of age and died on 12th September. His parents lived at 158, Church Street, Redcliffe, Manchester, but he had been lodging in Mexborough before enlisting in 1914. He is remembered in Gallipoli and on the Mexborough railway station memorial. The other was Private Harry Oxer who died on 24th October and is remembered along with Private Carroll at Hill 10 Cemetery, Gallipoli. He was from Swinton and a former pupil at the Swinton Bridge Council School and is remembered on the Swinton War Memorial

The conditions in which the men of the 6th York and Lancs were living is perhaps encapsulated in a letter written home to Barnsley by Private Thomas Gomersal shortly before his death in November. Thomas wrote:

> 'Things are pretty quite out here, but we have plenty of hard work digging trenches. We are out all night and it is very tiring. We never get much sleep. I think it is time we had a rest for we have been in the firing line for 16 weeks. Just fancy I have been sleeping on the ground ever since we left England with only one blanket so you can guess we have a hard bed.'

Private Gomersal ended his letter by thanking those at home for sending insect powder.

The withdrawal from Gallipoli was a massive strategic operation with the need to evacuate 80,000 men and tonnes of stores and materiels. It was hindered by continued sniper fire and heavy rain at Sulva Bay, where some men met their death through drowning. As far as the 6th Yorks and Lancs were concerned, their withdrawal proceeded on 10th December.

One of the last Mexborough men to die in the Gallipoli Campaign was Able Seaman Marsden Walker, a member of the 4th Platoon 'D' Company Howe Battalion of Royal Naval Reserve. He was killed in action sustaining multiple shell wounds on 13th December during the evacuation. Sub Lieutenant J.C. Hilton recorded these words in his diary, 'While I was away from camp several shells fell in our lines. One fell in the Howe gallery and killed a boy of 18; Born 4/5/1897. A railway servant. He lived with his father, Albert, at 52, Market Street, Mexborough, Yorkshire'. Walker is not remembered on the Mexborough station memorial, but may have been employed by the Midland Railway

Company rather than by the Great Central Railway Company. The employees of the Great Central Railway at Mexborough subscribed towards the erection of the memorial. on Mexborough station but there is no such local memorial for the men of the Midland Railway. However, there are other references in *The Times* that Marsden Walker had worked in his father business as an assistant butcher, which is more likely to have been the case. His father was Albert Marsden the well-known Mexborough butcher.

Three days after the death of Marsden Walker, another Mexborough man was killed during the days occupied by the evacuation. He was Private William John Haigh, another member of the 6th York and Lancs. A good deal of Private Haigh's army records survive, which enables us to evaluate a little of his life. He was a tallish man for the times, being near 5 feet 9 inches tall. Born in 1881 he worked as a carter, quite possibly on the railway. When living at 8, Quarry Street, Mexborough, he decided to join the army on 16th November 1914 in response to Kitchener's call. He was 33 years of age. Like many other Mexborough men he attested in front of Recruiting Sergeant Oddy. Private Haigh's attestation papers were witnessed by Justice of the Peace and well-known worthy Christopher Ward. We know that William Haigh was illiterate from the fact that he was not able to sign his name on his attestation papers making his 'mark' with a cross.

What motivated Haigh to join the army may have been poverty rather than patriotism. Records show he did not take kindly to the discipline of army life. His conduct record sheets far out-numbered that of the average soldier. While stationed at Harrogate with the 11th Reserve Battalion of the York and Lancs, Private Haigh was absent from duty from 28th February until 2nd March 1915. For this offence he received seven days 'Confined to Barracks' (CB). The army must have already formed of the opinion that they were dealing with a difficult soldier for they took the precaution of ensuring Haigh had an extra guard on this occasion.

With his transfer to the Farnley Camp, Haigh's discipline did not improve. Leaving the camp on the evening of 30th May he made the decision to make his way back to Mexborough, where he was apprehended by the civil police on the evening of 4th June. For this offence he received six days field punishment. At the end of June, Private Haigh decided once again to leave the camp in the evening in another attempt to see his family. As before, the civil police in Mexborough arrested him, this time at around seven o'clock in the morning which suggested he was able to spend the night with his wife and three children. For this offence he was given ten days CB and 96 hours detention. The military by this time must have been fully aware that the soldier they were dealing was unlikely to adapt to army life. Within two weeks of his last offence he broke out of Farnley Camp, he returned but this time under the influence of alcohol. On this occasion he was up before a Lieutenant Colonel Quill. Haigh's punishment was more severe this time; he faced 168 hours detention and fourteen days CB.

This difficult, reluctant soldier, as the military would have seen it, was finally moved to Penkridge Bank Camp in Staffordshire to undertake his last days of training. While at Penkridge Bank, Private Haigh 'overstayed his pass' from 9th October and was again punished with 168 hours detention and ten days CB handed out once more by the now familiar figure of Lieutenant Colonel Quill. On every occasion that Haigh was disciplined he forfeited a number of days pay.

Speculation leads one to think that Private Haigh's next move was one that the commanding officers of the 11th York and Lancs deemed to be a solution to Haigh's defiant conduct. On the 25th October he was examined and passed fit for active service. A decision was made to attach him to the 6th York and Lancs for service with the MEF in Gallipoli. There is no record of when Private Haigh embarked from England and arrived in Gallipoli but it may be fair to assume it would have been around mid-November. By this time the British 29th Division was contemplating withdrawal from the Peninsula and Private Haigh might have believed he had some hope of surviving the bloodbath which he would have been made aware of. It can only be speculated, but it is likely that the military's decision to send Haigh to the living Hell of Gallipoli was a punitive action. Here, far away in this inhospitable country it would not be easy to go absent without leave and to find his way back to his loved ones in Mexborough.

There is no record of when Private Haigh received the severe wounds of which he eventually died on 16th December. After receiving his wounds he was moved to a Military Hospital in Cattonened, Malta and it was here he passed away. The last Mexborough man of the 6th York and Lancs had given his life in the service of his country on the bloody Gallipoli Peninsula.

John Haigh's wife, Eunice and their three children were, at the time of John's death, living at 15, Cross Church Street, Mexborough. It's likely that Mrs Haigh was illiterate, for she appears to have had a guardian, a Mrs Sarah Breeze of 24, Main Street who dealt with all her correspondence. Eunice Haigh's correspondence from the army authorities included a letter telling her that the only personal property of her husband to be recovered was a photograph. The other was a letter advising her she would receive a War Widow's Pension of 20/6d with effect from 10th July 1916. Mrs Eunice Haigh had probably lived in poverty all her life and it is unlikely that from now on life for her would improve.

Private Haigh, like fellow Mexborough man Able Seaman Marsden Walker, was unlucky not to have survived, for the very last troops were evacuated from the Dardanelles in early January of 1916.

General Sir Charles Munro achieved the only success of the entire Campaign. He oversaw the evacuation on the final day on the Peninsula and with the aid of some deceptive strategies managed to depart from Gallipoli without further loss of life.

As for the 6th Battalion of the York and Lancs, the fortunate survivors sailed to Alexandria, then to Port Said and on to El Ferdan by February 1916. Later in 1916 the Battalion found itself posted to France to take up its engagements on the Western Front which by this time was considered to be the decisive theatre of war.

The Dardanelles debacle will always be considered by many as the one of the biggest blunders in British military history, notwithstanding the Somme offensive of 1916. It suffered from poor planning and was incompetently managed. This futile exercise was finally aborted at a cost of thousands of casualties. The total number of casualties on the Allied side is estimated to have been about 265,000 men of which 46,000 of them died either killed in action or of wounds or sickness. The Turkish casualties are said to have been even greater.

Chapter Ten

Flames, Gas, Death and Advancing Nowhere

The ill-fated Gallipoli Campaign ended in an appalling loss of life and without gain. Similar tragedies were a feature of the Western Front offensives throughout 1915. On the Western Front in 1915, German's were settled into positions that occupied the high ground with well-fortified defences and with effective machine gun positions which were a constant source of frustration to the Allied forces. The spring and summer of 1915 saw further Allied attempts to break these defences, push the Germans back and negate their gains of 1914.

The village of Hooge was just two miles east of Ypres, along the Menin Road which passes 'Hell Fire Corner' and was one of the most dangerous places on the Ypres Salient. On 19th July the British exploded a large mine under the German positions, leaving a massive crater around Hooge. The British infantry were, as a result of the destruction caused by the explosion, able to capture Hooge with relative ease. Eleven days later on 30th July, the Germans launched an attack using a terrifying weapon, the flamethrower, for the first time against the British. Although the weapon only caused minimal death the demoralising affect upon Allied troops was significant, allowing the German forces to easily take back their positions at Hooge.

Trench warfare in 1915 was one of stalemate with attack, counter-attack, success and failure. The British regained Hooge, by this time reduced to rumble, on 9th August. It was this offensive of 9th August that claimed the life of former Silverwood Collery miner and 'Sherwood Forester,' Private Thomas Ward. Thomas lived at 1, Athron Row with his wife and five children.

The next British major offensive was to take place around the French coal-mining town of Loos, about 40 miles south of Ypres. Commander Douglas Haig was not convinced of the feasibility of this operation. He was conscious of the strong fortifications assembled by the German forces and the difficult terrain which would have to be negotiated. Haig was also unconvinced about the ability of the existing strength of his artillery, including the availability of supplies and quality of shells with which to launch such an important offensive. However Haig was overruled by his Commander in Chief, Sir John French, who believed the numerical supremacy of the British would be the decisive factor. Additional Territorials and for the first time men from the 'New Army' had arrived at the Front, including Mexborough and district men of the York and Lancs and KOYLI regiments.

The Battle of Loos began on 25th September following a four day bombardment of the German lines. Before the troops went over the parapet, 250,000 shells were fired into the German positions. The British force's numerical superiority was, as Haig believed, initially an important factor in the battle, but the BEF's first use of gas was also a key factor. Not convinced that the bombardment of the German lines would be entirely successful, Haig ordered the release of 5,100 cylinders of chlorine gas at 5.15am on the morning of 25th. One of the best known events of the Battle of Loos was the less than successful nature of the gas attack. At various periods during the attack the wind direction changed, causing the gas to drift back into some of the British trenches. This was to affect over 2,600 of the advancing British troops, completely immobilising them from the offensive, although it caused only a few to die from gas poisoning. The gas, although said to be too small in quantity was, however, enough to see any German resistance collapse. This was helped by the primitive nature of the German gas masks, which at that time gave poor protection to its troops. By late evening the British had achieve significant gains including capturing the town of Loos. The strategic redoubt named Hill 70 was attacked by the British but was never sufficiently held by the BEF's in their efforts to break through to the second line of German trenches.

Often, breaking of the German first lines was achieved with relative ease. However, exploiting these gains and advancing behind them to take the strategically well-fortified German positions on high ground was a different matter. By 26th September, the Germans were able to launch counter-attacks with the German machine gun defences scything through the British in a way that was later witnessed at the Battle of the Somme in 1916. During this German counter-attack there was an absence of artillery support for the British troops. German machine gunners, seeing the slaughter of British troops, had difficulty in believing that men could be sacrificed in such a cavalier way.

Regiments containing Mexborough and district men, namely the 9th and 10th KOYLI and the 10th York and Lancs saw action at Loos. The 10th York and Lancs sailed from Folkestone on 10th September, arriving in the early hours of the next morning at Boulogne in readiness to move up to the front line for what was to be a bloody attack on the German second lines. The 9th KOYLI also arrived from England to take part in the same battle. Both battalions were newly arrived in the war zone and were to get their very first experience of actual warfare as a part of the BEF's 21st Division. The Division faced the immediate difficulty of reaching the front lines while travelling through the village of Loos itself. Their transport was slow, owing to the necessity for it to proceed in single file along difficult, rain-soaked roads. They were exposed on open ground which was heavily shelled while they were carrying heavy equipment, which was subsequently blown to pieces. One observer remarks that the troops were in 'no condition to endure prolonged strain'.

The 10th York and Lancs Battalion did not reach the outskirts of Loos until 8.30pm on 25th August. Here they watched the first casualties drifting back from the first day of the attack. Four companies of the 10th Battalion attacked towards Hill 70 in the early hours of the next morning, finding themselves having to dig in with entrenching tools at just before dawn. They were sighted by the German artillery and shelled, causing the four companies to lose formation in the confusion. Despite this, two companies were ordered to attack the slope of Hill 70 at 6.30pm.

In one of Conan Doyle's account of the attack at Loos, he cites the words of an Observation Officer as he watched the 10th York and Lancs advance towards the enemy lines. 'Their lines came under the machine guns as soon as they were clear of the Wood (Bois Hugo). They had to lie down. Many of course were shot down. After a bit the line went forward again and they had to go down again. Forward a little then down until the last five gallant figures rose up and struggled forward till they too went down.' The 10th York and Lancs had misunderstood their orders in the confusion of battle and were at the point of exhaustion and for this they suffered the consequences. The consequence being the Battalion's casualty figures were 14 officers and 309 other ranks killed. This included 'C' Company losing all its officers and a total of 69 killed or died of wounds.

On 27th September, the Yorkshiremen of the 9th KOYLI and 10th York and Lancs were moved out of the line, having suffered enormous casualties. By 28th September, the Battle of Loos had stuttered, with the British basically retreating to their original starting positions. The two days of intense fighting had seen 6,000 British soldiers lose their lives. The Germans recaptured ground in the following days, with the British making a final offensive between 13th to 19th October in an attempt to retake the ground captured by the German counter-offensive. From then on, the coming winter conditions dictated that the Battle of Loos should go no further. It ended with the British very much where they had been before the attack. Little had been gain at a cost of 50,000 British casualties.

Field Marshal Sir John French had been under criticism for his handling of earlier operations in 1915. Even French's supporters in the Government and the Army were unable to support him further and the decision to relieve him of the Command of the BEF was made. He was replaced by Douglas Haig in the December. Possibly not to provoke any demoralisation amongst its readership, the Barnsley Chronicle of 18th December described Sir John French's dismissal in this way, 'Sir John French being unable any longer to endure the strain of the Chief Commander of the British Army in France and Flanders, has at his own request been relieved of the post and has accepted the post of Chief Commander of the troops stationed in the UK with a seat in the House of Lords'.

The ordinary infantryman at Loos had no choice but to endure the strain of the battles they had faced. Among those killed on 26th September was Private Harold Stead of the 13th Northumberland Fusiliers, a regiment who fought alongside the 10th York and Lancs and the KOYLI Battalions in the battle for Loos. Harold's mother, Olivia Stead, while living at 51, Dodsworth Street, received the news of his death. Harold had worked at Mexborough Locomotive depot (the Plant). He is remembered on the Mexborough station memorial and alongside many of his comrades on the Loos Memorial. Olivia Stead was to hear, just twelve months later, of the death of another son, Newson on 29th September 1916.

There were two other local men of the 10th York and Lancs who died while fighting around the village of Loos. One was Lance Corporal Robert Vernon Truelove and the other, Lance Corporal Tom Beech. Truelove was born at Rawmarsh in 1896, came to Mexborough with his father Robert John, (a farrier) worked as a grocer's assistant and lived in the family home at 44, Church Street (known as Greno House) along with his mother Edith, three sisters and two brothers. Lance Corporal Truelove enlisted at Doncaster on 26th September 1914 with the KOYLI but transferred to the 10th York and Lancs on 1st October of the same year. Robert Vernon was a big man, for the time, standing nearly 5 feet 10 inches tall and weighing just over ten stone. He must have cut a fine figure in his army uniform. His official army records recorded him as 'Missing in the field' on 10th October. This was later revised to, 'Accepted as dead for official purposes' on 26th September. He was one of 69 men of the 10th York and Lancs who had died trying to secure this tiny piece of elevated ground named Hill 70. Lance Corporal Vernon was hoping to make a career in farming, but this aspiration and his life was cut short at Loos. He was just 21 years of age.

Lance Corporal Tom Beech, a miner, also died on 26th September after originally being reported as missing. Tom was from Swinton, where he lived with his wife, Elsie, who he had married in 1909 and his four children at 16, William Street. He had enlisted at the age of 27, with the 10th York and Lancs at Mexborough on 14th October 1914. Tom was said to have been well-known in the Mexborough and district area. He was described by *The Times* as a 'clever footballer' who had played outside left for both Mexborough Town and Denaby United. A comrade had written to his wife that he had seen her husband falling to the ground wounded. She would no doubt have had an extremely anxious time contemplating Tom's fate. Little can be gathered from Tom Beech's army records. We know that he had an older brother, William, who was promoted to Lance Corporal on 1st June a few weeks before leaving England for France and that his wife received a pension of just 22/6d (about £1.12p) for herself and four children. He is remembered alongside his fellow Lance Corporal and comrade, Robert Vernon, at the Loos Memorial.

Three other men from the 10th York and Lancs who escaped death, but who were wounded at Hill 70 were Privates W.Wright, J. Mason and C.L Schofield. Private Wright, who lived at 2 Cambridge Street, was hit by shrapnel and was evacuated back to the UK where he spent time in a Edinburgh hospital He was another keen footballer, having played for both Mexborough Town and South Kirby. Private J. Mason had lived at 19, Wragby Row, Wath Road. Private Schofield, who had six brothers serving in the forces, sustained wounds to the arm and head and he, too, was evacuated to the UK also spending time in an Edinburgh hospital. He was just nineteen at the time and had lived at 136, White Lee Road. There were many other local men from the Dearne and Don Valleys among the casualties fighting at Loos with the 10th York and Lancs.

The 9th KOYLI suffered considerably fewer casualties at Loos than their fellow south Yorkshiremen attached to the 10th York and Lancs. They suffered no loss of officers but 13 other men were killed together with 167 wounded and a further 34 were reported as missing. Among those to die was Mexborough man Private Peter Clarke, killed in action on 27th August, shortly before his battalion moved out of the line. He was originally reported as missing. Press reports stated that a Mr and Mrs Foster of 32, Oliver Street, with whom Peter once resided, were anxious for news of his whereabouts having heard nothing from the War Office. One of Peter's comrades had told the Fosters that Peter was among one of those in the forefront of an assault at Loos. Private Clarke's comrade noticed that he had disappeared and looked around for him but he was never to be seen again.

The 8th and 9th York and Lancs had arrived in France on 26th August. They travelled by train via Rouen, Etaples, Abbeville and on to Audriques. Here they de-trained for a place called Nordasques where they were billeted. From here the men could the hear rumble of the guns for the first time. Finally they settled into billets at Steenbecque where they took part in training during extremely poor weather conditions of continual rain. They were training in readiness for action in the big offensive at Loos along with many other 'New Army' men. The Battalions were ordered to advance up to the Front in early September.

On 25th September, the first day of the offensive, the 8th and 9th York and Lanc found themselves in reserve, 2,000 yards behind the front line at La Vesse and Rue Marle. They came under heavy artillery fire and experienced their first casualties of the war. One of these was Lance Corporal Charles Abey who was born in Market Rasen in Lincolnshire, but had joined the 9th Battalion at Mexborough. Both Battalions were warned that they might be sent into action to support the other active units but this order was never given. The ineffective use of reserves at Loos was believed to be critical factor in the failure to break the German second lines

There are four Calladines remembered on Mexborough's War Memorial. The first of this family was lost at the Battle of Ypres earlier in May. The catastrophe at Loos was to take one more. Private Arthur Calladine died at Loos while fighting with the 2nd Battalion Northumberland Fusiliers. Arthur wrote a letter to his father, addressed to 3, The Times Office Yard, Mexborough, shortly before his death on 1st October. The letter remarked that he had not slept in a bed since he arrived at the Front but appeared to be particularly proud of his commitment to the British cause. 'When I get home I can tell them all I have done my bit for my King and country and for home as well. I should not like to see in England what I see every day out here.' Arthur then made the, by now familiar, plea for those at home to join him and his comrades. 'All who can ought to come and help. You in England do not know what war is, but we do and don't forget it.' Arthur Calladine never saw home again and with it the comfort he longed to experience once more. He is remembered at Loos Memorial along with fellow Mexborough man Private George Morley of the KOYLI's who also died on 1st October.

The 9th KOYLI were moved out of the line at Loos on Monday 27th September to a place of relative safety. By 8th October they had moved into billets but then quickly moved up into the trenches south of Ypres at a place known as Ploegsteert Wood. They occupied these trenches from 14th to 18th October. According to their War Diary, the situation in this area was described as 'quiet'. However, their War Diary makes reference at this time to one 'Other Rank' killed on 15th October, this man being the only 9th KOYLI man killed in the trenches at this time. He was Swinton born Private Horace Shaw, who had attended Swinton Bridge School and is said to have played football for Swinton Town. He moved to Mexborough where he enlisted while living in Britain Street, but moved back to Swinton where he lived with his wife and four children.

Private Horace Shaw was by religion a Wesleyan. Mrs Shaw received a letter from the Battalion's Wesleyan Chaplain, detailing how Horace met his death. 'He was shot early this morning by a sniper in the trenches. He died to help secure your safety and all your young ones.' Horace Shaw's comrade Private Sugden also sent a letter of sympathy. In trying to give Mrs Shaw some comfort, he mentioned that Horace was 'buried in a pretty little cemetery'.

Later in October, a former engine cleaner at the Mexborough 'Loco', the 21 year old Herbert Hakin, met his death in a very unfortunate way. Attesting at Rotherham, Herbert joined the ranks of the 1/5th York and Lancs in November 1914. He arrived with his Battalion in France in April 1915 which was fighting around Ypres. On the morning of 9th October, Private Hakin was operating a sniperscope, a rifle that operated on the principle of a periscope allowing the operator to stay below the parapet whilst sniping the enemy. Many types of this new device were used in the British Army from the early months of the war. The weapon was very much a 'Heath Robinson' affair often being constructed by amateur inventors. The weapon was called by a variety names at the time of its introduction having no one recognised name. Later patented designs were made by the Royal Engineers in their workshops at Bethune in France. There was always a practical problem with them, as the trigger and the bolt were awkward to reach making them difficult to operate. This problem was responsible for the accidental death of Herbert Hakin. He was in a trench about 8.55am on sentry duty using the sniperscope against the German lines. Private Hakin's military records survive and give a good account of what happened. He was alongside a Lance Corporal Parish who placed the sniperscope over the parapet in readiness to fire. A sandbag had obstructed the Lance Corporal's view so he moved the weapon towards Herbert Hakin to get a clearer view and at the same time Parish brought the sniperscope down searching for the safety catch when the rifle went off killing Private Hakin.

A 'Court of Enquiry' took place on 16th October, the enquiry being a necessary requirement for the military authorities to establish whether or not there had been foul play. The proceedings appear to have been a cursory affair, taken 'in the field', in the present of a captain and a first and second lieutenant as presiding officers. Evidence was given by Lance Corporal Parish, another lance corporal and two privates who were on sentry duty with Private Hakin during the incident. The witnesses suggested that Hakin had told Parish to bring the sniperscope towards him in order that he could release the safety catch, it was at this point the rifle went off. The verdict, unsurprisingly, was one of accidental death. The findings of the Court of Enquiry, was officially typed up on 21st October, with Brigadier Lieutenant Dawson making the very brief, six line comment, 'I cannot help thinking that sufficient care was not taken in the handling of the sniperscope'. There was no recommendation as to the future handling of the weapon. The final word went to Major James E. Knight whose comments state that, 'After reading the foregoing statements I am of the opinion that Private Hakin met his death while on duty from accidental causes and that Lance Corporal Parish was in no way to blame'. Private Herbert Hakin had lived with his mother Annie and his late father Thomas at 42, Dodsworth Street. As a former employee of the Great Central Railway he is remembered on the Mexborough Station War Memorial, although unfortunately his name has been mis-spelt Hackin. One can only imagine this mistake deeply upset his mother and others who were close to this young man, a man who had not reached 22 years of age upon his tragic death.

Mexborough itself saw two military funerals taking place in 1915. On Friday afternoon 3rd September the first ever military funeral, with full military honours, took place at Mexborough Cemetery. This was the funeral of Private H. Sykes, a member of the recruiting staff at Wath-on-Dearne, a man who had recruited many to the 11th York and Lancs. He had been billeted at 6, White Lea Road whilst undertaking his role at Wath. Private Sykes had contracted a chill and died in the Montagu Hospital on 31st August. The funeral possession is said have started from Private Sykes' billet in White Lea Road accompanied by about 50 men of the York and Lancs and the band of the 1st York and Lancs from Pontefract Barracks. The procession was described as impressive as it passed through Mexborough town by way of Swinton Road, High Street, Bank Street and Adwick Road. As this was a funeral with full military honours, the coffin was draped in the 'Union Jack', three volleys were fired over it by the firing party and the 'Last Post' was sounded by buglers. Notably in attendance from Mexborough was Mr William Winstanley, the Chair of the Council and Mexborough's own recruiting officer, Sergeant J. Oddy.

The other military funeral took place on Thursday 14th October, again at Mexborough Cemetery. It was of Private Lee Danks an 'old' soldier of the York and Lancs who had often been engaged in assisting with recruiting at Mexborough's Hippodrome Theatre. He had lived at 56, Warmsworth Street in Denaby Main and was a member of the Denaby Ambulance Corps and well-known in the district. Private Danks died on 9th October in a Sunderland hospital with a diseased foot at the age of 43. The band of the York and Lancs again attended the funeral but there is no indication that full military honours were given to Private Danks on this occasion. What *The Times* does mention is that, as with Private Sykes' funeral, the event attracted a large crowd. Nevertheless, the public were excluded from the ceremony, owing to serious damage taking place at the previous military funeral. No details of this incident were given.

Privates Sykes and Danks are among the small number of servicemen who are remembered in Mexborough Cemetery with a Commonwealth War Graves Commission headstone.

One Mexborough man who has no memorial locally or abroad in a foreign field is Private Fredrick Turton who had lived at 116, Doncaster Road. This 29 year old, married man, with two children, had worked at Cadeby Main Colliery before joining the KOYLI Regiment. He was serving out in France when he suffered frost bite after which it was decided to ship him back to England to convalesce. He boarded the hospital ship HMHS Anglia at Calais bound for Dover on 17th November, but at about 12.30pm on that day the ship sunk after hitting a mine laid by a German U-boat. Information varies on the number of casualties, but it is believed of the 390 on board, 134 lost their lives, the unfortunate Fred Turton being one of them. Fred Turton is remembered on the Hollybrook Memorial, Southampton.

Chapter Eleven

Towards Social Upheaval and
Another Christmas at War

Registration for the National Registration Scheme took place in August, with the work of collecting the relevant information in the district being undertaken by teachers from local schools. The scheme, initially only seen as a half-way house to conscription, was to become the catalyst for change towards a system of military conscription, which in turn caused fundamental change in the social and economic life of the country. The results of this registration process were available as early mid-September when the registers were able to identity the numbers of men eligible to be considered for military service. Lord Derby's 'Report on Recruiting' identified that there were 2,179,231 single men of military age and of these only about 1,150,000 had attested. The figures for married men was not significantly different to that of single men, which gave rise to Lord Derby's assertion that every effort should be made to encourage single men to join the colours before their married colleagues.

A list of canvassers was drawn up for the urban district area of Mexborough, the task being to interview those who had not previously volunteered for service and to make them aware of the obligations under the 'Derby Scheme'. They were also tasked to make an assessment of the willingness of an individual to attest. The list of canvassers was made up largely of dignitaries and 'worthies' who were allocated various streets listing the numbers of eligible recruits in each street. The highest number of potential recruits was 71, in Garden Street, Flowitt Street, Glasshouse Lane, Simpson's Place, Raikes Street and Creswell Buildings.

The canvasser for these streets was to be a Mr J.P. Wright. The next highest was of 61 men possible for military service, canvassed by Mr Neild, taking in Herbert Street, Hirst Gate, Melton Street, Crossgate, Harlington Lane, Cross Church Street, Quarry Lane, Hewitt Street, Montague Street, Makin Street and Ferryboat Lane.

Dr J. Gardner had the lightest load in terms of his canvasser's role, just twelve potential recruits in Pym Road. He shared Pym Road with Dr J. Ram who was also responsible for Milton Road, Auckland Road and Carlyle Street. Dr V. E. Dodsworth was also a canvasser as was the Headmaster of Mexborough Secondary School, Mr Thomas Wilson Ireland.

The list of canvassers who were to cover other areas of the town also included six local councillors. It appears during this part of the war in particular, the town's local councillors had been extremely busy with the demands the war was placing upon them This can certainly be said of Councillor and Headteacher William Winstanley. The other councillors chosen as canvassers were Councillors John Thomas Rowen, John Ward, Chris Ward, John H. Watson and Arthur Goulding.

Throughout the war there had been heavy moral pressure on eligible men to join the colours. The pressure included the production of white feathers, an intensive poster campaign appealing to a man's conscience and appeals to women to ensure that the message was reinforced. The 'Derby Scheme' simply added more of this moral pressure upon the reluctant recruit. Now he was confronted on the doorstep by a local 'worthy'. All the members of the canvassing team commenced their work on the weekend of 20th November. Being a few weeks prior to Christmas, this was probably not the most convenient or welcomed time for the canvassers to inform male members of the household the news that they may shortly be heading for the Western Front.

In early November it was announced that khaki armlets, embroided with a crown, would be issued to men who offered themselves for military service. These were to be issued to men who had enlisted but were still waiting to be called up but were issued also to men who had offered themselves, but were deemed to be medically unfit, as well as men who were invalided out of the forces with good character. These armlets, each with their own distinctive marks, were a way of distinguishing those who had offered themselves for service, from those still reluctant, for whatever reason, to offer themselves to the military. This was a clear move to further pressurise men who had yet to attest.

The Times editorials were now reconsidering the newspaper's position on the voluntary system and giving some serious thought to compulsion. The newspaper believed that the register was not just a shapeless set of statistics and facts, but also contained deposits of information of great value. Seeing registration as the abandonment of the voluntary system, *The Times* noted, 'The day of grace enjoyed by the young man, particularly single, who has deliberately shirked his obligation to his country and to the brave fellow who is fighting his battles is rapidly drawing to a close'. The newspaper did nevertheless still hope that the voluntary system could be saved.

The driving force behind the move to try to solve the shortage of military manpower was Lord Derby, with his ideas becoming to be known as the 'Derby Scheme'. Conscription was, in essence, flying in the face of the political ethos of Liberalism, that of freedom of individual choice. Despite this, the Government was under pressure from the military and from right-wing militarists within the ranks of the Tories. A balancing act was necessary and originally there was no direct compulsion, but every man was to be persuaded to attest requiring them to serve in the armed forces if they were called up to do so. The Scheme did make a distinction between single and married men, a decision which appears to be based on an unclear, unsound and unfair foundation. Those married men who did attest were given an assurance that they would not be called up before all single men had been fully utilised.

There was to be exemption for the clergy, a decision which understandably caused great controversy. There was no such exemption for churchmen in France and Italy (Britain's allies) so what justification was there for this peculiarly British approach in relation to the men of the church? People may have wondered how was it that many clergyman could preach to members of their congregation, or from recruitment platforms, that the ordinary man should go forth and take up the sword? This war, they would claim, was a just and righteous one, but they were at the same time not compelled to follow their own example and take part in the conflict. This further inequality within the 'Derby Scheme' just added to the controversies which arose from it.

There was also to be exemption on the basis of having certain skills deemed to be of national importance or exemption on personal grounds. The category of skills of national importance gave rise to the publishing of lists of reserve occupations.

> *List A:* Occupations required for the production or transport of munitions supplied by the Ministry of Munitions. This would have covered the munitions factories and the production of steel and materials. South Yorkshire was well represented in this category.
>
> *List B:* Coal mining. Coal was the raw material which fired transport and its production were crucial to the war effort and south Yorkshire was of course was one of the key centres of coal production.
>
> *List C:* Agriculture. Other mining occupations and

railway servants. Agriculture was of course a nation-wide occupation although less so in the industrial north. The railway industry was also nation-wide but Mexborough and district was again well-represented in this occupational list.

List D: Described as occupations of cardinal importance for the maintenance of some other branches of trade and industry.

If a man left a reserved occupation he was immediately liable for service.

The lists were basically described as essential occupations, but particularly, as with List D, this was very much open to interpretation. In order to assess whether or not a man's occupation was essential to industry and the war effort at home, recruiting tribunals were set up throughout the country. Employers who wished to retain men in their employment had the right to appeal the tribunal for a ruling. By applying to this tribunal, employers and employees were making an application to be 'starred' and thus become exempt from military service. Later, when conscription was made compulsory these tribunals were the bodies which adjudicated on whether an employer or individual had a case for exemption.

Recruiting tribunal members were drawn from the ranks of local 'worthies'. Those elected to form the Mexborough Tribunal were from members of the Urban District Council. They were: Councillors Winstanley, J. H. Watson J.P., J. Wood, Tom Chambers and A. Goulding. Surprisingly, Mexborough's tribunal did have a direct representative from the trade unions, unlike Swinton who had Mr B.L. Smith on its own tribunal. This point had not gone unnoticed when one correspondent wrote to *The Times* remarking that the Mexborough Tribunal was not properly constituted, consisting of just five local councillors. It was argued that as some very delicate decisions would have to be made, industrial experience to represent workers at the tribunal was essential to the fair functioning of this type of body.

The others on the Swinton Tribunal were Councillor E. Tillotson, Councillor A. Greenfield, Councillor S.C. Ward and a Mr Verity representing the employers of labour.

It was also necessary for the Government to establish nation-wide Military Tribunals to deal with those who believed they should be exempt from compulsory military conscription. By the end of 1916 nearly 750,000 men had appealed to the Military Service Tribunals. Some of the applicants were given exemption if they joined the Voluntary Training Corps undertaking home defence duties. Of all the appeals, about 2% were from Conscientious Objectors (CO's.), but none, if any, were granted exemption. Many were granted the option of serving in non-combatant roles, which the vast majority did. Others were sent to special work camps, but about 6,000 suffered imprisonment for at least the period of their objection to military service.

Those objecting on the grounds of conscience did so largely on the grounds of religious belief. Quakers were well represented in the numbers of CO.'s refusing to fight. To a lesser degree, men objected on political grounds. There were many in the Labour Movement opposed to the war and many filled the ranks of the CO's. Their argument was based on their belief that the war was an Imperialist war, in which the working class was being asked to fight in a conflict that was essentially the making of the ruling classes of the warring nation states. Why should we, they argued, take up arms against our fellow worker in the cause of a war between capitalists? This position, taken by many socialists, was articulated by a London Socialist, Gerald Gray, when he told a tribunal, "I refuse to murder and butcher people that know as little as we do for what end they are fighting for". The military representative on the military tribunal remarked that Gray was of unsound mind. Another CO who went before a tribunal was told as a Socialist he could not possibility have a conscience.

It is not intended here to enter into any assessment of how widespread conscientious objection was in the Mexborough and surrounding areas. As with the role of the local women who were fighting for the vote, there is much scope for further investigation, but it is unlikely there was a great deal of activity by left-wing Socialists in the area over the question of conscientious objection. There was a presence of the British Socialist Party (BSP), a Marxist organisation, in the area. This organisation wrote a letter to the Mexborough Trades and Labour Council in October expressing strong views against conscription, but the BSP do not appear to have been influential in the Mexborough area. It is also unlikely that the pacifist movement had a great deal of influence in the district.

The subject of conscientious objection cannot pass, however, without the mention of Conisbrough's Bert Brocklesby. Out of the 6,000 CO's imprisoned, 42 were sent to France to potentially face death by firing squad. Of this number 35 were sentenced to death, although later reprieved to serve ten years penal servitude, Bert Brocklesby being one of them. Bert was an 'absolutist', he refused all offers to serve as a non-combatant and absolutely refused to serve in any capacity. Bert Brocklesby was a Methodist, a choirmaster at his local Chapel and by profession a teacher. He told a military tribunal panel that his refusal to join the military was based upon his belief that, "God has not put me on earth to destroy his children."

Bert came from a well-respected Conisbrough family, his father being both a lay preacher and a magistrate. His family was supportive of him in that his father, mother and brother supported his right to hold the religious belief that he did. His father had said, "I rather Bert be shot for his belief then to abandon them." It must have also been difficult for his brother, Philip, who served as a second lieutenant in the army. Despite this, he too respected Bert's views and paid tribute to his outstanding courage in maintaining his pacifism to the end. Bert Brocklesby was subject to cruelty and faced much provocation as a result of his conviction. He had to face some of this provocation in his home town of Conisbrough where the newspapers called for his sacking as a teacher. On his return from France he saw the war out in Maidstone Prison, and was prevented from returning to teaching until later in his life. It is clear from Bert Brocklesby's experience, CO's had very little sympathy from those living in the Don and Dearne Valley area.

It must have been difficult to distinguish between those who just did not want to go to war and used religion or politics as a convenient excuse and those of genuine belief. Certainly the Don and Dearne Valley area was one where there was an abundance of 'reserve occupations' which made it unnecessary for many to declare their thoughts on military conscription, making an assessment of the extent of conscientious objection more difficult to access beyond that provided by official statistics.

Opinion was very much divided on conscription, with opposition coming from across the social spectrum. The Labour and Trade Union movement was still basically opposed. In October the Parliamentary Committee of the TUC met the Parliamentary Recruitment Committee to discuss the best way to utilise the information from the registration process so as to preserve voluntarism. The Labour and Party and trade unions called a conference which appealed for 30,000 recruits per week, a call intended to stave off conscription.

Mexborough and District Trades and Labour Council also called a meeting on Sunday 21st November, as a part of the trade union's efforts to increase recruitment without the need for compulsory conscription. The meeting was held at the Hippodrome, with Mr W. Appleton, the General Secretary of the General Federation of Trade Unions, being the main speaker. The meeting was not well attended. A week later the local Trades and Labour Council tried another meeting on the issue of recruitment which was only moderately attended, despite managing to attract a 'big name' speaker in Mr Harry Gosling. Gosling, who later became the President of the TUC in 1916, reiterated the TUC's position of supporting the war, but at the same time being opposed to conscription and militarism. He went on to describe what he referred to as the evils of conscription. Harry Gosling wanted people to get it out of their heads that the voluntary system was failing, it had in fact, he argued, produced the greatest voluntary army in the world and as such had been an immense success. Great effort should be made to preserve the system of non-compulsion, particularly to defeat those militarists who wished to destroy the voluntary system once and for all. Gosling told the Mexborough audience, "The people who wanted conscription did not want it just for this war, they were desiring conscription for all time."

Harry Gosling may have looked around him noticing the Hippodrome theatre was by no means full to capacity. He would have known, as a member of the TUC's Parliamentary Committee, that those within the Labour and Trade Union Movement, who were struggling to keep voluntarism, were losing the battle. Gosling would have known moves were taking place in Parliament to vote through a Bill which would eventually see the enactment of compulsory military conscription. There were strong forces on the right of British politics, such as Lord Northcliffe, whose campaign for conscription was backed by his own newspaper editors, particularly in the Conservative supporting *Daily Mail*.

The 'Derby Scheme' was, as Arthur Marwick remarks, 'A gigantic engine of fraud and blackmail, but given the Government had to find soldiers somehow, it was a very astute piece of political tactics.' If the 'Scheme' was seen to be successful then all well and good and the Liberal ideal of voluntarism would left intact. If it failed what better argument was there for compulsion?

What was to become the 'last ditch' campaign to recruit volunteers did receive some response. In 30th October edition of *The Times,* a list was published of names of 104 recruits who had recently attested at the Mexborough recruiting office. The 'Mexborough Company' of the 11th York and Lancs was able to gain a further fourteen man, which included nine miners, eight of them from Mexborough. Up to this point the new recruits could still pick their own regiment. Some chose the RGA based at Rotherham and two thirds of the 104 chose the 40th Division of the Royal Engineers, based at Doncaster. Three Mexborough miners, Austin Fletcher, George Turner and Alfred Butler chose the Army Veterinary Corps. The list included a dental surgeon from Wath, Herbert David Wilson, who not surprisingly joined the RAMC. The Grenadier Guards attracted two Mexborough miners, George Brooks and Alfred Cope.

Recruiting campaigns in the last few weeks of the year continued unabated. On Thursday 4th November, the so called 'Mexborough Company' of the 11th York and Lancs arrived in the town from Cannock on an eight day long training and recruitment exercise. The company was said to have 166 men within its ranks, but could not claim to contain all Mexborough and district men. Nevertheless the exercise was designed to enthuse the locals with a concerted effort to fill the 'Company' with local men as well as hoping to attract men to other regiments. The 'Mexborough Company' arrived at Swinton railway station where they were met by members of the Wath recruiting staff, Lieutenant P.B. Richardson and Second Lieutenant Everitt. From here they marched to the Market Place in Mexborough where they were met by the usual dignitaries, including, as so often on these occasions, Councillor Winstanley and military personnel Major Charles. B. Skinner and Sergeant J. Oddy.

The men of the 'Mexborough Company' were to be billeted across various locations in the town, including the Montagu Hotel where sleeping accommodation was found for them. Others were billeted at Adwick Road School and the Cricket Pavilion, where there was still one Belgian refugee family housed. The military had commandeered the pavilion and alternative accommodation had to be found for the refugees. After intervention from the Belgian Relief Committee, John Clayton, chairman of the cricket club, was able to secure accommodation for at least one the Belgian families.

The Times appealed to readers with the message, 'We trust the townsfolk of Mexborough will do their best to make their own troops comfortable and happy during their stay.' The newspaper gave a promise it would award a gold medal to the member of the 'Mexborough Company', who was able to secure the greatest number of recruits during their stay in Mexborough.

The 'Mexborough Company' trained on the Athletic Ground throughout the week, but this training did not consist of purely 'square bashing'. A football match was arranged on the town ground between a Mexborough Town side and a team from the 'Company', the match being organised by Miss Dorothy Nicholson, a well-known local singer. The Town team eventual won 4 goals to 3 after being held 2 all at half time. The 'Company' had been entertained at a 'smoking concert' in the reception room at the Montagu Hotel on the Friday following their arrival. As usual the town's 'worthies' were in attendance including Dr Huey who had been made the Company's Medical Officer for the duration of its stay. Miss Dorothy Nicholson was again the centre of attention at this function. *The Times* noted that the local contralto sang, 'My little grey home in the West' and entertained her audience after an enthusiastic encore with amusing songs describing the varying joys of a cricket player. There appear to have been many contributions by local singers and artistes including Councillor Winstanley himself, playing a selection of war songs upon the piano.

The presence of the 'Mexborough Company' within the town for the week's duration is reported to have been a success, with streets during the week echoing with the sound of bugles and the thunder of drums. Young women were said to have been captivated by the large number of boys in their smart khaki uniforms. Even mature men were seen to be walking with a military style step, 'Carrying their umbrellas in all sorts of unaccustomed positions' as the parades proceeded through streets thronged with excited crowds.

The Company's visit was unexpectedly cut short when it was ordered to leave and return, on Friday 12th November, to an undisclosed destination. However their visit didn't end without some kind of farewell gathering. The men were up early at 4.00am to the sound of the last reveille, in readiness for their departure from Mexborough. They had a breakfast at the Montagu Hotel at 8.00a.m, said their farewells to a crowd of relatives and well wishers and were wished "God speed" by Dr Huey and Councillor Winstanley. The men marched through the town to Swinton Midland Station from where the 'Company', with their baggage safely aboard the 8.49am train, departed to wherever it was the military had ordered them. Their departure would no doubt have disappointed many Mexborough folk who had organised for a longer stay. George Travers, the manager at the Hippodrome had arranged another smoking concert. A dance and a whist drive had also been arranged by some of the locals, but these events had to be cancelled with the premature departure of Mexborough's military guests.

As the year drew to a close, local newspapers continued to report the area's recruiting campaigns in terms of overwhelming success. For those who had hitherto not attested there seems little doubt that the pressure placed on them by the 'Derby Scheme' was sufficient, for many ended any resistance to joining the 'colours'. The ranks of the recruiting staff of the Mexborough and district were added to by a dozen invalided soldiers from the York and Lancs, who had returned from France and the Dardenelles. The presence of these men was an addition to the already moral pressure applied through a recruiting system which was determined not to fail. The Mexborough and district recruiting staff, who covered Wath, Wombwell, Conisbrough and Darfield as well as Mexborough, were experiencing their own pressure, that of overwork. They and civilian volunteers, worked late into the night on the last days of the big recruitment push in December, in an attempt to see the 'Derby Scheme' succeed. Mobile recruiters went out to the collieries and workplaces where the 'starred' men were, according to the *Barnsley Chronicle*, 'attesting wholesale'. The *Chronicle* reported, 'A feature of the last stage of recruiting in the Mexbrough District has been the magical effect upon the single man by the enthusiasm of the married. Hitherto the shirkers were taking their place in the ranks on Saturday with a freedom and gaiety which no doubt surprised themselves'.

As expected, the 'gigantic engine of fraud and blackmail' of the 'Derby Scheme' came to an end with the introduction of the Military Service Bill in January 1916. The main provision of the Bill provided that all single men between the age of 18 and 41 would now be required to compulsory attest, but were now unable to choose their own regiment. The Bill was enacted in March 1916, but by May quickly modified to include married men. Those suffering from ill-health or in a reserved occupation were still exempt as far as the Act was concerned. The Government believed the Act was now the only way to fulfil the demands of the military, but its introduction prompted resignations from those in the Government who still disapproved of compulsion. The Labour Movement was, in general, still unhappy about such measures to force the working man to join the military by compulsion.

Most in Mexborough, towards the end of the year, would have been pre-occupied by the consequences of the Derby Scheme. Landlords and property owners perhaps had other concerns. The Mexborough and District Property Owners Association held their monthly meeting in November, a meeting which made some interesting observations. The Association argued that the purchasing power of money had greatly reduced, which in their view, saw property owners and builders facing difficulties. Their problems were increased by an escalation in taxes, rates of pay and materials and willful damage that was, at the time, happening throughout the district. As result of these issues and the 'fact' that rents were 9d to 1/- per week (about 4p to 5p) higher in other districts than in Mexborough and Swinton, rent increases for the area were inevitable. The local Labour and Trades Council, recognising the tenants had some protection in law under the Rent and Mortgage Interest (Rent Restriction) Act, reacted to any attempt to increase rents They declared that, while many of their members were away serving their country, it was up to the trade unions to challenge the imposition of unwarranted increases in rents.

In contrast perhaps to the property owners and builders, the local butchers recognised they had prospered, at least up to now, during the past year or so of the war. At the local butchers' annual dinner, held at the Montagu Hotel on 1st November, the Swinton Urban District Council's Councillor G. Tillotson J.P announced that the trade had never flourished as it had done during the course of the war. Speaking before Germany had re-launched its restricted U-boat attacks on British shipping, Tillotson said he was in indebted to the Royal and Merchant Navies for the way they had protected food supplies. *The Times* commenting on this, agreed that as a 'meat eating district', despite the price increases as result of the war, there was, in their view, more money available. The paper was somewhat amused by the butchers' honesty that trade, for them, was thriving. Farmers and others who had benefited from wartime conditions, 'not always legally' *The Times* remarked, were not so ready to admit their fortunes.

One hundred years on it is difficult to gauge the exact mood of people in the district as Christmas 1915 approached. Some stirring speeches would continue to be heard from the recruiting platforms, which may have gave some hope that the British Army was still filling its ranks with fine young men who would now quickly help to ensure a British victory. However, newspapers portray a general sense of despondency, punctuated with news of events which would give some distraction and light relief from news on the battlefields. Newspapers carried items about local sports, adverts and reports from the picture houses and theatres and of others events designed to rally the community into some sort of pre-war normality. Mr J. Verdi Popple, of 150, Doncaster Road, suggested that despite many men being away at the Front, Mexborough should attempt to set up a dramatic society which might of course give some diversion away from thoughts of the misery of those fighting in far-away lands. Mexborough, Mr Popple claimed, was behind such as Wombwell who had already taken such a initiative. Yet even Verdi Popple himself, at this time a railway clerk on the Great Central Railway, could not escape the demands of war. He joined the Royal Engineers, Doncaster, in the capacity of a telegraphist. Verdi was originally stationed at Newark, where his talents in amateur theatricals was much appreciated in the army camp from where he received both regimental and civil engagements.

As for local sport, football seems to have retained its popularity if not its best players. The Mexborough and District League was still functioning and taking on new players to fill its teams. At the beginning of the season the manager of the Empire picture house, George Beverley, entered a team called the Empire Electric Stars. Their first game was said to be a home game against Moorthorpe.

As for Mexborough Town FC, they had entered the Midlands Combination League at the beginning of the season, after making the decision to downgrade their ambitions and leave the more senior Midlands League. The club does not appear to have fared any better as a result of them playing in a less demanding league. After five games they were firmly at the bottom of the league with just one win and a draw. They managed a win in their next game, but still rested on at the bottom of the league while Rotherham County were well established in top position. Towards the end of the year the 'Town' had picked itself off the bottom and found itself in sixth position ahead of its old adversary Doncaster Rovers, who were now bottom. Rotherham County still led the small group of nine local clubs. Remarkably, on Saturday 20th November, Mexborough had one of their best performances of the season by beating the leaders Rotherham County three goals to one at Millmoor.

A football match was perhaps one event which could potentially lift the shadow now cast across the country. This might be particularly so at Christmas. Mexborough Town's Christmas Day match was played against Kilnhurst Town on the Athletic Ground, with a kick-off time of 2.40pm Mexborough's team was: E. Sylvester, G Beaumont, J. Seddons. J. Beaumont, T. Bolton, H. Frost, Winslow, R. Burkinshaw, W. Nicholson, R. Shaw and A. Cook.

As for 'Town' fans, who were still able to remain in the town or who were fortunately home on leave, they would have to travel away for the next Christmas programme match to Chesterfield. The 'Town' took on Chesterfield and came away with a very creditable 2-2 draw. Although the result left Mexborough Town still second from bottom of the Midlands Combination League, it would perhaps have given a little Christmas cheer to the townfolk.

Much of the activity around Christmas would have been over-shadowed by the impact of the 'Derby Scheme'. Many families must have directed their thoughts towards the very real possibility of more loved ones now having to endure the horrors of the battlefield, casting darkness in many corners of the family home. An evaluation of the local newspapers would suggest that the Christmas period was spent in a sombre atmosphere, although there appears to be a recognition that strenuous efforts should be made to give less fortunate individuals some Christmas cheer.

The Times published on Christmas Day of 1915 reminded its readers that there were two Christmases. One was been fought out in foreign fields and the other was being spent in more secure surroundings at home. Yet those at home were now more anxious and distressed than they had been a year ago. The extent of the horrors of war, which twelve months earlier could not have been contemplated, was now becoming realised.

Despite the distress that many were now feeling at home, the people of the district were not forgetting the other Christmas that would be spent on the battlefields. Earlier in December, Councillor Winstanley and Mr Arthur Brown, the Headteacher of Doncaster Road School, were instrumental in arranging a 'sacred concert' at the Hippodrome to raise money in order to dispatch gifts to British prisoners in Germany and Holland. The entertainers included the 'West End Glee Singers', and a number of violists, Mrs Brown and Miss Mary Ellis together with Miss Anne Green both violinists from Masborough. William Winstanley was an old colleague of Arthur Brown. Winstanley, who was now himself a headmaster at Mexborough's Central School, joined the staff at Doncaster Road School on 1st July 1899 as an Assistant Headteacher. He gained his teaching certificate at St Peter's Wigan in 1896 and trained at Liverpool between 1894-1897. Winstanley's first teaching position was at Hull Central, where he taught in the Science Department before moving to Doncaster Road School for a brief period. Mr Winstanley and Mr Brown would have still had a working relationship in their roles as 'Heads' of their respective schools and found the time to organise the worthy cause of giving assistance to British prisoners abroad.

There was, however, still a need for charity at home. There may have been now employment in abundance and more money in the pockets of workers, but there were still pockets of poverty as bad as any of the pre-war years. Many big families either had a father away or a father who was now never to return. Families in this situation would have to try to exist on the pittance of Separation Allowance, a War Widow's Pension, or handouts from the various relief funds. There would be no extravagance this coming Christmas in the homes of the poor, but it was fortunate there were those who continued to recognise their plight. The following letter written to *The Times* gives us a moving sense of the continued existence of poverty and neglect within the district:

An Appeal for Mexborough 'Bairns'

'Dear Sir, I should like through your valuable paper, space will permit, to appeal on behalf of the Rev t. Anderson's Christmas Fund for the poor bairns on Mexborough. Many readers will remember what a cold and foggy night last Christmas it was. I was present at the distribution of dolls, toys and games to the children in the Free Christian Church Hall. I shall never forget the sight as the poor boys and girls came trooping forward to receive the gifts allocated to them. I wondered how some of the little mites had found their way on such a miserable night and how their little faces lit up with happy smiles. I appeal to Mexborough to do it again this Christmas.'

Your's, Wilf Marrow
37, Pym Road, Mexborough

The Free Christian Church was able to repeat this happy event that took place in their hall during the Christmas of 1914. On the occasion of Christmas 1915 it is reported that over 100 poor children were given a treat by members and friends of the church when each child received a toy, an orange, an apple and a bag of biscuits. On receiving their gifts, the Reverend Thomas Anderson reminded the children that, although they were poor, someone thought about them at Christmas. The Reverend Anderson probably did not need to remind the youngsters of the fact that they were poor, but to acknowledge they were thought of at Christmas may have been of some additional comfort to them and their parents.

On Boxing Day evening a presentation took place in the Main Street Working Men's Club to John 'Blondin' Shaw, once described as Mexborough's most remarkable man.

John Shaw was the son of a barge skipper but, unimpressed with that type of life, he went off to join a circus, where he learned acrobatics and was said to be a master of his profession.

John come back to his native Mexborough, married Charlotte in 1894 and had two children Miriam and Joseph. Both Miriam and Joseph by this time were employed at the Hippodrome Theatre. John found work in the coalmining industry but never lost his desire to show off his theatrical and acrobatic abilities. He performed a balancing act on the top of the headgear at Denaby Main Pit and performed his skills at Manvers Main by somersaulting over the pit's haulage engine. On another occasion John handled a wheel barrow on a tightrope from Mexborough Red Lion Hotel to the 'tripping': the high ground opposite the Hotel on Bank Street.

By the time the Boxing Day presentation was made to John Shaw he was in his mid-sixties. He was presented with a medal for the medical work he was doing later in his life. John had set up a little chemist shop in his home at 13, Dodsworth Street and from here he practised homeopathy, making and dispensing pills and what he called 'Shaw Balsam'. He made a successful study of electrical treatment with the use of medical and electrical apparatus. John practised widely, treating members and friends of the Main Street Club, members of the Yorkshire Miner's Association and, by this time, soldiers wounded.

John Shaw did not live to see the end of the war. After a brief illness he died of pneumonia in 1917. His electrical equipment can still be seen and is now in the ownership of the Cusworth Hall Museum at Doncaster. The medal he was awarded at Main Street Club also survives and is a treasured possession of his granddaughter, Pauline Gibbons.

The local theatres were still doing their best to entertain the populace of Mexborough on its second Christmas at war. Over the Christmas period the Hippodrome offered Roland Carter and Company, a comedy vocal act and Mon Roelgin's Parrots described as 'The Greatest Bird Act in the World'. The Oxford cinema's special holiday attraction was a film called, *There's No Place Like Home* together with a comedy called Bachelor Boy. The Empire at Mexborough was showing what they called a domestic drama of the goldfields, intriguingly named '*The Governor's Lady*'. If, however, it was a traditional pantomime that was required to help forget some of the uncomfortable aspects of the present, then in order to see '*Dick Whittington*', it was, this year, necessary to travel to the Empire Theatre at Rotherham.

Every effort had been made to entertain patients in Mexborough Montagu Hospital, which by now was largely under military control. Patients, who were now mostly wounded soldiers, throughout the Christmas week were to enjoy what Montagu Hospital had to offer. The wards were tastefully decorated for the occasion and each patient received a Christmas stocking containing what was described as 'useful' presents. On Boxing Day, wounded soldiers were entertained by the 'Merrymakers' and various other local entertainers. The hospital employed a photographer, a Mr Twelves, whose pictures of the events were offered as a souvenir of the occasion. Towards the end of the week there were visits from local soldiers. A Private Briggs from Goldthorpe, Privates Garbutt and Butler from Bolton and two Mexborough men, Privates Spittlebone and Egden, were in attendance, the latter being a former goalkeeper for the 'Town'.

Mexborough's traders continued with what was called the 'Annual Xmas Pleasure Fair' offering 'attractions of all kinds' on the 'Top Market'. The event ran all week prior to Christmas Day.

Underneath all these praiseworthy attempts to engender a relative normality within people's experiences of Christmas 1915, there was the haunting spectre of a bloody war being fought out in the battlefields of Europe and elsewhere. There were now hundreds in the Mexborough and district who had lost their loved ones, wives without husbands, children without fathers. There were those who had become unrecognisable from the young, fit, energetic men their family and friends had previously known. They had lost limbs, bore dreadful facial damage, suffered from severe respiratory difficulties and psychological problems, with which, at this time, the military did not have much sympathy, in relation to working class soldiers and sailors. This would have been the backcloth to the Christmas celebrations in most homes. There would have been a toast to more absent friends this Christmas than there ever was before and a toast to those who were spending Christmas in the trenches, unable to enjoy the company of their family. There would also be servicemen lucky enough to be home on leave who would no doubt have had lingering thoughts as to whether or not it would be the last Christmas they would spend with their families. Their families would be thinking the same, as would those who had just attested in responded to the recent 'Derby Scheme' recruiting campaign.

After seventeen months of war, the British nation showed all the signs of being weary of it. Even the Mexborough recruiting staff was permitted a 'recruiting holiday', the first time since the outbreak of the war. The break extended for over a month, from late November almost into the New Year, with all offices temporary closed, including an office in the Free Library which had been established as the 'Central Recruiting Office.'

The Times in their 1915 Christmas Day editorial (Christmas Day fell on a Saturday) was not in any mood to offer any charity towards German troops, as in 1914 when fraternisation and the Christmas truce took place. The newspaper doesn't mention the British Military's fears over the repeat of events when strict orders were given to try and ensure there was no repetition. Yet *The Times* did make a very valid and poignant point when it remarked, 'Much has happened since then, the wholesale slaughter of British women and children by Zeppelin and submarine, but above all the fiendish resort to gas at Ypres and liquid fire at Hooge. These things can never be forgotten by the troops who faced them nor by their comrades who fell before them.' Indeed 1915 had been an experiment in how far man's inhumanity to man could extend.

The sentiments of *The Times* editorial would probably have been generally shared by the locals of Mexborough and district. The district was one of the areas which were prominent in witnessing riots after the sinking of the *Lusitania*. This was a sad episode in local history which led to the demise of a once respected member of the community. The atmosphere, both locally and nationally, must have been toxic with hatred for anything German and with what was perceived as, often wrongly, anti-British feeling. There was very little 'goodwill to *all* men' during the Christmas of 1915.

Thus the year came to an end amid more sombre feelings than hope. Yet hope was all many, both at the Front and at home, had to embrace. Hope that the New Year would bring an end to a war that many were led to believe would cease the Christmas before. We know in hindsight that those hopes were to be shattered in the blood-soaked battlefields of the Somme, when Mexborough and district would receive more than its fair share of its miserable legacy.

Bandsman Charles Higgins of the 2nd York
and Lancs was killed on 2nd April at the
second Battle of Ypres. He tried to enlist in
the regular army in 1911 by falsifying his
age, He finally fulfilled his ambition when
he volunteered in August 1914.

Soldiers of the 5th York and Lancs in their trench during the second
Battle of Ypres. This battalion contained a number of Mexborough men.
Courtesy Rotherham MBC Archives and Local Studies (578-K/6/6/1/1).

George Schonhut seated at the wheel of his vehicle. He and his family were victims of the anti-German riots following the sinking of the *RMS Lusitania* in May 1915.

Parts of Montagu Hospital were taken over by the military. The town saw many patients in their 'hospital blue' uniforms visiting Mexborough's shops and pubs. These are some of the wounded soldiers outside the hospital gates on Cemetery Road.

Private William (Bill) Ernest Bird survived the war, including the horrors of Gallipoli and the Western Front. Bill lived at 79, Victoria Road with his wife, Florence and daughter, Ann (insert in the photo). Courtesy of Susan Shaw.

Able Seaman John Hepworth, who served at Gallipoli and the Western Front.

Some of the first to arrive in the Dardenelles were the Royal Naval Division. Mexborough was well-represented in the RND. Courtesy of Mrs Dorothy Hepworth.

Private W H Biggs, one of many Mexborough men who joined the army early and found themselves fighting in Gallipoli. He was reported missing during an advance on 21st August 1915 and later declared dead on the same day.

Able Seaman Edward (Ted) Barker, who served with the RND at Gallipoli. He survived and, suffering from dysentery, was evacuated to Alexandria in Egypt.

MEN OF MEXBORO' AND DISTRICT

JOIN THE LOCAL COMPANY.

Who in this district has not read with pride of the gallantry of the local Territorials fighting in Flanders and France? That is because local patriotism is a degree more intense than general patriotism, and that is the reason why the Mexboro' and District Company of the 11th York and Lancaster Regiment ought to be, and will be, supported by the young men of that district.

Recruiting for this company has already commenced, and is now making satisfactory progress, thanks to the energetic anniversary campaign just concluded.

Local recruiting sergeants stationed at Mexboro', Conisboro' and Wath will be available to carry out enlistments.

Recruits will proceed to Pontefract to be uniformed, and then have the option of remaining there until the company reaches full strength, or of returning to their homes on pay and billeting allowance amounting to 3s. per day.

In the latter event they will go through daily drill at Mexboro' until the company is ready to go into full training.

Men of Mexboro' and district, here is a chance not only to "do your bit for your King and country," to take a voluntary share in the Empire's great task, to succour your comrades who have already gone from the district in their thousands, but also to uphold the credit of the town and district, to give it a name in the Army, and to identify it directly with one of the most gallant and heroic regiments in the United Kingdom.

The credit of your district is at stake. See that your district is not let down. It has poured men generously into the ranks of all branches of the Forces, and it is now to have a Company of its own. Make it a good one!

Mexborough did not have its own 'Pals' Battalion, but in 1915 there was an attempt to form a Mexborough Company, using adverts like this in local papers. It was not a success, as many men had already joined the Yorks and Lancs and KOYLI battalions.

The Reverend Hope of Mexborough Parish Church delivered a controversial sermon condemning trade union activity during the war.

Four Calladines are remembered on the Mexborough War Memorial. Private Arthur Calladine (above) died at Loos on October 1st 1915.

Guardsman Louis (Lewis) Calladine of the 1st Coldstream Guards died on 18th December 1915.

The gravestone of Guardsman Louis Calladine at Longuenesse (St Omer) Souvenir Cemetery. Note the incorrect spelling of the surname. Courtesy of Barrie Dalby.

MEXBOROUGH YOUTH MISSING.

Lce.-Cpl. Robert Vernon Truelove,
10th Y. & L.,

is reported missing since the fighting in France on the 26th of September. He is twenty years of age, and a son of Mr. and Mrs. Robert Truelove, of Greno House, Church Street, Mexboro'. Prior to enlistment he was learning farming at Red House, near Doncaster.

Lance Corporal Roberet Vernon Truelove, killed at the Battle of Loos on 26th September at the age of 20.

Private Harold Stead also killed at Loos on 26th September, aged 21.

Sergeant Albert Arthur Atkinson, orphaned early in his life and brought up by his grandparents. This picture was sent to them for Christmas 1915. Courtesy of Mr Gary Smillie.

John (Blondin) Shaw (centre) shortly before his death in 1917. His work in homeopathy and pharmacy helped many wounded servicemen (and others) in Mexborough.
Courtesy of Mrs Pauline Gibbons.

1916

Chapter Twelve

Enter Military Conscription

The Times recorded that the New Year was ushered in by great storms and gales, resulting in severe damage. The paper did not mention that this might be an omen for what could be expected during the coming year, but the prospect of storms ahead was on the minds of some.

Evidence that Britain had reached a new era in relation to how it raised its military forces was reflected in events in the early weeks of 1916. Some recruiting offices had closed for a period up to Christmas of 1915 giving the staff a break from the hectic activity of 'Derby Scheme' recruitment. Even though the Military Service Act had not come into effect, in the early weeks of the year most appeared to have resigned themselves to its inevitable introduction. Lord Derby, speaking at a meeting in Liverpool remarked, "I have done all I can to make the voluntary system a success up until the eleventh hour and the fifty ninth minute, so to speak". He would, however, do what he could to pursue the voluntary system to the end. Quite what Lord Derby was prepared to do to save the nation from conscription is not clear, particularly when the Military Service Bill was introduced on 5th January and was passing through Parliament at the time. As such, Lord Derby's proclamation that he wished to try to avoid conscription was, it might be suggested, as fraudulent as his scheme itself.

The Labour and Trade Union Movement generally was still against conscription. The Labour Party had called a conference on the day after the introduction of the Military Service Bill, to reaffirm its opposition. Mr J. H. Thomas, a prominent leader of the NUR, called the Bill, "a conspiracy against Labour". The Brassworkers Union put an amendment before the conference that single men should at least be conscripted, but this was soundly defeated by the 400 assembled delegates.

The miners' union, the MFGB, held its own conference and somewhat predictably voted to reject the provisions of the Bill. The men's union locally, the YMA, also voted to reject the Bill, somewhat to the disappointment of *The Times*. The newspaper argued that the miners had failed to notice the grave problem that the nation faced. Besides, claimed *The Times*, they had not given the opportunity for the 20,000 Yorkshire miners who were already serving their country to cast a vote. The fact that 632 Yorkshire miners had given their lives for their nation over the seventeen months or so, a figure rising to 673 by February, should have concentrated the minds of the YMA delegates, the newspaper argued. It may be a fair point that those at the Front may have been seeing matters from somewhat different view. Clearly *The Times* was now firmly of the opinion that conscription was the only answer to dealing with those men who still refused to attest. The paper talked scornfully of those who had to 'be fetched', especially the conscientious objector, although it added in the contemptuous language of the day 'we heard none of this curious species arising here'. Those now fully committed to conscription need not have had worried over its introduction. The Military Service Bill was being sped through the House of Commons as fast as the military authorities had desired. The Bill received an easy passage, passing into legislation by 431 votes to 39.

For those who were identified as having attested, but were awaiting for instruction from the military, or who for some reason were officially exempt from service, special armlets were made available. The commencement of the issuing of the armlets had started just after Christmas, on 30th December 1915, starting with Mexborough and continuing into the New Year for surrounding districts. Lord Derby received a letter from Buckingham Palace, written on 28th December 1915, from the King's Private Secretary. The letter read, 'Now that the work in connection with the King's appeal for recruits is over, His Majesty hopes every man who is entitled to wear the armlet will do so as proof to his fellow countryman of his response to that call'. This is further evidence that by the end of 1915 the voluntary system was dead and the previous frantic operations of its recruiting machinery, including its propaganda, were being run down.

The introduction of conscription would, theoretically at least, put an end to the reluctance of the so called 'slacker'. Yet there was continued pressure to ensure that the war effort would be served by all deemed able to offer themselves to it. If you were unable to serve your country at the Front then serious consideration should be given to joining the Volunteer Defence Corps. Mr Colin Snow of 'The Cedars',

Victoria Road, Mexborough was anxious to re-organise the Mexborough and Swinton section of the Corps in the early weeks of 1916. The Corps had previously disbanded because many of its members were not inclined to accept the conditions that, by joining the Corp, they could at some stage become eligible to be called up to the army. Under the new arrangements so called 'starred' men with slight physical defects were unlikely be called to serve in the new conscripted forces. The Corps were also hoping to attract men who had locally been placed in 'unstarred' colliery and munitions employment who might be able to give their services on a part time basis.

In a letter to *The Times,* Colin Snow outlined the purpose of the Corps and what its members could expect. Not dissimilar to the Second World War's Home Guard, the Corps would be asked to undertake some of the following:

a)   Assisting in repelling an invasion or raid;
b)   Garrison duties in towns and villages;
c)   Guarding railways and other voluntary points;
d)   Supervising removal of civil population, keeping order and allaying panic in case of emergency;
e)   Guarding communications etc.

In order to ensure that their duties would be undertaken efficiently, the Corps members were expected to regularly attend drill and rifle practice. One possible drawback to recruiting members to the Corps was that members were expected to supply their own uniforms. Mr Snow made it clear the necessity of purchasing a uniform by remarking, "I would point out that an ordinary suit is liable to spoil when engaged in 'trench' or 'field work' or in carrying a rifle at the slope on wet days. Would it not therefore be better to buy a cheap uniform and keep it specially for the one purpose. I know many men whose uniforms are getting distinctly dirty, but who are proud of the fact, as it showed that they had been doing useful work."

The inaugural meeting to revive the Mexborough and Swinton Volunteer Defence Corps took place at Swinton Bridge School on Tuesday evening of 4th January under the chairmanship of Swinton's Councillor E. Tillotson. JP. As was usual on these occasions, William Winstanley represented Mexborough. By all accounts the meeting was very moderately attended.

Mr W. M. Gichard of the Rotherham Corps, a man who had once approached Yorkshire Cricket Council to cease organising cricket during times of war, was the main speaker. Speaking of the low attendance, Gichard drew the audience's attention to the fact that the Rotherham Corps had grown from an initial two recruits to its present number of well over 200. It was expected that men who had attested would also join the Corps as an initial source of training. They would learn the rudimentary principles of rifle drill, bayonet practice and military drill. In the absence of well-trained military officers, older men who had military experience would make excellent training officers. Mr Gichard assured potential recruits that present officers were not in their positions through influence, but that they were chosen on merit.

With the speeches over, Councillor Winstanley moved that the Mexborough and Swinton Volunteer Corps be formed, a motion which was seconded by the Swinton councillor Mr A. Greenfield. The evening was at least able to attract the somewhat modest figure of 22 recruits to the ranks of the newly formed local Corps. The meeting was to be followed up in a week by a general meeting which took place in the evening at the Mexborough Roller Rink. This meeting was primarily to elect officers and confirm its affiliation to the Rotherham Battalion. The meeting itself was described as 'encouraging'. Mr R. Steel of Station Road, Swinton, was elected as the Corps secretary, with Mr E.J.H. Ford securing the treasurer's position. There was a five man committee which included Mexborough's Mr M. Hattersley and Colin Snow, the latter becoming the Corps's Commander. It was announced at the meeting that the Corps had 30 members who had commenced drilling under Mr Snow's command, which was taking place at the roller rink. The rink's proprietor, Mr R. Fowler, was to allow the use of his premises, free of charge, for purposes of the Corps. Mr Fowler's gesture was not surprising as most were anxious to demonstrate to the town's people their keenness to contribute to the war effort; to do otherwise was likely to be counter-productive. Mr Fowler was wise enough to hold a 'Skating Carnival' in mid-February with the entire proceeds going the Defence Corps. Within weeks of the reformation of the Corps, Colin Snow, who was a commercial representative for Messers Bakers' Engineering in Sheffield, had enlisted in the Royal Garrison Artillery and had to give up his position as Commander.

The move to compulsory military conscription saw a fundamental change to the labour market. The chance for women to demonstrate overwhelmingly their willingness and ability to enter into the man's world of work had now arrived. One profession, which even the most ardent opponent of women's emancipation would not deny entry, was that of the schoolteacher. The Mexborough Education Committee, at the beginning of the year, concerned itself with the shortage of teachers resulting from males responding positively to the recent recruiting activity. The Committee now gave serious consideration to the employment of 'suitable women', on what it called an emergency basis in elementary schools. These unqualified women would be given a short period of probation to establish their abilities. These women would probably be from the ranks of the lower middle classes or the upper working class; this class of woman probably being considered as 'suitable'. This gave them the opportunity to escape the mundane typist job or from even the environs of the restrictive parent.

The question of the organisation of female labour was discussed at a Mexborough and District Trades and Labour Council meeting just before the turn of the year. The delegate from the railway union, the NUR, reported that most of the women carriage cleaners had now been recruited to his union. The NUR delegate even claimed that the women were doing a better job than the men, although he assured the meeting men had nothing to fear from the women, provided the women received the same terms and conditions.

The local trade unions were certainly adapting to the influx of the new labour force. The Workers' Union had found themselves able to employ a 'lady' organiser who was about to visit the area shortly. Her task would be to recruit the women working in the 'powder works' at both Denaby and Kilnhurst which were now employing women in large numbers. Mr Murphy of the Workers' Union further reported there was a small number of women now employed on the tramways, an organisation said not to be eager to unionise women, although not eager to attract men into union membership either. The Trades and Labour Council were, by the middle of the year, prepared to allow the Mexborough and Swinton Women's Union to affiliate to their organisation. The YMA was not at all susceptible to the presence of women in the coal mining industry. In February, Nunnery Colliery introduced female labour into the lamp room. At a Council Meeting of the YMA on the morning the women were to commence work, the Council passed a resolution that they would take the question up with owners requesting them to withdraw any female labour. Refusal to withdraw the women would see a threat of industrial action. It was not the custom, therefore, to employ women in any occupation in south Yorkshire collieries, a policy that differed from that in as the Lancashire coalfields.

The whole of the trade union movement in the area was, however, united in their objection to the employment of German prisoners of war in local collieries. At a Trades and Labour Council meeting in late May, delegates condemned the prospect of the use of German POW's on the grounds they would be in the possession of explosives and as 'patriotic people would sacrifice themselves' by blowing up pits as an act of sabotage. Barnburgh Main Colliery miners also passed a resolution on similar lines. If a careless Englishman could blow up a mine so could a calculating German with homicidal tendencies.

It had been noted by the local newspapers that 1915 had seen the district working harder than it had done in any previous year. This was a result of a war effort demanding increased production in industry despite the reductions in manpower. With the increase in production came, in many parts of society, an increase in prosperity through a better standard of wage creating additional personal means and for some, family comforts. This was not of course the entire picture. The continuing casualty rate of war brought with it an ever-increasing abundance of widows and fatherless children and subsequently the corresponding hardship. The local distress funds were said to have declined, but so also, it was argued by *The Times*, had the level of distress. Certainly the assurance of more employment for the women and the young men of the extended family would help to compensate financially for the loss of the former family 'breadwinner'.

The Mexborough Military Service Tribunal members were finally chosen by the Urban District Council. Winstanley, Watson, Wood, Goulding and Chambers were initially appointed with the later additions of John T. Rowen and Levi I. Jones and David S. Humphreys. Although the Tribunal members were all councillors, there were now at least the latter three members who could be expected to view matters from a trade union point of view. Mr Alexandra Baron was also invited to join.

There was some controversy as to whether the press could freely report the proceedings of military tribunals. One chairman of a tribunal expressed the view that the press would actually assist the work of the tribunals. Reporting the proceedings would help to deter idle and frivolous appeals and raise public awareness of just what would and wouldn't be tolerated. Generally the tribunals were reported, but there was no reporting of the identity of those requesting exemption.

On the evening of Wednesday 1st March the first public sitting of the Mexborough Tribunal proceeded. The Chairman, William Winstanley, opened the Tribunal by pointing out that although the War Office understandably wanted all the men it could get, it was the duty of the Tribunal to consider the overall interests of both national and local communities. The decisions the Tribunal may have varied from granting total exemption, exemption for a certain period or temporary exemption, adjournment to be heard again, an order to appear in front of a Military Medical Board and of course outright refusal. Some who worked in the coalmining industry were referred to their local colliery tribunal.

One of the first cases for exemption was from someone who was described as a 'billiard hall proprietor'. No name was given, but the speculation as to who it might be, was probably more damaging than publicising the applicant's name in full. The applicant, who did not appear in person, but sent a representative, claimed exemption on business grounds. His business, it was argued, was a place for local miners, munitions and railway workers to relax. As such, it was claimed, it was in the national interest the business should be preserved. It appears the Tribunal members had some trouble in coming to a decision on this case and the applicant was exempted for a month. The Tribunal had no problem in outright refusal for others. An insurance company asked for exemption for an employee who was an assistant superintendent and the only eligible man left locally on the staff; the application was refused. Another refused application was from a chemist. The chemist wanted exemption for his young assistant who was partly qualified and helped with the dispensing. If this young man was not at work, the chemist argued, he would have to abandon his free dispensing to soldiers' and sailors' dependants. Probably much to the amusement of the Tribunal members, the chemist claimed his young assistant's services were indispensable. Another applicant to be refused was from a theatre scene-shifters. Perhaps not to have granted refusal in this case might have raised some difficult questions for Tribunal members to answer.

A bottle manufacturer applied for one of their bottle packers to be exempted. The company was now extensively employing women, but found them to be unsuitable for packing light and handling delicate bottles, although they were, argued their employer, quite capable of dealing with the heavier and clumsier type of bottle. The Chairman, William Winstanley, pointed out on refusing the application, that if their argument were reversed they may have stood a better chance of success.

A similar claim from a local glass bottle manufacturer came before the second sitting of the Mexborough Tribunal six days later. This manufacture asked for exemption for his son, who was the manager of the business as well as a glass packer. The company dealt with thousands of bottles a day and because of the shortage of labour they were failing to deliver orders. The company employed 32 women, but it was suggested by the applicant that one man could do the work of three women. The application for exemption was refused. The argument that female labour was often unsuitable for tasks once the preserve of the man, appears, from the early days of the tribunals, not to have found favour with its members.

The Times observed that tribunals often took a far too lenient view of some applications. Some of the local tribunals, the paper argued, were given exemption far too liberally, especially to married men. The problem of leniency was said to be worse in relation to the rural tribunals. Countryside tribunal members were, it was alleged, far too accommodating to the selfish interest shown by those with an agricultural perspective. Between March 1916 and March 1917, 780,000 men were granted exemption. Certainly there must have been immense pressure upon tribunal members from different influential individuals and organisations to grant their requests for exemption. Clearly the tribunal members were open to charges of bias and even bribery and corruption.

The Mexborough Tribunal had its third sitting on Monday 13th

March when it had its first conscientious objector (CO) before it. The CO appeared before the members of the tribunal displaying what they interpreted as arrogance. This applicant entered, wearing his cap which he was not inclined to remove until told to do so by the chairman. The objector said he was a trade union secretary. To the astonishment of the tribunal he began to read a prepared address without permission to do so. The applicant appears to have great confidence in himself and his arguments. Many CO's tended to be very articulate men, although often from a working class background, something which some tribunal members had difficulty in handling. This applicant put forward arguments on both religious and political grounds, although not always coherently. To take the life of any creature was inconsistent with Christ's teachings he said and further argued his faith was international and he believed in the brotherhood of man. William Winstanley, the chairman, asked a question often put to conscientious objectors and pacifists. What would the applicant do if he was attacked? "I have often been attacked and suffered some injury", was the reply, "but never once have I struck back".

Tribunals had the difficulty of assessing whether the CO was an absolutist, who would refuse to serve under any circumstance, or would accept an alternative and be prepared to take on a non-combatant role. Mexborough's first 'conchie' was an absolutist in that he declared to the tribunal that he, "would accept the hardest work imaginable, but he would not do nothing which would help to maintain the existing state of warfare".

Brigadier-General Copley, the military representative, was the most vigorous in the questioning of this objector. Copley asked whether the objector was a vegetarian to which he replied he was not, which somewhat contradicted his pronouncement that he did not believe in the killing of any creature. The objector claimed he had read the works of many philosophers whose views were similar to his own and he also followed the religion of the Puritans and took his lead from Charles Russell Lowell. "But", remarked the military representative, "the Puritans were the best fighters we ever had". From here the discussion became academic, with the military representative eventually making the CO aware, in no uncertain terms, he had no time for the applicant's claim for exemption. Copley's may have been a decisive influence in the tribunal's decision, which was taken in private. The CO was refused exemption of any kind, although it is not recorded what his fate was to be.

The press was generally scathing towards those who presented themselves to the tribunals. In their opinion applicants were no more than cowards and shirkers, simply wasting the time of the authorities. The press, like the military authorities, were always seeking to emphasise the 'normality' of patriotism. *The Times* was delighted to receive a letter from a young Mexborough school child who had written to a soldier at the Front. To this boy, the soldier was described as being 'all but god like'. The boy wrote, 'Do ask Lord Kitchener to let me come now. I am eight I can shoot a gun and use a bayonet'. *The Times* were only too pleased to publish these words to further ridicule many attending the tribunals, particularly CO's. This boy was, according to *The Times*, a sturdy young lad who, 'has not had time to develop into a conscientious objector yet. We fancy his conscience is going to be made of sterner stuff'.

Nevertheless there was sometimes a lenience and understanding shown by the military authorities. In February, Walter Nicholson, of the well-known Mexborough family of decorators, suddenly died at his home in Cromwell Road at the relatively young age of 39. He had taken over the firm from his father, the late Walter Wentworth Nicholson. Walter junior had been a keen footballer and a very good cricket player scoring 89 runs against the top side Wath just a few months before his death. The Mexborough UDC organised a petition to try to secure the release of Walter's brother, by then Private R. H. Nicholson of Bank Street, serving with the Army Service Corps, Motor Transport. In view of his brother's death the petition sought the release from army service of Private Nicholson in order he could take over the running of the decorating business. The petition was successful.

There were separate tribunals for those in the coalmining industry. There was always a difficulty in meeting the balance of retaining men in a reserved occupations and the continued need for men to serve in the armed forces. The miners' tribunal was a mechanism to try to ensure, as far as possible, this balance was maintained. The same problem of balance occurred in all industries deemed to be of national importance and the same 'combing out' system occurred. The same tasteless and de-humanising language was often used by the press when it referred to the process as 'weeding out' the slackers.

Despite the urgency prompted by the introduction of military conscription, there was no great need to force local miners to join the forces. Hickleton for example, employed a workforce of 2,426 at the beginning of the war, but by March 1916 this figure had reduced to 1,887. At the same time, Denaby Main Colliery had seen 447 of its men enlist and at Cadeby Main by March 1916 nearly a thousand, 997, men were serving. Having said this, it was the case that fewer soldiers were recruited in the 1916, in the period of conscription, than there were in the non-conscription period of 1915.

Those who remained working in the collieries were not immune from a military type discipline. Under the Employers' and Workmans' Act, a miner was liable to go before a magistrate and find himself prosecuted and fined for not turning up to work. The miners at Denaby and Cadeby had their own twelve member Absentee Board, where men, who were described as having 'slacking tendencies', would be dealt with without resorting to the courts. The offending men were judged by their peers, in an interesting industrial relations development of the time, where the incorporation of labour into governmental and workplace organisation was now being adopted. This method was described by *The Times* as being, 'so thoroughly English in character' that it has succeeded in many cases. 'Workmen are more susceptible to the judgement, opinions and censure of fellow workers rather than the employer or magistrate.'

Such was the pressure to deliver production for the war effort, *The Times* condemned the miners' customary act of refraining from working for 24 hours immediately after the death of one of their comrades killed at work. Such action by miners was regarded as paying tribute to their dead workmate. The newspaper did not appreciate this customary practice, described it as taking a 'holiday' and failed to see how this would help the families of their dead colleagues. The miners should, *The Times*, continued, abandon this illegal practice, as the situation now faced by the country didn't warrant such action. It was suggested that in the present crisis, miners should continue to work and hand their wages to the dependants of the deceased.

Work discipline was harsh in whatever industry or occupation one worked. The Munitions of War Act was a particularly authoritarian piece of legislation. Munitions factories became 'controlled establishments'. It became illegal to take strike action, workers could not leave their employment at free will, employers could not employ known 'shirkers' or those considered to be trouble makers. Munitions worker, who by now were mostly women, had to adhere strictly to time-keeping and very regular attendance.

Women also faced the dangers of possible explosions or 'blows' and the dangers of working with chemical such as TNT. Working with the TNT turned the munitionettes skin yellow, hence they became to be known as 'canary girls'. No amount of washing would remove the colouring. The younger women's hair would turn a golden colour and the older women, with grey hair, found they were 'fashioning' hair of a glass-green colour. Such would have been the working conditions for Mexborough and district women working in the nearby factories, the British Westfalite at Denaby Main (the powder works) and Baker's at Kilnhurst.

There was some compensation for the women of the munitions factories. Most were working class women, who in pre-war days were in 'service' as domestic servants or destined to be so. Although they were cheap labour compared to their male counterparts and they worked long hours, often twelve hours a day, they were able to earn a weekly wage beyond their wildest expectations. This allowed the women to have at least the potential to have some economic freedom previously out of their reach. The introduction of canteens into munitions factories at least provided a decent meal and a chance to socialise with, not only women of their own class, but sometimes with middle class supervisors, something they would never have experienced in domestic service.

Under the Munitions of War Act, local Munitions Tribunals were set. The tribunal for the Yorkshire and East Midlands was held at the Court House in Sheffield. This was the venue where munitions workers would have to attend if it was deemed they had contravened the Act. It was not only employees who could be fined or imprisoned, employers could also suffer from the harsh provisions of the Act.

There were a number of local firms penalised in the spring of 1916. If workers wanted to leave their employment, they were bound by the Act to receive a 'leaving certificate' which gave them the employer's permission to leave their place of employment. Equally the employer could not engage any worker without that worker presenting to them a certificate of permission to leave their previous employment. The Great Central Railway and Mexborough Locomotive Department weas brought before the Sheffield Munitions Tribunal charged with employing a man from John Bakers and Co without a certificate. Clearly the railway company was guilty of the offence, but in mitigation the Locomotive Superintendant Charles Hugill claimed that the Great Central Railway at Mexborough had lost 400 men to the military authorities and was finding it very 'difficult to keep things going'. Thomas Barrons at Mexborough had also breached the Act. They had employed a G. Smith, who despite receiving a certificate from C. H. Verity, did not appear on Barrons' books. Barrons' were fined £7 with two guineas (£2.20p) costs.

The harshness of the provisions of DORA, another piece of authoritarian legisalation, had seen the curtailment of the liberalism of the pre-war years. The sinister role of the state in curtailment of free speech is evident. In early April a NUR trade union organising secretary, living in Doncaster, was brought before the Barnsley Courts charged with contravening a section of DORA. The official, James Holmes, was prosecuted for making 'certain statements likely to cause disaffection to His Majesty, or likely to prejudice recruiting, training, discipline and administration of His Majesty's forces'. Captain H. Jacks of the Northern Command was prosecuting officer.

The NUR organising secretary was travelling in a railway brake van from Wombwell, as part of an investigation into an accident at Barrow Colliery. It was on this journey James Holmes was alleged to have said to a party of railwaymen that none of them should enlist and if they were conscripted they should, like him refuse to fight. Holmes was reported to have remarked, 'Why should I kill Germans who have done no harm to me?' His conversation was overheard by a Midland Railway locomotive inspector from Derby, Edward Wills. Wills was the main witness for the prosecution, but other railway company officials supported Wills' case.

James Holmes argued that the conversation was in regard to compulsory service and not meant to refer to voluntary recruitment which he believed was sufficient to attract men required by the military. He said he had addressed many meetings of his members advocating the necessity for recruitment.

Despite witnesses supporting the trade union official, the Bench fined Holmes £25 with costs or an alternative of two month's imprisonment. This was a hefty fine at this time and it might be assumed that the NUR were inclined to pay the fine on their man's behalf. At least it is known that local branches of the NUR came to the support of Mr Holmes. Frank Bailey of the Wath branch of the NUR was successful in getting a resolution passed in the branch expressing the view that the branch had every confidence in James Holmes and his ability as a union organising secretary.

A similar case in May, which involved restriction on speech, was again brought under a section of DORA against Michael Sheridan, described as a powerfully-built Irish labourer, living in Mexborough. Sheridan was said to be loitering around the railway lines near Mexborough, an offence under DORA in itself, late on the Saturday evening of 20th May. Private Joseph Waterfield of the Voluntary Defence Corps directed him to stop and declare who he was and what he was doing. This Sheridan eventually did and Private Waterfield placed him under arrest. After what Waterfield regarded as voicing anti–English sentiments, the Irishmen was handed over to the police. At Mexborough police station, PC Turner was said to have heard the prisoner articulating very hostile statements. The arrest had taken place just after the Easter uprising in Dublin, to which Sheridan made reference by stating, "the Irish in Dublin did the right thing, they ought to have shot all the ....English". The rebellious Sheridan had a number of witnesses willing to testify to his hostility to the English. Mrs Ellen, of 15, Adwick Road, gave evidence that Sheridan had been her lodger for a number of months and she and her husband had cautioned him to stop continually expressing antagonistic opinions against the English. If he did not refrain then, he was warned, he would have to leave his lodging, which he later did following his failure to heed the warnings.

It emerges that Michael Sheridan was a frequent visitor to the Red Lion public house in Bank Street, where Sam Cooper, the landlord, also witnessed the Irishman's anti-English utterances. There is little doubt that the Michael Sheridan's outburst against the English was influenced by the consumption of a good deal of alcohol. The chairman of the magistrates was in no mood to take this into account and sentenced the Irishman to two month's imprisonment.

It had by now been established in the minds of those at home that conditions at the Front were appalling. Yet it is clear that on the Home

Front, life, particularly for the working classes, was far from easy. The harshness of the draconian laws that curtailed liberties and even freedom of speech would have had a galvanising effect on the majority of the population, who would be keen to demonstrate their commitment to the war effort. According to *The Times* of 25th March, the female willingness to engage in the war effort was extending to unusual boundaries. The newspaper expressed it this way:

> '*The scope of women in the world's work of today has lost its horizons and the women's opportunities of usefulness have become limitless. Everywhere there is a demand for her services and more and more of the industrial burdens of the State are in exigencies of this great emergency, being shifted to her slender but willing shoulders.*'

What the paper was referring to were the local members of the Wath Wesleyan Chapel circuit, who were contemplating the appointment of women preachers. Non-conformists preachers were more likely to have sympathy with the CO's than the more orthodox churches, but this did not prevent them from joining the military in large numbers. Hence the shortage of Wesleyan preachers. There was now no hesitation to ponder the correctness or suitability of women preachers in Wesleyan chapels, such were the demands of the war effort. In *The Times'* view, 'Here is a duty which thousands of women are peculiarly fitted by temperament, education, and their nature to accept. It is work they might undertake a larger share of at any time. Feminine eloquence is quite as appropriate in the pulpit as the platform'. There never ceased to be such patronising words, even though women were now doing all kinds of work which two years earlier would have been hardly conceivable.

All classes of women were anxious to 'do their bit'. Much depended upon the class from which a woman came, as to the nature of her employment. Upper class women were the first to become involved in activities at the very beginning of the war, knowing full well their inclusion would be more acceptable to prominent men than that of the working class. Many committees were established under the authority of the more prosperous of women. In Mexborough the names of women from upper working and middle class backgrounds were associated with helping to run and organise charitable committees involved in assisting the soldier and sailor. The newspapers gave a list of some of these women who had been busy in the collection of gifts, clothing, boots and other comforts for British prisoners of war. Some of the names were familiar. Mrs Hope, the Vicar of Mexborough's wife, Mrs Thompson of 5, Melton Villas, Pinfold Lane, Mrs Popple, 150, Doncaster Road, Mrs Carter, 'Highbury', Church Street and Mrs Alderson, 16, Princess Road.

All had offered their time to serve charitable causes.

The Doncaster Road School log book has an entry as early as 8th September 1914 which records, 'Some of the older girls are making useful articles for soldiers. All classes and all ages of women turned their energies and skills to assist the boys at the Front'.

One such young woman, who gave her spare time to providing gifts to those serving abroad, was John 'Blondin' Shaw's daughter Miriam. Miriam had worked at the Hippodrome Theatre in Mexborough since 1911 (at that time the Prince of Wales Theatre). Miriam was about twenty at the time and like other women of her age encouraged to prepare parcels, containing items such as knitwear, cigarettes, chocolate and other provisions. Women were also encouraged to include a photograph of themselves with the purpose of helping to raise or maintain moral. Miriam, packaged her own parcel for dispatch to the Front and placed inside a postcard photo of herself, wrote her name and address, of 13, Dodsworth Street, Mexborough, on the back.

Where and at what time the package arrived at the Front and who it was destined for is unknown. Yet the parcel did arrive on the battlefields of the Western Front along with the photo of Miriam. Somehow Miriam's photo found itself pinned to a trench wall after being picked up by a Lance Sergeant Reg Bradley who was serving in the 20th Battalion of the Sherwood Foresters. Lance Sergeant Bradley returned the photo to Miriam's home in Mexborough with a letter which explains the story of how the photo was found:

'Dear Miss Shaw,
Just a few lines trusting they find you in the best of health as they leave me and the boys at present. I have no doubt you will begin to wonder who I am and how I have got your address. I will unravel the mystery. I had the pleasure of picking up your photograph along with others, and I asked all the boys in the platoon did they own the same, but the answer was in the negative. Your name and address was on the back of the same and as I picked it up in the Billets it evidently belongs to one of our boys. Of course you will be pleased to know that your photograph adorns the wall of one of our dugouts and my self and one or two of the boys wish the real thing was there to have a talk with us, as things sometimes get monotonous. I will be glad then the war is over and we can get back. What a time there will be when the boys come home. Well Miss Shaw I should be pleased to hear from you as to what I have to do with the photograph. Should you want me to return I will do so, otherwise I will keep the same. Sorry I have no photograph of myself here but my age is 23. In the meantime believe me to

be. Sincerely yours, Reg Bradley.'

Whilst Lance Sergeant Bradley clearly expresses the frustration of soldiers isolated from loved ones and a desire for the war to end and a return to social normality, his letter had every indication that he was keen to forge some kind of relationship with Miss Miriam Shaw, something he was later able to achieve. Miriam must have replied to Reg Bradley for her photo arrived back at 13, Dodsworth Street together with a photo of Reg himself, looking handsome in a police officer's uniform.

On the Lance Sergeant's return to England he met up with Miriam, who clearly took to the handsome young soldier, as they were to become engaged to be married. However, the relationship was not to last as it become obvious to Miriam that the sincere sounding words of his letter were not as plausible as they first appeared. She found that Reg was a 'ladies' man' and writing charming letters to young ladies may well have been Reg's regular pastime. Miriam broke off the engagement and in doing so made the symbolic gesture of seeing the engagement ring was appropriately destroyed. Miriam was shortly after to meet a Scotsman, John Graham, to whom she was happily married for the rest of her life.

The local MP for the Doncaster Division, Sir Charles Nicholson, spoke at the Division's Annual Meeting of the Liberal Party, justifying MPs salary of £400 per annum. He admitted he could do without it, but he argued that Kitchener had put him in change of over a thousand Military canteens and a Department of over 70 staff. The issue of this MPs salary in a time of austerity was soon to pale into insignificance when the news arrived that Sir Charles had lost his son in the service of his country. Sir Charles Nicholson, like many of his class, had sacrificed a son in a war, a war in which they passionately believed. His son was Captain George Nicholson, a Flying Officer in the Royal Flying Corps. George was on the platform in Doncaster when his father first won his seat in the 1906 election. There was talk of him being a prospective MP himself had he survived. Lord Derby had recently asked Captain Nicholson to become his secretary whilst he was acting as Joint War Air Committee chairman. The MPs son was never to take up his position in the Government, he was just another of a lost generation, who in the words of his class showed, 'a promise of greatness'.

The Mexborough Cricket Club held its Annual Dinner early in the year, as usual. This year it was hosted by Tom Athron at his Commercial Hotel with the club's president, John Clayton and Tom Chambers, the vice president, in attendance. William Winstanley, who was always a prominent figure in the Club, in his toast referred to the Club as the type of institution that made the Empire what it was and claimed the district was delivering the best in 'natural sportsman'.

John Clayton was able to tell those assembled at the dinner of the Club's investment in the new pavilion, but with it came a serious capital liability as the Club still owed £350 for its construction. The pavilion had been placed at the disposal of the Belgian Committee, free of charge. However the military, using the provisions of DORA, commandeered the pavilion for its own purposes. By this time there were seventeen Belgian refugees in the town with just nine left residing in the pavilion. One family of four was residing in Wellington Street and four other men were in lodgings around the town.

There was a growing concern that cricket in the town should not be played in wartime when, as it was described, the 'Empire was trembling in the balance'. Some were arguing that both married and single men were now away serving in the military and munitions workers had better things to do. It was the case that Mexborough Cricket Club was, by the beginning of the season, finding it increasingly difficult to raise a team and there was the prospect that only friendly matches would be able to be played. The whole question of cricket in the area being played in a time when money and manpower was of the essence, was discussed by the Mexborough and District League's Executive Committee in April. A Mr W.P. Turner was particularly concerned that clubs should not be registering professional players. It was inconceivable, Turner said, when the nation had to spend £5 million a day to maintain its war effort and with men killed and maimed daily, that any player should receive payment.

Mr J. Normanton from South Kirby believed that if the League did not pay 'good' money, then the bigger clubs in Yorkshire would pay and induce the best players with large inducements. Such was the conscience of the majority of the Committee that Mr Milner from Mitchell Main moved a resolution that the League would not engage professional players and would not pay fees in the forthcoming season due to start on 15th April. The resolution was passed unanimously. Furthermore, Mexborough's John Clayton put forward the proposal that all the gate money should go to charity. Such was the pressure upon all organisations to help the war effort in any way possible.

The start of the cricket season was to coincide with the Easter holidays. It was described as the 'First great Easter pleasure day' since the war began. There was an acknowledgement that, amid the gloom and the prospect of the war continuing, Mexborough and district should attempt some kind of relaxation from the stresses and strain of wartime life. The Easter holidays were to start on Thursday, 20th April, later than usual, but it gave the hard-working civilian population some opportunity for rest from their exertions in the mines, munitions factories, railways and other local industries. The weather was good after the heavy rains and flooding of the Don and Dearne in the early part of the year, giving many the opportunity to spend their leisure time getting out in the countryside.

The Good Friday Procession was led, as usual, by the clergymen from the Parish Church, the Reverend Edmund Hope, Reverend Lee and the Reverend C.W. Siran. Mr E Popple from St George's Parish Church was responsible for carrying the Cross at the head of the procession. Starting at the Parish Church, the procession halted at Montagu Square, where the various vicars gave their addresses before passing down the High Street towards St George's School.

As the hard working people of the district returned to work after the Easter holidays they would have done so well into daylight hours with hours of daylight going to waste. It had struck a certain William Willett back in 1908 that by advancing clocks by one hour this would adjust this seeming waste of daylight in the morning and so give more daylight in the evening for those, such as in agriculture, who might need it. Parliament decided that Willett's idea should be taken up and so introduced the 'Summer Time Act'. On Sunday, 21st May at 2.00am all clocks went forward one hour and were turned back again on 1st October. The result, it was observed by watchful parliamentarians, increased work efficiency and allowed for more healthy evening time leisure as well as work. It was, however, recognised that some parents now had difficulty in getting their children to bed at a reasonable time. It appears in the Mexborough district there were no real incidents occurring as a result of these changes, suggesting as least locally the innovation was readily accepted. The change was accompanied by outstanding weather and many took the opportunity afforded by the extra hour's sunshine to go 'walking abroad in the evening'. The success of the experiment was enough for daylight saving to become permanent.

Empire Day, on 24th May, fell on same week as the introduction of daylight saving. Remarkably, the occasion was not celebrated in the way that it might have been expected. The comment in *The Times* indicates surprise and indignation. 'Empire Day passed practically unnoticed in this district and at a time when the significance of the festival was never deeper. Save for a little casual display of bunting in some schools and from some public buildings, there was not an outward indication that May 24th had any greater claim upon the stolid and unemotional South Yorkshire Briton than any other day of the year'. The newspaper was puzzled as to this apparent, in its view, lack of patriotism when the 'greatest Empire the world has ever known' was at risk.

Despite Empire Day passing uneventfully, people of the district were aware of the importance of occasions and continued to support those events which demonstrated a more local solidarity. On 10th June, Mexborough's second Union Jack Day took place under the auspices of the Urban District Council. The event raised £52 17s 1d (£52.85p) with the proceeds going to the Mexborough Relief Fund and the YMCA's 'Hunt Fund'. Perhaps because of low key celebrations on Empire Day, the District School Committee of the Council thought it necessary to reinforce the importance of Union Jack Day. Doncaster Road School's Log Book records on 8th June, 'D.S.C. suggests the Mexborough Union Jack Day effort be brought prominently before the scholars by a special lesson on the Flag on Friday'.

Saturday, 24th June saw the third anniversary of Rose Day, again with the proceedings going to Montagu Hospital. Throughout the district, on this occasion a total of £187 was raised.

On the following Sunday afternoon, the Annual Demonstration took place, again in aid of Montagu Hospital. This saw a procession of local Sunday Schools, Friendly Societies, the Fire Brigade, Denaby Ambulance Brigade, Salvation Army and the Mexborough and Swinton Volunteer Corps, led by its Commander William Winstanley. The possession, as usual, assembled for the service on the cricket field at Hampden Road. The event raised the modest sum of £25.

If Easter holidays were spent with some relaxation for workers, then the Whitsuntide holidays were not. The Mexborough UDC was requested by the Government, as other local authorities were, to abandon the Whitsuntide festival. This was a universal request to the nation to maintain a continued effort in workplaces to increase production through the Government's machinery of total war. Another entry in the Doncaster Road School Log Book for 8th June records, 'Holidays previously arranged for Whitsuntide postponed in view of the Government's appeal'. The whole of the Don and Dearne Valley would have to forfeit its traditional festival. Any speculation that the Allies were preparing for a big offensive in France may well have been strengthened by this decision to abandon the 'Feast' holiday. Full production of shells and equipment was needed to fuel the 'big push' which was to start within weeks. The war was now beginning to enter its second year and the casualty lists in the newspapers grew longer. The reality of the war was now evident in district by way of grief and the sight of wounded men hoping to recover or of men who would never be fit again as a result their service in the frontline.

There was to be another military funeral and burial which took place at Mexborough Cemetery on 7th June. It was the funeral of the 20 year old Lance Corporal Joseph Venables of the Cameron Highlanders. Venables father, also Joseph, was the landlord of the Royal Oak Inn, Mexborough. The Lance Corporal, a butcher by trade, had enlisted in October 1915. While on sentry duty in France on 22nd May, he was struck by a German grenade in the back of the legs. Joseph was transported to a hospital in Rouen before reaching a hospital in Salford, Manchester. Joseph Venables had seemingly recovered well when gangrene developed in his badly cut and burned leg, but died as a consequence of these wounds on 3rd June. Like the other servicemen up to this time buried in Mexborough Cemetery, Lance Corporal Venables was afforded full military honours. The York and Lancs band from Pontefract was, as before, in attendance, along with military representatives from various regiments including, the KOYLI, RE and ASC. Mexborough Recruiting Officer, Sergeant Oddy, was, as always, there to pay his respects. There was a large contingent of family mourners. At the graveside the Reverend Lee officiated, his address was followed by the firing of a volley of shots and the sounding of the 'Last Post'.

It is doubtful if many people in the district could envisage that within less than four weeks of Lance Corporal Venable's funeral, *The Times* would be full of photos of his dead and wounded comrades who were to be slaughtered on The Somme. Of the dead only a few, such as Joseph Venables, would find a resting place in the peaceful surrounds of Mexborough Cemetery. For most there would be no homecoming and a last farewell from their loved ones.

Chapter Thirteen

At the Front: Preparing for the 'Big Push'

Militarily, 1915 had been a bad year for the Allied Powers. There was little doubt that the Central Powers had the advantage following the Allied disasters of 1915. Yet some valuable lessons had been taken on board and the military were optimistically anticipating better outcomes for the New Year. Issues were being 'solved' on the Home Front with the help of the restriction placed on society by DORA and the introduction of conscription reduced the worst concerns over the shortage of military manpower. Generally the trade unions were more cooperative and the labour market saw a plentiful supply of willing women workers. Preparation for an enormous offensive against the Germans was now gathering momentum, both at home and in France.

Chief of the German General Staff, General von Falkenhayn, was aware of the developing strength of the Allied forces. He was anxious to inflict a victory upon them before the advantage of the increased manpower and resources was placed at the disposal of the British and French forces. Both the Allies and the Germans had taken the decision that the war would be fought on the Western Front.

It was Germany's intention to commit its forces to an offensive against the French who were defending the well-fortified city of Verdun. The sector around the city was of great strategic importance, as it was in the centre of the French lines. As well as this, it was also of cultural importance to France and Falkenhayn knew it would be defended at all costs. Verdun had been symbolic in that it had become an important place in French national pride after being vigorously defended during the Franco-Prussian War. Falkenhayn cynically remarked of France's defence of Verdun, "If they do so, the forces of France will bleed to death", whether or not the battle for Verdun ended in a German victory. His intention was to "bleed the French Army white".

The German attack on Verdun was due to start on 12th February, but was postponed until the 21st due to blizzards and rains. At 7.00am on the first day, the fighting began with 2.5 million shells being fired on the German forces. So began the battles of attrition on the Western Front lasting throughout most of 1916. So furious and bloody was the fighting during the Battle of Verdun the whole sector was to become known as the 'Mincing Machine'. By the end of March both the French and German armies had collectively suffered over 80,000 casualties. The battle continued until 15th December with the distinction of being the longest battle of the entire First World War, resulting in 500,000 French casualties.

The French were at severe risk of a disastrous defeat at the Battle of Verdun between the start of the fighting and into July. The situation was critical for the French, so much so that General Joffre, the French Commander-in-Chief, was desperate for the British to initiate their offensive on the Somme and bring much needed relief for the French forces. Joffre and Haig had met at a conference in December 1915 to discuss the proposals for a massive Franco-British offensive. The offensive was originally to take place in the spring of 1916, but intervention of the German offensive at Verdun and a feeling of unpreparedness by Haig had put back the plans until the summer.

Many of the older established battalions of the York and Lancs and the KOYLI had been out in France for some time and suffered severely during the battles of 1915. The 'New Army' service battalions of both the York and Lancs and the KOYLI were now beginning to reach the Western Front to prepare for the long anticipated offensive. For example, the 9th York and Lancs found themselves in these preparations in the Fleurbaix sector in early January.

The 8th York and Lancs, another service battalion, which contained many Mexborough and district New Army men, were alongside the 9th York and Lancs during the period of the preparations on the Somme. One of the first Mexborough men to die in 1916 was from the 8th York and Lancs, Private Edward H. Briant, killed on 20th January. Edward Briant, known locally to his mates as 'Cockney', was 24 years of age and had previously worked at Wath Main Colliery. It was left to his sergeant to convey to Mrs Briant, who lived at 62, Kirby Street, that her husband had been shot through the stomach and died almost at once.

The 9th KOYLI had been operating in and around Ypres for some time prior to the start of preparations for the Franco-British offensive. The battalion's colleagues from the 10th Battalion of the KOYLI were to take part in a trench raid on the German position during the evening of

25th January. Such trench raids were a regular occurrence of trench warfare. The Germans responded to this particular trench raid by engaging in heavy shelling, over three days, on the front line where the 9th Battalion KOYLI was situated. There were a number of KOYLI dead as a result of the intense bombardment, including a Mexborough member of the 9th KOYLI, Private Herbert William Wright. A second lieutenant of the Battalion described how he was nearly killed by shrapnel and how 'D' Company, probably Private Wright's company, was affected by the shelling. The officer remarked, 'D Company had to leave their trenches and come along and take refuge in ours. They had eight to ten casualties, four or five were suffocated in a dug-out which fell in on top of them, pretty beastly, being buried alive. I think I'd prefer anything to that'.

A few days later, the 9th KOYLI suffered six more fatalities on 12th February, as a result of a 'tremendous explosion' from a German 'Minenwarfer', a mine launcher. On this occasion another Mexborough member of the Battalion, Private William Wilkinson, met his death. Private Wilkinson is buried near his Mexborough comrades in Cite Bonjean Military Cemetery, Armentieres.

A history of the 9th York and Lancs, records that February was a quiet and uneventful period, although the weather saw intermittent frosts and snow. The month of March was said to have been very much the same in terms of the weather, but that Fluerbaix was heavily shelled. Although there were periods which were relatively subdued, as experienced by the 9th York and Lancs, the shelling and the killing continued. Mr and Mrs Johnson of Commercial Row, Mexborough, heard news that their son, Sergeant Thomas Johnson, had been killed one 18th March. Sergeant Johnson, aged 24, was member of the RFA attached to the 164th Rotherham Howitzer Brigade. He had been in the choir at Mexborough Parish Church and played for their football team. Tom had been a clerk working for Messers Grocock and Company, Swinton and the secretary of the Mexborough branch of the Clerks' Association. Sergeant Johnson left a widow, previously a Miss A. Miller, who worked as a teacher at Garden Street School before the couple married in Preston in June 1915. Mrs Johnson returned to Preston to live.

Tom Johnson's officer, Captain H. C. Worrall, wrote to Tom's family with information about the events leading to his death and some consoling words, which was usually the purpose of such letter from a soldiers' officer. Sergeant Johnson had been hit in the head after inspecting a building which had just been shelled. He was performing the inspection to ascertain that all of his men were safe. He was quickly moved to a field hospital three miles away and underwent an operation. 'This bravery', remarked Captain Worrell demonstrated that he died as he lived, 'clean'. Captain Worrell continued, 'Tommy was greatly esteemed by all in the brigade and all the officers recognise that he is a serious loss'.

Tom Johnson had been a pupil at Garden Street School. On reading of his death, a former schoolmaster of his, Mr W.R. Hudson, wrote a letter from Harrogate to *The Times* expressing his sadness. It was not the first time that Mr Hudson had read of the death of one of his 'old' scholars in the service of his country. Apparently Tom Johnson was extremely well liked by both his teachers and school colleagues alike. Mr Hudson had particularly taken to Tom. Before departing to the Front, Tom had been stationed at Ripon and on his last Saturday afternoon, before embarking for France he visited his old schoolmaster's home in Harrogate. Mr Hudson remarked that he and his wife never had a son of their own, and were glad to have Tom Johnson's company and treated him as if he were their own.

The old schoolmaster would have been no different from hundreds of schoolteachers throughout the country. Many of their old pupils would have responded to Kitchener's call and paid the ultimate price on the battlefield. Mr Hudson referred to Tom Johnson and young men like him and of the sacrifice they made by writing, 'When war was declared Tom like so many more Mexborough lads needed no conscription. King and country needed him and he went. He has fallen and is now honoured in a foreign land'. The most telling sentence of his letter is a description of Tom Johnson's character that would probably apply to most young men who had died on the killing fields of France, Flanders and elsewhere, 'What a fine young fellow. How full of vigorous life and health.'

Ernest Goodbody was a cornet player with the Mexborough and Swinton Bands, but found himself as a bugler with the York and Lancs. While working at Manvers Main he had enlisted in September 1914 at the age of sixteen. He was probably serving with the 8th or 9th York and Lancs who, by the time of his death on 26th April, had arrived at Albert and taken over their first Somme trench from 1st April. Their position was heavily under shrapnel, grenade and rifle fire during this period and this was probably how he met his death at just nineteen years of age. He was said by his company captain to be one of the smartest in his outfit and had qualities which saw Ernest chosen as his personal orderly. In a letter to Bugler Goodbody's parents, who lived at 7, Alfred Place, Mexborough, his captain wrote in the language of the time, 'He died fighting for his country which is the noblest death of all'.

Mrs Depledge of 69, Frederick Street was to learn she had become a widow with three young children to support. She received a letter concerning the death of her husband, Private George Depledge of the York and Lancs, on 15th April. The letter was from two of George's sergeants, Sergeant D. Talbot and Sergeant R. J. Skelton. The two NCOs' wrote, 'We all know what a sad blow this will be to you and your children as we knew George was a good husband. All of us miss him. He was buried this afternoon at 3 o'clock in a quiet little graveyard in this town and we shall take care his grave is well looked after'.

Two Mexborough men, both from the 2nd Battalion of the York and Lancs, died on the same day, 21st April. They were Private Richard Hirst, known as Dick and Private George Horton. Dick Hirst, a small man of less than 5 feet 3 inches, a former miner at Manvers Main, had enlisted in May 1915 and was 20 years of age when he died. He had only arrived in France on 2nd February. His comrade Private Pat Finerty, who was later to die himself in September, wrote to Dick's mother, Mary, who lived at 258, Wath Road, Mexborough. In the usual attempt to give some comfort to the deceased parents, Private Finerty wrote that Dick died without pain and only spoke briefly saying, 'Lads I am hit in the stomach and I'm going home.' His comrade described how Private Dick Hirst, 'just lay back as if to go to sleep and the breath went from him'.

Little is known about Private George Horton. We know that he, too, was a miner and an older man of 34. After he attested, on 4th January 1915, he was quickly posted to France on 1st April of the same year. George and his wife, Ada, had lived at 27, Hall Gate, Mexborough with their three daughters, Mary, Alice and Doris and son George who on his father's death had not reached his first birthday.

While preparations were commencing on the Western Front for the big offensive, events elsewhere no doubt reached the attention of those in France and Flanders. The Royal Navy was to engage in the biggest sea battle since the days of the Battle of Trafalgar. The British Navy had taken part in action during the war in various parts of the world, but never as the complete 'Grand Fleet'. However, it was to engage the German fleet as a complete British naval force at the end of May 1916. A number of German warships from the German 'High Sea Fleet' had attacked Scarborough, Whitby and Hartlepool, killing over 100 civilians and seriously damaging property. More attacks on the British mainland were to follow in the April of 1916, as Vice-Admiral Reinhard Scheer decided upon an aggressive policy of sea warfare given the stalemate prevailing elsewhere in the conflict. A number of the German fleet put to sea in an effort to bombard the east coast towns of Great Yarmonth and Lowestoft on 25th April. On this occasion some damage to the towns was sustained, but, through important intelligence, the British warships marginally failed to intercept the German warships which were to make a hasty retreat. It was on the basis of such good intelligence that the British Grand Fleet were ready to engage the full might of the German navy.

The British fleet was of numerical superiority to that of Germany's fleet. Under Vice-Admiral Sir David Beatty the British fleet numbered 151 ships to the 99 of the enemy. This superiority was a problem for the German navy and one which the Kaiser was never happy with. It was the intention of German command to draw the British fleet into an engagement which would see sufficient destruction of the British navy so as to achieve some equilibrium of strength. The German fleet left their base at Wilhelmshaven on 31st May. Beatty had anticipated Scheer's intentions and with his total of nine ships had left the base at Rosyth some two and half hours earlier than the German fleet departed from its base.

British Admiral Sir John Jellicoe left his base at Scapa Flow with 28 Dreadnought battleships to assist Beatty. Beatty had sighted a section of the German fleet under the command Admiral Hipper at 3.35pm, although at the same time Jellicoe had not realised there was any urgency believing that the German Fleet had not put to sea. Beatty's ships raced to intercept Hipper's fleet believing Sheer's battleships were still in port at the time. Sheer was indeed at sea, but missed the opportunity to engage Beatty and it was Hipper and Beatty's ships who would engage in a horrendous sea battle. It was to be fought at Jutland off the coast of Denmark and to be the last great sea battle of all time, costing many lives. The Battle of Jutland, on the evening of 31st May, saw the loss of fourteen British and eleven German ships. Over 8,500 sailors lost their lives, over 6,000 British and about 2,500 German. Both sides claimed victory, the Germans on the basis of the greater British losses. The British claim of victory was on the basis that in the early hours of the morning of 1st June, despite the remaining German 'High Sea Fleet' managing to retreat back to port, it had effectively been forced into retirement never again to be put to sea during the war and never again engaging the British in such a massive force. From this time on Germany relied on submarine warfare utilising their U-boats as their main maritime force. Yet there can be little doubt that in reality British confidence in its naval supremacy had been seriously undermined.

The significance of the Battle of Jutland for Mexborough is that taking part in the encounter was Mexborough's youngest serviceman, the sixteen year old Able Seaman William (Willie) Barker. Born in December 1899, Willie originally lived in Kimberworth, Rotherham. By 1911 he and his family had moved to Mexborough and were living at 8, Ferry Boat Lane. Willie Barker decided to join the Royal Navy as a boy sailor in July 1915 when still at the tender age of fifteen. There is evidence to suggest that Willie, who trained at the Naval Barracks at Devonport, Plymouth, undertook his training with Seaman Jack Travers Cornwell. When only sixteen years of age Jack Travers Cornwell was posthumously awarded the Victoria Cross for his bravery during the Battle of Jutland whilst on aboard the *HMS Chester*. Barker and Travers joined the navy at the same time and both trained as sight setters. After completing his training, Willie Barker left Devonport for the Rosyth base in Scotland. He joined his ship, the *HMS Dublin*, a new, light cruiser in the same class as Jack Cornwell's *HMS Chester*.

At about 4.30pm on the afternoon of the Battle of Jutland the *HMS Dublin* was alongside one of Beatty's battle cruisers, the *HMS Queen Mary*. The *Queen Mary* was hit twice in a terrifying attack by one of the Hipper's German battle cruisers, *Derfflinderer*. The *Queen Mary* received a direct hit, immediately exploded and became a raging inferno. She sank within minutes with the loss of 1,200 men; only eighteen men survived. Able Seaman Willie Barker with the *HMS Dublin* would have witnessed this terrible incident. One of Willie's shipmates, William Cave, gave an interview to his local newspaper in June 1916 with an eyewitness account of what the crew of the *HMS Dublin* had seen. He described the horrifying scene in this way:

> *'In every detail we could see officers, signalmen and others. The Queen Mary was already doing about 20 knots with the fore section blown forward causing a higher bow than before only listing slightly to port, then skidding around starboard towards the Dublin. She actually parted our helm to avoid hitting us but it proved unnecessary with increasing list she dived her fore turret guns at full elevation, hot with firing off a loud and hissing as they met the water. It was terrible to hear those poor souls so near yet so far and being unable to help.'*

The *Dublin* scored some 'success' when it hit the German warship *SMS Elbring*. Able Seaman Barker was also interviewed by the press on his leave immediately after the Jutland battle. In *The Times* in early June Barker described what happen.

> *'Towards sunset we became aware that two enemy destroyers were making dead set for us, and were trying to track us down. We were standing silhouetted against the sunset and they were lying in the shadow. We were cruising at a tremendous speed so whenever we swerved in our course we heeled hard over and were washed by heavy waves. The sea was choppy rather than rough. One big wave caught me and threw me on to the gun. I thought my leg must have been broken for I could not raise my leg and I felt very sick. My mate picked me up and carried me down to the third deck where I spent the remainder of the action. What happened next I subsequently learnt from my mates.'*

Willie Barker went on to recall that as night fell the enemy destroyers closed in on his ship and threw their searchlights across the

HMS Dublin. One of the German destroyers was then distracted by a British cruiser's searchlights, enabling the *Dublin* to focus their own searchlight upon the enemy In Willie Barker's words, 'In a surprisingly short time the *Dublin* and other British cruisers pounded the two German destroyers to bits.'

Immediately before the *HMS Dublin's* success the ship found itself, just before sunset, amidst heavy fire. Although Willie Barker made light of the incident in his newspaper interview, his ship sustained damage when hit along with its sister ship the light cruiser *HMS Southampton*. The *Dublin* saw three of its crew killed with a further 27 injured.

During this historic sea battle, the young man from Mexborough, still only sixteen, witnessed horrors which resulted in the death and injury of his naval comrades. To witness the manner in which they were killed and injured must have had an immense psychological impact upon him.

Willie Barker had told his story to *The Times* in the June of 1916. Almost two years to the day he was home in Mexborough again, on leave, in June 1918. It had just turned the second anniversary of the Battle of Jutland. Willie had spent his leave days at his parents' house at 8, Ferry Boat Lane. He was due to return to his ship on 7th June, but for some reason decided to remain at home for another night. The next morning the young sailor left home, his family believing he was returning to his ship, albeit a day late. At about 9.30pm Willie Barker found his way to a railway bridge on the Midland Railway between Swinton and Kilnhurst stations. As an express goods train, travelling towards Sheffield reached the bridge, the young man threw himself into its path and he was killed instantly.

Local newspaper articles do not refer to William Barker's death as suicide but merely that he had been killed on the Midland Railway. As suicide at the time was a criminal offence it was a word that was discreetly used, especially in relation to active servicemen. At the coroner's inquest, in Rotherham during the following week, it was made known that, since the Battle of Jutland, poor Baker had suffered from headaches. The coroner returned a verdict of suicide whilst temporarily insane, suffering from a disturbed mind. The inescapable conclusion was that Able Seaman William Barker's experiences at sea were responsible for his state of mind and consequently the taking of his own life. There is probably little doubt that in today's terminology he would have been considered to be suffering from post-traumatic stress disorder. Had he lived in today's world, William Baker may have had the treatment necessary to assist him to cope with the impact of his dreadful experiences. In his time and in this war, such understanding and treatment were lacking particularly for those of his rank and social class.

William Barker was not the only Mexborough sailor to be on leave in the early days of June after serving at Jutland. Although it is not known what ship he was on, Seaman Gunner William Arthur Corbett arrived home at 6.30 on a Tuesday morning at his father's house in Argyle Street. His father, a well-known evangelist, had risen from his bed to let his son in after hearing him shouting, no doubt waking the whole street, 'We've broken the back of the German navy'. On Thursday of that week William Corbett had the uncomfortable task of travelling to Wath to break the sad news that his mate, Able-Seaman A. Oldhams, had died of injuries during the encounter with the German navy. Able Seaman's parents, who lived on Sandymount Road, Wath, had seen their son just one month before his death, Corbett told the Oldhams of their son's gallantry, no doubt in an attempt to ease the misery and pain of their loss.

Able Seaman Barker was the youngest 'man' from Mexborough to serve in the forces. One of the oldest was Sapper William Hackett. No account of Mexborough and district in the First World War can be written without mention of Mexborough's one and only, to present, recipient of the Victoria Cross (VC). Much has been written about William Hackett, both locally and nationally, although an in-depth study of his life remains to be undertaken. There are, however, a number of extensive articles written about Hackett and it is not intended here to give other than a brief account of William Hackett's life and bravery and his contribution as Mexborough's best known war hero.

William Hackett was not a native of Mexborough. He was born into great hardship and poverty in Nottingham on 11th June 1873. As a consequence of his poor upbringing, the young Hackett never received an education beyond that learned from the experiences of his social upbringing in a coalfield community. William was to remain illiterate for the rest of his life. He left his place of birth and is said to have walked to Denaby Main at the age of eighteen where he gained employment at the colliery, remaining there for over twenty years. Whilst in Denaby he married Alice Tooby at Conisborough Parish Church in April 1900.

There is no firm date as to when Hackett moved to 49, Cross Gate in Mexborough, but it is likely that it was just before the outbreak of war. He had gained work at Manvers Main Colliery as a repairer layer of the underground railway system. By the time he was settled into his home in Mexborough, William Hackett had two children, son Arthur and daughter Mary.

Hackett was one of those who, at the outbreak of war in 1914, responded to the Kitchener's call along with many of his colleague from Manvers Main pit. He attempted to join the York and Lancs, but was turned down, three times, due to a slight heart problem and on account of his age. He was by this time over 40 years of age. By the end of 1915, with the war having hit a stalemate there was a growing acknowledgement by the military that the conflict would need to be concentrated on the Western Front. Preparations for the 'big push' gave an opening for willing volunteers such William Hackett. On 25th October

1915 he was accepted in the Royal Engineers and was assigned firstly to the 172nd Tunnelling Company and later transferred to the 252nd Company who had first operated in Gallipoli.

Mining under the enemy's defences and blowing up their positions with explosives was a strategy often used by the military in a previous era. The revival of tunnelling was now believed to be a method of warfare which would greatly assist the infantry to make advances. As early as December 1914, commanding officer of the IV Corps, Sir Henry Rawlinson, had wanted to establish a special group to assist in mining duties. The Germans had already started using its own mining tactics. A Major John Norton-Griffiths first suggested employing 'Clay kickers', who had originally been employed in mining operation on the London underground. Norton Griffiths saw these men as most suitable for military tunnelling work. It had not escaped the attention of the military that coal miners were also eminently suited for tunnelling work under the enemy's defences.

The first British mine to be blown was at Hill 60, in February 1915, proving a successful operation. During 1915 there was an extensive use of this type of warfare and as a result the majority of the tunnelling companies were formed. Men like Sapper Hackett were primarily engaged for tunnelling work in preparation for the British-Franco offensive on the Somme in the summer of 1916. Men who volunteered for this type of duty, often lured by the extra pay they were afforded, found themselves quickly utilised for service underground at the Front within days of joining up. Hackett himself appears to have been hurried to the Front. After only two weeks training and a brief few day's leave, he arrived in Givenchy-lès-la-Bassée in northern France. Tunnelling operations in this region of France were, in the summer of 1916, mainly diversionary. The purpose was to keep German forces occupied and draw their attention away from the preparations taking place on the Somme.

William Hackett would not have spent Christmas 1915 at home with his family, such was the urgency with which his services were needed on the Western Front. He was never to see his family again. His fourteen year old son Arthur had only left school that Christmas in order to take up a job in Manvers Main Colliery. Within less than four weeks of Arthur starting work the boy was involved in an accident which resulted in his right leg having to be amputated below the knee. William Hackett himself had been involved in a roof fall at the same pit just a short period before his son's accident. He heard the news of his injured son within a couple of months into his duty in France. Through a friend, who wrote a letter back home on his behalf, Hackett was able to express his distress and frustration at being in France and unable to help his poor son.

Sapper Hackett was engaged in the very dangerous work, along with his fellow tunnellers, in laying mines under the German trenches on the Givenchy front on 22nd and 23rd June. (Dated as 27th June in some records). The British positions around Givenchy were very heavily shelled in the early hours of the morning. This included the saps in which Hackett and his colleague were working. The Germans had counter-mined and, it appears, undermined the British saps, blowing them up along with some of the British front line trenches at about 2.50am This caused a crater which was to be become known as the 'Red Dragon'. The explosion caused extensive damage below ground to the main drive from the Shaftsbury Shaft in which Sapper Hackett and his four comrades were working. The shock caused the timbers near the shift to move resulting in a roof fall which cut the men off. Rescue workers attempted to release the trapped men, but it took 24 hours before an opening made it possible for three of the men to escape to safety. Two men remained trapped in an area where a smaller roof fall had occurred near the face. One of these men being Hackett, the other his colleague, who was badly injured. The rescue party was able to establish an opening that Hackett could have released himself through, but the injuries of the other man were so severe that he was unable to help himself through the opening. As it was feared there was an imminent danger of a further roof fall, the Mexborough soldier was ordered to immediately withdraw from the danger area. He refused to accept the order and remained with his injured comrade. Just before a fall of clay which engulfed the two men, William Hackett spoke the now well quoted words, "I am a Tunneler, I must look after my mates." All efforts to reach the men once more failed. One of the first reports of Sapper Hackett's brave sacrifice was to appear in *The Times* four weeks after the incident on 22nd July. Captain G. M. Edwards of Sapper Hackett's company wrote to Mrs Alice Hackett:

> *'I find it very difficult to express to you adequately the admiration I and all the officers had for the heroic manner in which your husband met this death. Sad as his loss may be to his own people yet his fearless conduct and wonderful self-sacrifice must always be a source of pride and comfort to you all...... He has been recommended for the VC, that simple medal which represents all that is brave and noble. In token of our esteem the officers and men of this unit are sending you a small gift in the near future which I trust will be accepted.'*

The recommendation for Hackett to receive the Victoria Cross was quickly acted upon. On 4th August 1916 the London Gazette duly made the announcement of his conspicuous bravery, outlining to the British public the events of that fateful morning. It was not long before Mrs

Alice Hackett was attending a presentation in order to receive her husband's medal. On Wednesday 29th November Mrs Hackett received the posthumous award from King George V at Buckingham Palace.

With extraordinary rapidity the people of Mexborough rallied to support William Hackett's widow and children as well as expressing the wish to erect a memorial in the soldier's honour. The news that Mexborough was about to gain its first and, up to now, only recipient of the VC prompted the Urban District Council to set up an appeal to create a local memorial in Hackett's honour. The memorial fund drew donations from a wide range of subscribers, but local collieries, local business and individual leaders of local industry and commence were the major sources of funding for the monument. By the beginning of December the total fund amounted to, for those days, the considerable sum of in excess of £142.

William Hackett's Mexborough memorial came in the form of a tablet, made of granite and manufactured by the Swinton firm of Messrs Tyas and Guest, who at their own expense added the Mexborough coat of arms. On Saturday, 19th May 1917 the tablet was affixed to the frontage of the Market Hall and Council Rooms and unveiled in front of a large gathering of the general public, local dignities and military personnel. The tablet is inscribed, 'To the Memory of Our Comrade Sapper William Hackett Killed on 22nd – 23rd June 1916 in France, While Rescuing His Comrades'. The tablet was removed from its original position the Market Hall in 1997 to a perhaps a more fitting place alongside the War Memorial at Castle Hills on Doncaster Road, where it remains to the present. As to the date of Sapper Hackett's death there is some discrepancy. On official military documents and on the Commonwealth War Graves Commission records the date of death is recorded as 27th June 1916. It can be assumed that there was some confusion amid the 'fog of war'.

As far as William Hackett's military memorial is concerned he is remembered on panel 1 of the Ploegsteert Memorial. However there is now another fitting memorial to Mexborough's hero. A memorial costing £24,000 has been erected above the place where Sapper Hackett's body lay in the Shaftsbury Shaft near the village of Givenchy-lès-la-Bassée. The memorial was unveiled on 19th June 2010. Speaking at the unveiling military historian Peter Barton remarked:

> "The memorial is to honour the tunnellers and in particular Sapper Hackett, who fought a war underground that not many people are aware of. His V.C. medal was most deserved. That it is not to discredit the others but his actions were of the most noble kind. I don't think anyone can identify with what these soldiers went

through. But we can relate to being in a claustrophobic place. And this is where his moment of supreme bravery came, not on the battlefield but metres below in the cold and dark.'"

That fact that Sapper Hackett was posthumously awarded the V.C in 1916 was, at the time, something that was accepted in the town with great pride. William Hackett's name is probably recognised throughout the world today as symbolising the bravery of the military rank of sapper and tunneller, in fact being the only tunneller to receive the VC. Despite the town of Mexborough experiencing, in the late 20th and early 21st century, severe economic decline through the demise of the coalmining industry, it is not unreasonable to say that Sapper Hackett's name is still acknowledged with pride amongst the town's community.

It had been agreed between General Joffre and General Haig on 14th June that the combined offensive of French and British troops would take place astride the River Somme. The German attack on the French at Verdun, despite Haig's eagerness to relieve the pressure on the French, forestalled the original plan. The French army had suffered severe casualties as a result of the German attack on Verdun and it became clear that British forces would have less assistance from the French. Plans were altered to accommodate this. But by the spring, Joffre was desperate for the BEF to engage the Germans along the Somme as soon as possible. Haig was thinking in terms of the offensive commencing as late as August but he was under pressure from General Joffre. Eventually an agreement was reached that the offensive would begin on 25th June, the latest date being 29th June.

For many men from the Don and Dearne Valley area the Somme offensive would be their first experience of fighting in a full-scale offensive. The massive forces that the BEF had now assembled were about to take on an enemy they had vowed to defeat for King and country. Many had trained for months both at home in Britain and in France. Some would have hardly trained at all as new recruits drafted in as a consequence of the 'Derby Scheme'. There was a constant influx to the Front of men who had been in training at the notorious training camp at Etaples on the north coast of France. It would be Kitchener's New Army who would have to bear the brunt of the mission into which their country's military leaders were about to cast them into.

The diaries of officers of the 9th and 10th York and Lancs are revealing. On 22nd March, the 9th Battalion paraded at 5.45am for Major Willis to announce the sentence of a Court Martial of a private in 'A' company. We now know this to be Private Charles Bladen (14357) who was aged 26. Bladen had deserted in France, managed to reach England, but was brought back to face a Court Martial. Bladen was sentenced to death, his demise was to be witnessed by the entire 9th York and Lancs. The assembling of the whole of the Battalion would have been to make a point to others that desertion was not an option for coping with any anxiety about the forthcoming offensive. Private Bladen was shot at dawn, by a firing party provided by the Battalion under the command of Second Lieutenant A.W. Lamond.

Clearly the men, witnessing the great activity that was taking place on the Somme, were aware something big was about to commence but knew nothing of their specific roles. Activity in the weeks preceding the Somme offensive varied from labouring on trench work to raiding parties and occasional leisure, but there was always the threat of heavy shelling and sniper fire. The 9th York and Lancs arrived in Albert on 31st March and the next day took over its first Somme trenches and experienced heavy shrapnel and rifle fire. The Battalion was constantly in and out of the line in this period. They were back in the line on 14th April on the edge of Albert, where once again they were subject to a great deal of shelling from the German artillery.

The Battalion's diary describes this constant bombardment that the troops, engaged in preparation in or near the front line, had to endure. The 9th Battalion York and Lancs padre, Padre Farringtion, had been preparing a special dinner for the officers at their HQ on 29th April. Again heavy shelling from artillery rained down along with tear gas late at night. J.B. Montagu remarked that, 'The shelling continued until 10.30pm by which time the feast was ruined'. By 1st May they were in the line once more at La Baiselle when they were relieved by their colleagues of the 8th Battalion, with its large contingent of Mexborough and district men. Here the two Battalions were said to be just 60 yards from the German front line in a place the men came to know as the 'Glory Hole'. From here the Battalions made raids upon the German line which resulted in retaliation and temporary withdrawal by the 9th Battalion behind the lines into a reserve position. Later, in May, it is reported that the first draft of 'Derby Scheme' men were to arrive. The numbers were building and the various battalions beginning to reach full strength.

There would have been periods where the assembling British forces would have quieter moments. Despite this shelling, the raiding parties, sniping incursions and working parties of about six officers and 100 men would take place on a regular basis in the days before the offensive. The diary of Second Lieutenant R.M. Wilkinson writing of the activities of the 10th York and Lancs during this time, remarked, 'One soldier withdrew the pin from a Mills Bomb which dropped from his hand into the mud, exploded and killed him.' Clearly life was no picnic for the men who were about to commit themselves to the biggest battle of their army career. Working parties undertaking digging and repairing trenches would often take place at night time in very uncomfortable conditions. The battalions that were drawn from the coalfield areas contained miners and others from the labouring classes. These men always amazed officers with their resilience to undertake trench work with relative ease. One report on this work observed, 'A remarkable piece of digging, each man dug 70 cubic feet, in the dark in four hours'. The 10th Battalion's diary refers to the outstanding digging capacity of the Yorkshire miner.

There were moments for the men of relaxation and engagement in leisure pursuits. There were inter-brigade sports events which broke up the arduous tasks of trench digging and the dangerous activities of the raiding parties. One such event was a boxing tournament involving the 10th Battalion York and Lancs. The 10th York and Lancs diary mentions that during June the Battalion learned that the well-to-do English actor and singer Basil Hallam, famous for his rendering of 'Gilbert the Filbert', was in the area of the battalions' billets. With the full name Basil Hallam Radford, he was a Captain and an observer with a Kite Balloon section. He undertook a show for the Battalion but the men were said to be less than impressed. Captain Hallam was killed later in August when his balloon drifted into enemy lines. He attempted to bale out after being attacked, but his parachute failed to function and he plunged to his death.

The men of course sought their leisure and perhaps 'pleasure' in the rare moments of leave behind the lines. The private diaries of the York and Lancs regiments makes cursory mention of where the men might have spent their leave. R.M. Wilkinson reveals that while billeted at Heilly his men spent time in the Hotel de la Poste. Another centre of attraction was however the local bank. The bank was a billet for officers, but the bank often got overwhelmed by visitors. It appears the visitors were not intending to open bank accounts, but observe the bank manger's daughter. Another favourite retreat in Heilly was a café run by 'three fair damsels'. Whatever the attraction of the venue, the PBI (poor bloody infantry) had to take a back seat to the officers. The 9th Battalion York and Lancs diary also makes reference to the Hotal du Rhin Amiens which for reason, which we can only speculate upon, had been placed out of bounds by the General Commandant. No officers, NCO's or men were permitted to take billets or permanent quarters in Amiens without authority of army HQ.

What must have come as a shock to all was the death of Lord Kitchener on 5th June. It was the call from Kitchener to which thousands of Yorkshiremen and others responded, almost two years earlier. Kitchener was on his way to Russia for a conference when the ship he was travelling on, the *HMS Hampshire*, hit a German mine and was sunk. This iconic figure perished in the North Sea. News had filtered to the Somme the next day and the 10th York and Lancs diary simply records the shock with which the men received the news. The 9th

Battalion's diary remarks of Kitchener that it was, 'largely his administrative genius that the country has been able to create a place in the field for the Armies which today are upholding the traditional glories of the Empire'. The news must have been a psychological blow to the morale, at least momentarily, for the members of Kitchener's Army, at a time when it was least needed. Vera Brittain, in her book, 'Testament of Youth', expresses how many might have felt of Lord Kitchener's death, by saying of the event that it, 'seemed more startling, more dreadful than the tidings of Jutland; their incredibility may still be measured by the rumour, which so long persisted, that he was not dead...(and) would return in his own good time to deliver the final blow of the War'.

However there was no time in June to dwell on thoughts of events which might hinder the preparation for the massive offensive. The men of the 10th York and Lancs were to keep their spirits up with the songs of the day. Second Lieutenant Wilkinson recalled the gusto with which his men sang songs such as 'Tipperary' and 'Mademoiselle from Armentieres, parley vous'. But, remarked Wilkinson, 'The men of the Somme Battle, at a sing song, liked best of all, 'It's only a beautiful picture in a beautiful golden frame'.

The Somme offensive, which was originally planned to begin on 29th June, would be fought mainly on a fourteen mile front between Serre and Maricourt. The attack would be under the command of Sir Henry Rawlinson whose Fourth Army was made up of eighteen divisions. Of these divisions, the 70th Brigade of the 8th Division was made up of those regiments and battalions which drew a large number of Mexborough and district men of the 8th and 9th York and Lancs and the 8th KOYLI. The 21st Division, too, consisted of men from the area, although they would also have originated from the Doncaster area. The 63rd Brigade of this Division contained the 10th York and Lancs some who had seen fighting at Loos. The 64th Brigade contained the 9th and 10th KOYLI, 9th who, too, had suffered severe losses at Loos a year earlier. The 31st Division also had its 94th Brigade, which consisted of the three south Yorkshire 'Pals' regiments, the Sheffield City Battalion and the two Barnsley Pals Battalions. The 49th Division, the West Riding Division, was made up of territorials. The 148th Brigade of this Division consisted of four local battalions of the KOYLI and York and Lancs, the 1/4th and 1/5th from each Regiment.

The Somme offensive has been written about in great detail over the years. As it was the worst day in history, in regard to the number of casualties, it is not surprising that more words have been written concerning it than any other battle involving the British Army. It is sufficient to only briefly mention salient points.

The British artillery were issued with their orders on 5th June relating to the plan to bombard the German lines, continuously over a period of five days between 24th to 28th June. This was to be extended when Zero Day was postponed until 1st July as a result of the poor weather conditions. The artillery was able to deploy nearly 1,500 guns for the operations. It was a bombardment the like of which had never before been witnessed, with the eventual firing of over 1.5 million shells on to the enemy positions. The noise from the guns was said to be heard in parts of the south of England. The objective of this vast bombardment was to devastate the German defences and cut their defensive barbed wire system. This latter objective proved to be a patent failure. The air bursting shrapnel shells turned out to be ineffective with one third of the shells failing to explode and cut the German's barbed wire. Added to this failure, the bombardment only served to alert the Germans that an attack was imminent.

As for the plan to devastate the German trench defences, this too was a failure. The Germans, who held the high ground, were carefully accommodated in deep-dug, often concrete bunkers, with machine guns positioned for every conceivable angle of attack. The bunkers were equipped with electric lighting and steel doors, kitchens and capable of holding hundreds of men. This was the result of eighteen months preparation and the area in which south Yorkshire men were to fight was amongst the best defended on the Somme Front. With the bombardment having little impact on seriously destroying the enemy's defence, the idea that British troops would meet minimal resistance became an illusion. The British troops had rehearsed their attack time behind the lines, but the reality would be different. One diarist commenting on this rehearsal remarked, 'The troops marching through crops were instructed to advance as if on a parade. No thought was given to enemy resistance.' It appears that the men wearing the correct dress was more important to the military hierarchy than talk of the possibility and extent of enemy resistance.

The 9th York and Lancs diary records on 19th of June that the men were very cheerful. There can be little doubt however that as Z Day (Zero Day) approached there was tension and anxiety among all ranks. In the 10th York and Lancs diary, R.M. Wilkinson gives an insight as to the confusion and perhaps maneuvering which was taking place. On 29th June, Wilkinson wrote that the Brigadier General had informed the CO that in view of the coming offensive he thought that a Major Wallis was too young to be second in command. For this reason Wallis had relinquished his post. Wilkinson clearly saw this as unreasonable as his replacement would not appear in time, and '(be) left out of the show' until the worst had passed. The young officer continued, 'Eventually we become 'dizzy' with the succession of the seconds in command who joined us for a short period then fluttered away to some other appointment'. There was no such option for Second Lieutenant Wilkinson and men under his command to choose where they might be during the offence. Nor of course were the young men in the lower ranks of the 'New Army' considered too young, despite their inexperience, to face the horrors which were about to come.

The 120,000 infantrymen employed in the attack were moved up line to their positions on the originally planned Z Day of 29th June. Many would have been anxious to get it over with but were stalled by the bad weather of mist, rain and low cloud. As the artillery bombardment continued throughout 29th July, the Battalions formed of Yorkshiremen sat together in their trenches in the rain, their clothes thoroughly soaked, feeling most miserable no doubt. For some their thoughts would have been with their loved ones in Mexborough, Swinton, Wath, Bolton-upon-Dearne, Conisbrough, Denaby and elsewhere. Some would have written home to these loved ones and for many, these letters would be their last. Second Lieutenant Wilkinson expressed the view that he and his men were eagerly looking forward to the coming offensive, particularly as every man knew the part he was supposed to play in the attack, unlike the 'complete ignorance that had prevailed at Loos'. He also revealed the tensions and fears of the assembled troops in the early hours of the morning of Saturday, 1st July. The wait and the uncomfortable conditions the men found themselves in were clearly psychologically unfavourable to facing the enemy. Wilkinson wrote:

> 'The officers and men's spirits remained high although we found later that standing in the trench in the cold hours of early morning waiting for zero hour was not conductive to enthusiasm or to make us see red, unless the rum ration happened to be increased.'

As dawn broke on that first day of July 1916, the rain and mists of the previous days disappeared, rays of sunlight appeared, changing to glorious sunshine and clear blue skies. It was as if to send an invitation to the assembled infantrymen to believe their fortunes would also be as bright and clear as the day itself. The men had been briefed and told that it would only be necessary for them to walk at a steady pace in order to achieve their objectives of taking the German positions. It was Rawlinson's belief, 'Nothing could exist at the conclusion of the bombardment in the area covered by it'. Despite Rawlinson's belief, observers had reported that this in reality was not the case but had been rebuked with the suggestion that they were in fear of the enemy. This British commanders' mindset of self-delusion would consequently lead to the death of thousands of Britain's finest young men.

The infantry were also hampered by other orders they received. Kitchener had given the instructions that once captured German position were to be consolidated. For this the infantryman were to carry equipment that weighed around 66 lbs. This was of course to severely restrict mobility once into 'No Man's Land'. This is very well illustrated by the Operation Order No 1 issued by the Fourth Army, forwarded to the 9th York and Lancs by their commander Lieutenant Colonel A.J.B. Addison. Some of the orders included the instructions that:

> Every NCO and every man to carry two Mills Bombs each, plus in addition to 120 rounds of ammunition and are to carry two extra bandoliers making 220 rounds per man.
> Every NCO and man will carry four sandbags.
> Each Company will carry 16 picks, 32 shovels slung on their backs by cord. These tools will be carried by the men in the second line.
> Ten boxes per Company of Lewis gun ammunition will be carried forward by the Company. The boxes to be dumped in the German front line.

The zero hour of 7.30am was now approaching. The men must have been exhausted even before the battle had begun. They had marched from behind the lines through the communication trenches to their front line trench positions, burdened by the heavy weight of their equipment and the apprehension of their long wait for battle action. Some men had been able to sleep, for others this was an impossibility. The tension must have been palpable. Second Lieutenant Wilkinson, whilst waiting with 'D' Company of the 10th York and Lancs recorded; 'Rum was issued at dawn and who will forget the long wait to zero hour and the intense concentration of the barrage. Ladders were leaning against the sides of the trenches to assist everyone in leaving them'; Ten of the seventeen mines that were exploded were detonated early, warning the German of the imminent attack. Wilkinson described how at exactly 7.30am mines were blown at La Boiselle, east of Albert and how it 'literally rocked our trenches'.

The assembled infantry with bayonets now fixed, waited for their officer's whistle to sound. As it sounded, the first wave climbed the ladder to the parapet and into 'No Man's Land'. Many were no more than boys, or at least extremely young men, who could not have imagined in their deepest nightmares the horrors which they were about to face. Men, as an old campaigner once described, 'Who had never struck a child or never kicked a dog', had entered the killing fields. The war was now in the hands of the innocent youth of Britain who were about to be savagely cut down.

Chapter Fourteen

South Yorkshire's Finest in 'Hell's Parade': The Song of the Skylark, the Last Sound of Sweet Life

It is estimated that of the near 60,000 casualities on the first day of the Battle of the Somme, 9,000 were from Yorkshire regiments. The densely populated areas of the south Yorkshire coalfields had more than its share of mourning its dead. The Barnsley Pals, Sheffield City Battalion, the Doncaster regiments of the KOYLI and the Rotherham raised York and Lancs Service Battalions were certainly amongst them. Of all those from Mexborough and district the men of the 8th and 9th York and Lancs were to become the greatest victims on that fateful day of 1st July 1916. The list of Mexborough men, including Swinton men, identified as being killed on the first day, totalled 50. Of these, 25 were from the 8th Battalion York and Lancs and twelve from the 9th Battalion. Figures from Martin Middlebrook's book, *The First Day of the Somme*, with reference to the Battle of the Somme (or the Battle of Albert as it was officially known), records that the 8th York and Lancs saw a total of 597 casualties, including 21 officers (higher figures are recorded elsewhere). This casualty rate was higher than that of the well-known Accrington and Barnsley Pals.

It is not intended here to go into great detail on the minutia of the Battle of Somme itself. Thousands of men died because of mistakes of the commanding officers and the misunderstandings thrown up by the so-called 'fog of war'. The infantry were always at a strategic disadvantage, given false information about the resistance they were due to face and often with no protection from their own artillery. They were simply eliminated by the enemy's artillery and of course cut down like wheat in an English harvest time field by the continuing existence of powerful German machine gun units.

The 8th and 9th York and Lancs Battalions, made up the 70th Brigade of the 8th Division of Rawlinson's Fourth Army. The 8th was to form the frontline on the left of the attack, with the 8th KOYLI forming the right frontline. These two Battalions were to proceed in two waves, with the 9th York and Lancs behind them in support. The reserve battalion was the 11th Sherwood Foresters.

The 8th York and Lancs War Diary is typical of many as it described the last moment the Battalion went 'over the top' and the subsequent events:

> *'The first wave left the trenches in perfect order and to time, and at once met by exceptionally heavy fire from front and both flanks. Most of the men were killed or wounded, but the remainder continued to advance. In spite of the heavy fire the remaining waves advanced to the attack, but before getting half-way to the enemy trenches they were mown down by the machine-guns. About seventy men reached the enemy trench and some of these eventually reached the enemy's third line of his front system. Here they remained fighting for some time until all were killed or taken prisoner, one returned. The remainder held up in the enemy front line and considerable fighting took place here until all were killed; only three returned.'*

The diary records that eighteen of their 23 officers had been killed which included the Regiment's Lieutenant Colonel B.L. Maddison. Somewhere in this bloody advance of the 8th Battalion, towards the German positions, were 25 men from Mexborough and Swinton. Records of some of these men still exist and it is possible, at least, to tell a little about them. George William Oliver was one of the 25 men of 8th Battalion who died. Born in 1893, by the time of the 1901 census he was living at 12, Foundry Lane, Mexborough. He had two young brothers Samuel and Wilfred. His father, a glass bottle worker, was also named Samuel. George joined the army on 12th December 1915, just one month short of his 23rd birthday. Like many from Mexborough, he was recruited by Sergeant Oddy. George was a well-built man being 5 feet 10 inches in height at the time of recruitment. At the time he would have been considered as extremely tall. George's occupation on his attestation papers is described as 'labourer. This could have been his occupation within a number of local industries. Private Oliver was immediately sent to Pontefract Barracks where he joined the 11th Reserve Battalion of the

York and Lancs and after a few days there, and possibly a short leave, he was sent to Rugeley Camp in Staffordshire for training. By all accounts he never found himself in trouble with the army authorities, as his conduct sheet remained blank.

After going through what would have been a very rigorous training programme at Rugeley Camp, he was given his various vaccinations for foreign active service. Private Oliver then embarked from Folkstone to Boulogne on 27th May 1916, less than five weeks before he would enter his first and last full-scale action with the enemy. Still with the 11th Reserve Battalion, he was probably finishing off his training at the notorious training camp at Etaples before moving up to the front line. His records show that he joined the 8th Battalion of York and Lancs, 'in the field', on 23rd June 1916, this being about the same time as the massive British bombardment of the German lines had started. Nothing could have prepared the young Private George Oliver for such an experience. Within just over a week George would be going over the parapet into No Man's Land and to his death.

No real details exist of how George Oliver and many of his colleagues met their end, apart from the familiar stories and images of men being cut to pieces by shell and machine gun fire. All that is known is the story handed down by George's colleague, who was with him at the time, to his relatives, who still live in Mexborough today. The colleague was alongside George when a shell burst over his head. It was the last time the young George William Oliver was seen. Like many who were killed on that day, George was reported missing. On hearing the news that their sons or husbands were 'missing' families often sent out pleas to newspapers asking readers for any news as to the whereabouts of their loved ones. George Oliver's family made a similar plea on hearing the dreadful message concerning their son from the War Office.

Another 8th York and Lancs man and a comrade of George Oliver's, to lose his life on 1st July, was Private Levi Mountford. At the time of his enlistment on 8th February 1915, he was a bricklayer and living at 3, Pitt Street. As was often usual when a local man joined the York and Lancs he initially joined the 11th Reserve Battalion and went into training at Rugeley Camp. Levi married local school teacher Doris Yarnold of Queen Street, Swinton, the couple enjoying a very short honeymoon lasting just two days before Levi was sent to France on 26th May. Tragically Doris never saw her husband again, she was to become a widow within five short weeks.

Private Levi Mountford was a keen sportsman and well-known by many in the town as he had played cricket for Mexborough Cricket Club on many occasions. Levi's father Enoch, was himself a keen cricket enthusiast, but at the time of his son's death was extremely ill, something undoubtedly not helped by the sad news. In the September, a

Benefit Cricket Match was played on the Mexborough ground, between the Constitutional Club and the so called 'Mexborough Specials'. The proceeds from the match were to aid Enoch financially but it would have been surprising if Mrs Doris Mountford was not also a benefactor.

Corporal Thomas Alan Burgan was a Mexborough railwayman whose name can be seen on the Mexborough Station war memorial. He was to become one of the first employees of the Great Central Railway at Mexborough to attest as a volunteer soldier. This he did on 3rd September 1914, when employed as a passed cleaner or spare fireman at Mexborough Locomotive department. He was quickly posted to the 8th York and Lancs two weeks later. By November 1915 he had become a lance corporal and promoted to corporal on 8th April 1916, whilst the Battalion was preparing for the big offensive in France.

Corporal Burgan was killed along with his comrades in the 8th as it advanced east from Authuille Wood to the south of Thiepval. He was a single man of 25 years and had lived at 23, Lorna Road, Mexborough, a street well-known for the number of 'locomen' who lived there, earning the nickname 'Superheater Street'. Here, Cororal Burgan lived with his father Thomas, mother Sarah, a brother and three sisters, the youngest being Doris.

Corporal Burgan's colleague from Mexborough Loco, Fred Depledge, a boilermaker's helper, was killed alongside him. Fred was a Swinton man living at Brookfield Nurseries, Fitzwilliam Street. He was just approaching 25 years of age when he joined on 16th November at Mexborough recruiting office being, again, one of Sergeant Oddy's many recruits. He was quickly posted to Otley for his training a week later.

Fred Depledge was made a lance corporal on 27th July 1915. It is likely that he returned to his employment on the Great Central Railway for a while until he was recalled by the Army. This call came on 25th January 1916, when like many, duty in France beckoned.

As with many slaughtered on the first day of the Somme, Corporal Fred Depledge was recorded as missing as late as 16th July. It was not until the 4th October that his records declared that he was killed in action on 1st July. The sad news of his death was eventually to reach Swinton. It was news not to be received by his parent Richard and Annie, for by this time they had died, but by his sister Sarah Platts, living at 105, Queens Road, Swinton.

A good many residents of Queen Street Swinton were to receive the same message as Sarah Platts, namely the death of their loved ones. *The Times* reported, 'Many Swinton soldiers are among the missing since 1st July and Queen Street has been particularly hard hit in this respect. Queen Street is a veritable line of soldier's homes and almost daily news comes through of casualties from the War Office'.

Lance Sergeant Albert Valentine Brown was born in Bradford, but like many others, arrived in Mexborough to gain the type of employment the town was able to provide. Although little information about is available we know that he was one of the early recruits, enlisting on 4th September 1914 at the age of 32. At the time he was living at 22, Doncaster Road, Mexborough.

The remains of Lance Sergeant Brown's army records do not tell us when he embarked to France in the service of the 8th York and Lancs. He had been made a lance corporal in August 1915, a corporal in February 1916 and been given the position of unpaid lance sergeant on 25th May 1916. It wasn't long before he was paid for his rank as lance sergeant, obtaining payment on the 1st June, just one month before he was to be killed in action alongside his Mexborough colleagues of the 8th Battalion.

Another casualty of the 8th York and Lancs who died on 1st July was Private John Holt of 28, Crossgate. Little is known about him other than he had two brothers serving; Gunner George Holt with the RFA in France and Private Walter Holt serving with the Durham Light Infantry.

William Kershaw was born in 1890, lived with his mother Edith Kershaw at 9, Pinfold Lane, Mexborough, before enlisting on 11th November 1914, when he was just approaching his 25th birthday. He embarked for France on 28th August 1915 with 8th York and Lancs and become another 1st July casualty.

Yet another 8th Battalion man to fall on the first day of the Somme was Lance Corporal John Thomas Earnshaw. He was a big man for the times, standing 5 feet 9 inches tall and weighing 159 pounds, a good physique for his trade, a miner at Manvers Main. His army records do record, however, he had a slight eyesight defect, which it remarks, was not sufficient to cause rejection from the army. This was a small problem which, 'Would be greatly improved with glasses'.

Earnshaw, according the 1911 census, had once been a lodger at 25, Makin Street, Mexborough, in the days when he was a single man. He married an Adelaide Sharp on 23rd March 1913, and moved into 22, Wellington Street, Mexborough. Here the couple had a son they called William Henry, born on 13th April 1915. The birth of his son took place just shortly before Thomas Earnshaw joined the army on 18th May 1915. A day later Private Earnshaw, was posted to Sunderland where he firstly joined the 3rd Reserve Battalion of the York and Lancs. He must have seen very little of his new born son.

On 6th March 1916, Private Earnshaw, became Lance Corporal Earnshaw and was posted to join the 8th Battalion on 6th April, embarking for France the same day. By 28th April his records describe him as 'In the field'. Lance Corporal Earnshaw was not at home in Mexborough for his son's first birthday, but preparing to take part in the Battle of the Somme, which resulted in his wife Adelaide becoming a widow with the task of raising their son, William Henry, alone.

Mrs Adelaide Earnshaw received the news that her husband was missing, when he had in fact been killed in action, although his body was never found. By February 1917, she had moved to Leeds and in March 1917 Adelaide received a letter, like many other widows of the Battle of the Somme, which simply told her that her husband Lance Corporal Earnshaw had left no effects. Perhaps one piece of news that was welcome was received in February 1917; this was to inform Adelaide Earnshaw that she was to receive 15/- per week pension plus 2/-(10p) per week for her son. However this was little compensation for the loss of her husband; in fact it was less than she was receiving in Separation Allowance and Allotment Pay when Lance Corporal Earnshaw was alive.

With the 8th KOYLI and the 8th York and Lancs going over the top first in four waves, it is likely that the third and fourth wave suffered the greatest losses as a result of enemy machine gun fire. As the last man from these Battalions disappeared into No Man's Land the 9th York and Lancs had their orders to move into their own first line trench in readiness to climb on to the parapet and follow their comrades in support.

The 'Orders' issued to the 9th York and Lancs instructed them that once the first wave of the Battalion had crossed the parapet they were to move forward to the German front line. The instructions ran, 'The second wave of the 9th Battalion will remain in our front line trench until the first wave has evacuated the German front line, when they will move forward to occupy that trench.' The first objective was to be consolidated in 30 minutes, the second Germany trench in 1 hour 15 minutes. The theory was straightforward, the reality quite different.

At 7.40am the first wave of the 9th Battalion left the trenches and was immediately met from the left by alarming machine gun fire. The first wave reached the German frontline but with terrible consequences. The 9th Battalion diary records, the second wave were unable to advance at all, hampered by the barrage and the dead and returning wounded. Amongst the horror and commotion someone could be heard shouting the word "return" and it was evident that some of the men were trying to do just that. Things got progressively worse when the 11th Sherwood Foresters moved up, only to suffer heavy losses. All communication were cut and by now it was said to be impossible to stand anywhere in No Man's Land.

By 10.16am there were still a 100 men from the 9th Battalion left in their trenches; they were simply penned in by the intensity of German machine gun fire. No Man's Land was now described as impassible. The brave men of the 9th Battalion made repeated efforts to achieve their objectives, but with communication already broken down, they 'had become inextricably' mixed up with the 11th Sherwood Foresters.

The breakdown in communications just added to the mayhem and carnage. At 2.00 pm the last effort to re-establish communication across No Man's Land was made. The Battalion's machine gunners and trench mortars suffered heavily as the Germans were able to bring up reinforcements. The last of the 100 men of the 9th Battalion, who were waiting to cross No Man's Land, were quickly reduced to about 50 men. They did not attempt to enter the massacre they were witnessing, but instead spent time clearing their own trenches and helping to evacuate the wounded.

Those of the 9th Battalion who reached German frontline were attacking the enemy with Mills bombs (grenades) and engaged in some hand to hand fighting with the Germans. Finally, the men of the Battalion were pushed from the German trenches with many of the survivors in No Man's Land waiting for relief. A much needed respite from the fighting was afforded as a result of the fading summer light, but by 10.00pm the Battalion's casualties numbered 22 officers and 556 other ranks. The Brigade commander's report recorded these sobering words, 'The 9th York and Lancs fought for over six hours in positions won by them from the enemy, until they were dead.'

The 9th Battalion of the York and Lancs had not suffered quite the numbers of casualties as their comrades in the 8th Battalion. Of the hundreds that were casualties, 25 Mexborough and Swinton men had fallen fighting with the 8th Battalion. Elsewhere in the slaughter their comrades in the 9th Battalion saw twelve Mexborough and Swinton men killed in action. One of the twelve was Private Frank Blunt.

Frank Blunt came from a family whose men were, if there was ever such a thing, 'natural' soldiers. His father Isaiah was the landlord of the Albion Inn in Mexborough, a public house which came to be known as 'The Staff'. Frank had two younger brothers, Adam and Isaiah junior, who both returned from Canada to join Frank's regiment, the York and Lancs. Isaiah, an old soldier and a reservist had been killed in November 1914 in the first Battle of Ypres. The family originated from Denaby Main where both Isaiah and Frank started their occupations as miners. Frank married Myra Bamforth from Denaby in 1905, settled in Mexborough and had four children, the first one, a boy in 1906, who the couple named Frank.

At the time of his enlistment at the age of 37, on the 23rd February 1915, Frank Blunt and his family were living at 5, Mills Court, High Street, Mexborough. Private Frank Blunt probably left with his Battalion in the August for France as his records indicate he was in France in November of 1915. His records also suggest he was wounded on 21st July 1916. Such was the confusion of the actual whereabouts and fate of the men on 1st July, recordings such as this were commonplace. He was like many of his comrades recorded as missing, he had just 'disappeared' with nothing found to enable him to be given a grave or a headstone. His name is on the Thiepval Memorial, built to remember the 72,000 missing on the Somme. By the time the news of Frank Blunt's death reached his wife in Mexborough her oldest son Frank was ten years of age; another boy with his father's names but without his father.

Private Alfred Whaite, originally came from Gainsborough but moved to Mexborough for work and settled down to live at 20, Pitt Street. He decided to join the army in November 1914. By this time he was nearly 35 years of age and probably had been encouraged to join as a result of previous army experience in the 2nd Manchester Regiment. This experience saw him considered as a reserve soldier, and initially he was attached to one of the York and Lancs Reserve Battalions. His records tell us his statistics about his height, weight and physique which gives the impression of a powerfully built man. He was over 5 feet 7inches, weighed 161 pounds and had a 41 inch chest. It is likely that Private Whaite was posted to the 9th Battalion in November 1915, again in readiness for the preparations on the Somme and eventually his death on that battlefield alongside his Mexborough comrades.

Thomas Oliver was a Mexborough miner, single and living at 26, Doncaster Road. He was also one of the hundreds of men who emigrated from various parts of Britain to make their living in the local coalfields. It is fair to assume he came from Melton Constable where his father lived at the time of Thomas's enlistment on 29th December 1914 at the age of 28. Private Thomas Oliver, as he was to become, did his initial training with the 9th Battalion in England before going out to France in August 1915. He had a sister by the name of Lucie, who was a nursing sister in Alexandra, Egypt. The news of her brother's death on the Somme must have been a devastating blow despite her witnessing the sight of death on a daily basis.

Mexborough's Corporal Herbert Bentley's existing army records tell little about him. We do know his father went by the unusual name of Dan Sherry Bentley and lived at 5, Lorna Road, this being Herbert's home when he decided to enlist on 1st March 1915 when just short of his 22nd birthday. He had previously worked as a miner.

It is likely that, as a young recruit, Herbert would have had substantial training in England. Some of this training would have been at Lymirye, Kent before departing for France. Further training may have taken place at Etaples in France before joining up with the 9th Battalion in May 1916. At this time he was still Private Herbert Bentley. He was promoted to corporal on 26th June whilst the heavy bombardment of the German lines was taking place. He held his newly acquired rank of corporal for less than a week before he too was declared 'missing' and became another Mexborough name on the Thiepval Memorial.

Herbert Bentley was the youngest of a family of seven children, including three sisters. Apart from sister Sarah, who was living in Denaby, the other brother and sisters were still living in various parts of Mexborough after the war. Herbert's father received his son's campaign medals, like other relatives, in 1919, when living at Springfield Terrace, Garden Street. The receipt of these medals would have perhaps engendered mixed emotions, pride but also a sad painful reminder of the loss off the youngest member of the family.

Somewhere in the carnage experienced by the 9th York and Lancs was Private Sam Wright, yet another miner. He had lived at 2, Cambridge Street, Mexborough and had joined the army on 4th June 1915. He was just nineteen years of age and again, like his colleague Herbert Bentley, the youngest of a family of seven children. His mother was named Maria. Sam arrived in France on 20th April 1916 in readiness to join the other men of his Battalion. Still just twenty years of age, the Battle of the Somme would be what he had trained for during the previous twelve long months and his first experience of real warfare. This first day of Private Sam Wright's taste of warfare was to be the worst day any British soldier had ever faced or has ever faced since.

Private George Shenton was from Swinton and another to die with the 9th York and Lancs on that fateful day of 1st July. At the onset of the war he lived with his wife, Jesse, whom he had married in Swinton in 1902 and his four children at 12, Thomas Street, Swinton. A miner, George attested for service on 17th February 1915 at the late age of nearly 39. He was sent to France in February 1916 but after a short time in the trenches found himself in Etaples suffering illness, after which he rejoined his Battalion in May. George Shenton's wife was at this time receiving 21/6d Separation Allowance per week plus 3/6d a week 'Allotment' money that George had granted to her from his army pay.

A Mrs Beatrice Oxer, who lived a few doors away from the George Shenton and his wife, had the sad task of writing to the Infantry Records Office in York to inform them that Jesse Shenton had died. Mrs Oxer's letter also informed the army that George Shenton's sister, by now Agnes Stead of 31 Barker Street, Mexborough, was left to bring up Private Shenton's four children and that Agnes was in need of her brother's pension. A further letter explained that George had not left a will, believing that his wife would be able to provide for the children from his army pension. Jesse Shenton had however, as the letter said, 'left word for all to be distributed between the children'.

Within a short space of time the Shenton children had been orphaned. In 1920 the children were still living with Agnes Stead at Barker Street where Mrs Stead received her brother's campaign medals. With reference to the 1914-15 Star, she received the note that it would become the property of George's eldest son Walter, with the proviso that, 'it be kept in care until he becomes of an age to appreciate its proper value'. It can only be hoped that the young Walter Shenton did come to appreciate his father's sacrifice.

The 10th York and Lancs, containing a number of Mexborough

men, were to find themselves in the 63rd Brigade of the 21st Division. The Division's objective on July 1st was to take the well-fortified village of Fricourt, at that time held by the Germans. The 63th Brigade took up a position on the right of the Division just north of Fricourt, a position badly exposed to German machine gun fire. The 63th Brigade was made up of varied battalions. The 4th Battalion of the Middlesex Regiment and the 8th Battalion of the Somerset Light Infantry Regiment in the front of the attack were supported by the 8th Lincolnshires and the 10th York and Lancs. According to some accounts the 10th West Yorks were just in front of the 10th York and Lancs. The 10th West Yorks were to sustain the highest number of casualties of any battalion on the first day of the Battle of the Somme. This gives some indication of the furious nature of the attack in which the 10th York and Lancs were engaged.

The 10th York and Lancs had been out in France and Flanders since 1915 and had lost heavily at the Battle of Loos. It was now about to sustain its fair share of casualties in its attempt to take the Fricourt Salient. There was just one local soldier from the 10th York and Lancs who perished on the first day of the Somme, Private Charles Christopher White. Charles Christopher White came from a big family, was known as Charlie and had been born in Middlestown, Wakefield in 1897, before moving to Conisbrough shortly after. Charlie probably finished his education at school in Mexborough where the family had moved to 76, Victoria Road sometime before 1911. In 1911 his first employment was an errand boy, probably working in the grocer's shop opposite his house in Victoria Road. Charlie later became a miner. Charlie White attested on 2nd September 1915, another of Sergeant J. Oddy's recruits and made the decision to join the 10th York and Lancs. As was normal, the young recruits of the York and Lancashire Regiment, after attesting at Mexborough, were moved quickly to Pontrefact Barracks, for a further medical, 'kitting out' and awaited allocation to a training camp.

Private White was, within days of him joining up, sent to Rugeley Camp on Cannock Chase. This was also the training camp of the 12th York and Lancs, the Sheffield City Battalion and the two Barnsley Pals Battalions the 13th and 14th York and Lancs. It was also the training camp for the Accrington Pals. All these Battalions would be fighting alongside each other on the Somme in less than ten months. Training on Cannock Chase was in preparation for the Battle of the Somme and by all accounts, a very tough training regime. Charlie White and his comrades at that time may not have known what action they were actually training for, but when he received his vaccinations on 29th September for foreign service he knew he would be soon be leaving the shores of Britain.

Private White was given his first home leave in November, leave which should have lasted to 21st of that month, but he overstayed his leave pass by two days, arriving back at camp at two o'clock in the morning. For this offence he was 'admonished' and had to forfeit three day's pay. It was not at all unusual for men to be charged with this offence, many army records, record 'overstaying his pass'. We know that Charlie was a strong family man with extended family ties. His army records bear witness to this, when we read records which list his relations. The majority of his family lived on Victoria Road, Mexborough and he would have wanted to spend as much time with this extended family as he possibly he could. Home leave from the army was always for fixed days with the leave pass including the time it took to get home and back. Although it included free travel, the duration of the leave never took into account the time needed to travel from the camp to home and back again. The further distance a soldier was away from his base camp the more he was at a disadvantage. With this and travel problems, created by the chaos of wartime travel on the railways, it is not surprising many soldiers overstayed.

Private White was granted some leave over the Christmas period of 1915. One can only imagine the moment when Charlie set off to make the long journey back to his camp in Staffordshire. He would have done so very reluctantly, his close-knit family saddened to see his departure. The reluctant soldier should have arrived back at Rugeley Camp by 9.30pm on 27th December, but didn't turn up at the camp until late evening of 30th December. Again Private White was in trouble for overstaying his pass which saw a Captain Roberts impose the punishment of four days confined to barracks with a further four day's loss of pay. Charlie may well have thought that this punishment was small sacrifice for time spent over Christmas at Victoria Road. Whether or not Charlie White had further leave before his posting to France, there is no evidence. There is evidence that Private White's discipline was not always what the army expected of him and refusal of further leave was often used as a method of additional disciplinary action. What is certain is that Christmas 1915 was the last Christmas Charlie White spent with his family.

The medical officers at Rugeley Camp examined Private White on 14th February declaring him 'fit for service'. The next day he left Rugeley Camp and arrived with others of his Battalion at Folkestone bound for France. The first day of the Battle of the Somme was but a few short months away and Private White by now would have been fully aware of why he had joined Kitchener's Army.

On the first day of the Battle, the 10th York and Lancs was helping take the village of Fricourt, just behind the German front line and succeeded in capturing what was known as Quadrangle Trench and Junction Trench. These were the German third line trenches some two miles from the British trenches. The 10th were to see its A and B Companies go over the top first. They were initially helped by the detonation of three mines under the German lines, one of them just in front of the 10th West Yorks, and collectively known as 'Tambour'. Yet by all accounts the 63rd Brigade containing the 10th York and Lancs were subject to very heavy German defensive fire, described as a combination of heavy machine gun fire together with whistling rifle bullets and the occasional shells which was enough 'to daunt even the bravest'. There was a realisation that the sector containing Fricourt Salient was the strongest point in the German lines prompting a decision to surround the position rather than attempt a frontal attack. This, however, exposed the 10th York and Lancs to that daunting constant machine gun and sniper fire.

The poet, Second Lieutenant Siegfried Sassoon, witnessed that attack on Fricourt in which Private Charles Christopher White was to be a part. Sassoon's battalion was in reserve on 1st July sitting some 500 yards behind the frontline. His observations of the 21st Division attacking Fricourt are recorded in his diary. He described how the men attacked from the beginning of the day at 7.45am in small parties and not extended in lines, but attacking steadily all the same. He noted the brilliant sunshine with a haze of smoke drifting along the landscape. He wrote, 'Some Yorkshires a little way below on the left watched the show cheering as if at a football match'.

By 9.30am Second Lieutenant Sassoon observed that the 21st Division was still moving toward their objectives. He comments on how the sunlight flashed upon their bayonets and tiny figures could be seen quietly moving forward then disappearing into the distance and twenty minutes later, Fricourt was half hidden by what Sassoon described as, 'clouds of drifting smoke, blue, pinkish and gray'. As the shrapnel burst, the birds appeared to have become bewildered. A lark was observed making better judgement in not flying too high toward the bursting shrapnel. Sassoon continued to observe, 'Others fluttering above the trench with querulous cries, weak on the wing. On the left our men still filing across in twenties and thirties'. There was another big explosion in Fricourt and again Sassoon describes his observation of 'clouds of brown–pink smoke, but yellowish clouds too'. At just gone 10am Sassoon noted that the breeze gently shook the poppies and yellow weeds and remarks, 'I am staring at a sunlit picture of Hell'. The song of the skylark on the 1st of July was for 50 men from Mexborough and Swinton the last sound of life they were to hear.

Somewhere in this hell was Private Charles Christopher White and his comrades, bravely carrying out their orders in an attempt to achieve their objectives. The 10th Battalion of the York and Lancs fought on courageously during the first day, but it was not until Sunday 2nd July that Fricourt finally fell.

Although the Yorkshiremen of the 10th York and Lancs had been more successful in gaining ground than their fellow Yorkshiremen fighting further north of the lines, it had once again been at a heavy cost. The 10th Battalion suffered hundreds of casualties including seven officers killed; 53 other ranks were killed or died of wounds during the first day of the Somme offensive. Such was the mayhem and utter confusion that encompassed that first day, the 10th Battalion's diarist wrote, 'Although the majority of these casualties were officially registered as having occurred on 3rd July, there is not the slightest doubt that the majority occurred on 1st July'.

A Mexborough man who was also with the 10th York and Lancs and went 'over the top' on the first day was Private Alfred Hargreaves. He was a single man and miner living with his parents at Lillian Terrace, 111, Main Street when in November 1914 he responded to Kitchener's call at the age of nineteen. His army records tell that he was wounded in the ankle but also that he was later to die on 15th November 1916. Albert had a brother, George, who fought with one of the Territorial battalions of the York and Lancs. George had the unfortunate experience of being wounded five times during his time in France, the last occasion being on the Somme where he was severely wounded.

A good number of Mexborough and district men were to join the Royal Engineers. Many miners become Sappers as a result of their particular skills derived from their occupations in coal mining. Others, such as railwaymen, also brought their particular skills to the military originating from railway work. Sapper Tom Best was what is sometimes described as spare driver, employed at Mexborough Locomotive Department. He was a man who had fought in the South African War, had originally come from Sinnington in North Yorkshire, but moved to Mexborough for employment and settled to live at 56, York Street. On 1st July, Tom was serving with the 2/1st West Riding Field Company of the Royal Engineers, on this occasion waiting in reserve behind the lines. Despite the relative position of safety that Tom Best's unit was occupying, he too lost his life on the first day of the Somme at the age of 36. His officer wrote to his widow in Mexborough to inform her of the circumstances of his death. 'A stray shell burst among four men who were sat on the side of a trench some distance behind the firing line. His death was instantaneous. He was a thoroughly reliable and steady soldier and I offer you my deepest sympathy.' Sapper Tom Best was buried during the Battle of the Somme somewhere near where he was killed. After the conflict he was moved to the north of Albert to Aveluy Wood Cemetery. Tom is also remembered on the Mexborough Station War Memorial.

One of the four men who were sitting with Sapper Tom Best on the day of his death was his Mexborough colleague from 8, Leach Row, Lance Corporal Albert Henry King of the same battalion of Royal Engineers. Albert King was killed by the same shell as his colleague Tom

Best. Albert King's body was buried at the same place as that of Sapper Best, but like Tom Best, his body was also moved to Aveluy Wood Cemetery. Both men were to finally rest alongside each other. Lance Corporal King was 35 years of age and left a widow and two children.

As darkness fell upon the Somme on that first day of the Battle of Albert, the final death toll for the day at that point would not have been known. Trepidation over the final number of dead must have been felt by all those who survived. Of the near 20,000 who lost their lives on that bloody day, there were 50 of Mexborough and Swinton's finest young men. There would be more men from the local community who would be cruelly swept away in the coming weeks.

The Battle of the Somme continued, despite acknowledgement that the number of casualties would rise with its continuation and that a total breakthrough would not be realised. Many of the objectives of the first day had not been met, although there had been what was considered to be progress, in the southern end of the sector.

However, many had survived on that first day, one of them being 'Iron' Hague's brother Johnny Hague. Johnny was a boxer himself and took a keen interest in his brother's career and throughout his life was inseparable from 'Iron'. Johnny Hague, like many of his contemporaries, joined the local Yorkshire regiment, the KOYLI's. *The Times* received a letter written to Frank Law the proprietor of the Montagu Arms Hotel. Frank Law, being the entrepreneur that he was, had helped to finance 'Iron' Hague's boxing career. The letter came from a Lance Corporal Herbert Butler which the soldier had written from his hospital bed in Southport. Lance Corporal Butler wrote;

> *'Dear Sir,*
> *You will forgive me for writing to you, as I have not had the pleasure of knowing you personally, but have been in your place many a time before the war. But I thought I should like to say a few words about one of your boys from Mexborough. His name is well known in England.'*

The man being referred to was Johnny, who was in the same KOYLI company as Lance Corporal Butler. Butler refers to the tough physical and mental character of the men that Mexborough had sent out to the trenches. He had seen Johnny Hague fight many a competition whilst with his battalion, and was impressed with his sporting approach to his bouts, win or lose. Lance Corporal Butler describes how he and Lance Corporal Johnny Hague went over the top together on 1st July:

> *'I got stranded as our battalion was first over and things were a bit warm. I crawled to a place not far from the*

German lines and there was Johnny hard at it. There were a lot of us and he was dressing those brave lads just as if he was in the ring looking after the men as cool as a cucumber and a smile on his face. It was simply 'hell' as they say 'with the lid off'. I hope he came through all right and that I hope he gets want he deserves. I hear that he has been recommended for a DCM, which I am sure he was well worth.'

Johnny Hague did survive the war, and even fought an exhibition fight with his brother 'Iron' Hague in February 1919. He however did not receive that medal for gallantry that his comrade Lance Corporal Butler believed he merited.

Two local men were awarded a medal for their bravery on 1st July. They were Private Frank Oliver and Sergeant Charles Frederick Crowson, both of whom were awarded the Military Medal. Frank Oliver was killed fighting with the 8th Battalion York and Lancs. He was a 27 year old married man from Swinton.

Sergeant Crowson was a South Africa War veteran, worked at Cadeby Colliery before rejoining the army and also served with 8th York and Lancs. Charles Crowson received his Military Medal at Ovillers, where he took command of his platoon after his officer had been killed. He is said to have bravely led his men forward until only two were left. Despite this he was able to hold firm and incapacitate an attacking German officer who was leading a party of the enemy who Sergeant Crowson was able to drive back. All of Crowson's men were killed but he was able to escape. Without consideration for his own safety he assisted the wounded in No Man's Land, succeeding in bringing seven wounded men back to the British lines. This brave man, who had lived at 37, Quakers Fold, Mexborough, was not to see the war out. Sergeant Crowson was killed in March 1918 during the German's great 'Spring Offensive'.

The Battle of the Somme continued in what is said to be in three phases, the Battle of Albert being the first phase fought up to 13th July. For the ordinary British soldier and their families at home anxiously waiting to hear of their fate, this military 'speak' must have meant little. Phased slaughter must have seemed very much liked continuous slaughter. In an editorial under the headline 'Steady, Boys Steady', *The Times* of 22nd July, attempted to assure its readership back in south Yorkshire that the next phase of the Battle would be less dreadful than the first. Lessons had been there to be learnt and events would be more profitable in the coming phase of the offensive. The newspaper maintained that, 'The second phase of the British offensive on the Somme is developing quite normally and naturally'. Could this have meant that it was normal to continue with the carnage of the first phase, or there was anything natural about this man-made slaughter? Or were these words to try to reassure those at home that the loss of many in their community was not to be mourned excessively as, 'not a Briton may said to have given his life in vain since the new attacks were launched'?

The manner and language in which the local newspapers of the day reported the first few days of the Battle of the Somme is difficult now to understand. Sir Douglas Haig, *The Times* remarked, was anxious to be seen as not viewing his men as merely human resources or manpower. Yet quite contradictorily, in trying to justify the paper's claim that no one died in vain, quotes a local soldier who came through the first day unscathed as saying, 'We lost heavily, but we exacted the full price from every man'. However the newspapers faced the dilemma of attempting to sympathise with those who had lost their loved ones, whilst trying to maintain morale both at the home and on the Western Front.

The newspapers continued to fill its pages with news of the dead and wounded. One page of *The Times* published on 12th July, contains no fewer than 83 photographs of casualties from the opening days of the Battle of Albert.

One of those casualties was Private Fred Leach, killed fighting alongside his comrades in the 10th York and Lancs on 3rd July. Fred was a miner originating from Staffordshire, single and living at 53, Doncaster Road, Mexborough. He attested early in the war on 1st September 1914 at the age of age 27 and was soon given the rank of Lance Corporal, unpaid. There is some evidence to suggest that Fred Leach saw active service before the 'big push'. If he was out in at the Front in 1915 with the 10th York and Lancs he would have seen action at Loos. He most certainly undertook extensive training with the York and Lancs in the familiar venue of Rugeley Camp where his disciplinary records show him frequently absent, mostly overstaying his leave. For this he was eventually reduced in rank to a private.

The fact that Fred Leach appears to have been a sick man, may explain the reason for his frequent absence. He was referred to a RAMC hospital in London between late December 1915 and mid-January 1916. He was treated in the neurological section of the hospital with what his records describe as suffering from, or at least showing the symptoms of, 'Traumatic Neurasthenia'. Also described as 'post traumatic syndrome' the condition usually occurred following shock from head injury. Medical literature at the time sometimes referred to it as 'railway brain' owing to the frequency with which it occurred after railway accidents. The symptoms were characterised by headaches, dizziness, depression and a diminishing of concentration. The condition was commonly diagnosed during the First World War.

Where Fred Leach sustained his injuries may never be known. It could have been in his childhood past, as the result of a colliery accident, during his period in military training or at the Front. His army records refer to him receiving the 'usual treatment'. This tended to be electrotherapy treatment, a harsh treatment usually given to the lower ranks. No doubt there were some army medical personnel sympathetic to Fred Leach's illness, hence this admission to hospital, but there is a reference in Fred's military notes as being, 'Discharged under Home Office letter'. Certainly the Home Office and the military were not sympathetic to those they believed were no more than 'shirkers', particularly in a period when every man was needed for the forthcoming big offensive. Fred was discharged from the London hospital on 11th January 1916. In February and April 1916, Private Leach's conduct in relationship to overstaying his leave did not improve and he received two separate punishments of confined to barracks during these months.

It is easy to conjecture that Fred Leach's behaviour had a link with his illness and in today's more humane society he would be considered unfit for military service. However this was not the view of the military authorities whose records tell us that Private Leach embarked for France on 10th May to join his Battalion. He was in the field by 20th May, being expected to play his part in the massive Somme offensive. Whether Private Leach was fit enough or not, he went over the top on 1st July with his south Yorkshire comrades, into that 'sunlit picture of hell' around the Fricourt Salient. He is officially recorded as dying on 3rd July, but he could well have been added to the list who fell on the 1st July; such was the confusion of those first three days of the Battle of Albert. Fred Leach became another Mexborough soldier who has no known grave and is remembered with many others from the district at Thiepval Memorial. Mrs Emily Leach, Fred's mother, would have received the usual letter of sympathy from one of his junior officers of his death. Her home was 122, Doncaster Road, Denaby Main. A century later we can only speculate that she might have felt that her son had been cruelly placed under severe duress to fight. Today's more enlightened society may not have so readily pushed him into active military service.

Historically, there are surnames synonymous with the town of Mexborough, Barron is certainly one of them. Peter Barron was the youngest son of Thomas Barron, head of the Phoenix Glass Works, or as it was simply known, Barron's. Peter enlisted as a Private in November 1914 at Conisbrough in what was effectively the Doncaster Battalion of the 1/5th KOYLI, a Territorial battalion. This battalion was part of the Territorial Force which made up the 49th West Riding Division of the Fourth Army. It included Territorial battalions from across the West Riding of Yorkshire, including those from the York and Lancs and was known as the 149th Brigade.

On 1st July, Peter Barron's battalion was in the front British lines positioned to attack the German front line situated just east of Thiepval.

Private Peter Barron's battalion had the task of assisting in the taking the strong German positions around the fortified village of Thiepval. If there was to be any advance toward the ridges which lay north east of the Theipval, the capture of the village itself was crucial. Peter was killed on 5th July whilst he and his comrades battled to achieve this difficult objective. A single man, Peter was 35 years of age when he died.

Taking Thiepval village and the ground to the north east of it was key to the whole operation on the Somme. It did eventually fall to the Allies on 26th September, nearly three months after the original plan of taking it in the first hours of the first day.

One of Peter's brother's, Fred Barron, who lived in Glasshouse Lane in Mexborough, received a letter from his company sergeant major two weeks after Peter's death, informing Fred that Peter had been killed. The letter explained the circumstances of how he died. 'Peter, along with a few comrades, was doing some good work on the front line parapet when a German sniper caught him and killed him instantly'. The CSM goes on to say that Private Barron was buried with military honours just behind the lines.

Another letter was written home to his parents in Hartley Street, Mexborough by Private Jack Hobson, a close comrade. The main purpose of the letter was Jack's anxiety to tell of how Peter met his death. Jack wrote in his own words and his own way:

> 'We were at Thiepval a place you will no doubt of seen very frequently in the papers, and we took two lines of trenches from the enemy and held them two days, when they made an attack in main formation a thunderstorm and Peter and a Sergeant were the only two left on their feet and they held them for forty five minutes with bombs when they had to retire fighting like demons for every yard, two men to as many hundreds when Peter had the misfortune to get knocked out and the Sergeant came through all right, but poor Peter died like a Britton (sic) it was a wonderful feat and a credit to the town he comes from, and you ought to have another V.C. in Mexboro for never was one better earned. You can show this letter to his friends and relations if you like for it will be a bit of consolation to them to know he died like a true British soldier and a hero. I think this is all this time from your loving son, Jack.'

The letter, which was written to Fred Barron from Peter Barron's CSM, which appeared in *The Times*, makes reference to a burial. It would have been the case that Peter's body was buried by his comrades near the place he fell. It would have been a makeshift and hurried burial with little ceremony given the ferocity of battle around Peter Barron's mourners. Yet he is remembered on the Thiepval Memorial, a memorial to those whose bodies were never found. The likelihood is that Peter Barron's place of burial was simply ravaged by the continuous bombardment of the ground around the trenches.

Whether or not Jack Hobson had witnessed the death of his comrades at first hand or his narrative was secondhand is not known. Private Peter Barron's part in the offensive may not have been so heroic as Private Hobson's account, and was a mere description of events which was created to heighten morale of a community whose confidence in the outcome and justification for the war was waning. It could well have been that Peter Barron did deserve the VC, for there were many heroic deeds performed on the Somme in the summer of 1916 and not enough VC's to go around.

The day after the death of Peter Barron, another Mexborough man, Private William Wright, fighting with the York and Lancs, met his end. He had been a miner working at Wath Main and had joined in the summer of 1915. He had lived with his wife and three children in Market Street.

The Great Central Railway and Mexborough Locomotive Depot were to lose another of its staff. This time it was a locomotive fireman, J. Hinton. He had, like his colleague Tom Best, joined the 2/1st West Riding Field Company of the Royal Engineers at the same time. This Company was a part of 49th West Riding Division which contained a number of south Yorkshire KOYLI's and York and Lancs Battalions He was taken to a casualty clearing station, set up in readiness for the offensive, where he later died of wounds on 8th July. Sapper Hinton was buried in Puchvillers British Cemetery close to the casualty clearing station. Sapper Hinton was another man, like Tom Best, who had come to Mexborough for work on the railway. He was a native of Towcester, but while living in Mexborough lodged with a Mrs Braddock at 1, Belmont Road.

The Battle of the Somme continued relentlessly into the summer of 1916. There had been some British gains in mid-July with the capture of La Boiselle, Contalmaison and Mametz Wood, but not without great cost.

Private William Ramsey, fighting with 9th York and Lancs would have been in the area around La Boiselle at the time he was injured. William was a young miner enlisted on 2nd September 1915, at the age of nineteen, originally with the 11th York and Lancs, the Reserve Battalion. He may have been attracted by the advert which appeared in *The Times* around this date, to form a Mexborough Company. He was living at 25, Cromwell Road with his large family, being one of nine children.

As a young, single man William Ramsey's conduct record reads very much like many others. He was frequently overstaying his leave from Rugeley Camp in the early part of 1916. His time in England ended on 15th March when he embarked for France to join the 9th Battalion. The leave which he had taken, which he overstayed, was almost certainly the last time he saw his family at Cromwell Road. While fighting with his battalion on 14th July, Private William Ramsey sustained a severely fractured skull. He was immediately transported to hospital in Boulogne, but died of his wounds the next day and was buried in the Boulogne Eastern Cemetery. On Sunday, 30th July a memorial service was held in memory of young former miner at the Salvation Army Barracks in Mexborough.

Private R. J. Salkerd had been out in France with the York and Lancs since 26th May. He was declared missing from the offensive on the first day, but was later notified as being captured and sent to a prisoner of war camp in Germany. He had been wounded in the thigh but died of tetanus from the wound on 16th July. As a single man he had lived with his parents at 42, Highwoods Road, Mexborough. He is buried in Germany at the Hamburg Cemetery.

Charles Hart was, according to his military records formally a labourer and a powerfully-built man for the times. He lived with his parents at 9, New Street, Mexborough, joining the army at 22 years of age, as a result of Kitchener's call in December 1914, making the decision to join the York and Lancs.

Private Hart's army records tell of confusion over where, during 1915, he was actually serving. Some records show that he was posted to France in January 1915, whilst others show he was in England between December 1914 and April 1915. Even more confusing is that his records also show he was supposed to have embarked at Southampton on 1st May 1915 to join the 1st Battalion of the York and Lancs. Private Hart did reach Southampton around this time but was detained in a Southampton Hospital. He was, in fact, reported as missing from the 6th York and Lancs on 8th May 1915, a report that was later cancelled following a letter written later in the year, from his mother. She reported that she had frequently heard from her son since that date and he certainly had never served with the 1st Battalion. He was in fact serving with the 6th Battalion in Gallipoli.

Along with his other Mexborough comrades fighting with the 6th York and Lancs, we know that Charles Hart would not have had an easy time. His records do indicate that he received a head wound on 20th September of 1915 whilst in Gallipoli. Like his comrades he was evacuated in December 1916 after the struggles in Gallipoli were aborted, eventually arriving in Egypt in February. Private Hart arrived with his battalion in France on 2nd June 1916 just in time to play his part in the 'Battle'. The 6th York and Lancs were assigned to fight in the north end of the offence, some 25 miles north of Albert. His time in France was a short one. His records are in no doubt of the fact that he was killed in action on 21st July, after a bomb was thrown into his trench. The army chaplain, the Reverend T. Rees, performed a short burial service for

Private Charles Hart at what is now known as the Agny Military Cemetery.

A Mexborough comrade of Charles Hart in the 6th York and Lancs was laid to rest alongside him. He is Lance Corporal Henry Sydney Fruin of 11, Don View, killed in the same incident as Private Hart. He had enlisted in the 6th Battalion a little before his Mexborough pal, in November 1914 and, like Charles, served with the Battalion in Gallipoli. Mexborough had lost another young man who was just twenty years of age.

Just ten days later, on 31st July, Private Edward Hoggins of the King's Own Scottish Borders, from 79, Herbert Street, lost his life. He had signed up to the army in January 1915 and spent many months at the Front. He left a widow and three children. Edward Hoggins has no known grave and is remembered at Thiepval Memorial.

Tom King joined the KOYLI and lived with his sister, who had become a Mrs Manchester, at 7, Cross Gate, Mexborough. It was his sister who was first told of his death. He was struck by a piece of shell while in the trenches on 20th August. Private King's CO, Second Lieutenant R.W. Bowers wrote, as he had no doubt done on many occasions, to reassure the grieving relative that Private Tom King did not linger in any pain. Whilst praising the continuous good work of his man, Second Lieutenant Bowers mentioned that some recognition might be due to Tom in terms of military honour.

On 14th September, Mexborough lost Lance Corporal William Scales, a member of the Mexborough Concertina Band, who was fighting with the West Yorkshire (Prince of Wales) Regiment. He had lived at 33, Doncaster Road and had served in Gallipoli. On the same day, Private Walter Nettleton of the 4th Grenadier Guards was also killed in action. Walter was another railwayman who responded early to Kitchener's call. He was an eighteen year old engine cleaner at Mexborough Locomotive Depot when he enlisted on 8th January 1915. Walter was living at 14, Victoria Street, off Wath Road. (in Swinton at the time but in Mexborough today). The young Walter Nettleton was killed as his Battalion, engaged in the Battle of Flers-Courcelette, fighting their way towards Lesboeufs. He was officially declared killed on 14th September, although he was originally recorded as missing between 14th and 17th September. He is yet another to be commemorated on the Thiepval Memorial, but nearer home his name has its place on the Mexborough Station Memorial.

On the day the British deployed their new weapon, the tank, for the first time on 15th September, Mexborough lost the well-known William Waddington. He had been a frequent writer home with letters that regularly found their way into the pages of the *The Times*. What was probably his last letter appeared in *The Times* on 12th August. All William's letters were written in an interesting way, but this letter is particularly so. It is interesting not just as it is his last, but that it embodies an affinity with the community he had left behind and is written in a way that many Mexborough soldiers would have, or would liked to have, articulated their own thoughts. The letter is worthy of inclusion in full:

> '*Just a few lines to say I am in the land of the living and never felt better. I received the good old Times today and was very sorry to see the sad news of the death of my old pal Peter Barron. I can honestly say he will be missed by all who know him as he was always a jolly and goodhearted chap.*
>
> *I am afraid there is a good many more to go 'West' before this terrible and bloody war is over. I consider myself a lucky man. It is over two years since I left dear old Mexborough to join my Regiment....I thank God that I come out so far without a scratch, but as I have said before one never knows when he is going to stop one.*
>
> *I will close now by wishing all my friends in Mexborough the best of health and luck and my sympathy to the brother and sisters of my poor old pal Peter Barron.'*
>
> *P.S. I saw Iron Hague about a month ago, he said he rather be in Mexborough.'*

William Rowland Waddington was from the well-known Mexborough business family, being the youngest son of the late Harry Waddington, the auctioneer. The family lived at Beaconsfield House, Market Street. The family consisted of four sons and, apart from having an affinity with Mexborough, they all had a liking for army life. The eldest son Harry was in the Boer or South African War with the Imperial Yeomanry as a sergeant. Harry was to be mortally wounded in Kimberley being one of the two Mexborough men to die in South Africa. Both men are commemorated on a brass tablet in Mexborough Parish Church. William or Bill, as he was generally known to his friends, joined the Coldstream Guards at the time of the Boer War in the anticipation of fighting there, although he never saw action in South Africa.

As a result of his service with the Coldstream Guards in the early part of the century, Bill Waddington, being a Reservist, was one of the first half dozen to attest in Mexborough at the outbreak of the War in August 1914 and the first to be mobilised. He was present at what *The Times* describes as the 'Great Retirement' from Mons in 1914. With the exception of just a week's furlough (leave) sometime in 1915, he had been at the Front continuously since the beginning of the conflict. Private Bill Waddington's fortunes, up to his death were favourable, for he had come through completely unscathed during his time in Flanders and France. His army activities were closely followed by Mexborough people with great interest. His regular correspondence to the local newspapers captured the imagination of local readers with their lighted-hearted and cheerful approach to the unenviable task of soldiering on the Western Front.

As Bill Waddington's last letter remarked, all men at the Western Front, as elsewhere, never knew just when their luck might run out. His luck did run out on the fateful day of 15th September. Haig acquired his new Mark 1 tanks on 15th September. This day saw the start of the Battle of Flers–Courcelette, an offensive using the British reserve forces that it is thought would finally wear down what was perceived as a stumbling German Army. The Guards Division, which contained all the Guards regiments, including Bill Waddington's Coldstream and Iron Hague's Grenadiers were to attack the German front lines stretching from Ginchy to Combles, assisted by nine tanks. It is recorded that the Friday morning of 15th September was a typical, sunny, early autumn day as the guardsmen listened and waited for the sound of the whistle ordering them over the parapet. The whistles would have been almost inaudible as the thunder of the creeping barrage crashed towards the German lines at 6.20am. This was zero hour for the Guards Division.

Almost immediately the men of the Coldstream and Grenadier Guards entered No Man's Land, the Royal Artillery, which was firing its barrage with 100 yard gaps between the advancing tanks, saw that the tanks were too immobile or had failed to fulfil their function. The infantry Guardsmen were left without the cover that the creeping barrage should have provided. The two Mexborough soldiers, Hague and Waddington, and their colleagues were exposed to deadly German machine gun and other fire. They had made some progress but were to suffer heavy casualties. As history tell us 'Iron' Hague survived the war to live out his time in his home town of Mexborough, but 15th September was the day Bill Waddington's luck ran out just as he had feared.

The exact nature of Bill Waddington's death is not clear but a number of Mexborough men who were engaged in the same offensive on 15th September were to make mention of their concern at the death of their Mexborough comrade. A Battalion colleague Private Clarke, formerly from Kirby Street, Mexborough, was wounded in the same engagement. Clarke claimed that had seen Bill Waddington fall to the ground after being hit in the mouth from bullets from a machine gun. Clarke gave his pal a drink of water but whilst drinking he fell back and died.

Two RAMC men attached to the Guards also wrote home with concern for Mexborough's Bill Waddington. A Private Wressel wrote to his parents at Coach and Horse Inn in Barburgh shortly after the engagement and remarked, 'I was not able to attend Billy Waddington, it was a stretcher job I understand'. Lance Corporal Francis Davies, also with the RAMC, wrote home to his parents at 1, Crossgate, and remarked:

'I have made several enquiries for Bill Waddington and I am almost convinced now that he was bowled over. He had done his 'whack' if ever a chap has, and I am more proud of Bill than I am of the Mexborough V.C. If there is any query raised about him you can say that I was with him about a week before he went under and he was in the best of spirits and quite happy and above all died with his face to the Huns. I am half inclined to think that it was a fitting death for him, as he was a typical soldier and one of the kind that will win this war.'

The truth of the matter is that, despite Private Bill Waddington having his Mexborough comrade Private Clark with him at the end, Bill's body was never recovered. Somewhere in the confusion and horror of the Battle of Flers-Courcelette he was originally reported as missing, as was fellow Mexborough Guardsman, Walter Nettleton. Both men are remembered on the same pier and face at the Thiepval Memorial.

It is clear that Bill Waddington was a highly respected soldier, being described as an excellent soldier and as brave as a lion by his commanding officer Captain Ackland Hood, who had the duty of writing that dreaded letter of condolence to Private William Waddington's parents. Yet it is also evident that he was popular amongst the Mexborough community. Within a short space of time the killing fields of the Somme had claimed two soldiers whose surnames were synonymous with Mexborough, Waddington and Barron.

Locally, the Great Central Railway suffered more loss of its former employees as a result of the Somme offensive. Mrs Emma Stead, the widowed mother of Private Harry Newey of the 6th York and Lancs, heard that her son had been killed on 29th September. Harry, who had lived with his mother at 32, Main Street, Mexborough, was a locomotive cleaner at the Mexborough Depot and had enthusiastically joined the 6th York and Lancs as early as August 1914, lying about his age as he was only sixteen at the time. His age was clearly ignored, deliberately or otherwise, as he found himself at Gallipoli in 1915 alongside his 6th York and Lancs colleagues. Harry was wounded while serving out in the Dardanelles, sent to hospital in Cairo but recovered sufficiently to find himself on the Somme with his York and Lancs Battalion. Still only eighteen, Harry Newey was alongside Canadian troops with the 11th Division in the furious attack on the Thiepval Ridge, where Peter Barron had lost his life fighting nearly three months earlier. The eighteen year old former railwayman Harry Newey was killed by shellfire. His name is another on the Theipval Memorial and another to find its way into the Mexborough Station's Memorial.

Remembered on the Thiepval Memorial alongside Harry Newey is his colleague in the 6th York and Lancs, Private Newson Stead. Newson was fighting with Harry at the attack on the Thiepval Ridge, being killed with him on the same day, 29th September. Newson's mother, Olivia was to receive the news of his death when that dreadful letter arrived at 51, Dodsworth Street. It was almost a year to the day that Olivia had heard the news of the death of her other son, Harold, at the Battle of Loos.

29th September had been a particularly black day for Mexborough. The town had also lost Private Elijah Pearson again fighting with the 6th York and Lancs, Private W.H. Wesley and yet another Calladine, Private William Arthur Calladine.

The Somme offensive moved into its third phase with the Battle of Theipval. By the first day of October, the offensive had been in 'progress' for three calendar months with little gains and enormous casualties. On the night of 1st/2nd October Sergeant Percy Oswald Sale, fighting with the 9th Battalion York and Lancs, was to fall. Percy left his job as a miner at Denaby Main and joined the York and Lancs in September 1914 going to France in August with the rest of the 9th Battalion.

The letter of his death was received by his wife Jane, at 55, Victoria Road, Mexborough who by that time had three young children. Jane was previously Jane White, the sister of Charles Christopher White who had died on the first day of the Battle of Somme. This close-knit family lived near to each other in Victoria Road. Also living in the same street was another sister of Charlie White, Florrie, who had married Private Bill Bird. He had returned from Gallipoli and was fighting in France at the time of Percy Sale's death. Pain and grief must have absorbed the lives of this family during this period and for many years to come. With increased regularity throughout the streets of Britain, house curtains were being drawn out of respect for the fallen and began to be a permanent feature of life during this wretched war.

Percy had been killed acting as Sergeant Major Sales, (wrongly spelt Sayles in the press but Sales elsewhere). One letter to Jane Sales was from a Private T. Jackson. 'He was stuck by a bomb on the evening of 1st October. We had been through the worst part of the evening in which poor Percy did some excellent work everyone remarking on his coolness and bravery. He was always a good pal, and died a noble and heroic death fighting for his country.'

Another letter to Jane Sales was from one of Percy's officers, Second Lieutenant S. Riddle. The officer wrote of Percy Sales with similar reference to his bravery with the remarks, 'His death was instantaneous and, therefore painless. A heavy battle was going on but your husband was duly buried'.

Company Quartermaster T. Clarkson was also keen to inform Mrs Sales of the fact, designed to give some comfort, that Percy had died instantly. The Quartermaster added, 'I have to inform you that Percy was killed on the first of October. He died a hero's death leading his men into action. I am sending you a few things that belonged to him; they were given to me by his men'. This particular letter also mentions that Percy Sales was buried by a local comrade from Bolton-upon-Dearne, Private W. Day, who himself died two hours after his Acting Sergeant Major.

Sergeant Percy Sales had been in previous years a leading member and worker for the friendly society the 'Watson's Delight' of the Order of Druids in the so-called Rotherham Equalised District. He is remembered on the same panel of the Thiepval Memorial along with his brother-in-law, Private Charlie White.

As Mexborough itself was a close-knit community, grief was not far from most in the Town. Within a short distance from Victoria Road lay Pym Road. Mrs Selina Olby of 3, Pym Road would have been well aware of the men from Victoria Road who had lost their lives during the Somme Offensive. It was Selina Olby who would be next in this area to learn of her husband's death. He was Sapper R. Olby of the 2/2 West Riding Field Company of the Royal Engineers who was killed on 13th October. He was yet another former employee of the Great Central Railway and member of the Mexborough Locomotive Department staff who was employed as a spare driver. Sapper Olby had joined the Royal Engineers early in 1915 along with his colleagues from the 'Loco' Tom Best and J. Hinton. His name is remembered along with these colleagues on the Mexborough Station Memorial.

By this time, Mexborough's Hope Working Men's Club in Milton Road had seen 80 of its member join the armed forces. One of those was Joseph Vickers of 35, Hampdeb Road, which is situated within a few yards from the Hope Club itself. Joseph, a former miner, had worked at Denaby for 28 years and prior to enlisting in September 1915 was working at Barnburgh. He was one of the older experienced miners who, like Sapper Hackett, responded to the call to enter military service as a tunneller in the Royal Engineers.

Sapper Vickers had been home on his first ever leave of ten days, no doubt using some of his time at home to take a welcome pint in the Hope Club. He left Mexborough to return to his unit on 12th October. Two days later, Vicker's train, which had left La Havre for the Front, was involved in a collision in which he was seriously injured, resulting in the amputation of his left foot and also his left arm. In a letter to Joseph's family (he had a wife and four children), Reverend W.A. Timmins said that although Joseph was very ill, he hoped this brave and uncomplaining man would pull through as he had been an excellent patient whose strength would see his survival. Sapper Joseph Vickers did not pull through and succumbed to his injuries on 16th October. He is buried in St Marie Cemetery, Le Havre.

The final action of the Somme offensive was the Battle of Ancre which took place between 13th and 18th November. By now the conditions on the battlefields were appalling, becoming a quagmire of mud following the incessant heavy rains. It was the Fifth Army, the reserve army, led by Sir Hubert Gough which attacked north of Thievpal each side of the River Ancre in an attempt to make inroads into the German salient between Serre and the Albert-Bapaume road. The Beaucourt and Beaumont Hamel were captured. The capture of the village of Serre, which was an objective on 1st July of the Barnsley Pals and the 12th KOYLI, was never achieved and thus remained in German hands.

On the night of 17th/18th November the battlefields were hit by a snow storm making the conditions nigh impossible for any further attempts to make gains. The onset of winter, mud, snow and sheer exhaustion made it impossible for men on both sides to continue slaughtering each other. Human endurance had been tested to its limit and the Battle of the Somme was, as it is stated "closed down".

The 31st Division was engaged in the Battle of Ancre and with them were the 12th KOYLI. Mexborough's Sergeant Albert Arthur Atkinson was among the Yorkshiremen of that Division. He had endured the 140 days of the British army's bloodiest and costly of battles, but the last day of the Battle of the Somme on the 18th November was Albert Atkinson's last.

Albert Arthur Atkinson was born in 1892 in Mexborough. His father Arthur James Atkinson married a former Conisbrough woman, Edith Emma Hunt, a milliner, in Swinton in the summer of 1891. Four years later tragedy struck when Emma died in childbirth in 1895 while giving birth to their second child. This was not the end of the family's tragedy. In November 1898, Albert's father was found drowned in the canal at Mexborough at a place called Woffinden's Mast Wharf. At the inquest, the coroner, on the basis that there was not enough evidence to definitively say how Arthur James Atkinson entered the water, brought an open verdict. It is not surprising, however, that given the great trauma which Albert's father had faced, there was speculation that suicide was the actual cause of death.

As a consequence of the death of both his mother and father, from November 1898 Albert Atkinson was brought up as an orphan by his grandparents in various homes in Church Street, Mexborough. His grandfather was James Atkinson, originating from Boston, Lincolnshire, who established a prosperous grocery business in Mexborough in which his sons worked as assistants. There is no doubt that Albert grew up under the guardianship of James and Mary Atkinson as an articulate and intellectual young man. By 1911, at the age of eighteen, he was working as a 'confidential clerk' at E. Cottam and Company at the Don Steel Casting and Spring Works in Rotherham. Later he went on to become a teacher in commercial subjects at Clarke's College, Bristol.

Albert was one the early recruits to Kitchener's Army joining the 13th Battalion of the KOYLI in 1914. He was to undertake his initial training at various camps throughout north Yorkshire and as a result of excellent work during training was rapidly promoted to sergeant. Whilst training it appears Albert was always anxious to get home on leave to Mexborough. He was in regular communication by letter and postcard with his young aunt Phoebe, the youngest daughter of James and Mary Atkinson, being some six years older than Albert. There is probably little doubt that Phoebe was a great influence upon Albert's formative years, helping him through the early years of coping with life without his biological parents.

Sergeant Albert Arthur Atkinson was initially declared as missing following his involvement on the last day of 1916's Battle of the Somme. When the news reached 42, Church Street, there would have been unimaginable grief within the household. The family would have keenly supported and watched the development of Albert, but he was now cruelly taken away from their lives. A century later we perhaps can spare a thought for poor Phoebe in particular. Another life of great promise ended brutally on the blood-strained battlefields of the Somme and another name on the Thiepval Memorial.

For both the Allied and German armies it must have been hard to believe that the Battle of the Somme had actually come to end. But at what cost? There had been nearly 420,000 British casualties, of whom 131,000 had lost their lives, but what were the gains for this human cost? Some of the first day's objectives were never achieved. Serre, the graveyard of many of the Barnsley Pals still rested in German control. Another first day objective of Bapaume was over three miles from the British front line, with three lines of German trenches before it. That other 'bottom line' figure was that overall the British had only managed to penetrate six miles of enemy territory along a twenty mile stretch.

The debate as to whether the offensive was worthwhile was to begin immediately after Haig's 'closing down' of the battle; it continues today. Certainly as expected, Haig was keen to express his predictable assessment in a dispatch soon after the last day. 'Verdum had been relieved, the main German forces had been held on the Western Front, the enemy strength had been very considerably worn down. Any of these is in itself sufficient to justify the Somme battle. The attainment of all three is ample compensation for the splendid efforts of our troops and for the sacrifices made by ourselves and our Allies.' Such was the insensitive mindset of the military leaders at the time.

What of those at home? There was no indication in the local press that Haig's words were anything other than fully agreed upon. Any alternative view would have to be debated within the confines of privacy. One might venture to express some differing opinion within home or the meeting places of the various sections of society, but always, no doubt, with the utmost care. The fact remained that hundreds of families in Mexborough and district, like the rest of the country, had witnessed a war that had seen the death or mutilation of their loved ones. Some would cope better than others, but cope they somehow had to.

Private Herbert William Wright of the 9th KOYLI. One of the first Mexborough men killed in 1916, he was hit by shrapnel after his Company's trenches were bombarded by the Germans in retaliation for British trench raids.

With professional football suspended in 1915, women's football became very popular. This is believed to be the members of a team made up from the Mexborough railway carriage cleaners at the Mexborough Athletic Ground.

Able Seaman Willie Barker joined the Navy at just 15. He saw action at the Battle of Jutland. Willie took his own life whilst on leave in 1918, probably as a result of his experiences in the horrors of that battle.

A group of women at the Denaby Powder Works. With the onset of compulsory military conscription, women were required to work in previously male-dominated industries.

Mexborough Locomotive Depot engine cleaners. The Great Central Railway began to employ women engine cleaners now that so many railwaymen were joining the armed forces and Mexborough was the first Depot to employ women in this grade.

Women were now employed to work at Simpson's Mexborough Brickworks on Lower Dolclciffe Road.

Women working alongside soldiers assigned to assist them at Denaby Powder Works.

The photograph of Miriam Shaw (daughter of John 'Blondin' Shaw) sent to the Western Front, only to be returned by an admiring army sergeant. Courtesy of Pauline Gibbons.

Mexborough's VC, Sapper William Hackett. The only tunneller to be awarded the Victoria Cross.

Memorial to Sapper Hackett VC and the Tunnelling Companies of the First World War, situated at Givenchy les la Bassee, near the site of the Shaftesbury Tunnel in which Hackett lost his life. It was unveiled on 19th June 2010. Courtesy of Barrie Dalby.

Private Charles Christopher White who died on the first day of the Battle of the Somme aged 20. He had been a miner and was with the 10th York and Lancs. Courtesy of Geoff White.

Private George William Oliver of the 8th York and Lancs also died on the first day of the Battle of the Somme. Courtesy of Graham Oliver.

Private Frank Blunt died fighting with the 9th York and Lancs on the first day of the Battle of the Somme. His father ran the Albion public house in Mexborough. Courtesy of the late Peter Robinson.

Private Levi Mountford of the 8th York and Lancs died on the first day of the Battle of the Somme. He had married three days before his departure to the Front in May 1916.

A ticket for the film depicting the Battle of the Somme. This propaganda film, first shown in London in August, was shown in Mexborough in October 1916.

Two Mexborough comrades Sydney Fruin and Charles Hart of the 6th York and Lancs both died on the Somme on 21st July 1916 and are buried alongside each other in Agny Military Cemetery.
Courtesy of Barrie Dalby.

Sergeant Albert Arthur Atkinson (centre) was killed on the last day of the Battle of the Somme on 18th November 1916 whilst seving with the 13th KOYLI. Courtesy of Mr Gary Smillie.

Christmas cards typical of those sent home from the Front in 1916.

Chapter Fifteen

The Reality of War Reaches Home

The clandestine approach to the reality of the Western Front was somewhat broken by the release of an official film, made by the British Topical Committee for War Films, depicting the events leading up to and during the Battle of the Somme. The film was made by two officially appointed cinematographers, Geoffrey Malin and John Dowell. It premiered in London on 10th August before going out on general release a few days later. Within the first six weeks 20 million people watched it in over 2,000 cinemas across the country.

The film had its general showing in the south Yorkshire coalfields area in mid-October. Commenting on the film, *The Times* fully approved of its making and release of the film, declaring that it showed events and struggles in a way their newspaper and other literary forms of media were unable to. Not all agreed that it was right or moral to depict scenes of violence. The Dean of Durham described the film as undermining the 'very sanctity of bereavement'. Yet the makers of the film had been careful not to portray the most grotesque scenes of the bloody conflict. What brief scenes of death were shown were believed to be 'stage managed'; others mainly featured industrious and committed soldiers designed to stimulate, inspire and sober the audience at home. It was to bring to the screens the men's 'naked patriotism' and the sacrifices they were making on behalf of those who were safely at home watching from the more comfortable surroundings of their local picture houses. The film was, of course, a piece of propaganda which cleverly used the latest media technology to influence the mass public. Locally *The Times* had no doubt as to its worth. 'What could be more encouraging, for instance, to the munitions workers, than to be repeatedly shown the work of the guns at the Front, and to have it impressed upon them, by this means, that the responsibility of maintaining those engines of war at their highest point of efficiency is largely theirs.'

After the disastrous events on the Somme, it was necessary for the Government and the propaganda machinery to convince those at home of the overall worthwhile nature of the great offensive. It was important to continue to ensure a steady supply of men for the armed forces and likewise a supply of men and women for the production of armaments. Despite the advent of conscription, the difficulty in maintaining a balance between the supply of men to munitions work and the armed services still existed. There were still difficulties in getting men to enthusiastically join the colours even when compulsorily called to do so. The military's task was not made any easier by Britain's persistence in liberal ideals of allowing those who objected to armed service to put their case before a Military Tribunal. As military conscription proceeded, tensions began to exist between the local military tribunals and the military itself. The military's problem and main focus was to get men within its ranks as quickly as possible and not to involve itself with the finer arguments of business requirements. Nor did it have too much regard for the civil rights and liberties the tribunals were obliged to consider. By late in the year, with the urgent need to for more men, military authorities across the country were requesting the local tribunals to revise the ease with which they appeared to grant exceptions from military service.

The Mexborough Local Military Tribunal consisted of councillors, a number of them being businessmen. It could be said there was an element of bias towards the business classes, many of whom would have been colleagues seeking exemption for some of their employees. The Claytons were prominent within the Mexborough community. Ernest Clayton appeared before a Mexborough Tribunal in October, in support of one of his young assistants at his business, Messers E. and F. Clayton, the wholesalers and grocers. Clayton's case appeared strong. Mr Clayton pointed out that his male staff was already at a minimum, having let six men leave for the forces without appeal for exemption. Mr Clayton asked for exemption until the end of the year, which he was successful in achieving.

Evidently, the local military tribunals also had an expertise in judging the needs of local business which often militated against the needs of the army. This was not often appreciated by those who accused the local tribunals of being too lenient on those seeking exemption. The case of Mexborough's glass bottle industry was a case in point. The glass bottle industry was seen as an important contributor to the war effort.

The glassblower and bottle makers met the Board of Trade and it was finally agreed between them and the Army Council that such workers should be exempt from military service, unless the military representatives on the tribunals could prove otherwise. Councillor William Winstanley, the Chairman of the Mexborough Military Tribunal, argued that locally they spent a considerable amount of time looking at each case. The Mexborough Tribunal was to prove that Waddington's, for example, had lost sixteen of its men to the military and that, only 24 of what were described as 'holes', were working out of 41. If sickness prevailed then even this number of holes could not be kept going. By further looking at the invoices and orders of Waddingtons, the members of the Tribunal argued they could conclude that the greater part of the firm's production was of essential national importance. Although the appeal tribunals, which sat locally at Doncaster and Sheffield, were more likely to be sympathetic to the needs of the military, general employers and employees in the local glass industries at this time were always granted exemption.

The military appears to have been critical of the Mexborough Tribunal for its leniency with the town's butchers. In November, a butcher, aged 25, argued he was suffering from rheumatism and would be of no use to the army. He claimed it was impossible to find anyone who might take over running the business. The young butcher put forward the argument that his wife was suffering from mental illness. His wife, he claimed, was suffering from delusions and had imagined she was somehow responsible for the affairs of the Russian Empire. This bizarre evidence put forward as reason for exemption, on this occasion, was to find favour with the majority of the Tribunal.

A widow, who owned a butchering business, asked for the exemption of her single 23 year old son on the grounds that he was the only one to do her buying and slaughtering. Both her other sons had been taken by the military and she would be ruined if the remaining son were to go. The military representative on the Tribunal, a Mr R. Payne, was not sympathetic to the apparent keenness of Mexborough butchers to, as they would have seen it, protect their business. The military representative asked what Mexborough butchers were doing in the way of cooperating with each other to help run their businesses? The answer was there had been no attempt at coordination of this kind contemplated. Mr Payne went further and claimed it was his belief there were too many butchers shops in Mexborough at a time when the military's needs were of more importance. There were, he said, 23 butchers in Mexborough at the time, "rather more than was necessary". It was also necessary, suggested the military representative, to establish a public slaughter house, something that the Medical Officer of Mexborough UDC had long recommended., This would eliminate the need for slaughtering on the butcher's own premises. Others members on the tribunal disagreed that the number of butchers shops in Mexborough should be reduced. Councillor Watson thought it unfair that some should be closed at the expense of others. He was supported by Councillor Tom Chambers, although the latter admitted he was in the business himself.

One Mexborough butcher who was not so fortunate as his fellow traders, was 26 year old Albert Sinclair when he attended the Appeals Tribunal in Sheffield. The newspapers took the very unusual measure, in October, of naming this particular applicant who was seeking exemption. To name the applicant could be considered as a piece of unfair journalism on the part of *The Times*, exposing Sinclair to unnecessary and unjustifiable intimidation. The Sinclairs had recently changed their surname from Schonhut, Albert being the son of George Schonhut, the unfortunate target of anti-German riots. George was now said to be interned, whilst Albert had been making attempts to secure his father's liberty, without success.

Albert's case for exemption was, as might be expected particularly in view of news from the Western Front, not sympathetically received. Albert attempted to use a bargaining 'chip' and offered to willingly join the army if his father was released. His case floundered on the point that he was no longer carrying on his father's business. The military representative at the appeals tribunal was vigorous in his aim to secure Albert Sinclair for the army and indeed George Schonhut's son had no support from the rest of the tribunal. Alderman Fenton believed that the case had now gone on far too long, citing that exemption had been given to Albert Sinclair since February of 1916. Besides, it was the opinion of the tribunal that if the Albert Sinclair were to join the army it would probably help his father to secure liberty.

The pressure on businesses losing men to the armed forces is well illustrated by the Barnsley British Cooperative Society's store in Adwick Road, Mexborough. The Society applied to the local tribunal for exemption for its 32 year old branch manager. The Society's case rested on the point that the branch by this time, November 1916, undertook weekly business worth £480. They suggested this was because they were the nearest shop of any significant size to the new Barnburgh colliery where they delivered groceries twice weekly. The current manager was assisted by his wife, two other females and a young boy of seventeen. The position of the Cooperative store was not made any easier, the Mexborough Tribunal members heard, by the very recent death of another manager in the district. This and the fact that the Adwick Road store was doing vast amount of business, £480 a week income was a very considerable amount for the time, the Cooperative Society had no difficulty in being awarded a conditional exemption.

The Mexborough Military Tribunal, like others across the country, dealt with some extraordinary cases. Those engaged in what was considered essential work of national importance would have been less difficult to deal with than those who sometimes offered bizarre grounds for exemption. In December the Mexborough Military Tribunal had to deal with the case of a 33 year old married hairdresser who wanted an extension to his exemption on the grounds of business necessity and for domestic reasons. All those seeking exemption appear to have convinced themselves their work was of national importance, or at least closely allied to it. Mr R. Payne the military representative, not surprisingly was more than a little incredulous as to the Mexborough hairdresser's grounds for exemption to His Majesty's Armed Forces. Mr Payne asked the applicant, "Have you not tried to get a lady to run the business? Are there not any lady barbers in Mexborough?". The applicant was somewhat indignant to the question and replied "Well there is one in Mexborough, but I wouldn't allow my wife to go into the trade. It is not a business for a lady to be in". He made it perfectly clear that he would rather go into the workhouse than see a woman working in his shop. The barber received no sympathy for his threats or his arguments. He was placed on so-called class C2 work, and ordered to work on employment of national importance for four days a week.

The military were keen to 'comb out' the type of characters such as the Mexborough barber, at least into an occupation that it considered to be worthy of the war effort. Many workers found themselves orienting to the munitions factories, with many more advised to seek employment in such establishments.

The shock of the numbers of casualties on the Somme undoubtedly concentrated the minds of all sections of society. The military's focus was to get more recruits as replacements for those massive number of casualties. Others were critical of the military leadership's handling and tactics of the war which they saw as a senseless waste of life. The newspaper *The Nation* urged the military to 'go easy' with the men in order to reduce the number of casualties. The newspaper's editor was Henry William Massingham, one-time Liberal, who now favoured the Labour Party. *The Times, in* October, was critical of such thoughts and suggested that the *The Nation* was implying, 'What is the use of sapping our industrial vitality by 'combing out' a million men more men? Cut the losses and lie snug in the trenches'. This, suggested *The Times*, was precisely what the enemy was doing and it would give them the opportunity to reconstruct their underground complexes, regroup and once again become strong enough to 'hammer and batter our armies as they did in the autumn of 1914'. Pushing on much as before was believed by the local newspaper as the only answer to establishing a successful conclusion to the war.

The criticism of the handling of the war was also prominent at a national level, as it was at local level; but the voices of dissent were somewhat muted in the Mexborough area. At the end of July the Mexborough and District Trades and Labour Council received a circular from the Peace Negotiations Committee via Bradford Trades Council. The circular asked for the members of the Trades Council's support in an approach to the Government to begin a negotiated peace settlement with the German Government. The general consensus of the local Labour Movement was this was out of the question. One delegate to the meeting argued that this was not the time to think of peace. The meeting decided not to formerly discuss the circular, with a delegate moving that it be "bagged", and "be laid upon the table". In other words it was to be disregarded, at least for the present. If this was the approach by the local Labour Movement, on the question of a justification for carrying on the war very much as before, then it seems reasonable to suggest the general feeling within the district was not dissimilar.

Despite the general view towards the conduct of the war there were constant feelers for a peace and a negotiated settlement. The USA President, Woodrow Wilson, was constantly considering the prospects of a peace agreement and was prepared to place himself in the role of the honest broker to achieve this. The Germans announced in the Reichstag on 12th December that, through such neutral means as contact with the American President and indeed the Pope, they were prepared to talk peace with the Allied Powers.

Five days previous to the German's announcement of a proposed settlement to the war, Lloyd George succeeded Asquith as the British Prime Minister. Asquith, who was under fire for the lack progress being made on the Western Front, was effectively forced out of his premiership, when Lloyd George insisted that he himself should be given the responsibility of leading and directing war policy. Asquith refused to accept this suggestion and resigned, only to be followed by Lloyd George's resignation on hearing his rejected proposal. This gave Lloyd George the opportunity to become PM on the recommendation to King George V by the leader of the opposition, Bonar Law. David Lloyd George had skillfully manipulated himself into the highest office in British politics and had done so with the help of Conservative politicians.

Lloyd George's first task as the new prime minister was to deal with the German offer of the possibility of a peace settlement. The German offer was said to have been crouched in terms which portrayed a Prussian arrogance and was itself contradictory in tone. It was suggested that the German Government knew the offer would be rejected, thus allowing them to accuse the Allied Powers of casting away a real chance for peace and taking the responsibility for continued bloodshed. Further, the failure of the Allies to accept the peace offer would give the Germans the opportunity to declare unrestricted submarine warfare, which it was soon to do.

On 19th December the British Government did reject the German's peace settlement offer, and at the same time suggested that President Woodrow Wilson had little understanding about the Germans' real intentions. The truth was that the Britain and her Allies were in no position to get the kind of agreement they believed to be justified, when they were in fact in a position of weakness. This would amount to a capitulation which would be viewed by many as humiliation. Besides, the German proposals were not clear and Lloyd George told House of Commons, 'Without any knowledge of proposals she (Germany) proposes to make to a conference, is to put our heads into the noose with the rope in the hands of Germany'. It was, as the trade union delegate to the Mexborough and District Trades and Labour meeting earlier in the year had suggested, not the time to talk peace. This affair had only served to strengthen the majority of the public's support for the continuation of the war and with it the popularity of the man who would now direct it, Prime Minister David Lloyd George.

The support for the war and Government was not, however, universal. Sections of the Labour Movement, such as the ILP and a section of the BSP were still opposed to the war. What many trade unionists saw as that other struggle, the 'class struggle', continued to endure. There is no evidence of overt militancy in the Mexborough area at this time, but there were always local skirmishs of spontaneous strike action from time to time, nearly always portrayed by the local press as unpatriotic. In late August there was a problem at the newly opened Barnburgh pit, over wages and the sore point of having to forego holidays back in the spring. The President of the YMA, Herbert Smith, was however present in attempting to resolve such disputes, as was generally the role of the trade union official at a time of 'national crisis'.

Although there was no great militancy in the Mexborough area, the district could not have been unaffected by what was happening in nearby Sheffield. The engineering union, the Amalgamated Society of Engineers (ASE), was responsible for organising men in the engineering factories, vital to the war effort. A young militant from Manchester belonging to the Socialist Labour Party, John Thomas Murphy, settled in Sheffield during the war and helped form the Sheffield Workers' Committee within the metal and engineering industries in the City. The Committee organised around the formation of shop stewards' committees, throughout Sheffield's engineering industries. The shop stewards' movement would often have the ability to by-pass the wishes of their full-time union officials and take unofficial action.

In November Leonard Hargreaves complained to his union, the ASE, that he had been called up to the army when in fact he should have been exempt on account of his work in an industry of national importance. Leonard Hargreaves was, against his will, forced to join the

Army Service Corps. The union tried to resolve this dispute through official grievance procedures but without success. As a consequence the Sheffield Workers' Committee threatened to strike and bring its members out of the engineering works in which they were organised. Notably Hargreaves' case was supported by other key engineering workers across the country.

The Hargreaves' dispute, not surprisingly, reached the attention of the higher echelons of Government. The workers' potential action was seen as a serious threat to Britain's ability to continue supply the military with means to fight an effective war. The Government backed down, re-instated Hargreaves and was forced to issue all such men with a 'trade card' identifying them as employed in essential work and thus candidates for exemption to the military.

Trade union militancy as witnessed in Sheffield was then not too far from the borders of Mexborough and district. Such militancy does not appear to have spilled over that border to any significant degree and the Mexborough trade unionists would invariably accept the instructions of their moderate trade union officials. The local Mexborough Branch of the locomotive drivers' union ASLEF called a meeting at Garden Street School on the Sunday afternoon, 24th September. The meeting was chaired by Councillor David S. Humphreys, himself a locomotiveman. The meeting was addressed by the union's organising secretary Mr A. Mason. The union official expressed the view the men did not think enough of themselves, under-valuing their work and worth to the war effort. Mr Mason continued that it was an absence of a 'proper spirit of clannishness which was responsible for the position they found themselves in'.

Mr Mason's speech was a clear indication that generally railwaymen of all grades supported the war effort with little or no self-interest. But there were those employees in the railway industry who resented the fact that, despite their contribution and sacrifice, increased prices and profiteering by employers, their wages remained static. The more militant railwaymen who took this view tended to operate through their own rank and file organisations. The Executive Council of the NUR in September rejected a call for an ending to the industry truce and a strike for ten shillings a week in wages. Despite this official rejection of strike the South Wales district decided to declare strike action of its own. Just as in the Sheffield engineering dispute, which was to occur a little later, the Government were forced to intervene. The unions were told, in no uncertain terms, by the military representatives at talks on these industrial issues, that the position of the men at the Front was so serious that stoppage could not be contemplated for "even one hour". The Government was nevertheless forced to place pressure on the railway companies' directors to make an offer. This pressure was to result in an additional war bonus of five shillings with an agreement to operate from 16th September.

The Times editorial following the railway settlement commented that the country would be relieved that a national stoppage would not materialise. The newspaper was confident that good sense and patriotism of the railway workers would prevail, 'in the midst of the war, and at the moment when the tide of battle was turning in favour of this country and its allies'. Yet to ask for anything above this war bonus would, claimed *The Times,* be a demand exceeding the wildest dreams of any trade unionists. This point was challenge by an indignant local railwayman in a letter to the paper the following week. If the men had gained the full claim of an additional ten shillings it still would not bring then up to the same level of purchasing power that existed before the war. The raise was justified as the railway worker had done their duty to the country and to 'Tommy' in the trenches.

Despite the increase in the cost of living, *The Times* was correct in its assessment that most workers would remain committed to the war effort and would not vigorously pursue substantial wage increases. However, war bonuses were awarded to workers on account of their efforts and sacrifice. Mexborough UDC often awarded such bonuses to its workers, which included awards by the Education Committee to Mexborough schoolteachers.

Despite the awarding of war bonuses, industrial peace was always fragile. The pressures that were building up with the ever-increasing cost of living and the harsh terms and conditions imposed as a result of the incessant demands of wartime production would have their post-war consequences. As the ASLEF official was to say at meeting of Mexborough locomotivemen in the latter part of the year, men would have to, 'prepare for the inevitable struggle which would follow the end of the war'. The official's prediction was to be correct. The year 1919, was one of widespread industrial unrest, including a national railway strike which took place to gain the long-awaited improvement in wages and conditions.

The increase in the cost of living and the alleged increase in profits made by some employers on the backs of their compliant workforce, did not help the underlying and latent discontent which existed locally. The local Mexborough gas undertakings raised their price in July, followed quickly by price rises by the Mexborough Electricity Department. The price of milk increased by 6d per gallon, in October, from 1/6d to two shillings (10p), an increase of 33%. Farmers believed the price was justified on the basis that the Military Tribunals were insisting on taking too many of their farm labourers away from their employment. As a consequence it was difficult to obtain labour and it was necessary to increase wages to retain the remaining workers and as such the price of milk would also have to increase. There was scepticism over the farmers' claims in the pages of the local newspapers. One reader argued that the price increase was not comparable with any increase the farmer might be paying his labour. The answer, this reader suggested, was consumers should only buy half of their usual consumption of milk or tinned milk until the 'normal state of affairs were restored'.

Local farmers were blaming the military tribunals for the problems arising elsewhere in their industry and there were complaints about the lack of farming representatives on the tribunals themselves. There were 25,000 acres of land in Sheffield but not one member on its military tribunal was from the farming community. The tribunals' ignorance of farming issues and needs had led to the large quantity of land available going unused as a result of the reduction in the amount of labour available to work upon it. This meant that only 25% of wheat had been sown and similarly 25% of potatoes grown. These labour problems, the farmers argued, were chiefly responsible for a lack of supply of foodstuffs and a rise in food prices.

There was a suggestion by some rural parish councils that perhaps German prisoners of war could be ulitised for farm work. The deployment of prisoners of war in this way had been successful in Shropshire and Lincolnshire. The press agreed that this was far more ideal than the suggestion of employing German prisoners of war in coal mines, with the risk which might arise from such employment.

The rise in food prices and the cost of living were now leading to some unrest, the first indications a food shortage was beginning to appear caused by domestic problems rather than the losses from unrestricted German U-boat action which started in earnest in 1917. In November a meeting of the miners' union and other trade unions was held at the Empire Cinema, Mexborough to protest over the rising cost of living. It was now acknowledged that the pound was only worth 12/- (60p) due to wartime price increases. At a well attended meeting businesses were accused of, "breaking into the larders of the poor". The owners of big business were, according to Mr Sam Roebuck, a junior secretary with the YMA, profit-mongers and traitors, making enormous profits and "slowly starving the poor people". Sam Roebuck continued, "If the Government could feed the Army and the Navy cheaply then it could feed the people cheaply". What was needed, Roebuck suggested, was a mechanism by which they would take control of food prices. At the end of the meeting a motion was moved that read, 'That this meeting of miners and allied trade unions protests against the inactivity of the Government in respect of prohibiting prices which are being charged for the necessities of life'. The motion was passed without dissent and sent to the prime minister, still Mr Asquith at the time, the President of the Board of Trade and local MP, Charles Nicholson.

The Times had little sympathy for the position of local trade unionists. There were now better wages than ever before, which were being spent frivolously with 'criminal freedom', it said.

Towards the end of the year, the Board of Agriculture asked the owners of large greenhouses to utilise them in the winter to grow potatoes. The Government requested them to plant early crops of potatoes in the following January. The potato crisis was also recognised by Mexborough Council. It was announced at a Council meeting in late December that the Council had purchased one ton of 'Arran Chiefs' and one ton of 'Great Scott's' seed potatoes. These would be sold to local allotment holders at cost price with the appeal that every man should be his own greengrocer.

Mexborough UDC was desperate to acquire land for allotment use. They identified Glebe Farm as being ideal for cultivation. The Council had identified 27 men who would be prepared to take allotments on this ground. The owner of the land, Captain F. J. Montagu, agreed to allow Glebe Farm be used for allotment purposes, but requests for other fields for the same purpose was said by Captain Montagu to be "out of the question". The Chair of the Council, Mr Frow, expressed great disappointment at Captain Montagu's refusal to release additional land on which to grow local produce. Mr Frow was particularly disappointed that one of Mexborough's biggest landowners had turned his back on the Mexborough UDC when other landowners throughout the country were coming to the aid of their local authorities in this matter. The case for allotment land became more critical when it was found that Glebe Farm was not as suitable for growing purposes as first thought.

War weariness was beginning to set in amongst the hard pressed community of the Don and Dearne Valleys. Mexborough UDC cancelled its meetings for the whole of September. This was an unprecedented move which had never before happened in the history of Mexborough Council or for that matter anywhere else in the district. No explanation for such an unusual move was given. It was suggested by *The Times* that the Council's members were holidaymaking. At one time it would have been claimed by *The Times* that to cancel a meeting in time of war was unpatriotic. But it did not matter much, the newspaper continued, as it was the Council's officials who seemed to be those who deserved their holidays the most, hinting that councillors' absence on this occasion would make little difference. It can be argued, however, this was indicative of a war weariness which was now taking its toll.

The strain and stresses on the community throughout 1916 had been severe. The hectic introduction of the military conscription and all that it entailed placed pressure on those employees and employers who applied for exemption from military service. Those who sat on the military tribunals themselves were already engaged in other civic and public functions. William Winstanley, for example was performing an enormous number of duties, many created by the wartime necessities. The Medical Officer, Dr John Huey, was another who had taken on a number of additional positions as a consequence of the war. He was employed by a number of local collieries in a medical capacity as well as serving on the Montagu Hospital Committee. The war had also seen Dr Huey involved in the medical examination of new army recruits, whilst at the same time serving as a military representative on the tribunals.

Preparations for the 'Somme Offensive' were to see workers in the munitions industries, workers clearly of importance to these preparations, forfeiting their Whitsuntide and August Bank Holidays. There would have been some resentment building up amongst workers over their original loss of deserved and much needed holidays. These workers did eventually get their holidays, a Monday and Tuesday in late September. Many shopkeepers in Mexborough, taking the example of their Sheffield counterparts, decided to close their premises making it a complete holiday break. Munitions workers and other industries of national importance were also to benefit from two extra days over and above the usual festive days of Christmas Day and Boxing Day.

Not only was work fatigue the only stress and strain encountered by Mexborough and district's working population. It is likely that the heavy losses suffered during the Battle of the Somme had placed a critical psychological strain on many in the community, regardless of how the popular or 'yellow' press tried to justify the losses in terms of patriotic glory and honour.

Any undercurrent of discontent was not helped by the harsh application of DORA. Workers in the mining industry found themselves subject to some draconian decisions by the courts. Under the heading of 'Slackers at the Pit', *The Times* reported, in August, a punishment for a stoneman, Parker Shires, of damages to be paid to the coal owners of £5.16s 6d. for persistent absenteeism. Similarly it was reported that a large cohort of Hickleton miners were fined heavily by Doncaster West Riding magistrates on 7th November for their 'neglect of work'.

Miners, too, had also forgone their Whitsuntide holidays. Conscious of the sacrifice made by their workforce and perhaps aware that their own contribution to the war effort was somewhat disproportionate to that of their 'servants', the 'masters' in the coal industries were to make a redeeming gesture. *The Times* reported, 'Coal owners are not a popular breed, but a very substantial donation by the South Yorkshire Coal Trades Association has been made to the YMA for dependents of fallen miners'. This, the paper added, was for the patriotism of the miners who had worked through Whitsuntide. The donations would, in many cases, be equal to that contributed to by the men to the union's relief fund for miners' widows and families. Such donation, regardless of its source would have been gratefully received by the YMA. At the Association's Annual Council Meeting in Barnsley at the end of the year it was revealed that in the month of November an additional 119 Yorkshire miners in the union had died. In total over 2,000 widows and families of miners up to that time had received funeral benefits from union.

Although conditions at the front were almost indescribable, life was often unpleasant for many of those who remained at home. The munitionettes, the canary girls, were continually exposed to the dangers of toxic chemicals such as trinitrotoluene and sulphuric acid. There was always the risk of explosion, which was to happen in various parts of the country resulting in over 200 deaths in total. All this exposure to risk was often on shifts lasting twelve hours a day and continuously for two weeks at a time. We know in the summer of 1916, a Miss Elizabeth Ann Cope, munitions worker at Denaby Powder Works, living at 14, Lower Dolcliffe Road, Mexborough, died after a few week's illness. Not surprisingly the press reports gave no more than the bare details of Miss Cope's death. There is no explanation as to the cause of death, but exposure to lethal substances was an occupational hazard causing many health problems including severe harm to the immune system. It may have been that Elizabeth had succumbed to the harmful effects of the chemicals she was working with. It is unlikely that any great publicity about the hazards faced by munitions workers would find its way into the local popular press. The real nature of the hazards remained hidden to most.

Life was, of course, somewhat easier for some sections of society. It would be unfair and incorrect to say that life during the war for the aristocracy had not changed. They had lost many staff to the military, and faced difficulties in finding suitable replacements. They often volunteered their grand residences for use as hospitals or convalescent homes and other military purposes. Many of the female members of the aristocracy would take up important voluntary work, including roles in nursing, particular with the highly respected Red Cross. Yet it is evident in some aspects of life for the aristocracy had changed little as a result of the war.

The Fitzwilliams maintained their hounds with which to pursue their favoured sport of fox hunting. In early November the Wentworth hounds met at Great Houghton with Lady Fitzwilliam being very much present. The hunting, which had started on the Monday, found itself in Billingham on the Friday, where the Wentworth hounds were to take part in a cub hunt.

The press reports that after a few days of hunting, a 'good day's sport' was had when the Wentworth Hunt started from Swinton on the Saturday. In order that readers should fully understand the nature of a 'good day's sport' in terms of fox hunting, *The Times* reported the result of this hunting success. Altogether, with only 23 hounds being out on this occasion, there were thirteen brace of foxes killed with six brace run to ground.

During the height of the need to attract volunteers to the military, participation in sport had been frowned upon by some as a distraction, but it was now viewed as a necessary outlet from the harsh reality of wartime life. The Mexborough and District Cricket League was still providing the pleasures of this more sedate sport for those within the area. The fixtures for the 1916 season finished in September with South Kirby showing their superiority, topping the League from start to finish. Equally consistent were Darfield who finished bottom. Mexborough, after a reasonable start, finished just above the bottom place.

Locally, football had its setbacks as a consequence of the lack of suitable and willing players. The sport locally was reduced to colliery teams, being made up of very young men who had been formed into junior teams. Women's football teams formed from various workplaces were now becoming popular, despite disapproval by some more conservative males.

The sport which seemed to see little curtailment in Mexborough was boxing. Described as Mexborough's well-known favourite, Tommy Stokes was advertised as fighting in Doncaster in October. Stokes, an old adversary of 'Iron' Hague, was now fighting under the title of Bombardier Tom Stokes. On this occasion Tommy was to take on a young opponent from Sheffield, Private Gus Platts over fifteen rounds. Both these men had seen military service and now were 'doing their bit' by entertaining boxing spectators during a period when the spirits of the public would have needed lifting most. Tommy himself had lost his brother William Stokes in December of 1915.

The Mexborough Sports Syndicate was providing regular contests at the Empire Palace. The press reported, 'A good afternoon of sport was witnessed by a large crowd at the Empire Palace, Mexborough, on Saturday 15th October, when a boxing exhibition promoted by Messrs E. Rawson, and G. Townsend, was held. A number of spirited bouts were staged'. Ernest Rawson had been a local boxer himself, even doing a spot of bare knuckle fighting in the district in the past. All the fights featured local boxers from the Don and Dearne Valley area. The principle contest at this event was a fifteen round fight between a young lad called Rawson from Denaby and a Wath boxer by the name of G. Mapplebeck. Mapplebeck's experience proved the key on this occasion when he won on points.

Just as in football, the sport was providing young men, below the age of qualification for military service, with an opportunity to get established in their chosen sport and earn a little money into the bargain. The boxing programme arranged at the Empire in November saw George Hague, the young brother of 'Iron' Hague, taking on a George Stanton from Bolton-upon-Dearne. The fight was for a ten pound purse, again over fifteen rounds. Hague won the contest when the referee stopped the fight in the tenth.

The continuation of sport, albeit in a diluted form, would have offered some relief from the impact of war weariness and austerity. Throughout the year, the Government was tightening their grip on more and more aspects of socio-economic life. The war had shown the necessity for state control and with it the benefits which could derive from a planned economy. Paradoxically, the establishment of more central control gave political opponents of the Government strong arguments for the introduction of nationalisation of parts of the economy on a permanent basis at the end of the war.

There were then some benefits gained from more state control, but generally, Mexborough, like most of the country, suffered from the effects of austerity and a diversion of resource to the military. Supplies of petrol were rationed from July of the year.

On 30th October, the Early Closing Order, made under DORA, came into force. This gave local authorities the power to force shops and other businesses to close at 7.00pm on every day expect Saturday when hours were extended to 9.00pm. The Order did not include chemists and, strangely, barbers and hairdressers who could remain open until 8.00pm. Further, the provision for early closing did not include public houses or other places which sold intoxicating liquor. The pubs had their own hours licensed, although reduced from pre-war days. The Government appears to have taken the view that no constructive purpose could be served by further antagonising the working class men and women who liked a drink.

Newspaper establishments, too, were exempt from the Early Closing Order. Newspaper propaganda was essential in promoting the need for these wartime measure amongst the general public. Yet even newspapers themselves were to fall victim to Government austerity measures. By the end of the year there was a paper shortage, with the Government deciding to reduce the imports of paper from abroad. This, it was claimed, would free up more space on merchant ships bringing in foods and material for producing munitions. Every unsold newspaper was now considered to be a waste. From the beginning of 1917 all newspapers would need to be ordered at the local newsagents. By this time there was certainly a noticeable reduction in the numbers of pages and range of newspaper coverage.

The Early Closing Order had two purposes. It would reduce, particularly in the winter, the consumption of electricity and with it coal consumption. There were also concerns over the increasing number of Zeppelin raids over Britain; by curtailing lighting in commercial premises and streets the risk of successful raids just might be reduced. The district had been shaken by the visit of the Zeppelin raider of 25th September resulting in 28 deaths in Sheffield. Local councils in the district had given instructions to the public on how warnings would be given and how to respond to any air raids. Immediately after the September raid, a resident from Fitzwilliam Street in Swinton, which at the time had full electric lighting, wrote to the press to complain that the local police were neglecting to carry their duty to warn of impending raids. Other complaints were usually concerning the public's failure to reduce their lighting not only in their homes, but also on their vehicles. The Doncaster West Riding Police Court was constantly dealing with cases of breaches of the Lighting Order. Fines, usually of twenty shillings (£1), were imposed.

So alarmed by the recent presence of the German raider over Mexborough and district at the Mexborough UDC's meeting in October, the Highway Committee instructed the Council's clerk to write to the Mexborough and Swinton Tramway Company ordering them to reduce lighting from their cars. This could be achieved according to the Highways Committee by shading the inside lights or otherwise providing suitable blinds for the windows. At the same meeting the Electric Lighting Committee, with consideration to the finances of the UDC, decided, because of the high premium, not to insure the electricity works against air raids.

More of what Arthur Marwick describes as the 'pressures of necessity' were to bear down upon the masses in October by way of increased railway fares. The primary object of such a raise was to try to reduce passenger usage. Resources on the railway network were needed mostly for the transportation of goods and minerals. Most certainly the public tramways, of which there was a considerable network within the area and other forms of public road transport, would have profited by the particular railway fare increase.

There were accusations that wartime pressures were reducing parts of Mexborough to a state of neglect. Despite Mexborough being a major and important industrial town, other boroughs had the 'privilege' of having their own 'General Post Office' long before the town acquired its own. Under the headline 'A Pantomime Post Office', *The Times* was to accuse His Majesty's Mail service of being mean and creating unnecessary inconvenience. While admitting that since the beginning of the war the business of post offices had expanded enormously, the newspaper takes issue with the way the business is prioritised. The paper complained:

> *'On three days per week their whole resources are taxed to the utmost to deal with the business of Army and Navy allowances and old pensions, leaving out ordinary*

business transacted there. Mexborough's Post Office like its
railway station, is a continual insult to the town, and an
insult that is deeply resented in all parts of the town'.

How the editor of the *The Times* wanted the Post Office to deal
with the pressures placed upon them by wartime conditions is not
altogether clear. Those in receipt of Army and Navy allowances and old
age pensions would surely not have objected to their needs being met
above that of the undefined 'ordinary business'. Such allowances would
be necessary to sustain those who the Government deemed were entitled
to it, and every serviceman fighting for his country would be expecting
their families to receive it. The call for sacrifice and patriotism and the
need to endure the pressures of necessity, was constantly heralded
throughout the pages of the conservative and liberal newspapers. As
such, the attack on the Post Office by *The Times* might be regarded
somewhat contradictory.

The district suffered from an increase in juvenile crime. The lack
of parental guidance and supervision was to blame. The increase in the
number of men now serving away from home in the armed forces would
have a direct bearing upon the problem. Many young women who might
have given some assistance with the supervision of the young were now
partially removed from the home with their engagement in munitions
works and other important war service industries. The consensus to help
reduce youth crime appears to have been to encourge all male juveniles
to join the Boy Scouts or the Boy's Brigade.

By the end of the year the problems with child care, which had
blighted Mexborough for years, were still apparent. At the October
meeting of the UDC, in her final report, Health Visitor and School Nurse
Miss Margaret Cussack, set out a depressing picture. Although overall
babies born and reared in the district were up to standard, there were
areas about which the Council should be alarmed. Many infants and very
young children were still being subjected to the depraved atmosphere of
crowded halls at night. Some parents continued to give their infants
narcotics composed largely of paregorics which had the additive
properties of opium. These drugs were all too easy to purchase in the
Mexborough area. The lack of ventilation was a problem, even in 'better
class' homes, this being responsible for some respiratory complaints.

Miss Cussack's role included her involvement in overseeing the
health and welfare of school children. Her report starkly informs us that
wartime conditions did not improve matters in the area of child and
infant wellbeing. Margaret Cussack reported:

'While there is great improvement in the general condition
of cleanliness of school children, we are far from an ideal

state yet. The majority of children go to bed to late, and consequently do not get up in time to perform the necessary toilet duties properly. Many do not get proper breakfast foods, nor time to sit and eat that meal properly. It is regrettable to see so many badly shod children during the wet weather. Parents buy boots of cheap and showy variety which wear out quickly. At least one third of the children of this district are insufficiently shod for wet weather. Woollen clothing in the winter is not usual in fact some children are overburdened with clothes in the summer and not sufficiently clad in winter.'

What Miss Cussack believed, to the discredit of Mexborough, was that the town could not generate any great enthusiasm for a collective interest in child welfare. What was lacking was a body of people, principally made up of women, to help to brighten up the lives of both the children and their overworked mothers of large families. 'We really need the help and cooperation of the ladies of the town, to ensure that every baby has at least warm woollen underwear during the winter months.' The Health Visitor urged that a working party should be set up which would undertake to make, or re-make, suitable garments which could be sold and, if necessary, at a recoverable cost to mothers who did not possess the skills or time to make them. The difficulties in getting women, especially women of the higher classes in Mexborough, to give their time to the question of child welfare, was perhaps due to the ever-increasing demand the war was now placing on women from all classes. This together with a general war weariness was perhaps contributing to a decline in middle class philanthropy.

Such was the embarrassment of the Council towards their Health Officer's indictment of the poor state of child welfare within the town, William Winstanley and other councillors were forced to respond. Councillor Humphreys believed that someone within the Council was responsible for the town's seeming lack of interest in the subject. He could remember that sometime in the past the Council had set up a sub-committee to deal with the question of child welfare, but no such meeting had been convened. Humphreys was particularly alarmed that, although the rate of infant mortality in Mexborough had declined since 1913, it was still higher than the national average. Councillor Humphreys proposed that a Child Welfare Committee be immediately set up. In the circumstances this proposal had no trouble in being adopted with the following members appointed, Messrs, Winstanley, Humphreys, Allen, Rowan and Wood. Dr Huey was asked to convene the meeting.

Not only did Councillor Winstanley and his council colleagues feel themselves compelled to set up a committee dealing with the problems raised by Miss Cussack, but found themselves pressured to go further. In view of the appalling figures presented to the Council, Councillor Winstanley was more than convinced that it was now time to establish a maternity centre and public clinic in Mexborough. This decision was also driven by the fact that 17% of all big towns had taken this step as well as 40% of smaller ones.

Mexborough UDC was to take on board Miss Elizabeth Cusssack's suggestion to establish an ante-natal clinic and school for mothers, which would attract a Local Government Board grant. At Mexborough Council's November meeting Council members resolved to set up a clinic, once they had found suitable accommodation and committed themselves to employ a medical superintendent to oversee its work. The suggestion of setting up a maternity hospital was not, however, adopted. The clinic was not only a triumph for Miss Cussack, but also for Medical Officer Dr Huey. Dr Huey had, since 1902, stressed within his annual reports the need for such facilities as a result of Mexborough's high infantile mortality rate. During the period from 1902, the highest rate recorded was in 1904, the lowest in 1912. Despite the lowering of the national birth rate, with Mexborough following that trend, infant mortality had crept up again and was still far too high in the town. Now amid the austerity of wartime conditions, campaigners for this overdue medical facility of a maternity clinic were to fulfil their ambition.

Dr Huey had some good news to report in that the overall death rate for July 1916 was the lowest ever recorded in Mexborough. The irony of this figure for July 1916 was probably not lost on in the Council Chamber, when thoughts may have wandered to Mexborough's dead on the battlefields of the Somme.

Sanitary conditions were also improved in the town, leading to a decrease in infectious diseases. Although new sanitary laws were now enacted they were continually creating a great amount of clerical work and causing a distraction from some other important practical work. However, Mexborough's sanitary conditions were improving year by year. Great care was now being taken to control infectious diseases owing to the constant flow of soldiers and sailors in the district.

Health problems in the town, however, still continued and had always been a challenge for those appointed to help alleviate the worst of these problems created by the densely populated industrial environment of the Don and Dearne Valleys. The health visitor and school nurse positions appear to have been exceptionally stressful and frustrating employment. Mexborough UDC did not by all accounts succeed in holding on to its health visitor for long periods, possibly owing to the difficulties of convincing some of the councillors of the seriousness of the conditions they were observing on a daily basis. In November it was Miss Margaret Cussack's turn to depart to pastures new. She was to acquire employment as a superintendent of a maternity centre established by the Plymouth Corporation. Tribute was paid to by her former employers, the public and press alike. She had left the lasting legacy of helping to create Mexborough's first maternity clinic, a reward for her tenacious commitment, despite the limitation the Council placed upon her. Miss Cussack's position was taken over by Miss Margaret Swallow, a Church Street resident, in an announcement made by the Council just before Christmas. Miss Swallow's task may be said to have been made a little easier by the efforts of her predecessor and indeed by that of the long-serving Dr John Huey.

The third Christmas at war had arrived. The shock of what had happened on the battlefields throughout the year, with little prospect that it might end, was evidenced by a lack of real expression of seasonal joy within the newspapers. Over 170 servicemen from the Mexborough area had lost their lives during 1916. How would Mexborough's church and chapel congregations celebrate the birth of Christ while attempting to commemorate and pay respect to Mexborough's war dead? Religion would not find these two spiritual emotions of joy and sorrow easy to balance. It would have been even harder in the home for those gathered around a kitchen table containing the Christmas meal, a table in this year of 1916 that would be bereft of loved ones.

There were no large adverts within the newspapers informing the public of the delights of the theatre and cinema's Christmas programme. Nor were there the traditional pantomime shows of previous years. The Hippodrome featured a play called, *The Unseen Hand* performed by a London company. A supposedly famous baritone, Douglas Danes, and a 'well-known' comedian, Tom Burton, made up part of this seemingly dull Christmas programme. The Empire had at the head of their bill a group calling itself the *Six Greenless*, described as a clever group of artistes performing a play called *On Holiday*. This was a rather sombre Christmas offering by Mexborough's theatre and cinemas. At least the Royal was to offer a comedy drama starring the increasingly popular Charlie Chaplin.

Whatever the thoughts of Mexborough people were about the prevailing situation on the Western Front and other theatres of conflict, their thoughts would never be far from those who were, or had been, on those bloody battlefields. As from the beginning of the war, Montagu Hospital, with its wounded servicemen, was the centre of benevolent activity. On the Tuesday prior to Christmas day, a 'Concert Party' for the wounded was organised by Miss Dorothy Nicholson who also arranged a quantity of fruit to be distributed at the event. Entertainment was provided by a Mrs Strachan, a comedienne, and by Mexborough's Horace Hillerby, who was described as a humorist. A Mr Tolini performed on the musical glasses. Mr Brocklesby, likely to have been one of the Brocklesby family from Conisbrough, was on hand to entertain with his conjuring tricks. The singing was provided by soldier baritone, one Private Rawson.

On Christmas Day eve the wounded in Montagu Hospital were treated to yet another concert for their enjoyment, the event this time being arranged by Miss Phyllis Coules. On this occasion the event was entirely of a musical nature and to some extent a family affair. Mr Ernest Coules and Miss Phyllis Coules herself, were two of the concert's soloists, the other Miss Flo Addy. All were accompanied by Miss Horton on the piano.

The public houses, too, were thinking of and providing Mexborough's military wounded with some Christmas cheer. The landlord of the Red Lion Hotel, in Bank Street, Mr S. Cooper, encouraged his little granddaughter to approach customers with a collection box. No doubt assisted by her charm and a little audacity, this little girl was able collect the sum of £5 13s. 9d. Impatient to complete her mission she immediately proceeded to Montagu Hospital and presented one shilling (5p) and 25 cigarettes to each of the 33 wounded soldiers in the hospital's care.

The military authorities had ordained that 10% of the armed forces would be allowed leave during the Christmas period, but by all accounts it is doubtful if Mexborough was to see is fair share of this limited number.

The Government had requested that during the Christmas period the public should curtail their travel by railway. By and large this was heeded, for the Great Central Railway was to announce that civilian passenger usage during the period was down. Priority was given to the thousands of soldiers and sailors who would be eager to be getting home to enjoy their priceless army and navy Christmas leave. The London railway stations of St Pancras, Kings Cross and Marylebone were the gateways to industrial south Yorkshire and its vast Don and Dearne Valleys' coalfields. These great railway terminals would have been massed with those making their way home to such places as Sheffield, Doncaster, Barnsley, Rotherham and of course Mexborough. If they had left it late, they would have witnessed the beginnings of a white Christmas, at least in London, when the snow fell and covered the station platforms. This was perhaps a brief glimpse of a magical traditional Christmas, a Christmas they would attempt to enjoy.

For those who made it home for Christmas there would be some joy for them and their families. As *The Times* remarked, 'Happy were those households who could include one or more of their fighting men in their fireside company'. But overall Christmas in Mexborough and district passed, as it would elsewhere in the country, 'soberly' and with little joy, devoid of the traditional Christmas festive spirit.

Those who were fortunate enough to get Christmas leave often did so without their comrades. The reality of war was more than ever upon them and their families' minds. Shortly after the Christmas break, in the language of the period, *The Times* remarked:

> '*It was not our first wartime Christmas. We have learned more of the realities of our situation and of the immensity of the crisis through which our Empire and the civilisation of the world are passing, in the past twelve months than in the sixteen months which preceded it. The year 1916 has taught us to look out toward what 1917 holds in store and to face it not only with courage and hope, but with fortitude and understanding.*'

For those who survived the Great War and for those of future generations like ourselves, we are sadly, with historic hindsight, aware that 1917 held much the same for the people of Mexborough and district as it had done in the blood-stained year of 1916.

Appendix I

Mexborough Men Who Died From 1914 to 1922

Mexborough Men Who Died in 1914

September 1914

11th September: Sergeant George Ernest Jones, 1st York & Lancs, 8736, Age 25
Addenda Panel, Tehran Memorial

October 1914

18th October: Private Ernest Oxer, York & Lancashire Regiment, 8502
Panel 8 Ploegsteert Memorial

21st October: Private Frank Firth, 2nd York & Lancs, 10206, Age 21
Panel 33 Ypres (Menin Gate) Memorial

22nd October: Private Daniel Hughes (Born Mexborough), 2nd Battalion KOYLI, 9231
Panel 31 Le Touret Memorial

26th October: Private Joseph Morley, 2nd KOYLI, 7376
Panel 31 Le Tuoret Memorial

28th October: Private William Hutchinson, 2nd KOYLI, 7329
Panel 47, Le Touret Memorial

**30th October: Private Fred Archer (Born Bentley), 2nd
Battalion KOYLI, 8934 Age 24**
Panel 31 Le Touret Memorial

November 1914

**1st November: Leading Telegraphist Alfred Henry Perry, Royal
Navy J.867, Age 24**
RN 3 Portsmouth Naval Memorial (Lost on HMS Good Hope)

**8th November: Private Isiaih Blunt, 2nd York & Lancs, 7365,
Reservist (Canadian Division) Born Denaby, lived
Mexborough**
Panel 8 Ploegsteert Memorial

**28th November: Private Harold Rodgers (Born Mexborough),
10th York & Lancs 15824, (Died at his billet in Bedfordshire)**
B 8 St Thomas Church Yard Extension, Kilnhurst

Mexborough Men Who Died in 1915

February 1915

**25th February: Private James Hill, Royal Scots (Lothian
Regiment), 9861, Age 32 (Born Mexborough lived Denaby)**
A 7 Dickeburgh New Military Cemetery

March 1915

**12th March: Company Sergeant Major Arthur Jackson
Goulding, 1st Battalion Wiltshire Regiment, 3970, Age 32**
Panel 53 Ypres (Menin Gate) Memorial

April 1915

2nd April: Bandsman Charles George Higgins, 2nd York & Lancs, 9147
Les Gonards Cemetery Versailles

5th April: Private Joseph Cliff, KOYLI, 20894
I E 33 Birr Cross Roads Cemetery

8th April: Private Fredrick Ramsey, 1st KOYLI, 20592, Age 20
Panel 47 Ypres (Menin Gate) Memorial,

8th April: Private Isaac Whitehead, 1st York & Lancs, 18745, Age 27
Panel 36 & 55 Ypres (Menin Gate) Memorial

11th April: Driver Wilfred Drury, Royal Field Artillery, 35715, Age 21
III D 88 Boulogne Eastern Cemetery

18th April: Private George Henry Dickenson, 2nd KOYLI, 31102, Age 22
Panel 47 Ypres (Menin Gate) Memorial

27th April: Private Herbert Heald, KOYLI, 16683
VI T 18 Railway Dugout Burial Ground

29th April: Gunner George Twigg, RFA, 43742
III A 9 Perth Cemetery (China Wall)

May 1915

7th May: Private Wilfred Higgins, 2nd KOYLI, 3/1741, Age 34
Panel 47 Ypres (Menin Gate) Memorial

8th May: 1915: Private John Calladine, 1st York & Lancs, 18131, Age 24
Panel 36 – 55, Ypres (Menin Gate) Memorial

8th May: 1915: Private Joseph Cliff, 1st KOYLI, 20894
IE 33 Birr Cross Road Cemetery

8th May: Private Frederick Ramsey, KOYLI, 20592, Age 20
Panel 47 Ypres (Menin Gate) Memorial

9th May: Private Thomas Ward, Sherwood Foresters, 6614
Panel 39 and 41 Ypres (Menin Gate) Memorial

11th May: Private George Truelove, Sherwood Foresters (Notts & Derby) Regiment, 14617
Merville Communal Cemetery

15th May: Private Richard Robert Douglas, Royal Army Medical Corps, 2163
Panel; 56 Ypres (Menin Gate) Memorial

24th May: Gunner Andre Kelly, RGA, 339
B 2 Railway Chateau Cemetery

25th May: Private Albert Clark, 1st KOYLI, 20874
II B 2 Hazebrough Communal Cemetery

July 1915

2nd July: Corporal Arthur Andrews, KOYLI, 1735, Age 22
II F 9 Talans Farm Memorial

3rd July: Private Walter Stead, 1st York & Lancs, 9345
J48 Kemmel Chateau Military Cemetery

7th July: Private Herbert Falkingham, Lancaster Fusiliers, 13821,
Panel 33 Ypres (Menin Gate) Memorial

17th July: Private William Shaw, 2nd KOYL, 20488, Age 25
VII C.7 Voormezeele Enclosure No 3

29th July: Private John Boynton, 2nd York & Lancs, 8504, Age 29
II B 27A Etaples Military Cemetery

29th July: Private Albert Jackson, 2nd Northumberland Fusiliers, 2987
I C 982 Balleul Communal Cemetery Extension, Nord

August 1915

2nd August: Private Joseph Walter Fox, 1st KOYLI, 21655, Age 28
5. 13 Kemmel Chateau Miliary Cemetery

5th August: Private H. Moore, 1st KOYLI, 20975
II G 7 Hazebrouck Communal Cemetery

8th August: Private Jesse Senior, 6th York & Lancs, 18596
Panel 171 to 173, Helles Memorial (Gallipoli)

9th August: Private Thomas Ward, Sherwood Foresters, 6614
Panel 39 and 41 Ypres (Menin Gate) Memorial

10thAugust : Private Thomas Humphries, 6th York & Lancs, 15266
Doiran Memorial

11th August: Private James Timmins, 6th York & Lancs, 15334
Panel 171 to 173 Helles Memorial (Gallipoli)

13th August: Private John Galbraith Hunter, RAMC, 1776, Age 20
Panel 199 and 200 or 236 to 239 and 328 (Lost on the Royal Edward)

13th August: Private John Smith, RAMC, SS/14037
Panel 199 or 233 to 236 and 351 (Lost on the Royal Edward)

15th August, Private Henry Whittlestone (Born Mexborough, Enlisted Wakefield), 6th KOYLI
Panel 47 Ypres (Menin Gate) Memorial

21st August: Private William Henry Briggs, 6th York & Lancs, 10894
Panel 171 to 173 Helles Memorial (Gallipoli)

29th August: Private John Atkinson, 1/5th York & Lancs, 2723, Age 30
IV A 30 Talana Farm Cemetery

31st August: Corporal Irwin (Reginald) Day, 7th York & Lancs 3/2978, Age 21
Voormezeele Enclosure Vijanderaan Region, Belguin PA VIII C 6

31st August: Private Herbert Sykes, 11th York & Lancs (Reserves), 11154
New D 'U' 101 Mexbrough Cemetery

September 1915

9th September: Private George Reynolds, York & Lancs, 3/2216
K 30 Kemmel Chateau Military Cemetery

12th September: Private Robert Carroll, 6th York & Lancs, 10672
Hill 10 Cemetery (Gallipoli)

25th September: Lance Corporal Charles Abey (Born Market Rasen, Lincs)
9th York & Lancs, 15329, Age 27
Panel 105 to106 Loos Memorial

25th September: Lance Corporal Tom Beech, 10th York & Lancs, 15963, Age 28
Panel 105 to 106 Loos Memorial

25th September: Corporal James Clarke, Kings Own Royal Lancaster Regiment, 13087, Age 21
II H ii Le Touret Military Cemetery, Richbourg L'Avouve

26th September: Private Harold Stead, 13th Northumberland Fusiliers, 15595,Age 21
Panel 20 to 22, Loos Memorial
Employed at Mexborough Locomotive Depot. Named on station memorial

26th September: Lance Corporal Robert Vernon Truelove, 1st and 10th York & Lancs, 23242
Panel 105 and 106 Loos Memorial

27th September: Private Peter Clarke, 9th KOYLI, 19023
Panel 97 and 88 Loos Memorial

October 1915

1st October: Private Arthur Calladine, 2nd Northumberland Fusiliers, 16908, Age 18
Panel 20 to 22, Loos Memorial

1st October: Private George Edward Morley, KOYLI 22017, Age 22

Panel 97 & 98Loos Memorial

1st October: Private Francis Osborne Rowland, 6th York & Lancs, 22033
Panel 9 Vis – En – Artois Memorial

9th October: Private R. L. Danks, York & Lancs, 3409
New D "C" 96 Mexborough Cemetery

9th October: Private Hiran Foote, 2nd York & Lancs, 8212, Age 32
Commonly known as Hiran Prince
Div 19 J. 4 St Marie Cemetery, La Havre

9th October: Private Herbert Hakin, 1/5th York & Lancs, 2754, Age 21
I. J. 27 Bards Cottage Cemetery

10th October: Private Matthew Graham, 6th York & Lancs, 21448, Age 24
Sp Memorial C. 231 Twelve Tree Copse Cemetery

14th October: Lance Corporal Harold Edgar Woodhead, Sherwood Foresters (Notts & Derby) Regiment, 2160, Age 25
Panel 87 to 89Loos Memorial

15th October: Private Horace Shaw, 9th KOYLI, 19046
Born Swinton, Enlisted Mexborough
III G. 6 Ploegsteert Wood Military Cemetery

24th October: Private Harry Oxer, 6th York & Lancs, 17428
I. G 10 Hill 10 Cemetery (Balkans)

26th October: Private Isaac Beardsley, 10th Duke of Wellington's Own West Riding Regiment, 14528
Panel 6 Ploegsteert Memorial

29th October: Private Matthew Thomas, 6th York & Lancs, Age 24
Sp Mem C 231 Twelve Tree Corpse Cemetery

November 1915

2nd November: Private Fred Turner, 9th York & Lancs, 16919, Age 41
II K 16 Rue-Petillon Military Cemetery

7th November: Private Herbert Roberts, 1/5th Battalion York & Lancs, 1973, Age 25
I L 39 Bard Cottage Cemetery

17th November: Private Frederick Turton, KOYLI, Lost on HMHS Anglia
Hollybrook Memorial, Southampton

29th October: Private Matthew Thomas Graham, York & Lancs, 21448, Age 24
Sp Mem C. 231 Twelve Tree Copse Cemetery

December 1915

10th December: Private David Murray, Argyle and Sutherland Highlanders, S/3845, Age 28
Panel 125 to 127 Loos Memorial

12th December: Private (Guardsman) Louis Calladine, 1st Coldstream Guards, 14789
1. A. 171 Longuenesse (St Omer) Souvenir Cemetery

13th December: Able Seaman Marsden Walker, Royal Naval Volunteer Reserve, Tyneside Z/4771, Howe Battalion
Special Memorial A 20, Skew Bridge Cemetery, Helles (Gallipoli)

16th December: Private John William Haigh, 11th & 6th York & Lancs, 17208, Age 34
C II 2 Pieta Military Cemetery

20th December: Private Robert Marshall, 2nd York & Lancs, 2965 , Age 38
I. J 15 Bard Cottage Cemetery

Mexborough Men Who Died in 1916

January 1916

3rd January: Private/Fusilier Ernest Samuel Hornsby, 25th Battalion Royal Fusiliers, 13721
II 13 II Vio Cemetery

20th January: Private Edward H. Briant, 8th York & Lancs, 13965
1J 63 Rue-Petillon Military Cemetery Fleurbaix

22nd January: Private R. Jones ,York& Lancs, 2835, Age 20
Croix-Rouge Military Cemetery, Quaedypre

25th January: Private Herbert William Wright, 9th KOYLI, 16371
IXE 72 Cite Bonjean Military Cemetery, Armentieres

February 1916

12th February: Private W Wilkinson, 9th KOYLI, 17271
1X6 94 Cite Bonjean Military Cemetery Armentieres

March 1916

2nd March: Private Willie Hall, Duke of Wellington's (West Riding) Regiment 17252, Age 33
Panel 20 Ypres (Menin Gate) Memorial

18th March: Sergeant Thomas Johnson, Royal Field Artillery, 164th Rotherham Howitzer Brigade, L/1986, Age 24
A61 Millencourt Communal Cemetery Extension

22nd March: Private George Frederick Pinder, 6th York & Lancs, 16422 Age 24
Bay 8, Arras Memorial

April 1916

1st April: Private John Scott, 8th York & Lancs,14263
Died of wounds, St Margarets Churchyard, Swinton, NM 10 M

4th April: Drummer Ernest Goodbody, York & Lancs, 15097
I C 23 Albert Communal Cemetery Extension

9th April: Private Percy Dyson, South Wales Borderers, 19868
Panel 16 to 62 Basra Memorial

15th April: Private G. Depledge, York & Lancs, 17422

IX G 59 Cite Bonjean Military Cemetery, Armentieres
21st April: Private George Horton, 2nd York & Lancs, 18196, Age 36
III H 20 New Irish Farm Cemetery

21st April: Private Richard (Dick) Hirst, 2nd York & Lancs, 21326 Age 20
II L 11 Essex Farm Cemetery

21st April: Private Walter Smith, 2nd York & Lancs, 21442 (Born Wath)
II N 10, Essex Farm Cemetery

25th April: Private H. Harrison, Duke Of Wellington's (West Riding) Regiment,14929
IX G 37 Cite Bonjean Military Armentieres

26thApril : Drummer Ernest Goodbody, York and Lancs, 15097
I C 23 Albert Community Cemetery Extension.

30th April: Private Harry Johnson, Grenadier Guards, 22717, Age 29
II. B. 5. BrandHoek Military Cemetery

30th April: Private Levi Vernon, (Born Heathhayes, Staffs), 8th KOYLI, 21115
Becourt Military Cemetery, Becordel-Becourt

June 1916

3rd June: Lance Corporal J. G. Venables, Cameron Highlanders, S/21194, Age 20
New B "U" Mexborough Cemetery

8th June: Private Frederick William Jenkinson, 17th Prince of Wales Own (West Yorkshire Regiment)
II G 20 Le Touret Military Cemetery, Richebourg L'Avoue

8th June: Sapper William Williams, Royal Engineers, 79342
Pier & Face 8A & 8D Thiepval Memorial.

16th June: Private George Sims, York & Lancs, 21501, Age 21
1C 63 Norfolk Cemetery Becordel–Becourt

22nd/23rd June: Sapper William Hackett VC, Royal Enginners, 136414, Age 43
Panel 1 Ploegsteert Memorial and Givenchy les la Basse. Memorial also

in Mexborough and remembered on Manvers Main War Memorial.

27th June: Gunner Ernest Hill, Royal Field Artillery, Rotherham Howitzer Brigade L/ 20024, Age 26

IID 16 Mesnil Communal Cemetery Extension.

July 1916

2nd July: Private William Harrison, 8th York & Lancs, 22031, Age 26. Died of wounds from 1st July

1. B 7 Heilly Station Cemetery Mericourt–L'Abbe

2nd July: Private Thomas Smith, 1/5th (TF) York & Lancs, 4234 (Enlisted Barnsley)

Pier & Face 14A & 14B Thiepval Memorial

2ndJuly : Private Arthur Steel, 9th York & Lancs,17432, Age 24

A II Millencourt Communal Cemetery

3rd July: Private Luke Barker, (Born Wombwell), 9th York & Lancs, 21441 Age18

Pier & Face 14A & 14B Thiepval Memorial

3rd July: George Hakin (Shoeing Smith), Royal Field Artillery, 111284

Panel 3 & 60, Basra Memorial

3rd July: Private George Jenkinson, (Born Pontifract), 10th York & Lancs, 14914

Pier & Face 14 A & 14B Theipval Memorial

3rd July: Private Albert Marshall, 1st Kings Own Scottish Borderers, 21120

Pier and Face 4A & 4D Thiepval Memorial

3rd July: Private Fred Leach, (Born Chadsmoor, Cannock), 10th York & Lancs, 13938

Pier & Face 14 A & 14B Theipval

4th July: Private George Taylor, 8th York & Lancs, 13368, Age 26

Puchevillers Britsh Cemetery

5th July: Private Peter Barron,1/5th Battalion KOYLI, 3439 (Enlisted Conisbrough)

Pier and Face 11, C and 12A Thiepval Memorial

6th July: Private William Wright: York & Lancs, 16891
I. D 31 Heilly Station Cemetery Mericourt, L' Abbe

7th July: Lance Corporal F. Fisher, Royal Fusiliers, G/238
VII 19 Ovillers Military Cemetery

8th July: Sapper J. Hinton, 2/1 Royal Engineers (West Riding Field Company) 2394, Age 26 ID 37 Puchevillers British Cemetery

9th July: Private William Ramsey, 9th York & Lancs, 23235, Age 19
VIII D. 121 Boulogne Eastern Cemetery

12th July: Private Fred Hall, 8th York & Lancs, 14028, Aged 39
Old E 'U' 150 Mexborough Cemetery

14th July: Sergeant John Thomas Morris, RGA, 21390
VII A 17 Lijsenthoek Military Cemetery

15th July:Private William Ramsey, 9th York & Lancs, 23235 Age 19
VII , D1 21 Boulogne Eastern Cemetery

16th July: Private R. J. Salkeld, York & Lancs, 21858
Died of wounds in internment camp,VC 5 Hamburg Cemetery

19th July: Private Edgar Stephen Hallford, Machine Gun Corp (Infantry Battalion) 6182, Formerly KOYLI 662
II E 6 Louez Military Cemetery Duisans

20th July: Private L. Aubrey, Cameronians (Scottish Rifles), Age 28, 43113 xxx IIIJ. 5 Delville Wood Cemetery Longueval

20th July: Private Samuel Boyce, Gloucester Regiment, 26440, Age 21
Pier & Face 5A & 5B Thiepval Memorial

20th July: Private Arthur Tilson, 13th York & Lancs, 13/976, Age 25
X 904 Barnsley Cemetery

21st July: Private Charles Hart, 6th York & Lancs, 17660, Age 24
D 18 Agny Military Cemetery

21st: Lance Corporal H.S.Fruin, York & Lancs, 176033. Age 21
D 18 Agny Military Cemetery

25th July: Private Percy Wilkinson (Born Adwick-upon-Dearne enlisted Bolton-upon-Dearne, 13th York & Lancs (1st Barnsley Pals)
1A 19 Pont ODU Hem Military Cemetery, La Gorgue

31st July: Private Edward Hoggins, Kings Own Scottish Borderers, 17765
Pier & Face 4A & 4D Thiepval Memorial

August 1916

8th August: Sapper Samuel Wooding, Royal Marine Divisional Engineers, Royal Navy Division, 21991
I A. 17 Fosse No 10 Communal Cemetery Extension Sains-en-Gohelb

6th August: Private John Mason, (Born AshtonUnder Lyme), 10th York & Lancs, 19768, Age 19
Bay 8 Arras Memorial

20th August: Private Tom King, KOYLI, 26047, Age 20
Pier 11C & 12A Thiepval Memorial

21st August: Private (Pioneer) James Bennett, Corps of Royal Engineers 23863
Formerly York & Lancs 5th Special Brigade of Royal Engineers, Pioneers, 12896
Pier & Face 8A & 8D Theipval Memorial

26th August: Private G. Tingle, KOYLI, 20305, Age 26
II B 38, Lahana Military Cemetery.

31st August: Private H. Sykes, York & Lancs, 11154
New D "U" 101, Mexborough Cemetery

September 1916

3rd September: Private Charles Norman, Sherwood Foresters (Notts & Derby Regiment), 31120
II C. 8 Mesnil Communal Cemetery Extension

3rd September: Rifleman Harry Soar, West Yorkshire (Prince of Wales Own) Regiment, 5070,   Age 24

Pier & Face 2 A2C 2D Thiepval Memorial

4th September: Acting Bombardier George Henry Dean, Royal Horse & Royal Field Artillery, 35616 (Awarded M.M.) (Born Stafford)
Pier & Face 1A & 8A Thiepval Memorial

7th September: Gunner George Henry Askin, Royal Horse Artillery & Royal Field Artillery, 32806
IX G 27 Amara War Cemetery

11th September: Private Harry Butler, York & Lancs, 21216
1F 4 Blighty Valley Cemetery Authuville Wood

14th September: Private George Dobson, (Born Kilnhurst) 8th Duke of Wellington's, 15792
Pier & Face 6A & 6B Thiepval Memorial

14th September: Lance Corporal William Scales, West Yorkshire (Prince of Wales Own), 18702
Pier & Face 2 AC &2D , Thiepval Memorial

14th September: Private Walter Nettleton, Grenadier Guards, 21813
Pier & Face 8D Theipval Memorial

15th September: Private William Ronald Waddington, Coldstream Guard, 3185, Age 36
Pier & Face 7D& 8D Thiepval Memorial

15th September: Rifleman Raymond White, 8th KRRR, R/20169 Born Mexborough, lived in Doncaster, enlisted Mexborough
Pier & Face 13A & 13B Thiepval

16th September: Private Jonathan Davies, (Born Barnburgh), 9th York & Lancs, 16241,Age 43
Pier & Face 14 A & 14B Theipval Memorial

17th September: Private B. Eckford, Kings Liverpool Regiment, 3892, Age 25
B19 28 St Sever Cemetery Rouen

18th September: Private Patrick Finerty, 2nd York & Lancs, 23044
Pier & Face 14A & 14B, Thiepval Memorial

25th September: Private: Sydney Brown (Born Mexborough), 9th Sherwood Foresters
Pier and Face 10 & 10D & 11A Thiepval Memorial

25th September: Corporal E. C. Morton, Royal Field Artillery, 34956, Age 35
I E 19 Grove Town Cemetery, Meaulte

28th September: Private Benjamin Abson, Machine Gun Corps, 39032
Pier & Face 5C & 12C, Theipval Memorial

29th September: Private William Arthur Callandine, Lancashire Fusiliers, 7662
I Q 24A Wimereux Communal Cemetery

29th September: Private Harry Newey, 6th York & Lancs Regiment, 11178, Age 18
Pier and Face 14A & 14B Thiepval Memorial

29th September: Private Newson Stead, 6th York & Lancs, 21056
Pier and Face 14A & 14B Theipval Memorial

29th September: Private Elijah Thomas Pearson, York & Lancs,19417
Pier & Face 14 A & 14B Theipval Memorial

29th September: Private W. H. Wesley, York & Lancs 3/21209, Age 23
V II J 15 Regina Trench Cemetery Grandcourt

October 1916

1st October: Sergeant Percy Oswald Sale, 9th York & Lancs 15440, Age 28
Pier & Face 14 A & 14B Theipval Memorial

3rd October: Private Wilkinson Day, 9th York & Lancs, 15449, Age 24
Pier & Face 14 A&14B Theipval Memorial

5th October: Gunner C. Monk, Royal Field Artillery, 107651
Pier & Face 1 A & 8A, Thiepval Memorial.

10ᵗʰ October: Private George Henry Foster, York & Lancs, 8406, Age 42
Pier and Face 14A & 14B Thiepval Memorial

11ᵗʰ October: Albert Edward Baker, York & Lancs, 25795, Age 22
VI E 8. Struma Military Cemetery

12ᵗʰ October: Private T. A. Crowcroft, 2ⁿᵈ York & Lancs
IV M3 Bancroft British Cemetery

12ᵗʰ October: Corporal J. A. Ellis, Seaforth Highlanders, S/9189
Pier & Face 15 C Thiepval Memorial

13ᵗʰ October: Sapper R Olby, Royal Engineers 3600, Age 31
VIII F10 Guards Cemetery, Lesboeues

16ᵗʰ October: Sapper Joseph Vickers, 132701, Age 43
Div 3. M7 St Marie Cemetery, Le Havre

16ᵗʰ October: Sapper Fred Stanley, Royal Engineers (2/2 West Riding Field Company), 2446
Pier & Face 8A & 8D, Theipval Memorial

23ʳᵈ October: Private Charles Lawton, Lincolshire Regiment, 13537
Pier & Face 1 C Thiepval Memorial

27ᵗʰ October: Private Thomas Hendley, (Born Normanton), Depot Battalion KOYLI 19030, Age 28
55 Denaby Main (All Saints) Burial Ground

November 1916

7ᵗʰ November: Private John Thomas Jackson, (Born Parkgate) 3ʳᵈ KOYLI
(Reserve), 22916, Age 34
Haugh Road Cemetery, Rawmarsh

15th November: Private Alfred Hargreaves, 10ᵗʰ York & Lancs, 16868 Age 21
Pier & Face 14 A & 14 B Theipval Memorial

13th November: Able Seaman P Stables, KW/335 Royal Navy Volunteer Reserve
IE 36 Ancre British Cemetery, Beaumont Hamel

18th November: Sergeant Albert Arthur Atkinson, 13th KOYLI, 2/1510
Pier & Face 11 & 12A Thiepval Memorial

18th November: Private Herbert Gelder, 2nd KOYLI, 20861, Age 19
Pier & Face 11C & 12A Thiepval Memorial

December 1916

6th December: Private Bernard Walker, 13th York & Lancs (1st Barnsley Pals), 27243, Age 20
II K 12 Mont Huon Military Cemetery Le-Treport

11th December: Private Richard Burke, 14th York & Lancs, 14/1572
V C 8 Couin British Cemetery

18th December: Private Walter White, York & Lancs, 17427
VIII G. 18 Brown's Road Military Cemetery

Mexborough and Swinton Men Who Died on the First Day of the Somme

Private David Askin, (Born Mexborough), 14th York & Lancs (2nd Barnsley Pals) 14/2
Pier & Face 14A & 14B Theipval Memorial

Lance Corporal Albert Henry King, Royal Engineers, 2456 (2/1st West Riding Field Company), Age 35
II F. 2 Aveluy Wood Cemetery, Lancashire Dump, Mesnil Martinsard

Private William Batty, 8th York & Lancs, 16951 (Swinton enlisted Mexborough)
Pier & Face 14A & 14B Thiepval Memorial

Private James William Batty, 9th York & Lancs, 15321, Age 21
Pier & Face 14A & 14B Thiepval Memorial

Corporal Herbert Bentley, 9th York & Lancs, 18899, Age 22.
Pier & Face 14A & 7C, Thiepval Memorial

Sapper Tom Best, WRD Royal Engineers, 2422
III H 1, Aveluy Wood Cemetery, Lancshire Dump, Mesnil, Martinsart

Private Willie Bradshaw (Wilfred elsewhere), 8th York & Lancs, 15142
Pier & Face 14A & 14B Thiepval Memorial (Swinton – enlisted Mexborough)

Private Arthur Bramall (Bramhall on CWGC) 8th York & Lancs, 14068
Pier & Face 14A & 14B Thiepval Memorial

Sapper William Brookes, Royal Engineers, 2nd West Riding Field Company (Boer War veteran)
Pier & Face 14A & 14 B Thiepval Memorial

Lance Sergeant Valentine Brown, (Born Bradford) 8th York & Lancs, Age 34
Pier & Face 14A & 14 B, Theipval Memorial

Private Frank Blunt, 9th York & Lancs, 18861
Pier & Face 14A & 14B Thiepval Memorial

Lance Corporal Albert Bucknell, 8th York & Lancs, 14327, Age 21
Pier & Face 14A& 14B

Corporal Thomas Alan Burgan (Burgin), 8th York & Lancs, 15099
Pier & Face 14A & 14B Thiepval Memorial

Private George Bywater, 9th York & Lancs, 16859 (Swinton enlisted Mexborough)
Pier & Face 14A & 14B Thiepval Memorial

Lance Corporal George Alfred Catling (Born Diss, Norfolk), 2nd KOYLI, 21962
11 C 18 Bouzin Court Communal Cemetery Extension

Private William Chipp, 10th KOYLI, 19679, Age 22
Pier & Face 11C & 12A Thiepval Memorial

Private Thomas Arthur Cooke, 8th York & Lancs, 24309, Age 23
Pier and Face 14A & 14B Thiepval Memorial)

Private Percy Crookes, 8th KOYLI, 21113
Pier & Face 11 C & 12A, Theipval Memorial

Private Joseph Frederick Currie, 12th York & Lancs (Swinton enlisted Mexborough)
Pier & Face 14A & 14B Thiepval Memorial

Lance Corporal Fred Depledge, 8th York & Lancs, 17200, Age 25
Pier & Face 14A & 14B Thiepval Memorial

Corporal Wilfred Dickinson, 8th York & Lancs, 14073 (D Company), Age 25 (Swinton enlisted Mexborough)
Pier & Face 14A & 14 B Thiepval Memorial

Private Isaac Dobson, (Born Canklow Rotherham) 8th York & Lancs, 19670
Pier 14A & 14B Thiepval Memorial

Lance Corporal J. Thomas. Earnshaw, 8th York& Lancs, 21194
Memorial at I I G 7 Blighty Valley Cemetery, Authville Woods

Private John Holt, 8th York & Lancs, 14966
Pier & Face, 14 & 14B Thiepval Memorial

Lance Corporal John Henry Gaunt, 8th York & Lancs, 14080 (Swinton enlisted Mexborough)
Pier & Face 14A & 14B Thiepval Memorial

Private Herbert Gelder, 2nd KOYLI, 20861 (Swinton)
Pier & Face 11C& 12A Thiepval Memorial

Private Joseph Hague, 8th KOYLI, 19010, (Swinton)
VC 37 Blighty Valley Cemetery, Authuille Wood

Private William Jackson, 8th York & Lancs, 15144 (Swinton enlisted Mexborough)
Pier & Face 14A & 14B Thiepval Memorial

Private Bernard Jowett, (Born Todmorten) 8th York & Lancs, 16573, Age 20
Pier & Face 14A& 14B Thiepval Memorial

Private William Kershaw, 8th York & Lancs, 16948
Pier& Face 14A & 14B Thiepval Memorial

Private L. Lynam, 2nd York & Lancs, 14/70
VT6, Euston Road Cemetery, Colincamps

Private Patrick Manix, 9th York and Lancs, 16259 (Born Claremorris, County Mayo, Ireland, enlisted Mexborough)
No record on CWGC

Private Thomas Henry Mansell (Born Wortley) 2nd KOYLI, 19058, Age 42
Pier & Face 11Cc & 12A Theipval Memorial

Private Jesse Mole, 9th York & Lancs, 15339, Age 36
Pier & Face 14A & 14B Thiepval Memorial

Private Levi Mountford, 8th York & Lancs, 21855, Age 25
V.B 21 Blighty Valley Cemetery, Authville Wood.

Private Clement Nichols, 9th York & Lancs, 3/3774 (Swinton)
Pier & Face 14A & 14B Thiepval Memorial

Private Frank Oliver M.M., 9th York & Lancs (Swinton)
Plot II Row P 10 Lonsdale Cemetery, Authuille

Private George William Oliver, 8th York & Lancs, 24322
Pier & Face 14A & 14B Thiepval Memorial

Private Thomas Oliver, 9th York and Lancs, 18121, age 24 (Born Norwich, enlisted Mexborough)
Pier & Face 14A & 14B Thiepval Memorial

Private Herbert Oxley, 8th York & Lancs, 24320 (Born Mexborough, lived Rotherham)
Pier 14 A & 14B Thiepval Memorial

Private John Thomas Parkinson, 8th York & Lancs, 140004 (Swinton enlisted Mexborough)
Pier & Face 14A & 14B Thiepval Memorial

Private George Shenton, 9th York & Lancs, 18829, (Swinton)
Pier & Face 14A & 14B Thiepval Memorial

Lance Corporal John Willie Southway, 8th York and Lancs, 14366 (Born Mexborough, lived Rotheram)
Pier & Face 14A & 14B Thiepval Memorial.

Private John Thomas Smith (Born Hunslet Leeds), 2nd KOYLI, 21549, Age 28
Pier & Face 11 C & 12A Theipval Memorial

Private John Taylor, 8th York & Lancs, 14366 (Born Burdall, Chesterfield)
Pier & Face 14A & 14B, Thiepval Memorial

Private Alfred Whaite, 9th York & Lancs, 16950 (Born Manchester)
Pier & Face 14 A & 14B Thiepval Memorial

Private Charles Christopher White, 10th York & Lancs, 23234, Age 20
Pier & Face 14A & 14B Thiepval Memeroial

Private Richard Winfield, 8th Battalion York & Lancs (Swinton enlisted Mexborough)
Pier & Face 14A & 14B Thiepval Memorial

Lance Corporal Sam Wright, 9th York & Lancs, 21517
Pier & Face 14A & 14B Thiepval Memorial

Mexborough Men Who Died in 1917

January 1917

1st January: Private Thomas Freeth Allen, West Yorkshire Regiment (Prince of Wales Own), 7000
II J 7 Warlengcourt Halte British Cemetery, Saulty

1st January: Pioneer John H. Lockett, Royal Engineers, 9th Field Company, 107236
I V C. 8 Metz – En – Couture Communal Cemetery Extension

1st January: Private Robert Wood, 9th York & Lancs, 24169, Age 21
VII D 8 Railway Dugouts Burial Ground

3rd January: Private John Hill, 13th York & Lancs (1st Barnsley Pals), 31713 Age 23. (Formerly 5603 West Riding Regiment)
II G 16 Sailly–Au Bois Military Cemetery

3rd January: Private Thomas Watson, 13th York & Lancs, 27259
Sailly-Au-Bois Military Cemetery

7th January: Private R. Wood, York & Lancs, 241669, Age 21
VII D8 Railway Dugouts Burial Ground

22nd January: Private Herbert Sheridan, 9th York & Lancs, 23236, Age 21
VII F11 Railway Dugout Burial Ground

February 1917

5th February: Lance Corporal Charles Ernest Rolfe, Royal Engineers, 106687 Age 43
La Neuville Commumal Cemetery, Corbie

16th February: Private Harry Tatton, 7th York & Lancs, 18242, Age 24
I D 12 Guards Cemetery, Combles

March 1917

4th March: Corporal Alfred Dunham, 1st Worcester Regiment, 24235
VIII D. 20 Fins New British Cemetery Sorel-Le-Grand

April 1917

6th April: Sergeant Thomas Hughes (Born Mexborough enlisted Hameworth), 12th KOYLI, 12/750
I A 12 Anzin St Aubin British Cemetery

9th April: Lance Corporal William Beech, 1st Northumberland Fusiliers, 17061
II C 14 Tilloy British Cemetery, Tiloy-Les-Mofflaines

9th April: Private John Maurice Ellis, 26th Northumberland Fusiliers (Tyneside Irish), 41372, Age 24
III A 11 Roclincort Military Cemetery

9th April: Private Thomas John Reed, 8th York & Lancs, 32129, Age 24 (Formerly 4104, Yorkshire Dragoons)
Panel 36 to 55 Ypres (Menin Gate) Memorial

10th April: Private Richard Charles Rose, 8th York & Lancs, 10590, Age 20
XI C 34A Lussenthoek Military Cemetery

11th April: Private George Bernard Davidson, Cameron Highlanders, S/22976, Age 37
Bay 9 Arras Memorial

12th April: Private David Lees: 2nd York &Lancs , 15143, Age 22
Panel 104 and 106 Loos Memorial

14th April: Private John William Hodgson, KOYLI, 19048
Pier & Face 11 C & 12A Theipval Memorial

17th April: Lance Corporal Thomas William Lee, Royal Engineers (West Riding), 476224, Age 22
III F 6 Tilloy British Cemetery Tilloy-Les-Mofflaines

17thApril: Sergeant Charles Henry Petty, York & Lancs, 21393
Bay 8 Arras Memorial

18th April: Private Thomas Trueman, 2nd Cameronians (Scottish Rifles) 40889, Age 31. (Former York & Lancs 22606)
X A 6 Warlincourt Halte British Cemetery

19th April: Private John Edward Smith, 2nd Prince of Wales Own (West Yorkshire Regiment), 22486
III G. 27 Peronne Communul Cemetery Extension

20th April: Private William Ernest Peplow, 14th York & Lancs, 25683, Age 22
III J 62 Aubigy Communal Cemetery Extension

21st April: Lance Corporal Albert Atkins, 10th York & Lancs, 14326
Bay 8 Arras Memorial

21st April: Sergeant Charles Henry Petty, York & Lancs, 21393
Bay 8 Arras Memorial

23rd April: Leading Seaman George Hakin, Drake Battalion, Royal Naval Volunteer Reverse Division, KW/ 597
Addenda Panel Arras Memorial

23rdApril : Able Seaman John William Dickinson, Royal Naval Volunteer Reserve Division, KW/653
Bay 1 Arras Memorial

26th April: Private Ernest Akers Bayes, Highland Light Infantry, 40457 Age 22
IV E. 43, Duisans British Cemetery, Etrun.

26thApril: Private Frederick Smith, 19864
I G 32 Aubigny Communal Cemetery Extension

28th April: Private A. Henshaw, York & Lancs, 20975, Age 29
B. 21 Beaumetz Cross Road Cemetery Beaumetz-les-Cambrai

28thApril: Private Elyah Share, 10th York &Lancs , 38312 (Formerly 17/1217 West Yorkshire Regiment)
F 17 Athies Communal Cemetery Extension

28th April: Private Thomas Wharton, Northumberland Fusiliers, 23538 Age 38
Bay 2 and 3 Arras Memorial

30th April Sergeant Alexandra Dodds, 10th KOYLI, 18418 (Born Conisbrough enlisted Doncaster)
B 46 Cojeul British Cemetery, St Martin-Sur-Cojeul

May 1917

2nd May: Private James Harold Brumby, 12th East Yorkshire Regiment (HullPals)
 Canadian Cemetery No 2, Neuville St Vaast

2nd May: Private Willie Whitehead, York & Lancs, 21344, Age 21
XIX O 6, Etaples Military Cemetery

3rd May: Private Ernest Calladine, 2/5th York & Lancs (TF), 241347
Bay 8 Arras Memorial

3rd May 1917: Private Edward Poulson, 2/5th Duke of Wellington's (West Riding Regiment), 241777, Age 37
Bay 6 Arras Memorial

3rd May: Private Arthur Preston, York & Lancs, 240913, Age 34
Bay 8 Arras Memorial

3rdMay: Rifleman Fred Nettleship, Kings Royal Rifle Corps, 12651, Age 20
Bay 7 Arras Memorial

5th May: Private Charles O'Brien, KOYLI, 235194, Age 24
Bay 7 Arras Memorial

6th May: Private Merle Hobson, 6th KOYLI, 22263
Bay 7 Arras Memorial

6thMay : Lance Corporal Albert Victor Robinson, Royal Engineers, 10662, Age 26
P I D 7B St Sever Cemetery Extension Rouen

8th May: Private W. R. Woolridge, York & Lancs, 21432, Age 19
III K 44 Duisans British Cemetery, Etrun

9th May: Lance Corporal George Conway, 14th York & Lancs, 14/1289, Age 31
Bay 8 Arras Memorial

16th May: Gunner Henry Dryden, Royal Field Artillery, 73533, Age 24
II. E 14 Feuchy British Cemetery

27th May:Driver Joseph Tilson, Royal Army Service Corp, T/293527 Age 42
New D "C" 75 Mexborough Cemetery

June 1917

19th June: Corporal Reginald Taylor, 12th York & Lancs, 24249, Age 22
III L 27 Duisans British Cemetery, Etrun

23rd June: Private Herbert John Minchin, South Wales Borderers, 24116, Age 25
PII 1 3A St Sever Cemetery Extension, Rouen

30thJune:Private Willie Varney, 8th York & Lancs, 41017, Age 31
Panel 36 to 55 Ypres (Menin Gate) Memorial

July 1917

6th July: Private Arthur Harold Chadwick, 2nd KOYLI, 33387
V B I Ramscappelle Road Military Memorial

8th July: Private (Guardsman) F. Howard, Coldstream Guards
I B 11 Canadian Farm Cemetery

8thJuly : Private (Guardsman) Edgar Adams, Coldstream Guards, Age 21
I B 12 Canadian Farm Cemetery

8th July: Private (Guardsman) John Archibald Nicholson, Coldstream Guards, 3424, Age 37
I B 13 Canadian Farm Cemetery

9th July: Sergeant Richard Alfred Jones, 2nd KOYLI, 6261, Age 36
I E 33 Coxyde Military Cemetery

12th July: Private Ernest Cutts, Royal Fusiliers, G/13793
6 M. I. Dar Es Salaam War Cemetery

16th July: Private Clarence Whitham, 6th York & Lancs, 15270
M 2 Pond Farm Cemetery

25th July: Private James Severn, 3rd Battalion Grenadier Guards, 21503
Panel 9 & 11 Ypres (Menin Gate) Memorial

25th July: Acting Bombardier Richard Street, Royal Field Artillery, 26601
II N 14 Brandhoek Military Cemetery

28th July: Sapper Headley Thomas Mawson, Royal Engineers, 47664 Age 20
V A 28 Duisans British Cemetery, Etrun

August 1917

7th August: Private Alfred Cope, 4th Grenadier Guards, 24295, Age 22
Panel 9 &11 Ypres (Menin Gate) Memorial

8th August: Private Harold Carr, 6th Bedfordshire Regiment, 204014, Age 31, Formerly Cambridgeshire Regiment, 328943
XVI C 15 Voormezeele Enclosure No 3

18th August: Rifleman George Morris, King Royal Rifle Corps, 43447 Age 28
I E 23 Perth Cemetery (China Wall)

25th August: F. D. Poxton, Durham Light Infantary, 43970, Age 35
Panel 106 and 107 Loos Memorial

28th August: Private James Adamson, West Yorkshire Regiment (Prince of Wales Own), 42606
I A 18 Lagnicourt Hedge Cemetery

September 1917

17th September: Private C. Hood, York & Lancs, 23626
VII A. 13 Dozinghem Military Cemetery

19th September: Sapper John William Briggs, Royal Engineers, 136270 Age 41
C7 Potijze Chateau Lawn Cemetery

20th September: Corporal Ernest Speight, KRRR, R/12994
Panel 115 to 119 & 162A & 162A, Tyne Cot Memorial

21st September: Lieutenant William Rutherford Tiptaft (Born Mexborough lived in Kilnhurst), Machine Gun Corp (Infantry), Age 24
II D 7 Klein-Vierstraat British Cemetery

21st September: Private E. Winstanley, KOYLI, 21813
V. D. 13 Dozingham Military Cemetery

23rd September: Archie Samuel, KOYLI. 30118, Age 28
C. 24 Bethleem Farm West Cemetery

26th September: Private Blucher Barley, 2/5th Leicestershire Regiment, 241935
Panel 50 to 51, Tyne Cot Memorial

28th September: Corporal Patrick Blythe (Born Craggs County Galway), 10th York & Lancs, 19657 (Formerly KOYLI, 16214)
Panel 125 to 128 Tyne Cot Memorial

October 1917

4th October: Lance Corporal Arthur Hickling, 2nd Kings Own Scottish Borderers, 18170, Age 31
XII B. Hooge Crater Cemetery

4th October: Private Albert Price, Yorkshire Regiment, 24712, Age 26
I F. 12 Fins New British Cemetery, Sorel-Le Grand

8th October: Lance Corporal Louis Dawson, KOYLI, 37857, Age 36
XXX A 6A Etaples Military Cemetery

8th October: Private Walter France, 205th Company Machine Gun Corps, 65824, Age 20
Panel 154 to 159 & 163 Tyne Cot Memorial

9th October: Private James Henry Hinchcliffe, KOYLI 425151 Recorded as York & Lancs, 204498 elsewhere.
Panel 125 to 128 Tyne Cot Memorial

9th October: Private George Thomas Hurst, York & Lancs 1/4th Hallamshire (TF) Battalion, 21938, Age 27
Panel 125 to 128 Tyne Cot Memorial

9th October: Private Ralph Senior, 6th York & Lancs, 18597, Age 28
125 to 128 Tyne Cot Memorial (His brother Jesse who joined the 6th York & Lancs on same day as Ralph, was killed in 1915)

10th October: Gunner Joseph Ramsey, Royal Field Artillery, 152928, Age 23
Panel 4 to 6 & 162 Tyne Cot Memorial

10th October: Sergeant Samuel Trethewey, York & Lancs, 240553, Age 23
XXV. D 11 Tyne Cot Memorial

10th October: Private John Lomas, 'A' Company, 6th York & Lancs, 17912
XI J. 17 Dozinghen Military Cemetery

14th October: Gunner Ralph Blackwell, Royal Field Artillery, L/26599 Age 24
XXI F. 16 Lijssenththoek Military Cemetery

18th October: Lance Corporal Louis Dawson, 1st KOYLI, 37857
XXX A. 6A Etaples Military Cemetery

18th October: Private Charles William Lyons, 9th York & Lancs, 17317
Panel 125 to 128 Tyne Cot Memorial

18th October: Private Herbert Ramsden, 2nd York & Lancs, 18384 Age 38
AA1 Potijze Chateau Lawn Cemetery

18th October: Lance Corporal Ernest Stephenson, York & Lancs, 201325 Age 22
AA I. 45 Bard Cottage Cemetery

18th October:Private Charles Williams, York & Lancs, 17317
Panel 125 to 128 Tyne Cot Memorial

18th October: Private John James Wagstaff, York & Lancs, 26743
I VE II Nine Elms British Cemetery

19th October: Private Henry Charlesworth, Sherwood Foresters (Notts & Derby Regiment), 92302
Panel 99 to 102 & 162 to 162A Tyne Cot Memorial

19th October: Private Albert William Jackson, Royal Army Medical Corps, 32240, Age 26
X E. 21 Dozingham Military Cemetery

25th October: Private Walter Skirrow, 7th York & Lancs, 16443, Age 28
VI A 45 Bard Cottage Cemetery

26th October: Private George Hawcroft, Royal Warwickshire Regiment, 29907
LX H. II Tyne Cot Memorial

27th October: Corporal William Houlbrook, East Yorkshire Regiment, 9395, Age 25
Panel 47 to 48 163A Tyne Cot Memorial

31st October: Private George William Cusworth, 6th or 2nd York & Lancs, 7647
XXX H. 12 Etaples Military Cemetery

November 1917

1st November: Lance Corporal Arthur Finch, London Regiment, 23rd County of London Battalion, 702192, Age 21. Formerly RAMC, 79992. Died in the Egyptian Theatre
J 23 Beersheba War Cemetery

10th November: Private John Harry Hinds, Sherwood Foresters (Notts & Derby) Regiment, 92284, Age 26 (Formerly York & Lancs, 43593)
Panel 99 to 102 & 162 to 162A Tyne Cot Memorial

10th November: Corporal George Edward Meek, 1st South Wales Borderers 9847, Age 28
Panel 65 to 68 Tyne Cot Memorial

14th November: Rifleman John Marsden, West Yorkshire (Prince of Wales Own) Regiment, 48835, Age 32
Panel 42 to 47 & 162 Tyne Cot Memorial

15th November: Lance Corporal George Sheppard Hirst, 26th Northumberland Fusiliers, 41397 (Formerly York & Lancs, 230131)
II D II Bucquoy Road Cemetery Ficheux

22nd November: Private William Henry Buncall, 9th Leicestershire Regiment, 39556 (Formerly Sherwood Foresters, 88229)
I A 8 Hersin Communal Cemetery Extension

25th November: Private John Thomas Smeaton, 12th South Wales Borderers, 24106 (Lived in Wath)
Panel 5, Cambrai Memorial, Louveral.

December 1917

1st December: Private Thomas Naylor MM, Grenadier Guards, 21812, Age 21, Panel 2 Cambrai Memorial, Louveral.

2nd December: Private William Henry Bedford, KOYLI, 21334, Age 32
Panel 108 – 111 Tyne Cot Memorial

10th December: Gunner C. R. Adams, Royal Field Artillery, 185937
IX E 13 Grevillers British Cemetery

12th December: Lance Corporal Walter Hare, 1/4th (TF)York& Lancs, 241780
VIII C. 30 Duhallow ADS Cemetery

27th December: Lance Corporal Harold Hill, KOYLI and 8th York and Lancs 40724, Died at Home. Remembered on Swinton War Memorial.

31stDecember: Able Seaman Sydney Lake, Royal Naval Volunteer Reserves, Tyneside Z/5257
Pier & Face 1A Theipval Memorial

Mexborough Men Who Died in 1918

January 1918

1st January: Private Charles Dunstan, KOYLI, 20368, Age 35
IX B 12. Mendlingham Military Cemetery

3rd January: Private Lawrence Cain, 12 Lincolnshire Regiment, 29255, Age 27. Transferred to 17th Labour Corps
Plot 9, Row G, Grave 9, Morbecque British Cemetery

9th January: Private Herbert Curtis, 1/5th York & Lancaster Regiment, 111027
Menin Road South Military Cemetery

10th January: Private Henry Severn, North Staffs Regiment, 50663, Age 32
1X C9 Rocquigny Equancourt Road British Cemetery

March 1918

21st March: Private Willie Axe, 2nd York & Lancs, 44031
IV A6. La Kreule Military Cemetery, Hazebrouck.

21st March: Private Harold Morton (Born Wath), 12th/13th Northumberland Fusiliers, 20311, Age 24
Panel 16 to 18, Pozieres Memorial

21st March: Private George Overend, 8th York & Lancs Regiment, 13941 Age 24
Bay 8 Arras Memorial

21st March: Rifleman Horace Phillips, Kings Royal Rifle Corps, A/203924
Panel 61 to 64 Pozieres Memorial

21st March: Private Malcolm Francis Watson, 1/5th Sherwood Foresters, (Notts & Derby Regiment), 78946
Bay 7 Arras Memorial

21st March: Private Reginald Frank Waller, Machine Gun Corps, (Infantry), 15043, Age 21
Panel 90 to 93 Pozieres Memorial

21st March: Sapper Henry Wilcock, Royal Enginners, 112477, Age 37
II E. 18 Bancourt British Cemetery

22nd March: Private William Andrew Durham, Leicestershire Regiment, 46927
Panel 29 & 30 Pozieres Memorial

22nd March: Private George Fred Pinder, 7th York & Lancs, 16442, Age 24
Bay 8 Arras Memorial

23rd March: Private Patrick Conlon, Army Cyclist Corps, 4945. (Formerly York & Lancs, 10676)
Bay 10 Arras Memorial

25th March: Gunner Albert Batty, Royal Engineers, 107025
VI E. 14 Puchevillers British Cemetery

25th March: Private Frederick Carratt (Born Mexborough), 10th Battalion Sherwood Foresters, 27239
VD 29 Doullens Communal Cemetery Extension No 1

25thMarch: Private Horace Parker, (Born Boston, Lincs), 13th York & Lancs (1st Barnsley Pals), 25799, Age 22
Bay 8 Arras Memorial

27th March: Rifleman Horace Phillips, 9th KRRC , A/203924 (Formerly RASC T/3/026370 CWGC records)
Panel 61 to 64 Pozieres Memorial

27th March: Private E. Rodgers, Grenadier Guards, 21062
VI A1. Bucquoy Road Cemetery, Ficheux

27th March: Private Jesse Shaw, Royal Horse Artillery & Royal Field Artillery, 107652
II D. 24 Bucquoy Road Cemetery Ficheux

28th March: Private William Henry Phillimore, 18th Durham Light Infantry204240
II 3 22 Douchy –Lles – Ayette British Cemetery

28th March: Sergeant Charles Fredrick Crowson. MM, 8th York & Lancs Regiment 8/16372.
II. B 30 Abbeville Communal Cemetery Extension

28th March: Private John William Shaw, 4th Battalion Machine Gun Corps (Infantry), 73544, Age 20
Plot V I Row A. 4. Browns Corpse Cemetery Roeui, Pos –de Calais

29th March: Private Thomas H. Green, Durham Light Infantry, 301876
Panel 68 to 72 Pozieries Memorial

30th March: Private James George Beresford, 2/4th KOYLI, 36823, Age 19 (Formerly York & Lancs)
41006) A4 St Hilaire Cemetery Extension, Frevent

April 1918

2nd April: Private Arthur Clothier, 'A' Company, 2/5th Battalion, KOYLI, 240344
XXX III C II Etaples Military Cemetery

4th April: Gunner Walter Dakin, Royal Field Artillery, 222717, Age 19
G. 10 Hedauville Community Cemetery Extension

4th April: Private Roland Ainstock, Machine Gun Corps (Infantry), 129222 (Formerly York & Lancs, 46310)
III D 28 Chocques Military Cemetery

4th April: Lance Corporal John Wilfred Harrison, 6th York &Lancs, 19999
St Margaret's Churchyard, Swinton

4th April: Private Arthur Lewis, (Born Mexborough enlisted Featherstone) 12th KOYLI, 12/437, Age 26 Panel 8 Ploersteert Memorial

4th April: Private Alfred Wilson, 15th Durham Light Infantry, 81649, Age 29. (Formerly York & Lancs – 14458)
IV F 13 Wytschaete Military Cemetery

12th April: Private Fred Durose, 5th York & Lancs, 240532
Panel 125 – 128 Tyne Cot Memorial

12th April: Private Frank Halstead, York & Lancs, 28889, Age 32
Panel 8 Ploegsteert Memorial

12thApril: Private Frank Matthews, 13th York & Lancs, 425508, Age 23
Panel 8 Ploesteert Memorial

12th April: Private Joseph Pinches, East Yorks Regiment, 30378
Panel 4 Ploegsteert Memorial

13th April: Private Arthur Lewis, 12th KOYLI, 12/437, Age 26
Panel 8 Ploegsteert Memorial

15th April: Private George Fell, 2nd Duke of Wellington's, 268947
Panel 6 Ploegsteert Memoial

15th April: Private Harold Irving Gill, 4th Lincolnshire Regiment, 44720
Panel 3 Ploegsteert Memorial

15th April: Private Frank Thompson, 1/5th (TF) York & Lancs, 43990
Born Swinton
XXA 2 Cabaret-Rouge British Cemetery, Souchez

17th April: Sapper James Flint, Royal Engineeers, 476699
1F 17 Haringhe (Bandaghem) Military Cemetery

17th April: Private Charles Victor Clark, 4th Lincolnshire Regiment, 44701
Panel 3 Ploegsteert Memorial

17thApril: Private Edward Robins, 9th York & Lancs, 19776
Panel 125 to 128Tyne Cot Memorial

18thApril: Private Claude William Tretheway,Seaforth Highlanders S/400061, Age 24?
A6 Le-Vertannoy British Cemetery Hinges

21st April: Gunner Reginald Scholes, Royal Field Artillery, 203762
PV. II A 7B St Sever Cemetery Extension Rouen

22nd April: Private Roland Ainstock, Machine Gun Corps (Infantry), 129222 (Formerly York & Lancs 46310)
III D 28 Chocques Military Cemetery

24th April: Gunner George Edward Booth, Royal Field Artillery, 14099, Age 22
XIII C. 1 St Pierre Cemetery Amiens

25th April: Private William Cutts, West Yorks, (TMB), 201410
Panel 42 to 47 & 162 Tyne Cot Memorial

25th April: Private John Dyson, York & Lancs, 240116
V K 6 Perth Cemetery (China Wall)

29th April: Lance Corporal Thomas Ashcroft, 2nd York & Lanc, 41635 Age 21
Panel 102 to 104 Tyne Cot Memorial

May 1918

1st May: Private Albert Charlesworth, 5th Kings (Liverpool) Regiment, 99291 Age 19
11 A 36, Pernes British Cemetery

2nd May: Gunner Harry Cater, Royal Garrison Artillery, 15331, Age 35
XIII D 8 Bienviller Military Cemetery

9th May: Private Charles Edward Booth, Royal Defence Corp, 38955, Age 29
North of Church, Tansley (Holy Trinity) Churchyard

13th May: Acting Leading Stoker Sydney Marsden, Royal Navy, K/8582 HMS Attentive, Age 28
New D "U" 85 Mexborough Cemetery

June 1918

1st June: Private William Drabble, Royal Engineers, (Road & Quarries) Pioneer, WR/22344. Formerly KOYLI, 2445
A 14 Montigny Communal Cemetery, Somme

2nd June: Corporal P. Ashmore, York & Lancs, 22104
XXI B 9 Bienvillers Military Cemetery

8th June: Ordinary Seaman Willie. Barker, Royal Navy J/43351, HMS Dublin
Old B "C" 245 – Mexborough Cemetery

13th June: Private Horace Hepworth, 1st East Yorks, 31330, Age 21
VIII C. 6 Cologne Southern Cemetery

15th June: Sergeant Henry Livingstone Davenport , 9th York & Lancs, 17211
Plot 1 Row D Grave 15, Granezza British Cemetery, (Kia, Italy)

18th June: Sergeant Joseph Samual Rothery, Army Service Corps, Motor Transport, M2/019330, Age 28
Q II J. 14 St Sever Cemetery Extension, Rouen

26th June: Private John Worrall, KOYLI, 3/1685, Age 37
Old B "C" 310 Mexborough Cemetery

28th June: Private Isaiah (Buller) Hague, West Yorkshire Regiment
17/1306 Panel 3 & 4 Ploegsteert Memorial

July 1918

3rd July: Sapper Percy Frogatt, Royal Engineers, WR/327893
A 'C' 195, Haugh Road Cemetery, Rawmarsh

14th July: Private George Gabbitas, (Born Mexborough), 10th York & Lancs   15375 (14211 on CWGC), Age 24
I B 29 Staglieno Cemetery, Genoa, Italy

17th July: Corporal Eli Clothier, 2nd York & Lancs, 203422, Age 23
II C I Hagle Dump Cemetery

27th July: Private William Stocks, 2/4th York & Lancs, Regiment Hallamshire TF Battalion, 46307, Age 22
IV D 7 Marfaux British Cemetery

30th July: Lance Corporal Albert Edward Denham, KOYLI, 37856 (Formerly York & Lancs, 23338), Age 23
XV II B22 Terlingcthum British Cemetery Wimille

August 1918

2nd August: Private Edward Adshead , 1st Royal Fusiliers (City of London Regiment), 76748, Age 19 (Formerly TR 10/75557, 107th TR Battalion Royal Fusiliers)
VI A 4 Bully Grenay Communal Cemetery British Extension
6th August: Private William Burgess, RAMC, M/285588
1476 Saklonia (Lembet Road) Cemetery

6th August: Private Clarence Victor Marsden, Royal Army Medical Corps – M2/269602, Age 21
IVC 19 Abbeville Communal Cemetery Extension

19th August: Lance Corporal R. Colby, Norfolk Regiment, 320072, Age 24
Outter Steene Communal Cemetery, Bailleul

26th August: Private Cyril Ibbotson (Born Wath), 2nd KOYLI, 51405, Age 19 (Formerly 91st TR Regiment)
III F 31 Daours Communal Cemetery

28th August: Rifleman Doulglas L. Lubley, London Regiment Queen's Westminster Rifles, 43571. Posted from 1st Battalion Kings Royal Rifle Corps
Queant Road Cemetery Buissey IV B. 27

31st August: Private Arthur Edward Chappell, West Riding (Duke of Wellingtons Regiment), 33862 Age 19
1B 55 Vis-en-Artois British Cemetery, Haucourt

September 1918

6th September: Private Arthur Crowcroft: ASC. (MT), M2/176631
VII H. 16 Queant Road Cemetery, Buissy

6th September: Guardsman John Henry Brooks, 2nd Grenadier Guards 19679 Age 25
Pier & Face 8D Thiepval Memorial

6th September: Private George Harris, East Yorkshire Regiment, 9106, Age 33 (Lived in Sheffield)
Panel 4, Ploegsteert Memorial

9th September: Sergeant H. E. Woods, 7th Leicestershire Regiment, 41449
VI. E. 7. Gouzeaucroft New British Cemetery

16th September: Flight Lieutenant George Leonard Bryers, R.A.F.
3. Bevillers Communal Cemetery

18th September: Gunner Edward Robert Shaw,Royal Field Artillery, 32804
294 Mikra British Cemetery Kalameria

19th September: Private Walter White, 2nd Sherwood Foresters, 93729
Panel 7 Vis-en-Artois Memorial

24th September: Private Thomas (Tom) Barron, Durham Light Infantry, 92003,
Age 18
Panel 9 Vis-en-Artois Memorial

27th September: Private George Herbert Sykes, West Yorkshire Regiment 58712,
Age 19
I A 19 Chappelle British Cemetery, Holnon

27th September: Lance Corporal Fred Thorpe, York & Lancs, 34156
VII D. 10 Gouzeaucourt New British Cemetery

October 1918

1st October: Private Samuel Harrott Henson, York & Lancs, 44103, Age 23
North Side Artes Communal Cemetery

1st October: Private Francis Osbourne Rowland, 6th York & Lancs, 22033
Panel 9 Vis-en-Artois Memorial

2nd October: Gunner T. H. Howlett, Royal Field Artillery, 72852
Old B "U' 186, Mexborough Cemetery

2nd October: Lance Corporal Arthur Edward Mann MM, 2/4th York &Lancs 201168, Age 22. (Was an Acting Sergeant at time of his death. Died in University War Hospital, Southampton)
SM 22. C. St Margaret's Churchyard, Swinton

3rd October: Lance Corporal Fredrick Charles Morton, 1st KOYLI, 25782
C4 Guizancourt Farm Cemetery, Gouv
3rd October: Private Richard Rownsley, 2/5th Sherwood Foresters (Notts & Derby) Regiment, 92387, Age 32
A 12 Ramicourt British Cemetery

3rd October: Private Frederick Charles Shaw, 1st KOYLI, 25782
Born Mexborough, enlisted Rotherham
C4 Guizan Court Farm Cemetery, Guoy

5th October: Private R. William Ernest Anderson, East Yorkshire Regiment, 205629, Age 23
428 Mikra British Cemetery, Kalamaria

5th October: Private Jesse Thornton, 2nd York & Lancs, 24129, Age 23
B 10, La Baraque British Cemetery, Bellenglise

8th October: Lance Corporal E. Hannan, Northumberland Fusiliers, 38869
Bois-Des-Angles Britissh Cemetery, Crevecouer Sur-Lescaut

10th October: Gunner Harry Flinders, Royal Field Artillery, 263548
I D. 24 St Souplet British Cemetery

11th October: Private George Clark, 25th Battalion Royal Fusiliers
Vis-en-Artois

13th October: Private Samuel Harrot Henson, 3rd York & Lancs, 44103
Memorial near North Side, Artes Communal Cemetery

13th October: Private Matthew Senior, 1/5th York & Lancs (TF), 43399
B 3 York Cemetery, Haspres

13th October: Private C. E. Haldenby, 1/5th York & Lancs, 46947
York Cemetery, Haspres

14th October: Rifleman William O'Brien, Royal Irish Rifles, 10609
I D 6 Dadizeele New British Cemetery

18th October: Private R W.E. Anderson, East Yorkshire Regiment, 205629
428 Mikra British Cemetery.

19th October: Private Arthur Willey, Machine Gun Corps (Infantry), 129179 (Formerly York & Lancs, 46339)
V C 12 Tournai Communal Cemetery Allied Extension

23rd October: Private Thomas Grindle, South Wales Borderers, 40962
K2 Heestert Military Cemetery

25th October: Rifleman John Pepper, Kings Royal Rifle Corps, R/17545 Age 25
St Sever Cemetery Extension Rouen

27th October: Private Henry Dobson, (Born Kilnhurst), 2nd York & Lancs, 60266, Age 21
I B 39 St Souplet British Cemetery

28th October: Private Leonard Corbridge, 2nd York & Lancs, 15388, Age26
LXXI E 4 Etaples Military Cemetery

November 1918

2nd November: Private Harold Fletcher, 15th Lancashire Fusiliers, 55023, Age 23 (Formerly Lincolnshire Regiment, 50842)
A3 Landrecies British Cemetery

7th November: Private Gordon Ernest Straw, 15th Durham Light Infantry, 100997, Age 26.
II A 16 Dourlers Communal Cemetery Extension

8th November: Lance Corporal Harold Hadfield Chappell, 1st KOYLI Formerly York & Lancs, 60893
I C 4 Dourler Communal Cemetery

8th November: Lance Corporal Fredrick Charles Morton, 1st KOYLI, 25782
C. 4 Guiyancourt Farm Cemetery

14th November: Driver W Reginald Hallford, Army Service Corps,
SIII AA 20St Sever Cemetery Extension, Rouen

Mexborough Men Who Died 1919 -1922

February 1919

23rd February: Private Henry Keenan, Lancashire Fusiliers, 25553, Age 24
Old B "C" 101 Mexborough Cemetery

27th February: Private J. W. White, Sherwood Foresters (Notts & Derby Regiment), 4558, Age 24
Mexborough Cemetery

March 1919

24th March: Sergeant E. Foster, York & Lancs, 21433
New C"C" 21 Mexborough Cemetery

May 1919

1st May: Sergeant H. E. Snipe, KOYLI, 11264, Age 36
Extension D "C" 608 Mexborough Cemetery

April 1919

4th April: Able Seaman Harold Andrew Siddall, Tyneside, Z/8905 Machine Gun Battalion, Royal Navy Volunteer Reverse
Engelbelmer Communal Cemetery II B. 9

12th April: Sergeant Cyril Joseph Levi, 302572, RAF Observers' School Egypt, Age 20
P 9, Cairo War Memorial Cemetery

July 1920

16th July: Lance Corporal Hirst, Military Foot Police, 18300
Mexborough Cemetery (No record with CWGC)

March 1921

24th March: Private M. Gavin, Essex Regiment, 19492
Extension D "U" 588 Mexborough Cemetery

May 1922

18th May 1922 : Private Robert Keenan, Royal Army Service Corps, Age 28
Mexborough Cemetery (No record with CWGC)

Appendix II

Soldiers and Sailors Buried in Mexborough Cemetery

Ordinary Seaman William Barker, Royal Navy, J/43351, HMS
Dublin, Age 18. Died 8th June 1918
Old B "C" 245

Private Frank Brown Chattell, 49th Battalion Australian
Infantry (AIF), 2645. Age 35, Died 4th June 1919
Old A"C" 262

Private R. L. Danks, York & Lancashire Regiment, 3409. Died
9th October 1915
New D "C' 96

Private Frederick Dawson, (Mapplewell), RAMC, 21900. Died
10th April 1918
Old 'U' 110

Sergeant E. Foster, York & Lancaster Regiment, 21433. Died
24th March 1919
New C'C' 21

Private M .Gavin , Essex Regiment,19492. Died 21st March 1921
Extension D "U" 588

Private Frederick Hall, 8th York and Lancs 14028, Age 39. Died 12th July 1916
Old E 'U' 150

Lance Corporal Hirst, Military Foot Police, 18300. Died 16th July 1920

Gunner T. H. Howlett, Royal Field Artillery, 72852. Died 2nd October 1918

Private Henry Keenan, Lancashire Fusiliers, 25553, Age 24. Died 23rd February 1919.
Old B "C" 101

James Robert Keenan, Royal Army Service Corp, Age 28. Died 18th May 1922.

Acting Leading Stoker Sydney Marsden, Royal Navy K/8582, HMS Attentive, Age 28. Died 13th May 1918
New D "U" 85

Sergeant H. E. Snipe, KOYLI, 11264, Age 36.Died 1st May 1919
Extension D "C" 608

Private H. Sykes, 11th Yorks & Lancs, 11154.Died 31st August 1915
New D "U" 101

Driver Joseph Tilson, Royal Army Service Corp, T/29352, Age 42. Died 27th May 1917
New D "C" 75

Private J. W. White, Sherwood Forseters (Notts & Derby Regiment), 4558, Age 24. Died 27thFebruary 1919

Lance Corporal J .G. Venables, Cameron Highlanders, S/21194, Age 20. Died 3rd June 1916
New B "U" Mexborough Cemetery

Private John Worrall, KOYLI, 3/1685, Age 37. Died 26th June 1918
Old B "C" 301

Appendix III

Mexborough Schoolteachers Who Joined the Armed Forces

Adwick Road
Mr W. Sykes (Headmaster)
Mr Walker

Central Senior
Second Lieutenant Ernest Elliott: RHA
Second Lieutenant L. Stevens: York & Lancs
Second Lieutenant W. H. Popple: RGA
Mr William Winstanley: (Headmaster)

Doncaster Road
Mr Edward Alfred Phillips: 12th York & Lancs (Sheffield City Battalion)

Doncaster Road Mixed School
Mr Frederick J. Horne: RAMC

Garden Street
Mr J. L. Haddon (Headmaster)

Mexborough Secondary School
Mr H. Alderson: Royal Engineers
Mr E. Sutcliffe
Mr J. Thorpe

National School
Mr C. R. Cockcroft: KRRR. Returned from Germany as prisoner of war to his home in Halifax
Mr Garwood: 12th York and Lancs (Sheffield City Battalion)

Roman Terrace School
Mr Steel, Headmaster (Active member of Mexborough and Swinton Home Defence Corps)

Note: All Mexborough teachers named above survived the Great War.

Appendix IV

Mexborough Soldiers Awarded Military Honours

Victoria Cross (VC)

Sapper William Hackett : *Royal Engineers, 136414*
Gazetted 4th August 1916

'For conspicuous bravery when entombed with four others in a gallery owing to the explosion of an enemy mine. After working 20 hours, a hole was made through fallen earth and broken timber, and the outside party was met. Sapper Hackett helped three of the men through the hole and could have easily followed, but refused to leave the fourth, who was seriously injured, saying. "I am a tunneller, I must look after the others first". Meantime the hole was getting smaller, yet he still refused to leave his injured comrade. Finally the gallery collapsed, and though the rescue party worked desperately for four days, the attempt to reach the two men failed. Sapper Hackett well knowing the nature of sliding earth, the chances against him, deliberately gave his life for his comrades.'

Distinguished Service Medal (DSM)

Sergeant J. M. Atkinson: 1st Battalion York & Lancs, 17331
Gazetted 16th November 1915

'For conspicuous gallantry on 29th September 1915, near Vermelles, when he crossed over 300 yards of open ground under heavy fire to bring back a message and take one back to the fire trench, which had been cut off from the communication by the enemy. It was due to his bravery and devotion that the support company were sent up to retake the trench and re-establish our line.'

Sergeant J. Brown: 1st York & Lancs, 8336
Gazetted, 16th November 1915

'For conspicuous gallantry on 29th September 1915 near Vermelles, in holding an advanced trench against repeated bomb attacks of the enemy when no officer or NCO was left in the platoon. He continued to discharge his duty with the utmost courage and devotion until he himself was wounded'.

Private H. Cavil: 2nd Battalion : Leicestershire Regiment, 6550
Gazetted 3rd June 1915

'For conspicuous gallantry from 24th–26th January 1915, when communication with one of our advanced picquets was broken, he went out of his trench three times in daylight and repaired wires under the enemy's shell and machine gun fire.'

Company Sergeant Major Walter H. Cooke: 9th Battalion York & Lancs Regiment 7722– Woolwich (Italy)
Gazetted 10th January 1920

'For conspicuous gallantry and ability during the battle 29th - 31st October 1918. During an attack on the first day when the enemy were putting up a determined resistance, he rushed forward with about thirty men taking a number of prisoners and capturing the objective. Later he again by his leadership and entire contempt for danger succeeded in capturing a position of the village and many prisoners.'

Company Sergeant M. W. Collingwood: 1/4th Battalion York & Lancs Regiment T.F., 10700 (Mexborough)

'During attack at Avesnes le sec on 13th October 1915. He displayed great courage and ability to command. After all the officers became casualties he took charge of the company and reinforced at the critical places with rapidity and decision.'

Sergeant Eric Downing: Royal Field Artillery (Bombardier, 68505 and later 1 'B' Reserve Brigade)
Gazetted, 30ᵗʰ June 1915

'For conspicuous gallantry from 25ᵗʰ to 30ᵗʰ January 1915, when in charge of a trench mortar often under heavy fire during German attacks.'

Private A. Gwynnette: 1/5ᵗʰ York & Lancs Regiment (TF),2156
Gazetted, 6ᵗʰ June 1915

'For great gallantry and devotion to duty on the 10ᵗʰ July 1915, on the Yser Canal. During the heaviest period of the bombardment, where the stretcher bearer was isolated from his company. Private Gwynnette attended to about twenty wounded men, his courage and example gave great encouragement to all ranks. Later he collected a party and under heavy fire assisted to bury several of the dead left by the battalion previously in occupation of the trench.'

Private T . Jones: 1ˢᵗ York& Lancs, 18165
Gazetted, 16ᵗʰ November 1915

'For conspicuous bravery on 29ᵗʰ September 1915 near Vermelles. Private Jones displayed the greatest bravery in continuing to throw bombs under constant heavy fire. The enemy had cut off the left flank, and he helped to bomb them out and retake the trench. The whole action lasted six hours, and nearly all his fellow bomb throwers were killed or wounded. His gallantry and devotion to duty were most marked.'

Company Sergeant Major John W. Gill: 5/28118
Gazetted, 18ᵗʰ June 1917

'For conspicuous gallantry and devotion to duty. He carried out a difficult reconnaissance under very heavy fire and brought back most valuable information.'

Sergeant A. Hammond: ASC/C/S/M – M/2/018414,(Army Service Corps)
Gazetted, 25ᵗʰ August 1917

'For conspicuous gallantry and devotion to duty in extricating and bringing into safety lorries of ammunition which had been blocked by fallen trees and debris, under very heavy fire and continued shell fire. He worked strenuously and gallantly for two hours during which he carried one of the drivers to a dressing station under heavy shrapnel fire the whole time.'

Company Sergeant Major G. W. Richards: York & Lancs

Sergeant F. Riley M.M.: *Royal Engineers, 476735*
Gazetted 3rd October 1918

'For conspicuous gallantry and devotion to duty. He rescued a wounded comrade killing two of the enemy. Subsequently he again displayed great courage in clearing the enemy. On at least one occasion killing an additional two of the enemy in hand-to-hand fighting.'

Sapper James Leadbeater: *Royal Engineers*
Gazetted, 3rd March 1917

'For conspicuous gallantry in action. Accompanied by a sergeant he crawled to a sap head of a mine shaft and went down. After 2 hours work they succeeded in rescuing the wounded man and brought him back safely to our lines. He has previously done fine work.'

Private J. W. Shaw: York & Lancs

Private A. Steel: York & Lancs

Private J. F. Whitehead: *2nd Battalion Leicestershire Regiment, 15910*
Gazetted, 15th April 1918

'For conspicuous gallantry in carry messages under heavy fire. Later he joined the firing line and set a fine example.'

Croix de Guerre

Private Alfred Newey

Military Medal (MM)

Private Clement Allen: West Riding Regiment
(Worked for Mexborough & Swinton Times)

Sergeant J. Bramhall

Signaller William Carr: C. Battery 160 Brigade (Parents lived in
Park Road)

Sergeant Charles Frederick Crowdon: 8th Battalion York & Lancs
Received his MM for gallantry at Ovillers on 1st July 1916

Sergeant E. E. Dainty: Duke of Wellington's

Bombarier H. Edwards: Canadian Artillery (Lived in Mexborough
before emigrating to Canada)

Second Air Mechanic H. Flather: RAF (Workedfor Mexborough
and Swinton Times)

Corporal Archie Freeman: South Wales Borderers

Sergeant Sam Goodman: KOYLI

Private John T. Halleron: 2nd York & Lancs, 7737 (Reservist)

Sergeant John Horton: York & Lancs

Lance Corporal Albert Hudson Robinson: Royal Engineers (West
Riding) Posthumously awarded

Private Thomas King: KOYLI

Private David Kirbyson: Royal Army Medical Corps

Corporal G.E.S. Lowe: York& Lancs

Lance Corporal Edward Mann: 2/4th York & Lancs – 201168
Died of wounds. Buried St Margaret's Churchyard, Swinton

Sergeant Agnus McLaghlan: Royal Field Artillery

Sapper Fred Meanwell: Royal Engineers

Company Sergeant Major George Oldfield

Private Walter Oldfield: York & Lancs

Private Frank Oliver: 9th York & Lancs (Killed 1st July 1916)

Private E. Roblns: York & Lancs,

Private E. Rose: KOYLI, 1719

Lance Corporal William A. Scott

Gunner Mark Thompson: Royal Field Artillery Awarded on 24th October 1917

Sergeant John Horton: York & Lancs
Lived 20, Oxford Road. For bravery in February 1916. Gazetted, 9th November 1916

Private Harry Jevons: Coldstream Guards

Sergeant J. Mc Call: Kings Royal Rifle Corps

Private Thomas Naylor: 4th Grenadier Guards
Gazetted, 21 December 1917

Lance Corporal William A. Scott: Trench Mortar Battery

Private Samuel Smith: 9th York & Lancs

Sergeant H. Wrigley: ASC (Worked for Mexborough & Swinton Times)

Mentioned in Dispatches

Private W. Beaumont

Sergeant George Walker: Royal Engineers

Bibliography

Adie, Kate, *Fighting on the Home Front, The Legacy of Women in World War One* (2013)

Ashby, Julia, *The First Thirty Years are the Worst; History of Doncaster Road School..* (Undated and unpublished)

Bagwell P.S., *The Railwaymen* (George Unwell & Unwin Ltd, 1963)

Bailey, Catherine, *Black Diamonds, The Rise and Fall of an English Dynasty* (2007)

Bowmen, Timothy, *Irish Regiments in the Great War* (2003)

Brearley, Giles, *The 'Iron Man'*, The Story of James William Hague (2011)

Bridger, Geoff, *The Great War Handbook,* Pen & Sword (2009)

Cahalan, Peter James, *The Treatment of Belgian Refugees in England During The First World War* (1977 PhD Thesis)

Cesorani D. and Kushner T.(ed), *The Internment of Aliens in 20th Century Britain,* (1993) (Routledge)

David, Saul, *100 Days to Victory, How the Great War was Fought and Won* (2013)

Dangerfield, George, *The Strange Death of Liberal England,* Paladin (1970)

De. Groot, Gerald J, *The First World War, Twentieth Century Wars* (2001)

Ellisworth-Jones, Will, *We Will Not Fight* (2008)

Gilbert, Martin, *First World War,* London (1994)

Ferguson, Norman, *The First War World – A Miscellany,* Summersdale (2014)

Hazlehurst, Cameron, *Politicians at War, July 1914 to May 1915* (1971)

Hochschild Adam, *To End all Wars* (2013)

Holmes, Richard, *Shots from the Western Front, The British Soldier 1914 -1918* (2008)

Holton, Bob, *British Syndicalism, 1900 -1914,* Pluto Books (1976)

Liddell Hart, B.H., *History of the First World War,* Pan Books (1972)

MacArthur Brian (ed), *For King and Country, Voices from the First World War* Abacus *(2009)*

Marwick, Arthur, *The Deluge, British Society and the First World War* (1965)

Middlebrook, Martin, *The First Day of the Somme* (1971)

Montagu J. B., *The History of the 9th Battalion York and Lancaster Regiment, 1914 -1919* (London) (Unpublished and undated, thought to be circa 1930)

Neiberg, M.S., *The Western Front, 1914-1916,* Amber Books (2008)

Panay Panikos (Edited), *Germans in Britain Since 1500,* Hambleton Press (1996)

Russell, D, *Popular Music in England, 1840 – 1914,* (1987)

Sassoon, Siegfried, *Memoirs of an Infantry Officer,* New York (1930)

Sherry, Dave, *Empire and Revolution, A Socialist History of the First World War* *(2014)*

Simkins, Peter, *Kitchener's Army – The Raising of the New Armies, 1914 -1916*, (1988)

Smith. Stuart, *The Cinemas of Mexborough and the Dearne Valley* (1995)

Stevens, Philip, *The Great War Explained*, Pen and Sword Books (2012)

Strachan, Hew, *First World War, Oxford Illustrated History* (1998)

Wilkinson. R.M., *The 10th (Service) Battalion, York & Lancashire Regiment* (Unpublished, dated circa 1934)

Willmott, H.P.,*Ultimate Book of World War 1* (2003)

Wilson, Donald M., *Short History of Montagu Hospital, Mexborough,* Times Printing Company (1926)

Wylly, C.B. (Colonel), *The York and Lancaster Regiment* (1930)

Diaries

Mexborough Doncaster Road School Log Book, 1894-1924

Official Diary of the 2nd Battalion of KOYLI. (KOYLI Museum, Doncaster)

Journals and Newspapers

Barnsley Chronicle: 1914 - 1918

Daily Mail: 5th May 2010

Forward: The Journal of the Great Central Railway Society. Articles by Ken Grainger

Mexborough and Swinton Times (The Times): 1910 – 1920

Mexis: Mexborough and District Heritage Society Newsletter, April 2006 Sapper Hackett VC of Mexborough by Julia Ashby

Malvern News: 10th June 1916

Rotherham Advertiser: 1910 - 1911

The Suffragette: 7th May 1915

Websites

www.pontefractus/co.uk (Accessed 31.10.13)

www.pocklington history.com (Accessed 31.10.13)

www.chrishobson/sheffieldfirstraid1916.htm (Accessed 31.10.13)

ALSO FROM LEB BOOKS

IT'S ALWAYS THE CHILDREN

GILLIAN LARGE

Gillian Large began life the hard way in the West Midlands in the late 1940s.

Although her mother had a wealthy, privileged upbringing, Gillian was born into an inner world of squalor and chaos.

In *It's Always the Children*, Gillian takes you on a roller coaster ride of her early family life in the 50s and 60s to womanhood with courage, inner strength and humour.

"A very honest account of shocking emotional and physical abuse"

⭐⭐⭐⭐⭐

ISBN 978-0957314177
£11.99

ALSO FROM LEB BOOKS

Bill Cawley has been described as "a continual seeker after facts".

This collection of over 80 original articles will entertain and amaze you in equal measure.

Bill's knowledge of the Staffordshire Moorlands - its people, its culture and its history - is encyclopaedic. *Tales From The Hills* takes you on a journey into the past culled from the archives of local newspapers and Bill's own personal encounters.

"something for everyone"

⭐⭐⭐⭐⭐

ISBN 978-0957314191
£11.99

ABOUT THE AUTHOR

Bill Lawrence was born in Doncaster, but brought up in Luton. His first employment was as a railway worker before attending university where he graduated in British History and Sociology, later gaining a post graduate degree in Industrial Relations.

Bill is now retired after 30 years as a lecturer and spends much of his retirement organising, researching and writing for Mexborough and District Heritage Society. He is particularly interested in the history of the early 20th century in Britain including the First World War.

Picture Courtsey of Mick Pettinger

47153963R00224

Made in the USA
Charleston, SC
07 October 2015